Shifting Views & Changing Places

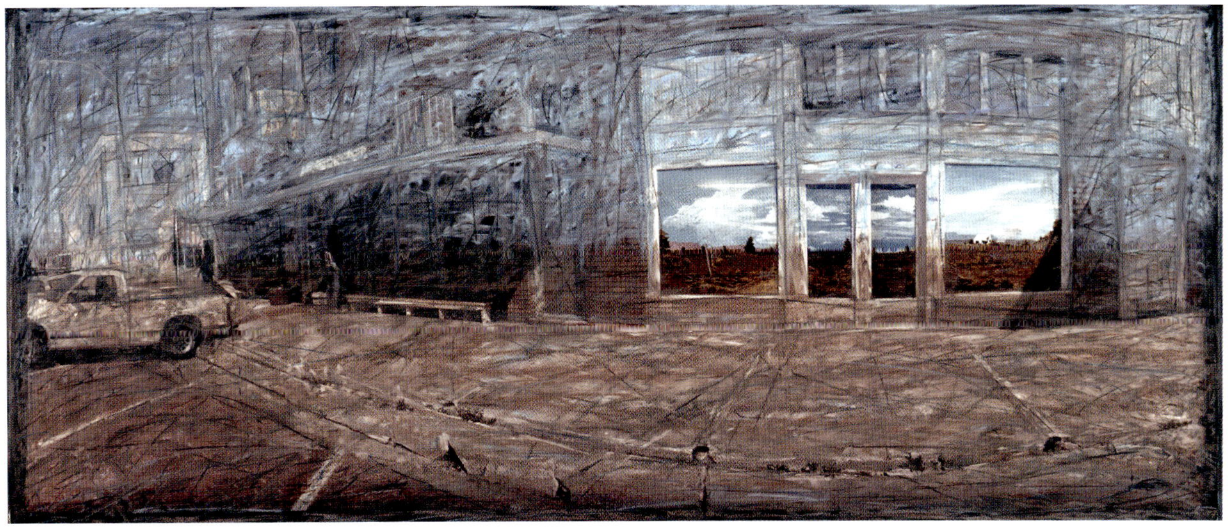

SHIFTING VIEWS & CHANGING PLACES

THE PHOTOGRAPHS OF RICK DINGUS

BY RICK DINGUS
EDITED BY PETER S. BRIGGS

FOREWORD BY TOBY JUROVICS

WITH CONTRIBUTIONS BY
SHELLEY ARMITAGE
PETER S. BRIGGS
LUCY R. LIPPARD

UNIVERSITY OF OKLAHOMA PRESS : NORMAN

Publication of this book is made possible by the generosity of the Helen Jones Foundation, Inc.

Unless otherwise indicated and credited, all photographs are by Rick Dingus.

The following image appears uncaptioned on page iii:
Storefront Landscape, Texas Panhandle, 1998 (see pages 56–57)

Library of Congress Cataloging-in-Publication Data
Names: Dingus, Rick, 1951– photographer, author. | Briggs, Peter S., editor.
Title: Shifting views & changing places : the photographs of Rick Dingus
by Rick Dingus ; edited by Peter S. Briggs ; foreword by Toby Jurovics with
contributions by Shelley Armitage, Peter S. Briggs, Lucy R. Lippard.
Other titles: Shifting views and changing places
Description: Norman : University of Oklahoma Press, [2016] | Includes
bibliographical references and index.
Identifiers: LCCN 2015043761 | ISBN 978-0-8061-5281-3 (hardcover : alk. paper)
Subjects: LCSH: Travel photography. | Photography, Artistic.
Classification: LCC TR790.D56 2016 | DDC 779—dc23
LC record available at http://lccn.loc.gov/2015043761

The paper in this book meets the guidelines for permanence and durability of the Committee on Production Guidelines for Book Longevity of the Council on Library Resources, Inc. ∞

Manufactured in China.

1 2 3 4 5 6 7 8 9 10

Book design by Skip McKinstry

To Carolyn, and our shared journeys ahead

CONTENTS

FOREWORD

Two Easy Pieces

Toby Jurovics

PHOTOGRAPHY IN THE AMERICAN WEST BEGAN IN earnest when Timothy H. O'Sullivan exposed his first wet collodion plate in the vicinity of Donner Pass in July 1867. He was not the first photographer to work beyond the Missouri River, but this event instigated an approach to the landscape that remains incisive to this day—an enthusiasm for the salient visual facts of western topography, no matter how raw or unassuming, and a rigorous commitment to describing the landscape as it appeared before the lens, without giving in to our inclinations toward the picturesque. This same aesthetic fired the second great wave of photographic surveys a century later, one equally committed to that tough version of the landscape, as Robert Adams, Lewis Baltz, Joe Deal, Frank Gohlke, and others of the New Topographics community battled their way through the cities and suburbs of the post–World War II West. As Gohlke recently noted,

> Ansel Adams represented a strain in American Art that goes back to nineteenth century landscape painting, and it's pretty undiluted . . . that's where Muybridge and Watkins and Jackson learned a lot of their stuff. And we wanted to look at Timothy O'Sullivan, who, even if he had learned things from the painters, chose not to use them. Almost without exception, O'Sullivan's work denies those conventions. . . . We thought that was a pretty good way to describe a lot of what America looked like now—uninhabitable, unhospitable.[1]

Less than a generation younger than these artists, Rick Dingus began his photographic explorations by wading into the deepest stretch of that river, with his lens fixed directly on O'Sullivan. Dingus is, in fact, most widely recognized for an image he made after his predecessor, *Tertiary Conglomerates (Witches Rocks #5)*, 1978 (figure 18), a view of Witches Rocks in Utah, along the route of the Union Pacific Railroad. Dingus was a member of the Rephotographic Survey Project (RSP)—a consortium of photographers who bookended the century between the West's first photographers and the modern West by carefully duplicating images originally made by O'Sullivan, William Bell, William Henry Jackson, A. J. Russell, and others and presenting them as side-by-side comparisons, then and now. Of all the photographers engaged in the RSP, Dingus unpacked more about O'Sullivan's working method from a single frame than did the remaining weight of the project combined. He did not just show a highway where a trail had been, or the face of a dam spanning a canyon, or the edge of suburbia creeping into the sagebrush. From the perspective of thirty years later, in fact, one of the most notable things about the RSP is how little the landscape had changed in most of the views they selected to rephotograph. But *Tertiary Conglomerates* exposed the process of making a photograph; it revealed O'Sullivan's intentions. How does one ascertain such things, especially about a photographer who was dead by 1882 and left no diary or written record? Dingus unveiled O'Sullivan's deliberateness—his willful choice to tilt the camera off level to amplify the instability of the formations as they pitch sharply against the horizon. In revealing O'Sullivan's use of the camera beyond its most literal application in order to create an image that was suggestive of personal experience, Dingus pulled the curtain back on the presumption of topographic accuracy and revealed the metaphor beneath the surface.[2]

Why dwell on this single image, one that Dingus arguably didn't make but copied, and that he is tired of discussing? Because it signals the possibilities of the camera and the landscape, and it establishes one pole of Dingus's understanding of photography. It is easiest to assume that artists work sequentially, engaging in single discrete projects one at a time—perhaps because as a viewer, it can be difficult to reconcile multiple simultaneous viewpoints—but Dingus was making another very different body of work during his participation in the RSP. At first glance, the works in the "Photo Drawings: Vernacular Landscapes" chapter might seem somewhat of a mad release from the precision demanded by the RSP—after a while, setting the viewfinder by compass and triangulation must have felt like having a hand tied behind the back. Nor is it exactly photography—yes, a sheet of film was exposed, but it takes away some of the fun when you know exactly what the picture you are going to make will look like before starting the truck in the morning. The frenetically incised, hand-drawn graphic practice of the photo drawings—which continued as an aspect of Dingus's work for two decades—undid the earnestness of the RSP. They are lighthearted and funny, subverting the dearness of the print surface and the rigor of the topographic document. And Dingus's incisions again recall O'Sullivan and the careless scratches he made on his plates for the Wheeler survey, as he crossed out and corrected their numbers, exhibiting a disregard for visual purity that maddens collectors to this day.

As he notes in the interview with Peter Briggs in this book, Dingus drew directly on the surface of his prints to acknowledge them as artifacts, ones that pitted the presumed objectivity of photography against his own subjective experience. *Untitled (Hole with Board: Gravel Mound)*, 1977 (figure 19), has a laugh at the expense of archaeological earnestness. A scrap section of two-by-four lumber is posed as if uncovered during an excavation and photographed in situ, with rapid squiggles indicating what is and is not real—the heavy shadow that creates its own jagged horizon knocked back to return your focus to the two-by-four. This simple image becomes a riddle about photography, where the real—the board—is less interesting and less present than the imagined landscape articulated to its side. *Lightning Snake Shadow*, 1977–81 (figure 20), draws even closer to this truth—a serpentine crack or crevice, scale indeterminate (where is O'Sullivan's yardstick when you need it?), zigzag silver pencil running beyond every edge—is it landscape, animal, atmosphere, energy? *Lightning Snake Shadow* undoes the purpose of the survey photograph—to provide a transparent, easily read, and descriptive image. Its uncertain space is not unlike O'Sullivan's mysterious 1868 image of Mono Lake,

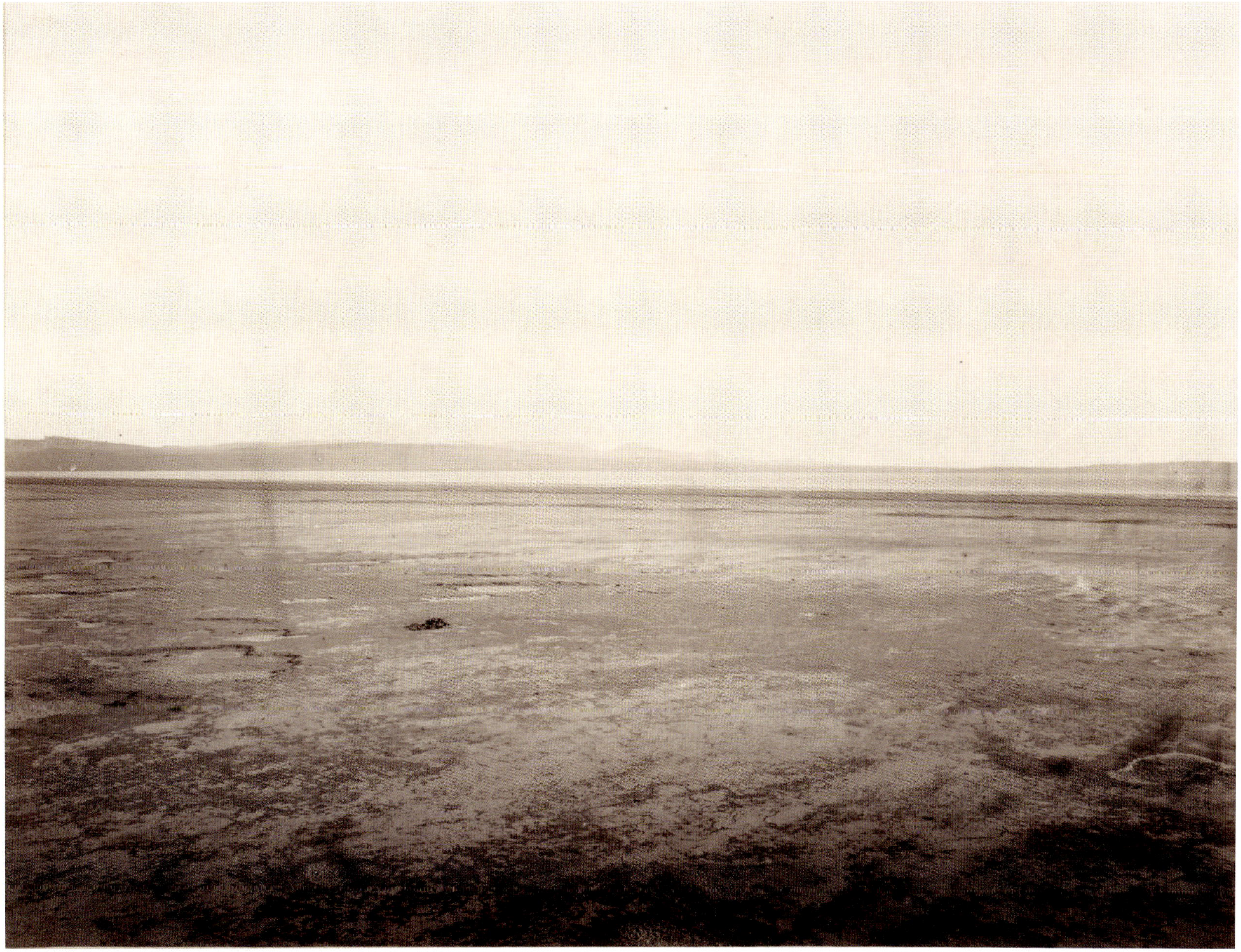

1. *Salt Lake Desert, Utah*, 1869, by Timothy H. O'Sullivan. Albumen print. Courtesy the Library of Congress Prints and Photographs Division, Washington, D.C. (LC-DIG-ppmsca-11964)

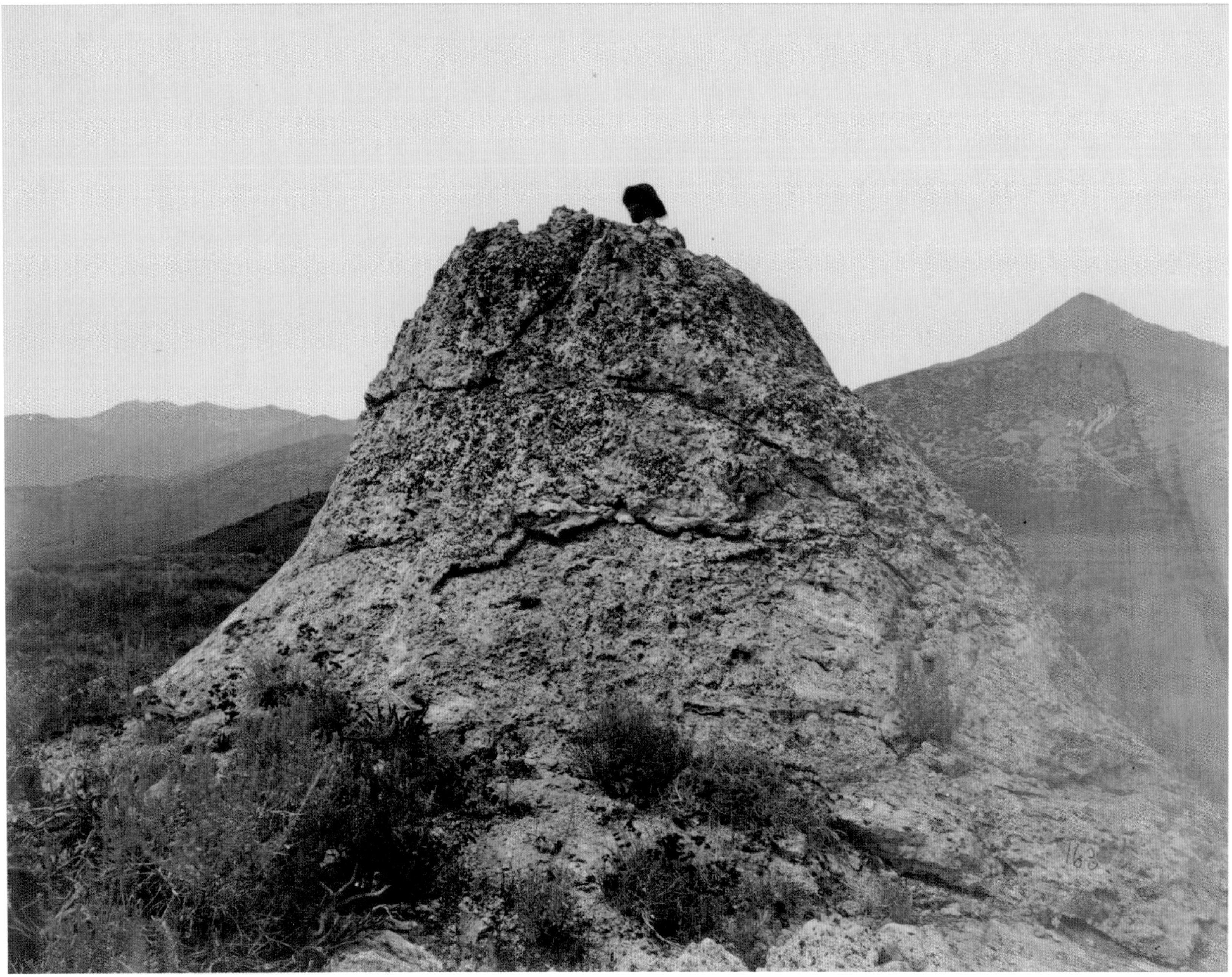

2. *Hot Spring Cone, Provo Valley, Utah*, 1869, by Timothy H. O'Sullivan. Albumen print. Courtesy the Library of Congress Prints and Photographs Division, Washington, D.C. (LC-DIG-ppmsca-11950)

California, whose islands hover along an indeterminate horizon, or of the Salt Lake Desert in Utah from the following year (figure 1), which appears to be a photograph of almost nothing. Instead, *Lightning Snake Shadow* reflects a self-consciousness of the act of photography and the intensity of the photographer's experience—a virtual stand-in for being there as the shutter was tripped. Like O'Sullivan, Dingus understood that the edges of a photographic print were resilient enough to contain both empirical and metaphorical truths, the descriptive and the personal, the past and present.

Dingus recently explained, "O'Sullivan fundamentally rejects the idea of the 'best general view' of Watkins and Jackson—the idea that there is one way to see a place. He understood that his photographs were quotations, and he could show the same place in different ways. Rather than go for the view, as Jackson did, I think O'Sullivan wanted to try it all out."[3] Dingus got his message from the start—that landscape is about the long view, and there is more than one way to approach it. O'Sullivan's multiple images of sites like the Montezuma Range in Nevada or the buttes outside Green River City, Wyoming, did more than show how the appearance of topographic features changed as his camera navigated; they put us into the picture, on the ground, prowling the landscape. O'Sullivan's best pictures remind us that the landscape has a long history, one that can be seen in all directions. Were we tasked with summing up Rick Dingus in a single image, it would not be that rectangle hanging over Witches Rocks; it might be *Journey Within*, 1987–88 (figure 28). Again, he recalls O'Sullivan, reminding us that his old friend was not without a sense of humor either. In *Hot Spring Cone, Provo Valley, Utah*, 1869 (figure 2), a gentleman in a hat appears to pop his head up like a gopher from the inside of a dry spring and give the landscape a once-over—O'Sullivan was clearly willing to spare a plate for a good one-liner. A century later, Dingus photographed a dry soda well against a stretch of New Mexico desert that is at once familiar and completely anonymous—the vernacular topography of the West. A daypack lies tossed in the foreground, as an arm grapples for purchase along the lip of the vent. It is hard to tell if this hidden figure is lowering himself down or clawing his way back to the surface, but either way he is literally *in* the landscape. It's funny, too, but it doesn't let us forget that the landscape is serious business, and getting it right is an act of complete immersion—this is Rick Dingus's "best general view."

Notes

1. Frank Gohlke, "New Topographics: Landscape Photography Then and Now" (panel discussion, Association of International Photography Art Dealers Photography Show, New York, March 20, 2010).
2. See the discussions in Rick Dingus, *The Photographic Artifacts of Timothy O'Sullivan* (Albuquerque: University of New Mexico Press, 1982); and Toby Jurovics, Carol M. Johnson, Glenn Willumson, and William F. Stapp, *Framing the West: The Survey Photographs of Timothy H. O'Sullivan* (New Haven, Conn.: Yale University Press, 2010).
3. Jurovics et al., *Framing the West*, 20.

ACKNOWLEDGMENTS

THE FOLLOWING PEOPLE DESERVE MY THANKS for intentionally or unwittingly contributing to my work. My parents fostered an early interest in traveling and wandering back roads and encouraged me to travel on my own. My older brother Larry gave me my first 35mm camera to record my journeys. And my other older brother, Ron, infected me with his enthusiastic curiosity and playful penchant for experimentation.

At the University of California at Santa Barbara, Richard Dunlap, a jazz musician and painting professor, supported my early interests in improvisation, theme, and variation; sculpture professor Miles Varner helped me understand "process" as immersive experience and extended metaphor. Painter Jim Alford encouraged my enthusiasm for natural settings and arranged a summer job for me in Grand Teton National Park, a life changer.

From my graduate studies at the University of New Mexico, I owe debts of gratitude to many faculty members, especially Betty Hahn, Anne Noggle, Thomas Barrow, Van Deren Coke, Beaumont Newhall, and Rod Lazorik. Artist Roger Sweet, also at UNM, became a close friend and collaborator in making artworks about time, place, and process. Steve Fitch, a fellow UNM graduate student, introduced me to J. B. Jackson's writings, and he traveled and collaborated with me on projects that continue to this day. David Stephenson, another graduate student, explored the landscape with me and later guided me to some of the places in Tasmania that appear in this book. In Tasmania, Martin Walch also guided me to many locations that prompted me to consider the "untamed" elements that remain within culturally affected places. During a one-year teaching position at the University of Colorado in Boulder, I met William S. Sutton and Michael Berman, whose ideas about "being in the landscape" influenced me. I also made friends with Robert Adams, who shared ideas and resources, as well as confirming the importance of Timothy O'Sullivan to contemporary photographers of the new American West.

After moving to Lubbock in 1982 to teach at Texas Tech University, I continued to travel, studying with medicine people on the Navajo Reservation and a meditation teacher in India. Their insights into the relations between the landscape of the mind and the exterior world continue to affect me daily. At the 2006 national conference of the Society for Photographic Education, I met writer and curator Liz Wells, who introduced me to landscape artists and initiatives in various places around the world.

People I worked with and who supported me on various projects include Manuel Davila, who mentored me as a scientific photographer at the Civil Engineering Research Facility at Kirtland Air Force Base, New Mexico; geologist Stephen G. Wells, who honed my repeat photography skills, Mark Klett, Ellen Manchester, and JoAnn Verburg, who invited me to join the Rephotographic Survey Project; Charles Roitz, Steve Fitch, Linda Connor, and John Pfahl, who helped me consider rock art in its contemporary context for Marks in Place; and Will Tsosie, Kent

Thompkins, Lawrence McFarland, Linda Connor, Mark Klett, Krista Elrick, Barbara Gilson, and Rich Rollins, who invited me to join them in recording and studying the importance of rock art to traditional Navajos in Dinétah-Hajiinei: Place of Emergence.

Bill Tydeman and Steve Bogener supported my proposal to create the Millennial Collection at the Southwest Collection/Special Collections Library of Texas Tech University, as well as securing funding for the Llano Estacado: An Island in the Sky project; photographers Andrew Liccardo, Peter Brown, Steve Fitch, Miguel Gandert, and Tony Gleaton worked with me on the Llano Estacado project; and Shelley Armitage, Darryl Birkenfeld, Paul Carlson, Andy Wilkinson, Monte Monroe, Curtis Peoples, and Barry Lopez, among others, participated in roundtable discussions that helped guide the project. Toby Jurovics shared his keen knowledge about Timothy O'Sullivan and the evolution of landscape photography since the nineteenth century; and Lucy Lippard's writings continue to feed my interests in relationships among place, art, and community.

Faculty colleagues at Texas Tech University deserve my thanks: Robin Germany, who helped me to establish the Millennial Collection and to plan a conference on Shifting Landscapes; Jorgelina Orfila, Chris Taylor, and Carolyn Tate, who partnered with me in Landscape as Knowledge, a year-long series of events, exhibitions, and lectures at TTU; and Lydia Thompson, director of the School of Art, who supported a reduction of teaching duties so I could finish this manuscript.

Many photographs in this book were made for projects supported by the National Endowment for the Arts; Polaroid Corporation; Sun Valley Center for the Arts and Humanities; Art Matters; Mid-America Arts Alliance; Arizona Commission on the Arts; Texas Tech University Arts Humanities Research; Texas Tech University's Institute for University Research; School of Art at the University of Tasmania, Australia; Chadron State College, Chadron, Nebraska; and the *CH* Foundation.

Peter S. Briggs's proposal for a retrospective exhibition of my work at the Museum of Texas Tech University inspired this book. Briggs acquired most of the photographs reproduced herein for the museum and secured a grant from the Helen Jones Foundation to support the exhibition and this book.

I thank the Museum of Texas Tech University and the Southwest Collection/Special Collections Library at Texas Tech University for their willingness to collect and archive my work.

I want to thank the staff of the University of Oklahoma Press, especially Kent Calder, Stephanie Evans, and Tony Roberts, who provided vital assistance in the acquisition, editing, and production of this book.

And most all, I thank my wife, Carolyn, my children, Cody and Nikki, and their extended families for their unstinting support and patience. My grandchildren, Jaxon, Carson, London, Jayden, and Mikayla, inspire me with their eager and joyful sense of discovery for what is yet to come.

Shifting Views
& Changing Places

Shifting Views, 1972–1978

When I was a child, I set aside a drawing that I wanted to keep. Later I accidentally stumbled across it, and it looked naïve. I was bemused that I had once thought it was good. From then on I have had an interest in collecting and gathering different sorts of references to revisit, rethink, or rework.

In 1972, before phone companies automatically rerouted misdialed long distance calls to local recordings, I dialed without an operator's assistance what I knew would be a "wrong number" for every possible area code. I made an audio recording, *Sixty-three Wrong Numbers,* of the varied dialects used by operators across the country repeating the same phrase.

I experimented with media and processes to disrupt my expectations and to test my blind spots. I wanted to photograph a landscape with an aesthetic aimed at seeing subtle changes over time. For the entire month of February in 1973 I visited the same place and shot a color slide every day at exactly 5 P.M., looking down a set of stairs at the beach in Isla Vista, California. I visited that spot often because I was fascinated that every time I revisited, I knew a lot had changed since my last visit, but I could never put my finger on the details of those changes because the experience of being in the present overrode my vague memories.

I studied the resulting slides and experimented with viewing them. I projected them as a slide dissolve in the same order in which each had been shot. This made it easier to view things I did not otherwise recognize: the cycle of tides slightly out of sync with my twenty-four-hour photographing cycle, the appearance and disappearance of distant islands because of daily changes in haze and weather, or the sandy beach disappearing after a storm, revealing the stark underlying bedrock of the coastal shelf.

Since the early 1970s I have experimented with making stereoscopic images to perceive depth in other ways, including stereo images of time as space (shooting left and right images at different moments) and enhanced depth for distant or near subjects (changing the distance between the left and right images). This led me to create other artworks such as films, installations, and process pieces that explored layered simultaneous experiences. Looking at old snapshots repeatedly and recording stories connected to them confirmed for me that memories change over time.

During my graduate study at the University of New Mexico, I worked as a scientific photographer at Kirtland Air Force Base, making high-speed motion pictures and still photographs of experimental tests. The challenges I faced in accurately representing events made me question the documentary capabilities of photography. I began to think of photographs as incomplete visual quotations, or as misquotes.

In 1977 and 1978 I worked with geologist Dr. Stephen G. Wells on a study of the aftereffects of a forest fire in Bandelier

National Monument, New Mexico. I photographed evidence of transformations after the burn, such as erosion patterns, falling trees, and the frost wedging of soil.

While I was working in Bandelier, the National Endowment for the Arts (NEA) funded the Rephotographic Survey Project (RSP). During the summer of 1977 the RSP focused on repeating the 1873 photographs that William Henry Jackson had taken in Colorado for the Hayden expedition. A year later the RSP invited me to work with them. I joined Mark Klett, Ellen Manchester, JoAnn Verburg, and Gordon Bushaw, and we expanded the focus of the RSP to include sites throughout the American West shot not just by Jackson, but also by photographers for the King, Powell, and Wheeler surveys. Many of the sites I photographed looked nothing like what I had expected. I experimented with making alternate views to investigate how particular scenes might continue to yield new interpretations. Looking back and forth between the "then" and "now" photographs led me to consider the role played by each viewer of a photograph.

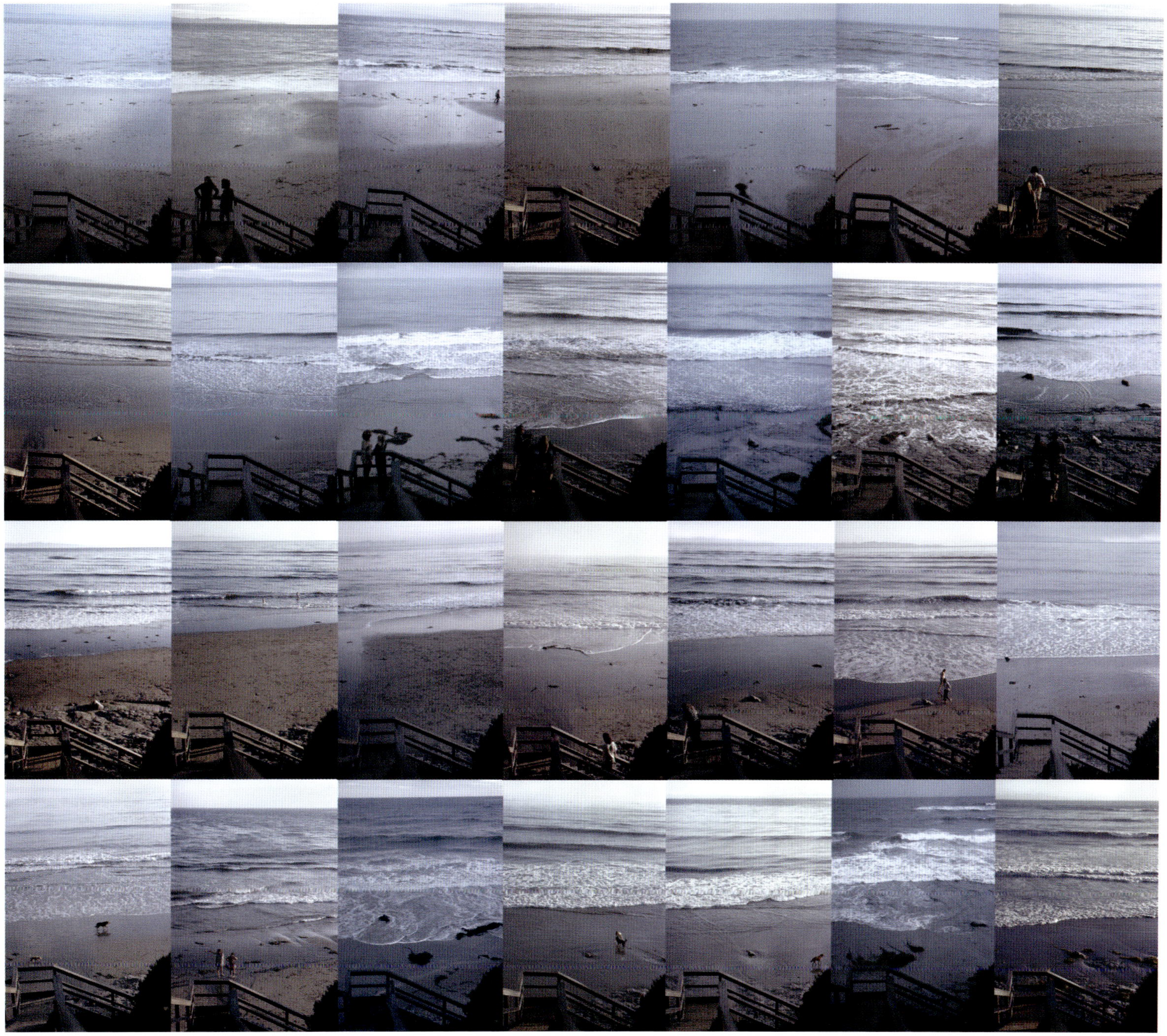

3. *Every day at exactly 5 P.M. in February 1973 (Beach at Isla Vista, California)*, 1973.
Twenty-eight 35 mm color slides, originally presented as a slide dissolve.
Archival pigment print, 22 × 25½ in.
In the collection of the Museum of Texas Tech University, Lubbock

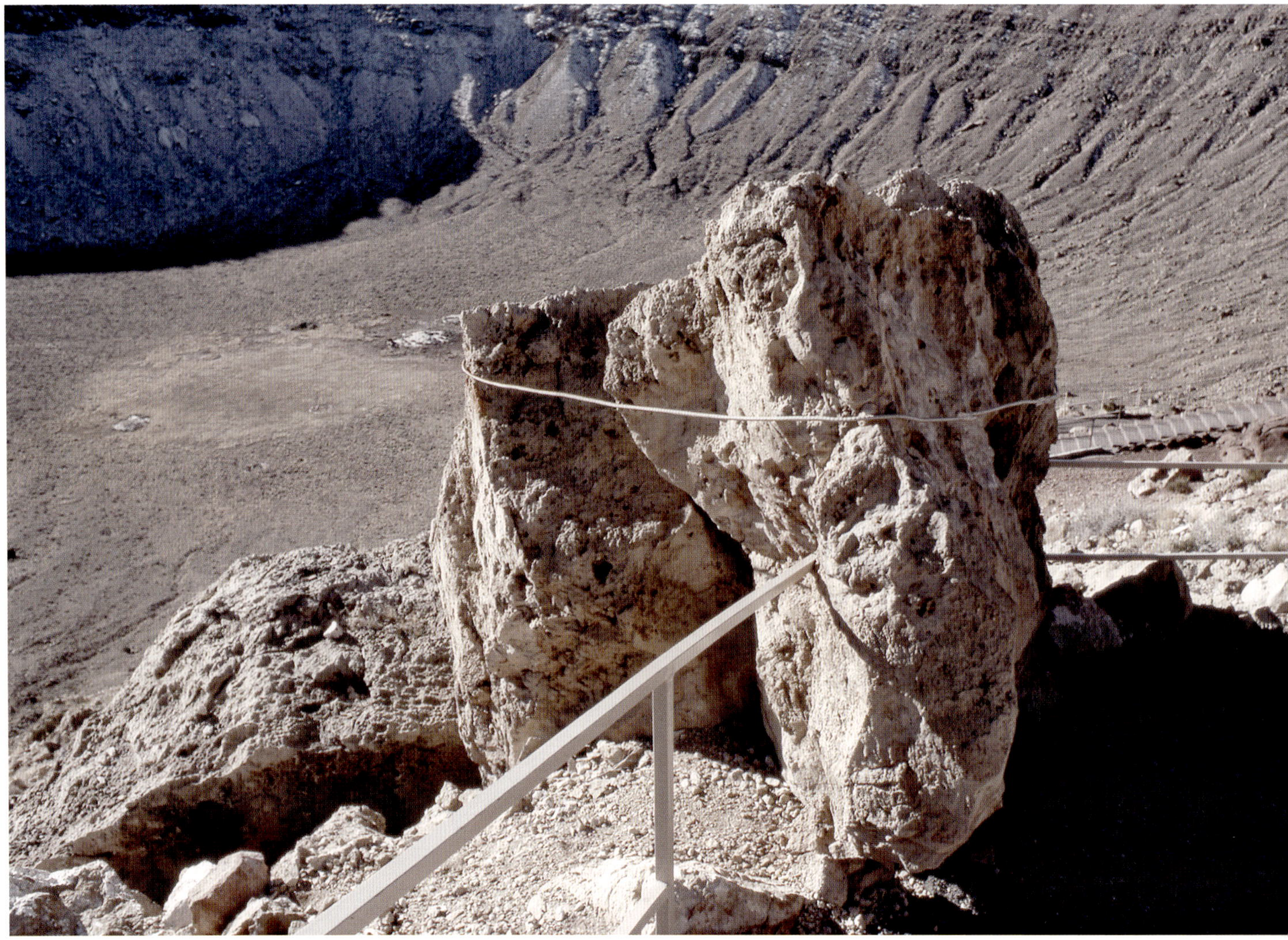

4. *Bound Rock, Meteor Crater, Arizona*, 1976.
Two 35 mm Kodachrome slides, presented as a polarized stereo projection; also printed as a 3½ × 7 in. stereo card.

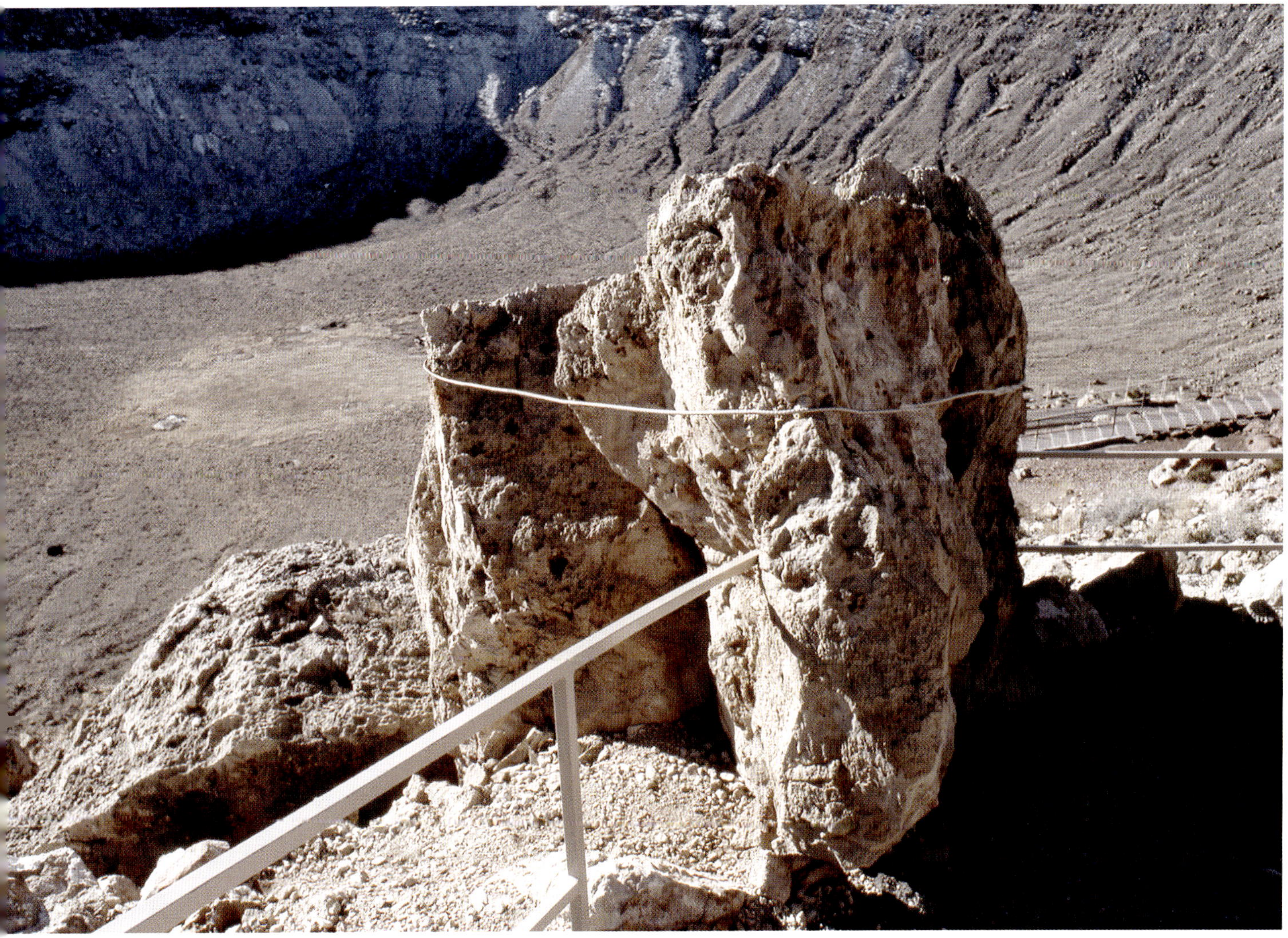

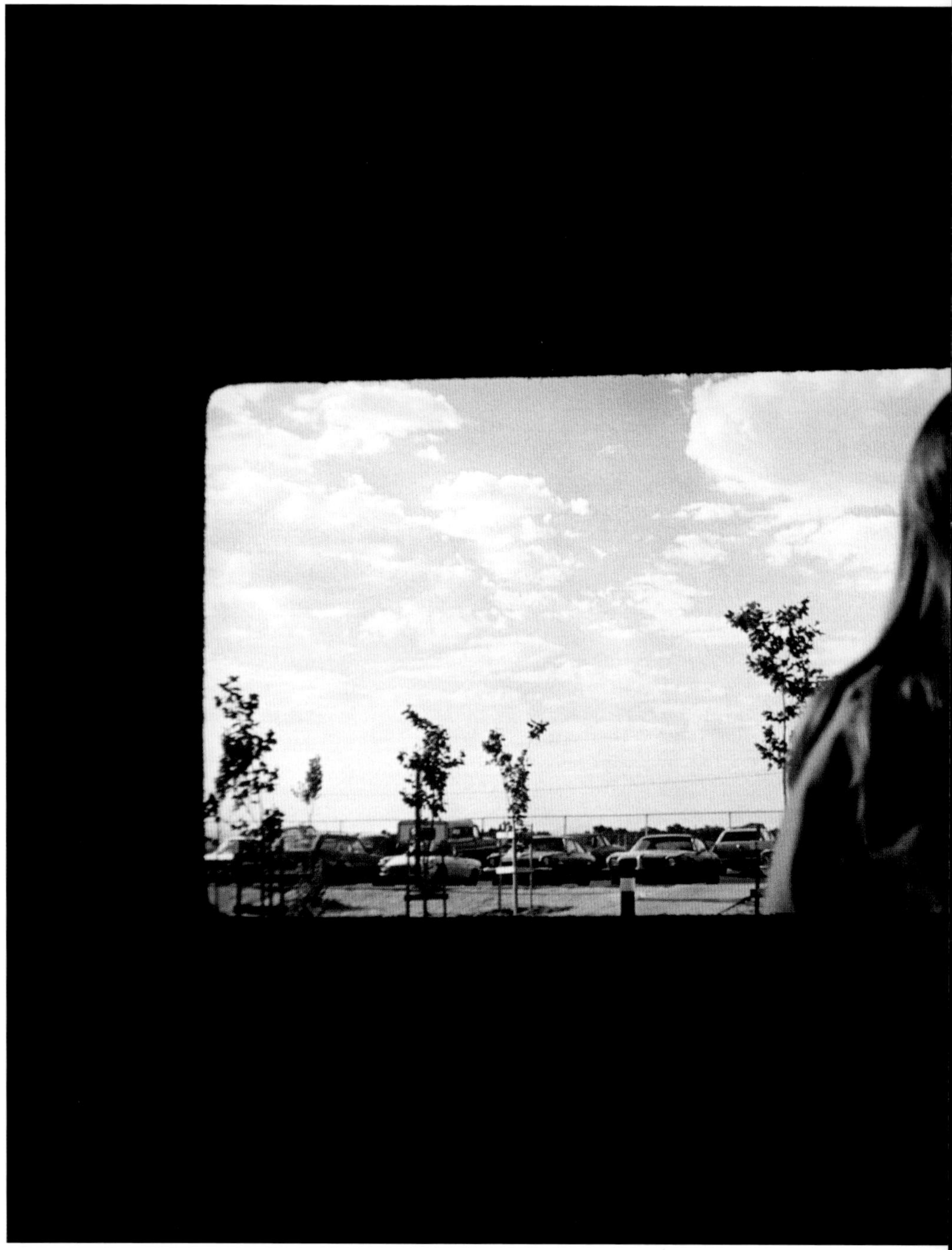

5. *Merged Moments*, 1976.
Gelatin silver print, 5½ × 9 in.
In the collection of the Museum of Texas Tech University, Lubbock

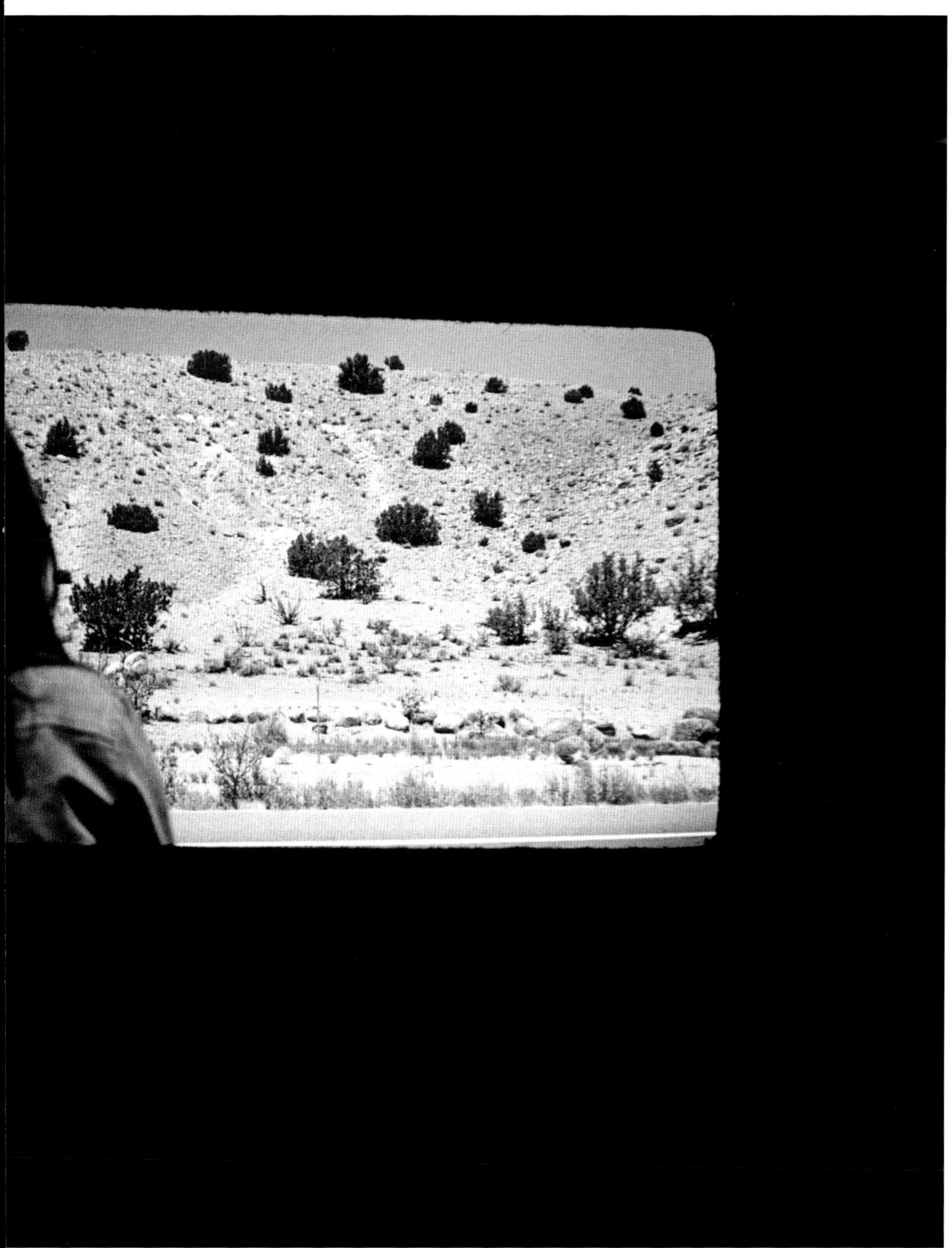

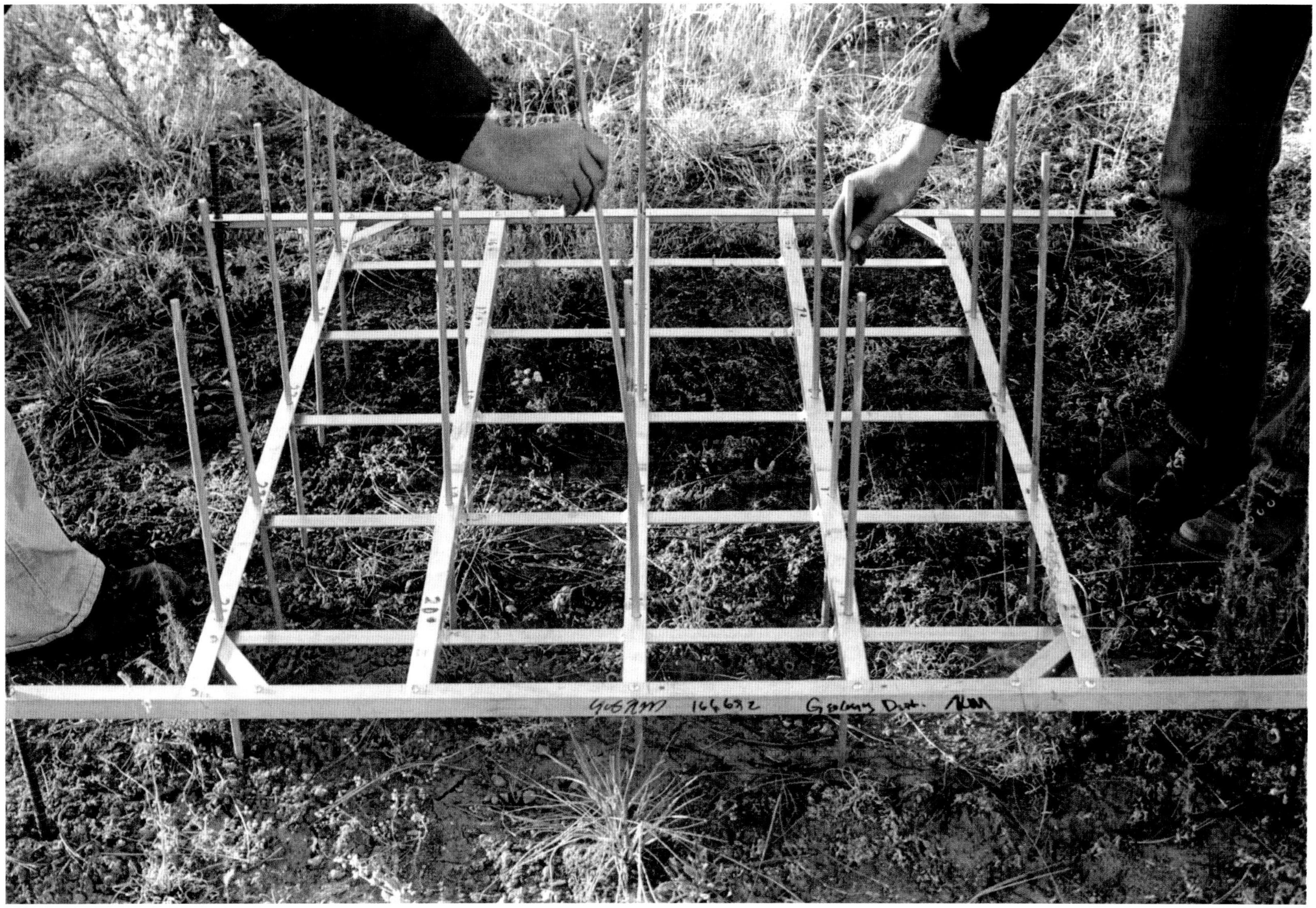

6. *After the Fire, Bandelier National Monument, New Mexico (Topography Grid)*, 1977–78.
Gelatin silver print, 5 × 7 in.
In the collection of the Museum of Texas Tech University, Lubbock

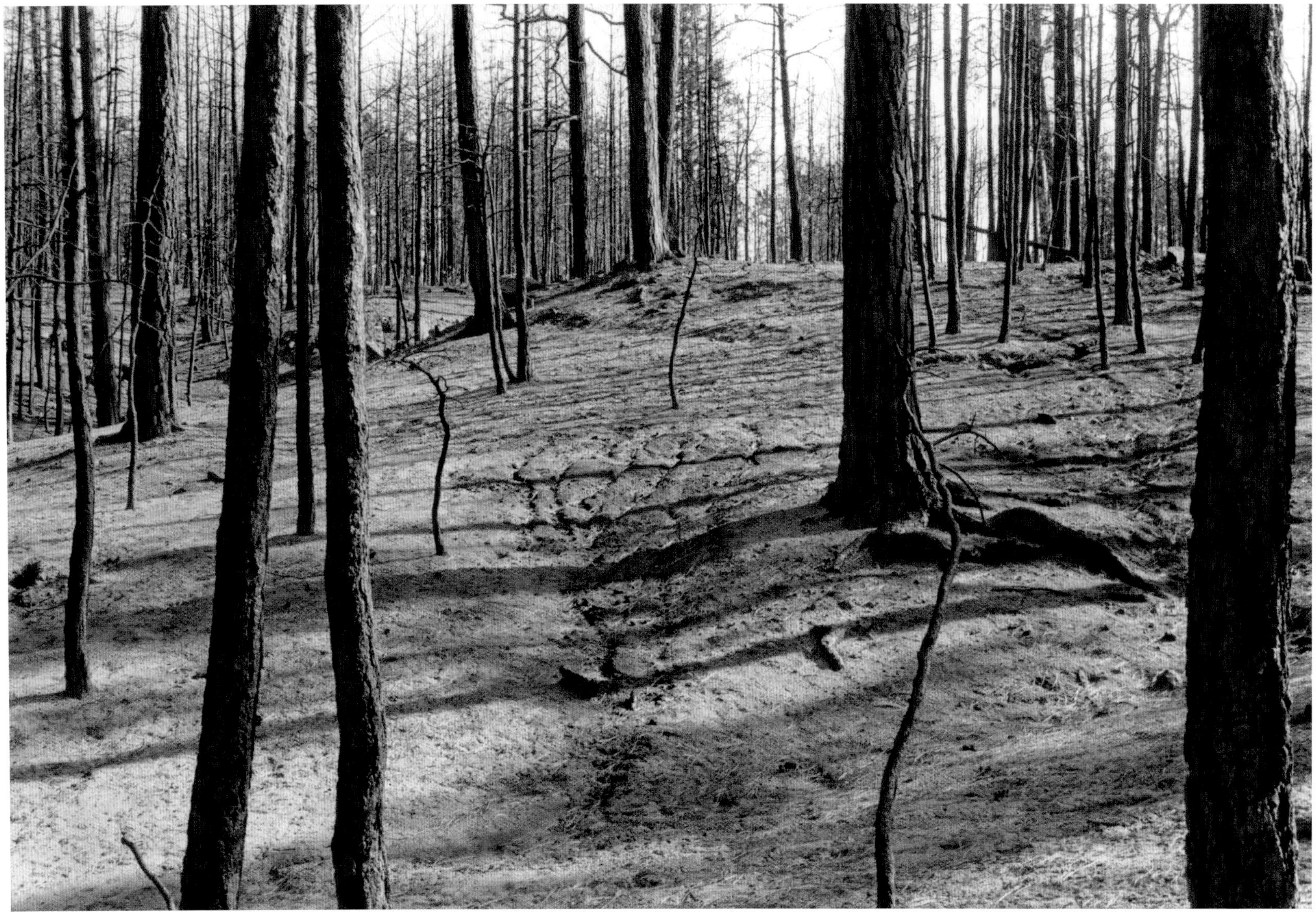

7. *After the Fire, Bandelier National Monument, New Mexico (Denuded Slope Erosion)*, 1977–78.
Gelatin silver print, 5 × 7 in.
In the collection of the Museum of Texas Tech University, Lubbock

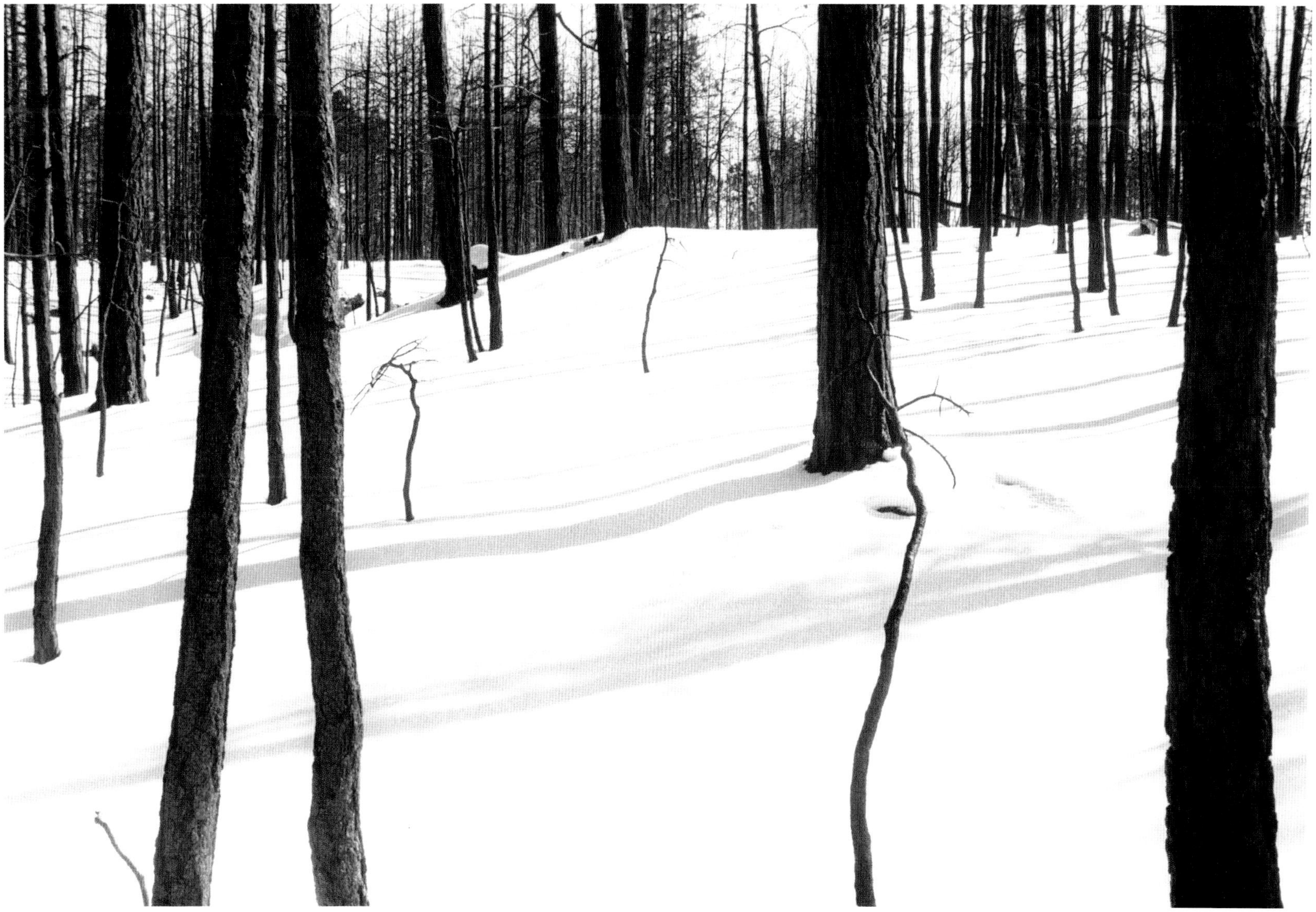

8. *After the Fire, Bandelier National Monument, New Mexico (in Snow)*, 1977–78.
Gelatin silver print, 5 × 7 in.
In the collection of the Museum of Texas Tech University, Lubbock

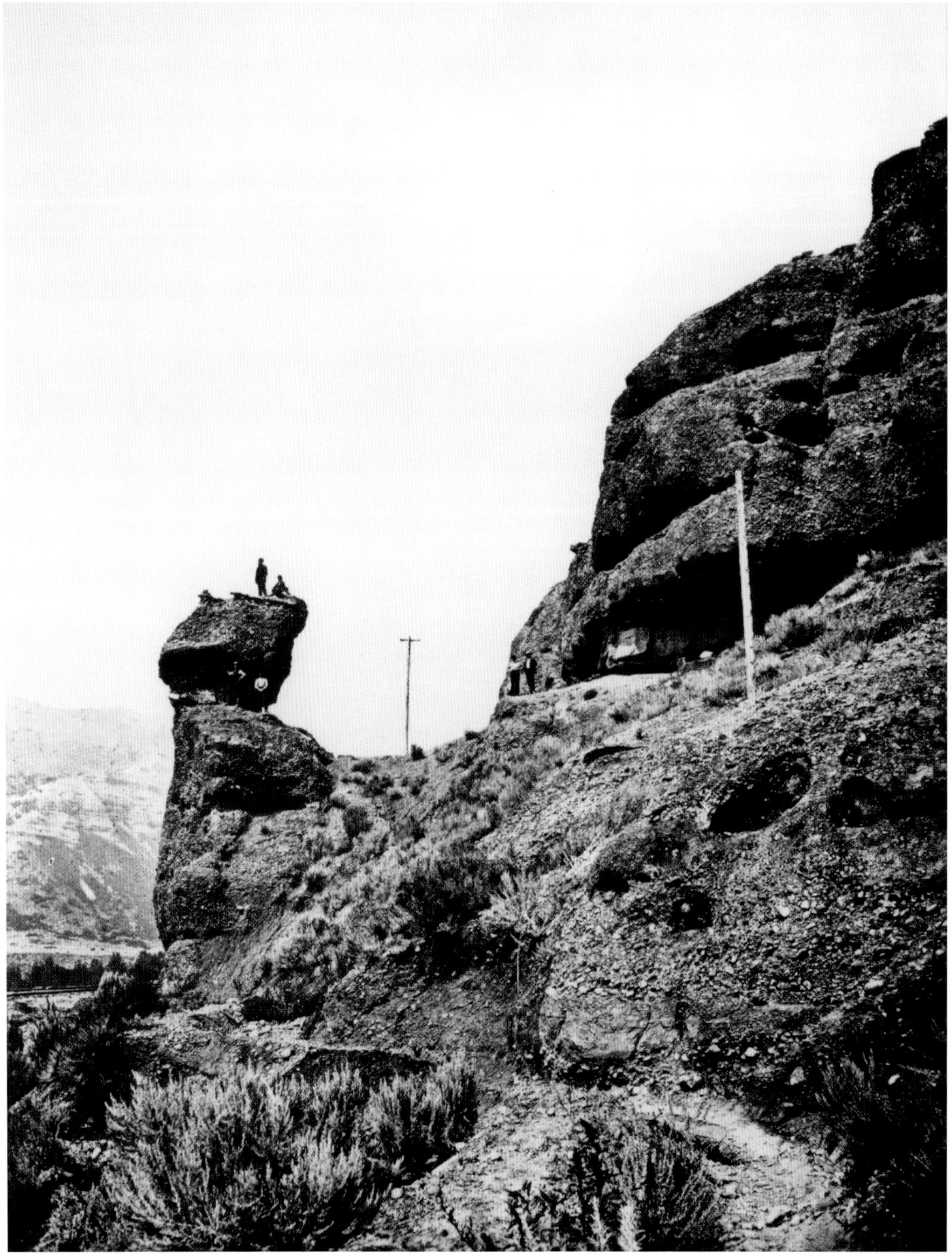

9. *Pulpit Rock*, 1869, by W. H. Jackson.
Gelatin silver print copy of an albumen print, 9 × 7 in.
Original albumen print in the photo collection of the U.S. Geological Survey Library, Denver.
Gelatin silver copy print in the collection of the Museum of Texas Tech University, Lubbock

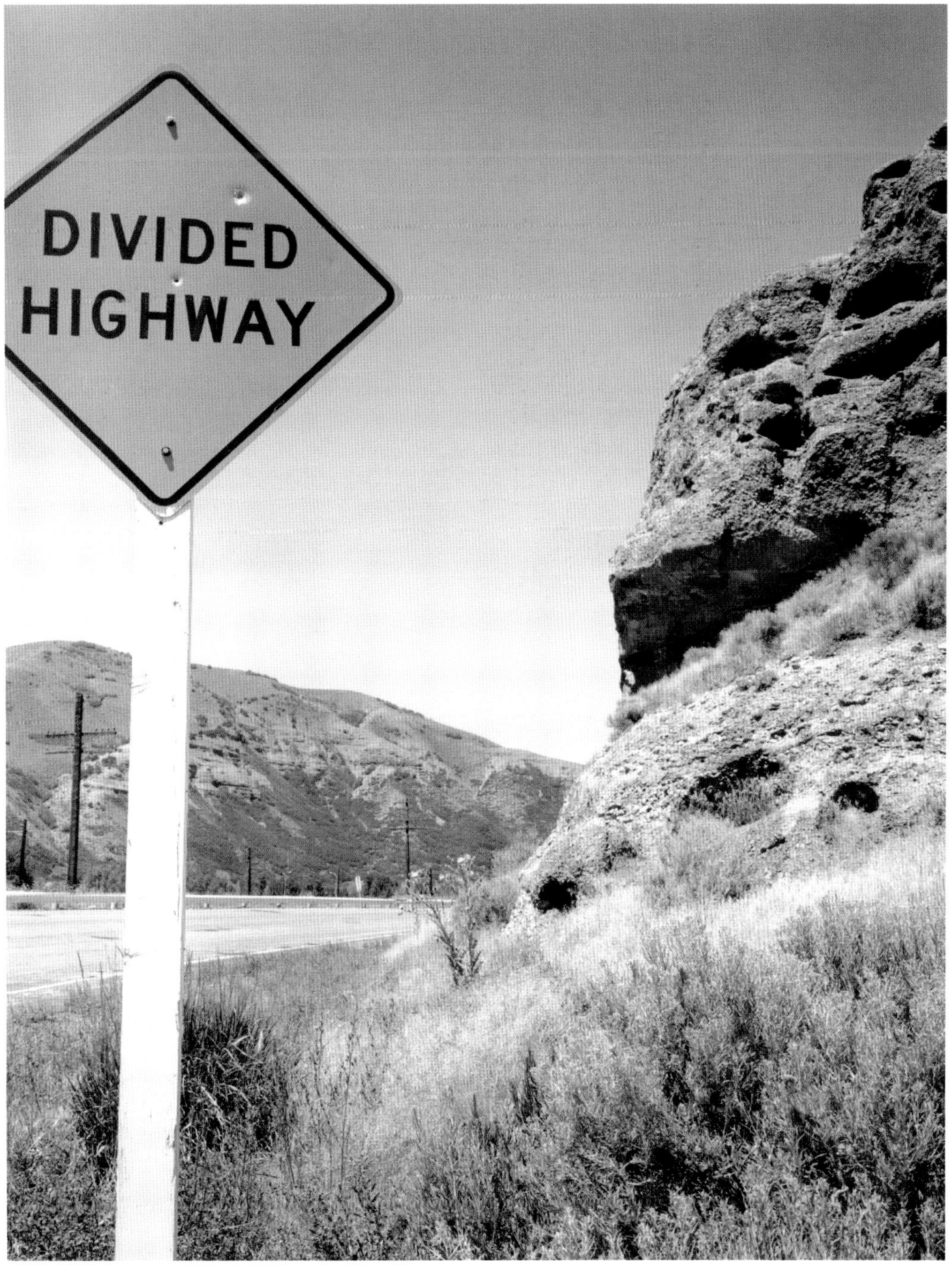

10. *Location of Pulpit Rock*, 1978, by Rick Dingus for the Rephotographic Survey Project.
Gelatin silver copy print, 9 × 7 in.
In the collection of the Museum of Texas Tech University, Lubbock

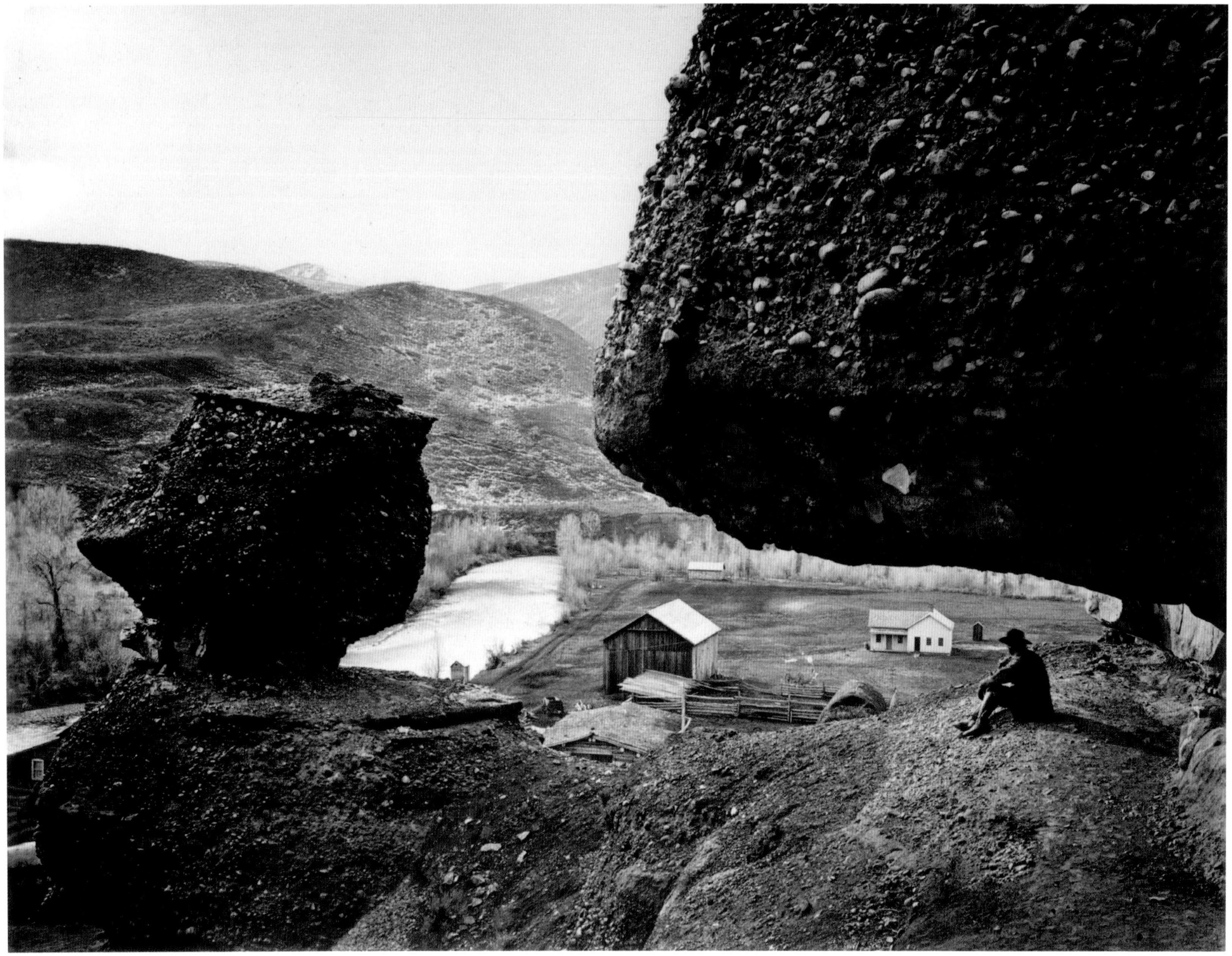

11. *Hanging Rock (and Pulpit Rock), Echo City, Utah Territory*, ca. 1868, by A. J. Russell.
Gelatin silver print copy of an albumen print, 7 × 9 in.
Original albumen print in the photo collection of the U.S. Geological Survey Library, Denver.
Gelatin silver copy print in the collection of the Museum of Texas Tech University, Lubbock

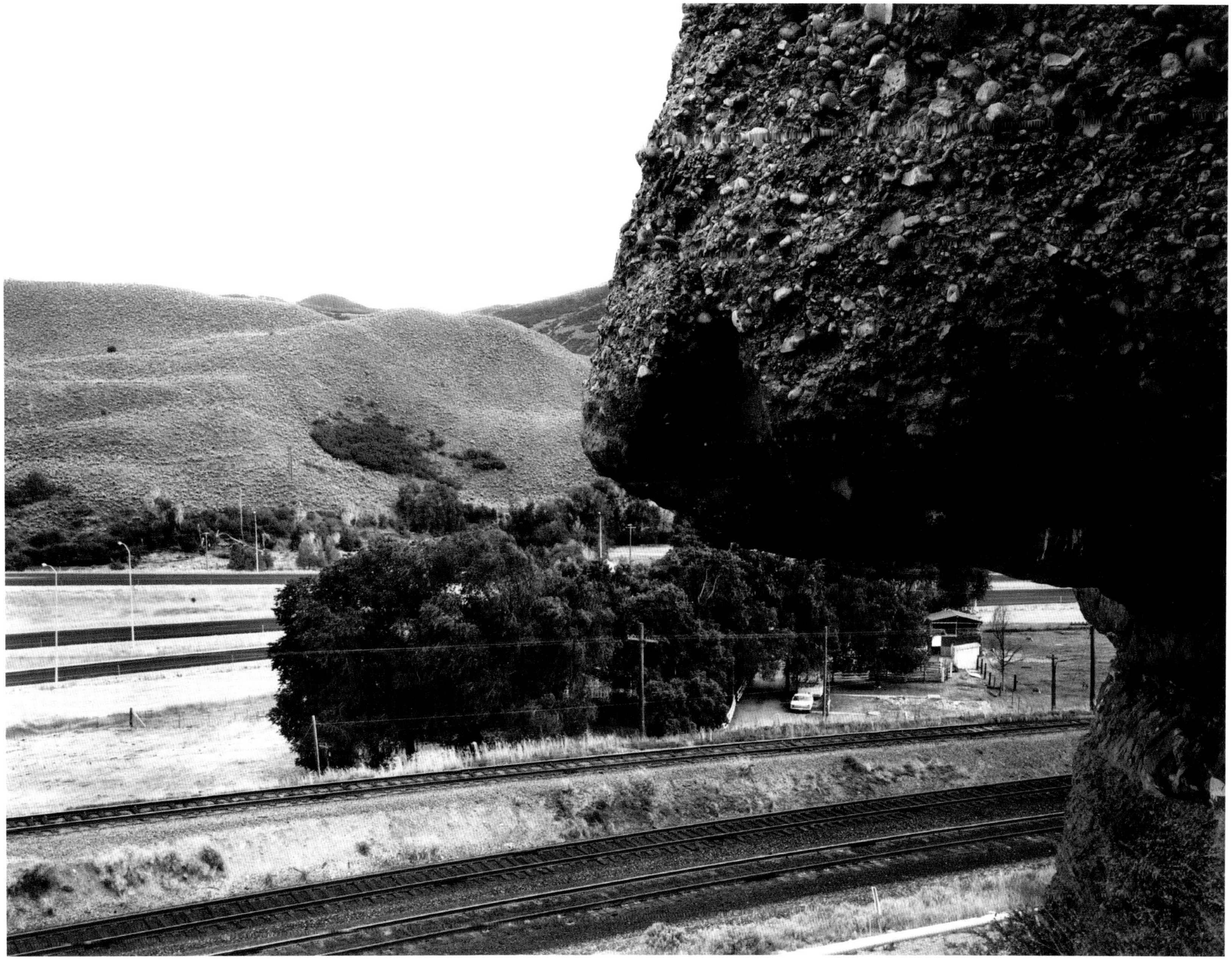

12. *Hanging Rock*, 1978, by Rick Dingus for the Rephotographic Survey Project.
Gelatin silver print, 7 × 9 in.
In the collection of the Museum of Texas Tech University, Lubbock

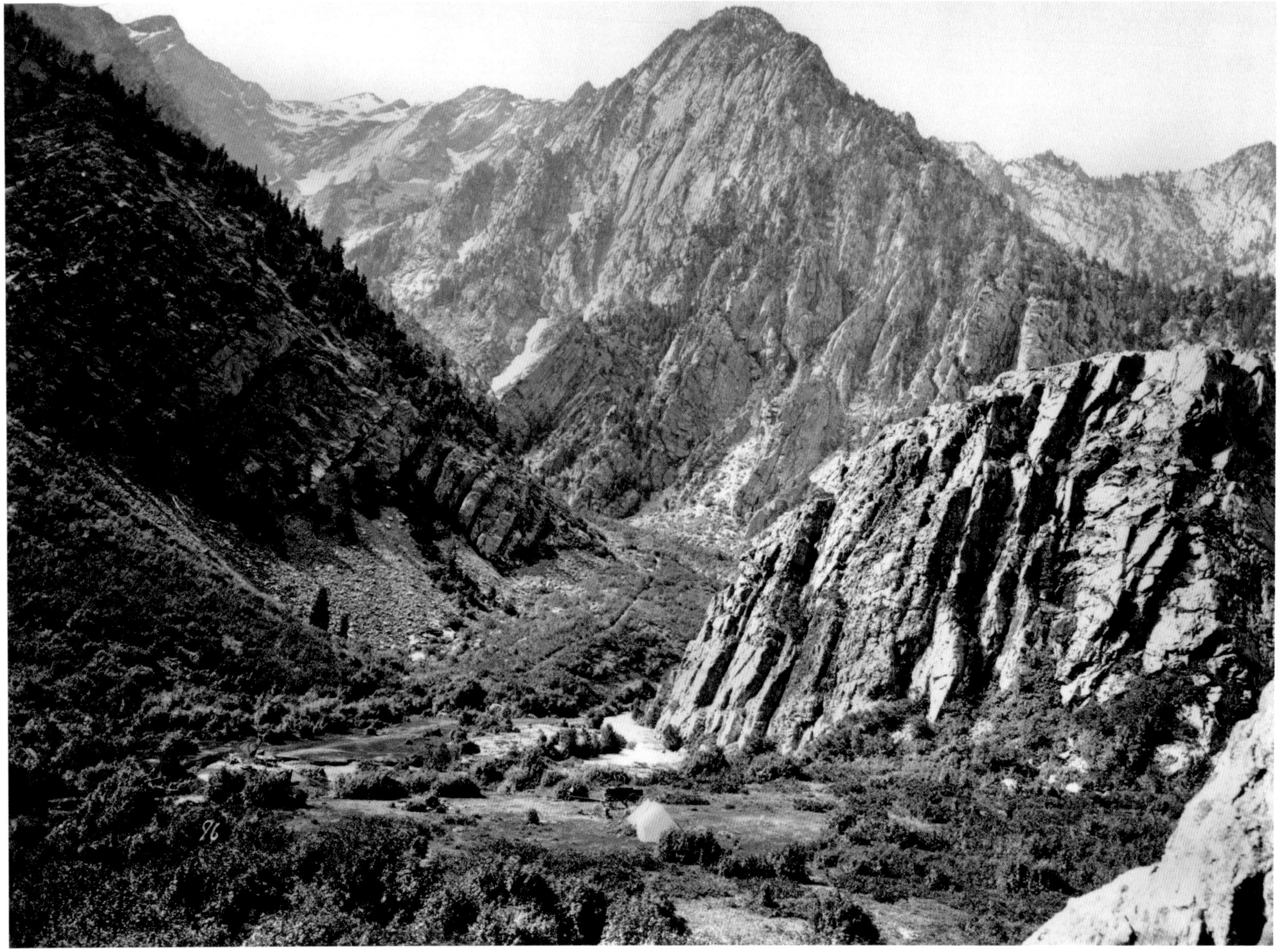

13. *Big Cottonwood Canyon*, 1868, by T. H. O'Sullivan.
Gelatin silver print copy of an albumen print, 6½ × 9 in.
Original albumen print in the photo collection of the U.S. Geological Survey Library, Denver.
Gelatin silver copy print in the collection of the Museum of Texas Tech University, Lubbock

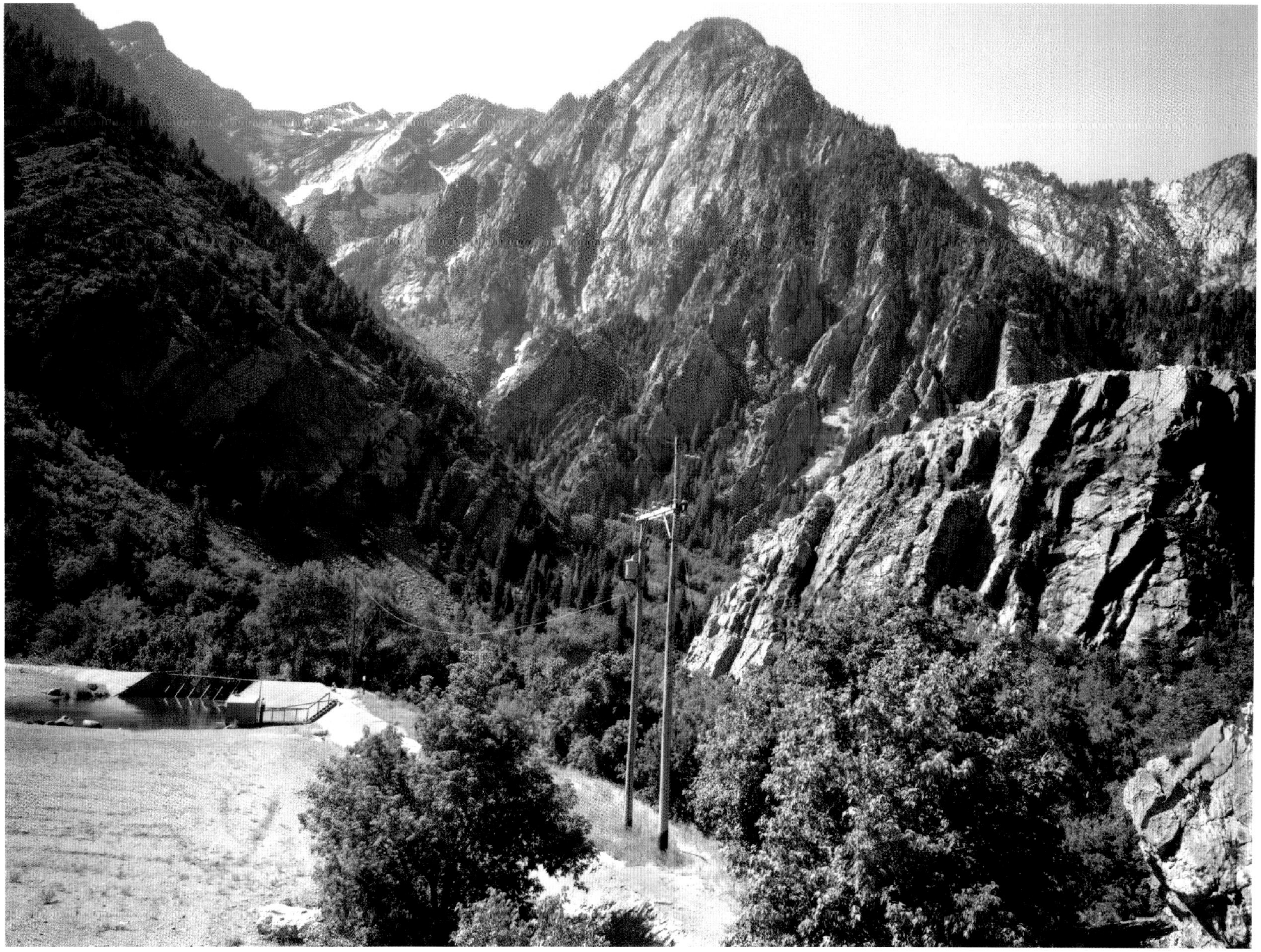

14. *Big Cottonwood Canyon*, 1978, by Rick Dingus for the Rephotographic Survey Project.
Gelatin silver print, 6½ × 9 in.
In the collection of the Museum of Texas Tech University, Lubbock

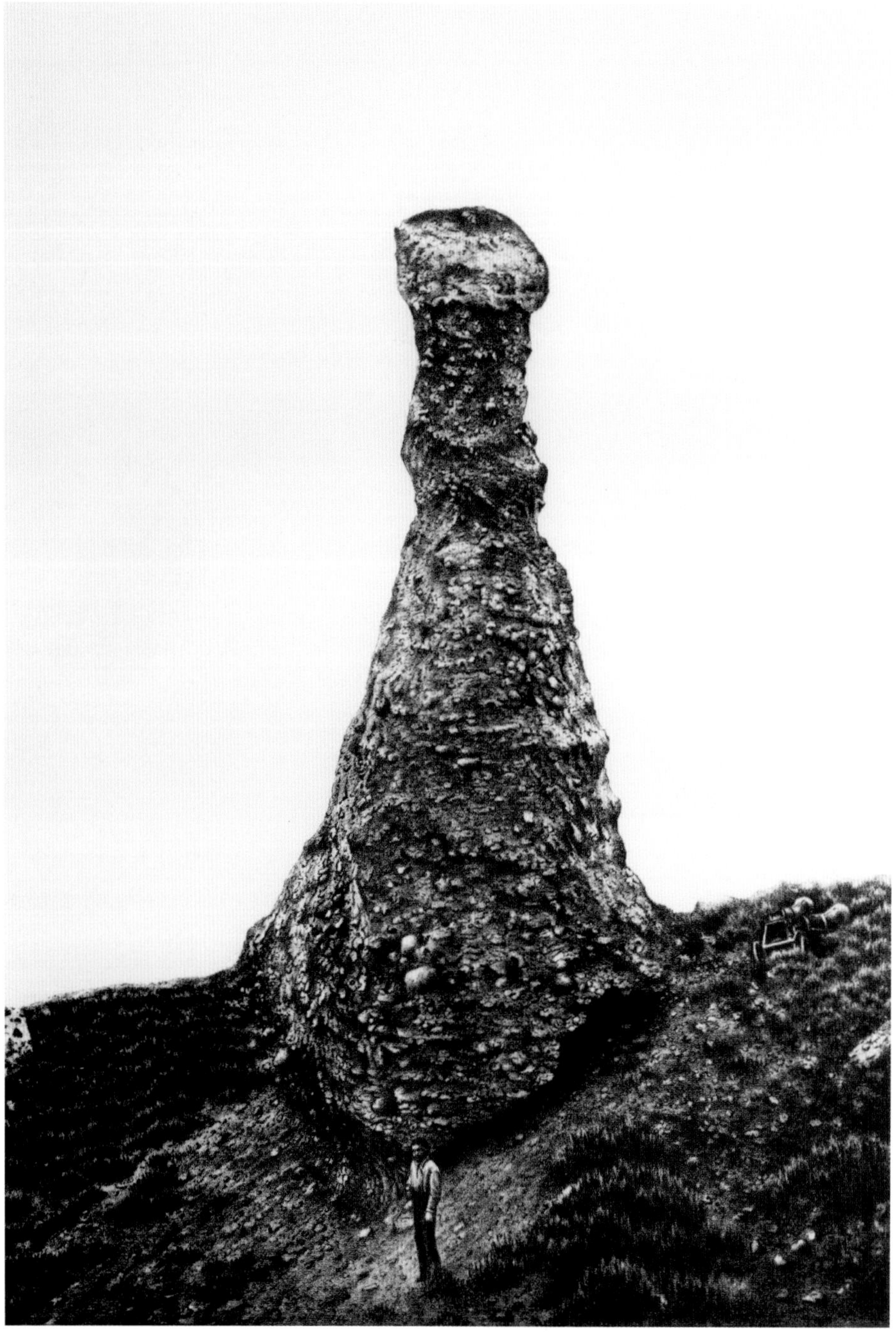

15. *Conglomerate Column (Witches Rock #1)—Weber Valley, Utah*, 1869, by T. H. O'Sullivan. Gelatin silver print copy of a lithograph from Clarence King's *Report of the Geological Exploration of the Fortieth Parallel, Volume II—Descriptive Geology*, after an 1869 photograph by T. H. O'Sullivan, 9 × 6 in.
Original photograph in the collection of the U. S. Geological Survey Library, Denver.
Gelatin silver copy print in the collection of the Museum of Texas Tech University, Lubbock

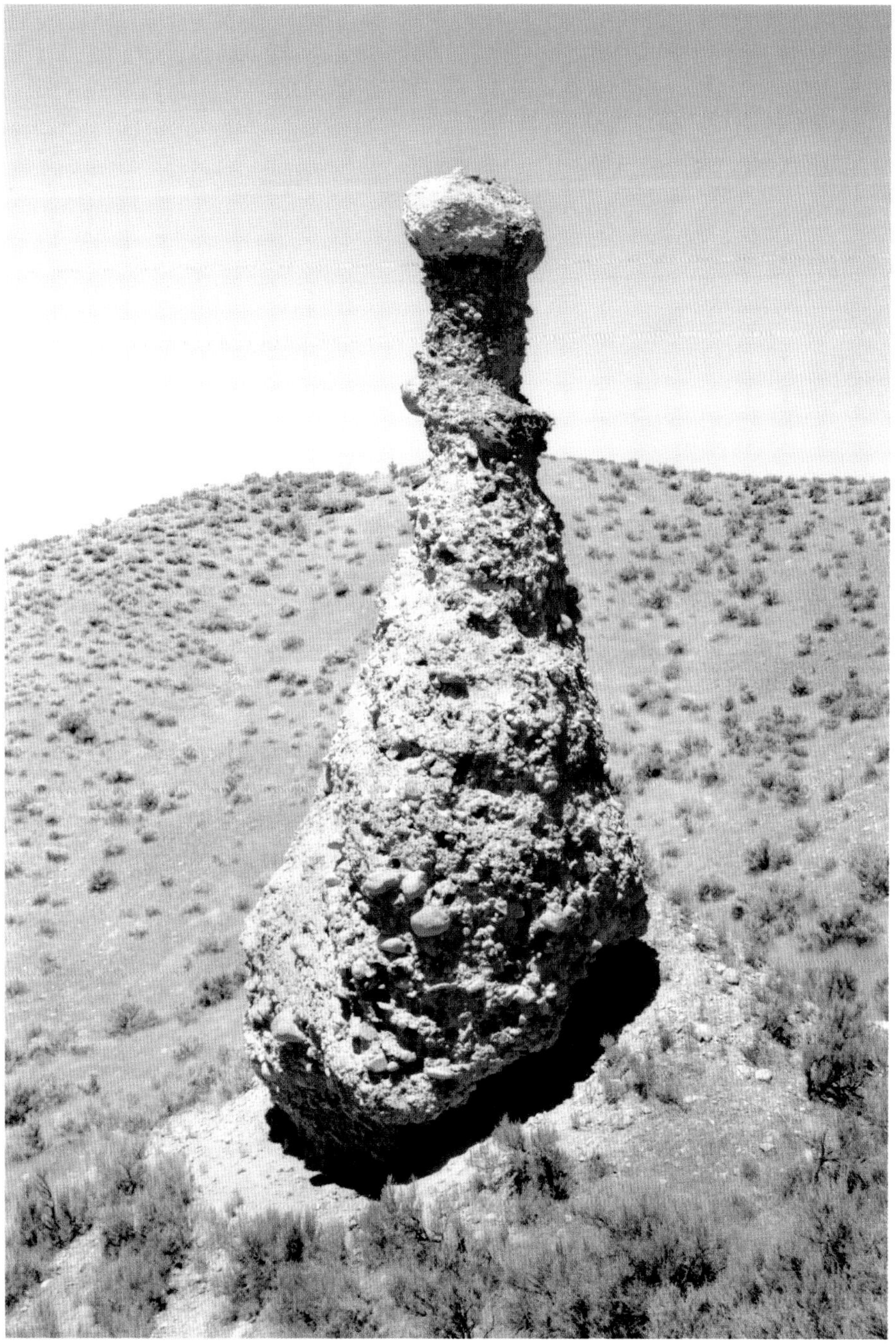

16. *Conglomerate Column (Witches Rock #1)*, 1978, by Rick Dingus for the Rephotographic Survey Project.
Gelatin silver print, 9 × 6 in.
In the collection of the Museum of Texas Tech University, Lubbock

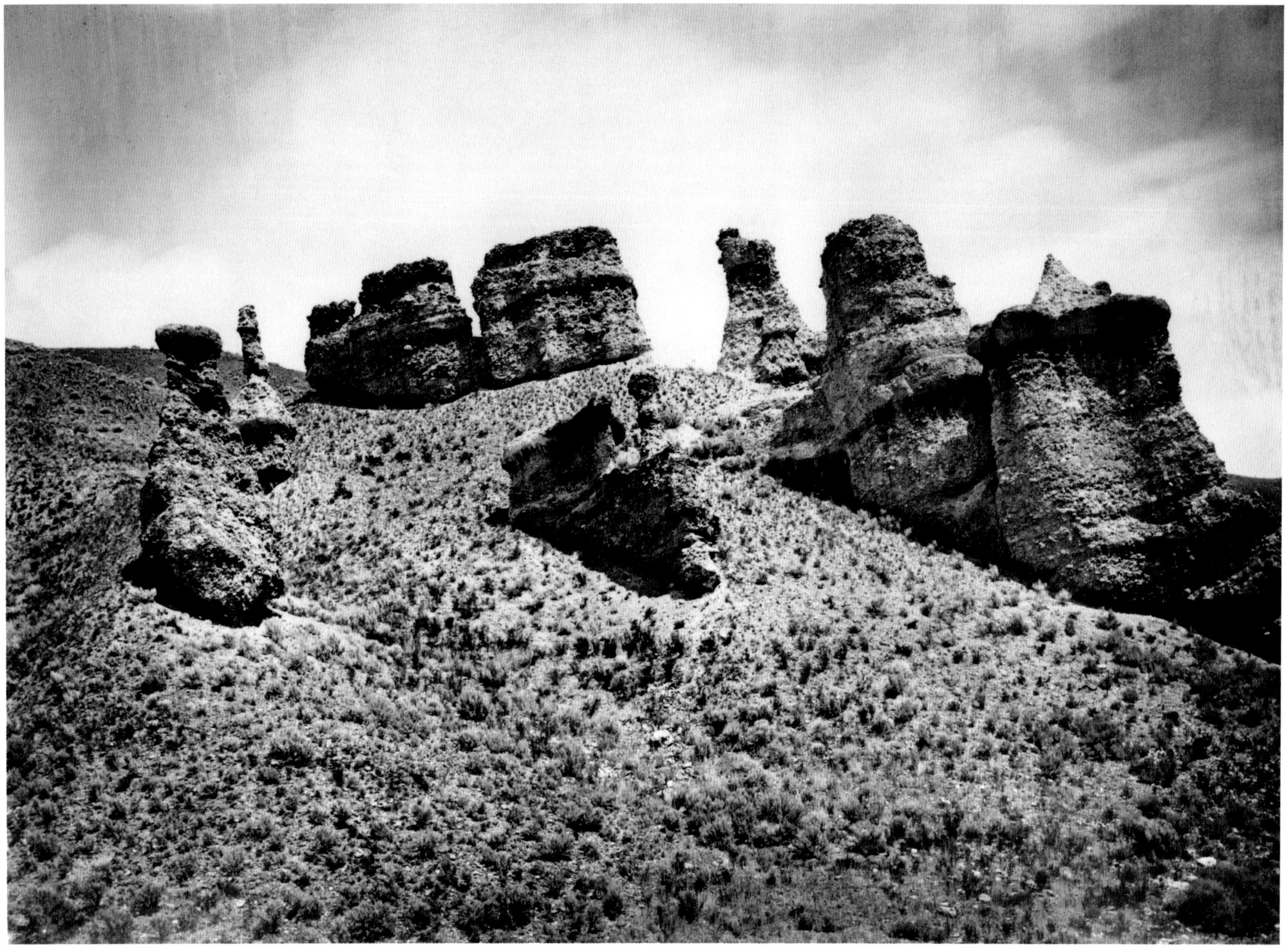

17. *Tertiary Conglomerates (Witches Rocks #5)—Weber Valley, Utah*, 1869, by T. H. O'Sullivan.
Gelatin silver print copy of an albumen print, 6½ × 9 in.
Original albumen print in the photo collection of the U.S. Geological Survey Library, Denver.
Gelatin silver copy print in the collection of the Museum of Texas Tech University, Lubbock

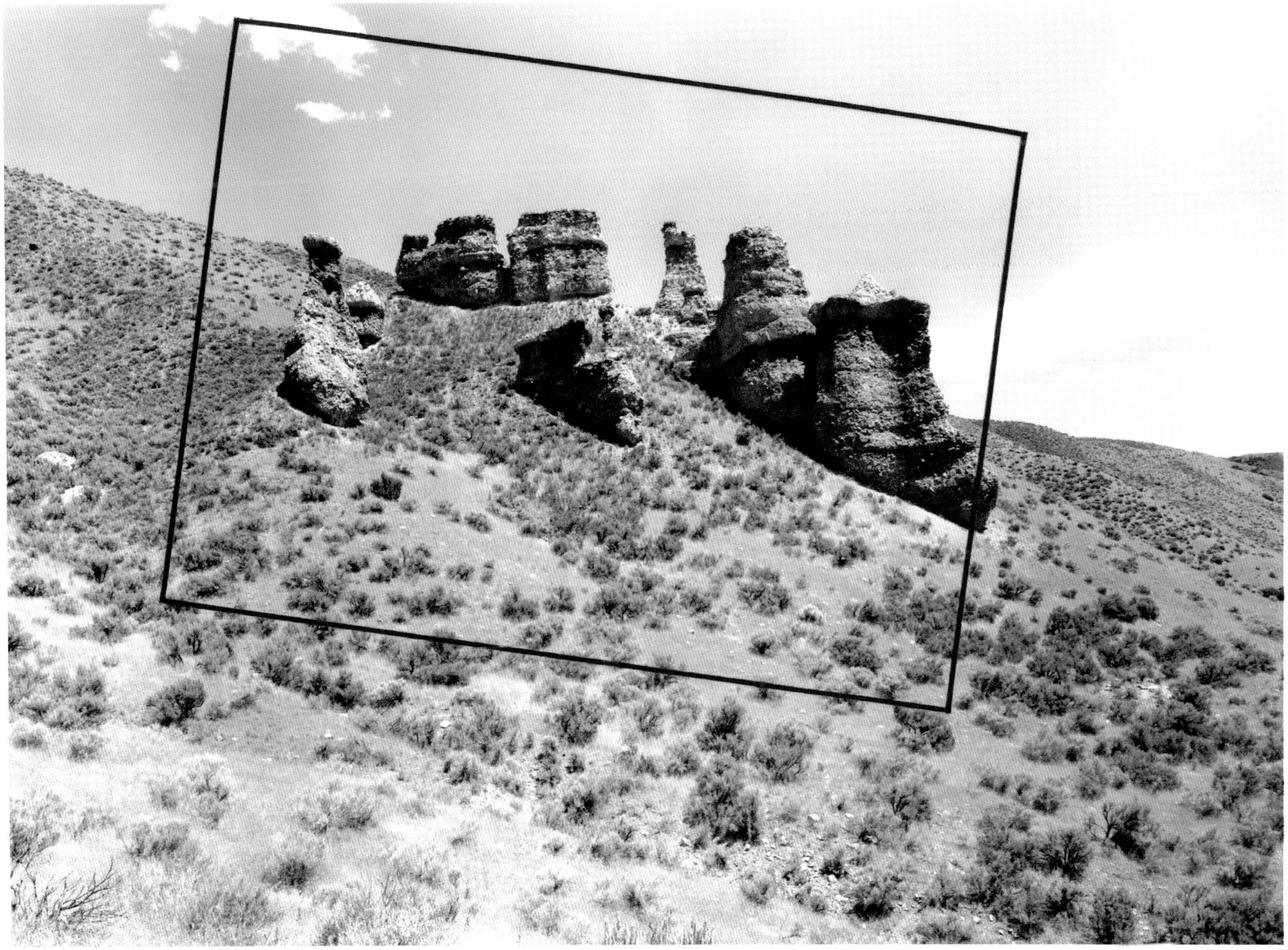

18. *Tertiary Conglomerates (Witches Rocks #5)*, 1978, by Rick Dingus for the Rephotographic Survey Project.
Gelatin silver print, 6½ × 9 in.
In the collection of the Museum of Texas Tech University, Lubbock

Ground Level

An Interview with Rick Dingus

Peter S. Briggs

THIS EDITED INTERVIEW between Rick Dingus (RD) and Peter Briggs (PB) was gathered from several discussions in Lubbock, Texas, over the last ten years. While the conversation tends to focus on formative aspects of Dingus's art-making practice, it concludes with the artist's observations on his most recent work, Star Party and IR Aerials.

PB: What is the importance of the relationship between a place where you find yourself and your camera?

RD: In some ways my photographs are souvenirs of having been somewhere, in a particular place at a given time. When I am traveling I am often focused on identifying places to go back to, to explore and walk around. If I end up photographing, it becomes about being in that place with a camera.

PB: Are the images or photographs you make, then, a mnemonic, a means to reinvent a physical or emotional moment that might also be a memory?

RD: That's part of it. But while preserving references to past experiences, I'm also interested in acknowledging that memories are continually replaced and new experiences are constructed every time we look at photographs. We always perceive in the present moment, and our experience constantly varies depending on our engagement. I've been interested in photographs because of this. Photographs are imperfect records, like quotes taken out of context, or selected and edited recollections. They connect the past to the present. Looking at them can't help but create new impressions; they change how we experience and what we remember. Looking at photographs is an unremitting negotiation.

PB: Do you think in this world of fluctuations, or to use your word, negotiations, that there are any general principles, principles that seem like a scientific law?

RD: I imagine there are probably general patterns that guide the way things work. And we might agree to recognize or trust some of these as rules or principles. But I'm not sure we ever see enough of the pattern to avoid being deluded by limited perspectives.

PB: When or how did your disposition toward variability, toward change and fluctuation develop?

RD: As a kid I liked science experiments, but I also liked to draw pictures, write stories, and make photographs. My parents made snapshots with different cameras that we passed around. They bought a home movie camera when I was in junior high school, and my friends and I made films that mocked the TV shows and movies we liked. In high school I had good art classes taught by practicing artists, and the teachers took us on field trips. I remember studying themes and variations in serial artworks, like Monet's Impressionist paintings, and seeing Ed Kienholz's controversial *Back Seat Dodge '38* (1964) at the Los Angeles County Museum of Art. I also took a photography class during my senior year of high school. But I was afraid that becoming an artist or photographer might not be practical. I had two older brothers who had pursued professional careers: Larry was a lawyer, and Ron was a physicist. Ron's enthusiasm for experimentation and the abstract concepts of theoretical physics influenced me at first to consider science as a career. I thought it might provide a better chance for making a living. But I knew I would always want to make art, even if I couldn't earn a living as an artist.

When I went to college, I thought I might follow in Ron's footsteps. But I wasn't interested in the math that was required and I didn't trust the reliability of clinical distance that science espoused. I liked how art blended abstract thinking with spontaneity and the primacy of firsthand experience. With photography it seemed as if the world itself could become an experimental lab. I could go out and collect information to bring back and study later. I liked how photography seemed connected to memory and conditioning, and how images could be recorded in chronological order. It was also a means to explore perception and how a translation of an experience through media alters things.

I thought of accumulated images as evidence that fed my continued deliberations. I liked that art encouraged interdisciplinary exploration so you didn't have to stick to a single field. I valued the methodologies of science, but I was suspicious of the goal and possibility of ever attaining neutrality—"objectivity" only seemed possible in limited ways, and no matter how close you might get, you were left with the problem of interpretation, which was not neutral. Besides, I wanted to include and not ignore the mythical, symbolic, and freely associative subconscious and unconscious aspects of the human condition as part of what I was investigating.

PB: Your undergraduate education at the University of California, Santa Barbara (UCSB), between 1969 and 1973, seems to have been a seminal period in the development of your approach to making art that addresses variability of time and space.

RD: I tried altering public spaces in subtle ways, and created studio environments that changed as one moved through them. I experimented with how photographs recorded space and time and how that altered experience. I made stereoscopic time exposures, for example, of colored light drawings to be viewed in three dimensions. Inspired by Robert Smithson, Zen koans, and Tony Delap's magical trick sculptures, I shot color slides of mirrors stuck in the sand to create "illusions" that showed their tricks and questioned "reality."

I put different kinds of paint on blocks of solid ice. As the ice melted and everything dried, visible evidence of the process remained that could be read like a geologist might read processes that are visible on the earth's surface. On another occasion, I went to a particular spot at a local beach and dug a deep hole with a posthole digger. I filled the hole with concrete to make a solid column that served as a benchmark for the changing levels of sand. Afterwards, I kept returning to photograph it. One day the concrete marker disappeared because it was completely covered by sand. Later, a small corner of the column reemerged, just barely visible midway along a sandy ridge. Then a major storm came through. It took away all the sand that was on the beach as well as the concrete column. During the next few days, the previously hidden bedrock of the coastline was revealed.

I was intrigued but frustrated at how elusive these beach transformations seemed. My memory was not detailed enough to bring much into focus, and the photographs I had been making were too casual to record what I wanted to see. The varied positions and angles of my camera made it hard to track and follow subtle changes. This led me to become interested in using the camera in a more controlled fashion. I came across Eadweard Muybridge's photographic studies of humans and animals in motion. It occurred to me that Muybridge's use of multiple images to study brief time intervals could be adapted to studying change over long time spans. If Muybridge had made things visible that were happening too fast for us to see in standard time, I wondered if it was possible to make things more visible that we might see but not notice because our attention was directed elsewhere.

This led to my first repeat photography experiment during February in 1973 at the same beach in Isla Vista, California, that had held my concrete column. I thought of this as a performance piece. It required that I rearrange my life to be available every day at precisely 5 P.M. to revisit and be anchored to the same place in order to make the same photograph. Instead of intuitively responding to the beauty of that place, I embraced a mock scientific aesthetic for this project, a systematic and seemingly detached study of change. Instead of shooting when the beachfront looked appealing, I wanted to see how the place might look if I just made the same photograph at precise twenty-four-hour intervals over the course of a month. So I inverted Muybridge's technique—instead of freezing individual moments that occurred in the span of a few seconds, I shot recurring moments over a month-long period. If motion pictures recorded twenty-four frames per second to duplicate the look of "normal" time, I wanted to see what a month would like if each frame was shot twenty-four hours apart.

Throughout February 1973, I returned every day to the same staircase overlooking Isla Vista beach. At exactly 5 P.M., I shot basically the same image, creating a series of color slides. I tried viewing them in several ways, usually as slide dissolves with the images gradually shifting one by one in chronological order. This made it possible to experience changes I had not been fully aware of when I was exposing the film. The cycle of the tide gradually coming in and going out became visible. Islands in the distance appeared and disappeared. Colors, sunlight, and weather varied constantly. The beach was crowded on sunny days, empty on rainy ones. The sand level went up and down. Another storm uncovered the bedrock that was more often than not hidden beneath the sand.

I tried printing these images on paper as well as projecting the slides in tandem. As these experiments progressed, I began to consider photographs less as end products and more as catalysts for experience and engagement. I became interested in the idea that the "images" actually resided more in the minds of viewers than on projection screens or sheets of paper.

PB: Does a viewer become like sand and water or the tides that move and define an image within a particular moment?

RD: Sort of. . . . I think of it as a triangular relationship among the photographer, subject, and audience. Each plays a role. Instead of emphasizing one to the exclusion of the others, I wanted to acknowledge and explore all sides of that equation as never resolved, as ongoing.

You can't guarantee or definitively predict how people will

experience or understand anything, and I'm not interested in just sharing a canned experience. I want to encourage viewers to pay attention to their experience. Presenting images in ways that confound expectations invites observers to study more closely, to spend more time looking, to see more. If they really get invested, they may begin to realize that what they are seeing is as much a product of what they bring as it is about what the photographer brings.

PB: Can you give me an example?

RD: Consider the photo drawings I did for many years. I made these mixed media pieces by altering my own photographs of natural landscape processes (e.g., erosion) and traces of human activity (e.g., cultural artifacts). Like other photographers in the 1970s, I was interested in posing questions about relationships between culture and nature. I was visualizing how the human condition was not separate from nature but part of it. I also sought to acknowledge how all black and white photographs frame the world, alter it, change the context, and translate a three-dimensional world into a flat tonal plane. On the surface of these photographs, I drew gestural and expressive marks with graphite and silver-colored pencils. These marks served as counterpoints of intuitive and imagined responses to challenge the documentary associations that were commonly projected onto photography in those days.[1] A lot of people were talking about photographs as transparent windows you looked through. I wanted to acknowledge them as artifacts.

My drawn marks mimicked, but also remained at odds with, the physical marks in environments recorded by the camera. I was challenging the assumptions about a photograph's ability to represent objective reality. I wanted to acknowledge that photographs were physical objects. My marks altered what was visible in the photographs and changed how a viewer read the images. When the prints were installed and lit, the reflected light from the graphite and silver marks caused shifts in the images as viewers moved. At times it was hard to tell what was drawn and what was photographic. A slight shift might cause the silver to stand out as a highlight sitting on the surface. I wanted the viewers to move around, come close, back up, shift from side to side, and explore the consequences of their own participation.

PB: You attended the University of New Mexico (UNM) for graduate school. Why there?

RD: Throughout my undergraduate career I had wanted to work more with photography, but that wasn't much of an option when I was at UCSB. I happened to visit my brother who was working as a physicist in Los Alamos. As soon as I arrived in New Mexico, I thought, "This is a place I want to be." By then I had lived in the farmlands of the Midwest, near the beaches of both coasts, and in the Rocky Mountains of Wyoming, but there was something compelling and magical about New Mexico that made me want to stay. I discovered that there was a reputable graduate program in photography at UNM. Back in California, I saw a photo exhibition in Los Angeles that included works by UNM faculty—Van Deren Coke, Beaumont Newhall, and Tom Barrow. I applied without knowing much more than that. I didn't quite realize what I was getting into when I was accepted in January 1976. In some ways the academic focus at UNM was very different from the open-ended, free-wheeling environment I had worked in at UCSB in the late sixties and early seventies.

At UNM we were likewise encouraged to experiment and push the edges of the envelope, but it was different. There was an equally strong emphasis on history, criticism, and scholarship. I thrived on the challenge. I learned from the various photo faculty, from studying photographic history, and by meeting contemporary photographers, historians, curators, and critics that passed through UNM. And I learned a lot from just living in New Mexico.

PB: So, you received your MFA from UNM in 1981.

RD: A lot of graduate students back then only completed an MA at UNM because an MFA at that time involved substantial historical research and writing a dissertation. I finished my course work in just a few years, but it took several more to finish my writing. While I was doing that, I became involved in working on the Rephotographic Survey Project, writing my dissertation based on the repeat photographs I had made of sites originally photographed by Timothy H. O'Sullivan. However, somebody broke into my studio and stole a knapsack with all my notes and drafts, so I had to start over. That added at least a year. But the delay caused me to review and rethink things more carefully. UNM Press by then had agreed to publish my dissertation as a book. At the time I was in love with living in New Mexico, and I didn't really want to go anywhere else. Albuquerque was a good base camp. I was teaching part time at New Mexico Tech in Socorro and photographing near and distant landscapes throughout the Southwest. I was also beginning to exhibit my work around the country. I took a temporary job offer at the University of Colorado in Boulder to get moving again.

PB: It's almost a cliché, for a photographer to fall in love with New Mexico. . . . What did you fall in love with?

RD: I liked the "magical realism" of the place, the strange mix of time frames and cultures comingled in the present, people with competing cultures, rituals, and histories continuing to coexist. I liked the vast continuum of geologic and cultural time— land formations with fossils that looked like an autobiography of the earth's own making; artifacts and ruins that referenced an unbroken record from prehistory to the present; competing frictions and perspectives among Anglos, Hispanics, and Native Americans. And this caldron boiled alongside problematic cutting-edge technologies and scientific research at Los Alamos and Sandia National Labs.

I liked the sparseness, austerity, and isolation of the desert, the crystalline clarity of the atmosphere that made it possible to see into the far distance. Yes, I liked the "light." But not just because of how beautiful it made things appear. I liked how it seemed to expose and reveal each thing it illuminated for more incisive scrutiny. There seemed to be an inexhaustible store of meaning connected to everything.

The land seemed to contain all of these things. I had been suspicious for some time of popular landscape photographs because to me they looked like nostalgic platitudes. And they glossed over the problematic realities that I wanted to recognize and study. Living in New Mexico caused me to think differently about the landscape. I became interested in it as a constructed vernacular environment instead of as a beautiful picture or a pristine natural setting. I saw it as the world reflecting our changing choices, roles, and understandings. Landscapes became any environment—interior or exterior— where visible intersections of culture and nature existed that seemed worth pondering. The land became a localized symbol of the earth, the universe of forces in which we live, the larger context, that all-inclusive place that we call home.

PB: What about influences on your work from within the history of photography?

RD: Timothy O'Sullivan was probably the biggest influence. The strategies and issues explored by him seemed relevant to my practice as a young artist interested in process and conceptual art.[2]

Following O'Sullivan's trail and rephotographing his images taught me two things: the significant potential of details and just how much photographs alter and translate information. He taught me to experiment with framings, angles, and distances to explore multiple interpretations. At first glance his landscape photographs may seem like simple records of places, but if you look closely, his carefully chosen subjects implied significance and ambiguity. His images seemed slyly subversive, dryly expressive, sometimes humorous, ironic, or skeptical. Some of O'Sullivan's landscapes reminded me of moments from a time-lapse film of geologic time. His use of human figures for scale made me wonder about the human frame of reference within that time frame.

I was especially interested in using repeat photography to learn more about O'Sullivan. The more I rephotographed the sites he had photographed, the more certain I became that, unlike the history I had been taught, O'Sullivan was not a "primitive" who was merely recording the world. He created carefully selected interpretations and experimented with techniques that manipulated visual information. The manipulations he used are not always obvious.

PB: What kinds of manipulations?

RD: Like masking out a background, or canting the horizon, or moving around and photographing the same places from several drastically contrasting angles and distances: exploring totally different aspects of what was there and translating each of those features into separate images. Most other survey photographers didn't push the interpretive possibilities in so many directions. They might make several views, but mostly they just seemed to be trying to make the "best picture," one that conformed to the expectations of landscape paintings or photographs.

Consider O'Sullivan's shots of Bridal Veil Falls near Provo, Utah. He made two images that were meant as separate pictures. One is centered on the waterfall. The other is centered on layers of tilted strata, although the waterfall is included. If you place these two photographs side by side, you can see how they overlap. One of the photographs is drastically tilted, while the other maintains a level horizon. The level image is a picturesque view of a waterfall; the tilted one isolates the rock wall and follows the tilt of the inclined layers of strata. After that, I began to recognize that O'Sullivan sometimes canted the horizon at other places too. But you can't always tell this simply by looking at his images. At first I thought such adjustments may have been accidental, but I soon found several views of individual scenes that included level and canted horizons, so it seemed clear that the canting was intentional.

PB: And how do you embrace in your work that O'Sullivan-like dialogue between a perpetually shifting view of the world and any uniformity of a particular process?

RD: I like venturing deeply into places that seem new and foreign to me, to try and discern larger patterns, which I imagine probably exist but elude me. But I try to keep one foot grounded in a familiar and present context to keep my bearings. As I search to reach beyond my limits, the goal is not to reject where I came from, who I am, or get lost in something new and not be able to return. I look for continuities within diversity because everything, at least at some fundamental level, is part of the same story.

PB: Your more recent bodies of work, Star Party and IR Aerials, exploit infrared light and move from the earth to the stars and back to the earth again, extending the literal and figurative space of your vision.

RD: In 2011 I audited an observational astronomy class because I was interested in learning more about how scientists and amateur astronomers create and manipulate photographs, and I was interested in examining relations among the history of optics, telescopes, and photography. I discovered that Johannes Kepler had coined the term "camera obscura" and used telescope lenses to project images for astronomical studies and for surveying purposes. When smaller camera obscuras evolved as drawing aids for artists, the desire to capture camera images, which could then only be traced by hand, led to the invention of photography. Photography, in turn, became essential to astronomy because serious research telescopes today are not made to look through, but for capturing images with cameras.

I wanted to adapt astrophotography techniques to subjects closer to home so I sent away a DSLR camera to be modified to record visual information from the full spectrum of light. I experimented with this camera by shooting earthbound landscapes in different parts of the spectrum with special filters. The Star Party and IR Aerials series emerged as fitting subjects for infrared.

Straddling the fence between actual science and weird science, the *Star Party* series records mock documentary "evidence" about the activities of amateur astronomers. Although I enjoyed looking through telescopes at the star parties, the activity of the astronomy buffs engaged in obscure tasks fascinated me more than what they were observing. Intrigued by their quirky inventions and methods, I saw this as a vernacular landscape like others I had photographed. Wacky, obsessive, and geeky, but not that different from other niche gatherings I had attended, like those with photographers.

It occurred to me that if I used my modified DSLR and shot with an infrared filter taped over my electronic flash, the illumination would be visible to the camera but not to the people I photographed, nor would it disrupt the night vision they needed for seeing through telescopes. Without a viewfinder, I photographed in the dark, guessing at the framing.

IR Aerials was the second series in which infrared seemed appropriate. Before making these images, I had experimented by shooting ground-level landscapes in infrared; but the images didn't satisfy me. . . . They looked mannered. Mulling that over, I happened to fly home from a trip and ended up with a seat by one of the plane's windows. I shot some infrared photos through the window of the ground below just to see what would happen. When I later studied these photos on my computer, I was amazed by how the infrared had cut through the blurred smears on the window and the haze of atmosphere in the distance. These images contained sharp details of visually separated forms on the earth's surface with tones that didn't look anything like what I had seen when I shot them. Cryptic evidence of human activity was etched in odd patterns on the ground that contrasted with, yet also followed, cogently visible features of topography, erosion, and drainage. The skies looked black like outer space; the curvature of the earth was apparent; the ground's surface looked familiar but alien. Although these were just shot from a passenger airplane, at first glance some of the images might be mistaken for photographs taken from a space station, or confused with pictures of another planet. From then on I paid extra for window seats whenever I flew anywhere in order to accumulate more of these strange photographs. For the duration of each flight, I remained glued to the window, shooting constantly, because I never knew what would come into view, nor how the resulting photographs would look until later when I reworked them in Photoshop.

Making these reminded me of the first time I peered at the sun through a solar telescope and was stunned to see unexpected forces boiling on its surface. Before that I had taken the sun for granted as a familiar bright spot in the sky that provided warmth and security. Astronomy introduced the awareness that our lives on earth depend on maintaining a precarious position within the sweet spot of just the right distance from this dangerously explosive star. With IR Aerials, I'm visualizing the earth as a space rock spinning in proximity to the sun in the midst of a vast universe of unimagined possibilities, and pondering the significance of our role and impact on this isolated planet.

Notes

1. Van Deren Coke provides context for this face to Dingus's work in *Photography: A Facet of Modernism* (San Francisco, Calif.: San Francisco Museum of Modern Art, 1986), 21, 23, 154–55, 171.

2. Dingus discusses this further in "The Ironic Abstractions of Timothy O'Sullivan," *Luna Córnea* 7 (September 1995): 30–37, 132–34.

Photo Drawings

I made a series of manipulated photographs to acknowledge photographs as constructed objects, neither neutral witnesses nor transparent windows on the world as it is. I recognized that once details are translated into a photographic image, they inevitably yield symbolic, expressive, or literary associations.

For nearly two decades, I made mixed media prints by drawing directly on the surface of my photos. I drew on black and white prints with silver-colored pencils and graphite. These images shifted and changed as the viewer moved and looked at them from different angles to see the light reflect differently. In about 1990 I began to shoot in color and to draw on these photographs with color crayons.

VERNACULAR LANDSCAPES, 1977–1998

Vernacular landscapes focused on the intersections of human activity and natural processes.

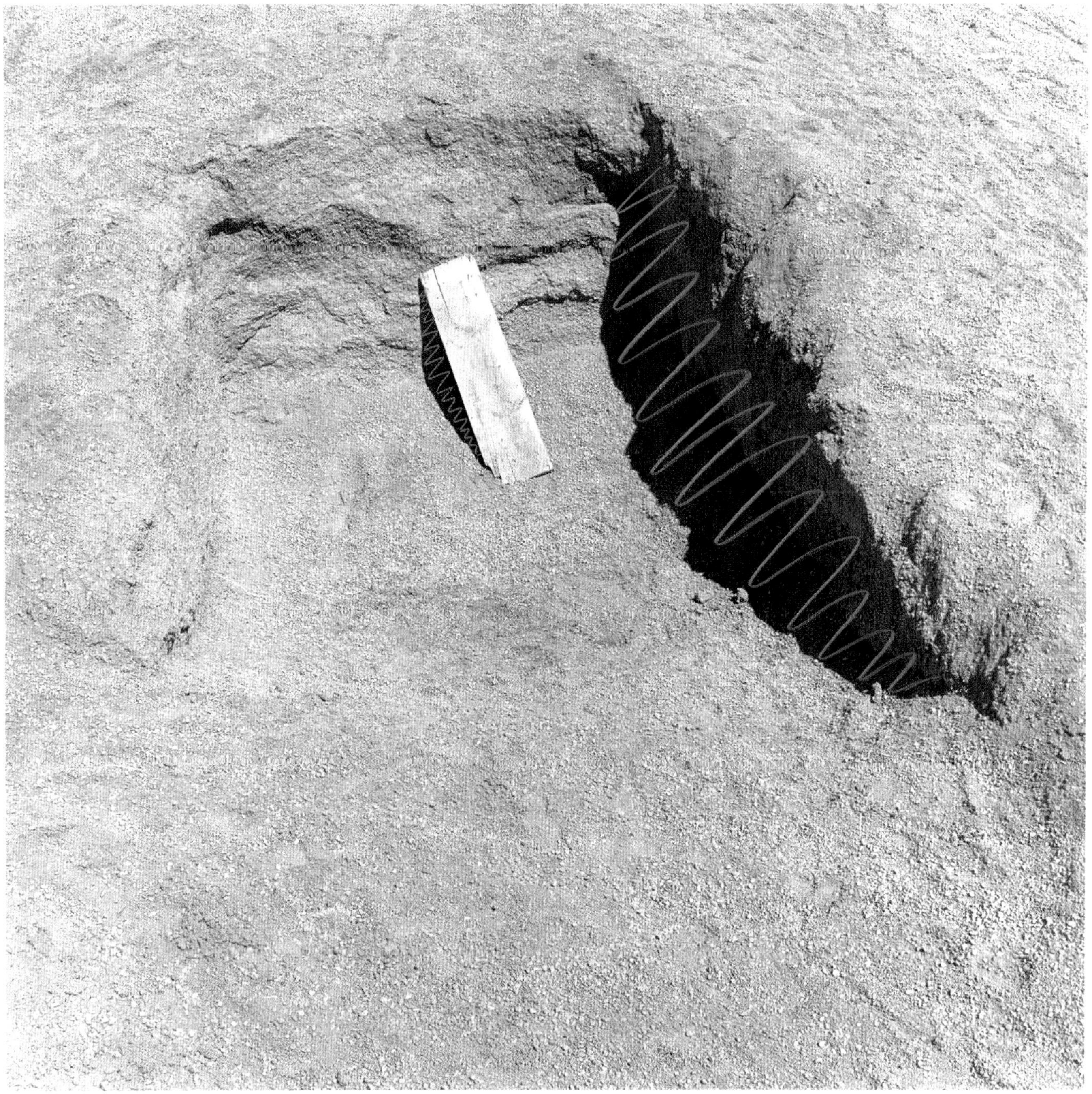

19. *Untitled (Hole with Board: Gravel Mound)*, 1977.
Silver-colored pencil on gelatin silver print, 12 × 12 in.
In the collection of the Museum of Texas Tech University, Lubbock

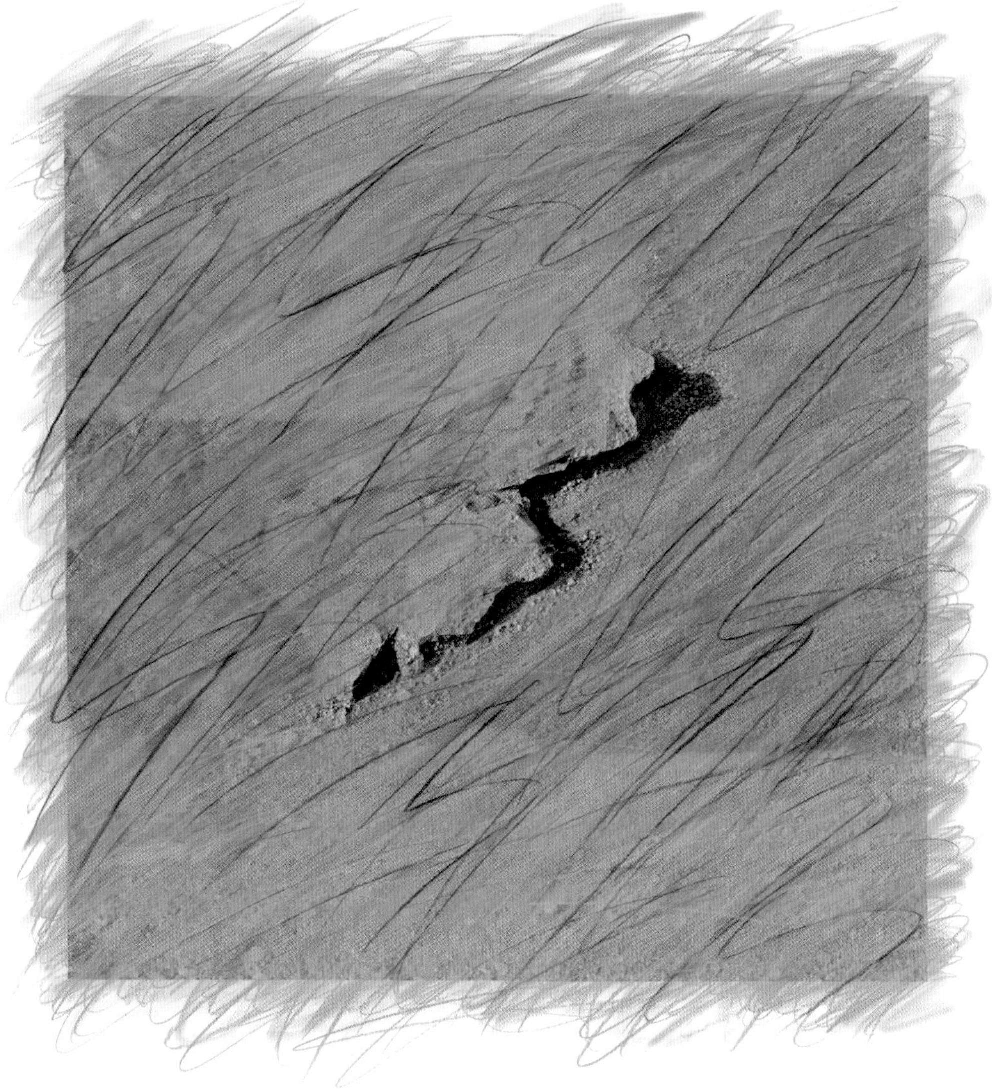

20. *Lightning Snake Shadow*, 1977–81.
Graphite and silver-colored pencil on gelatin silver print, 20 × 16 in.
In the collection of the Museum of Texas Tech University, Lubbock

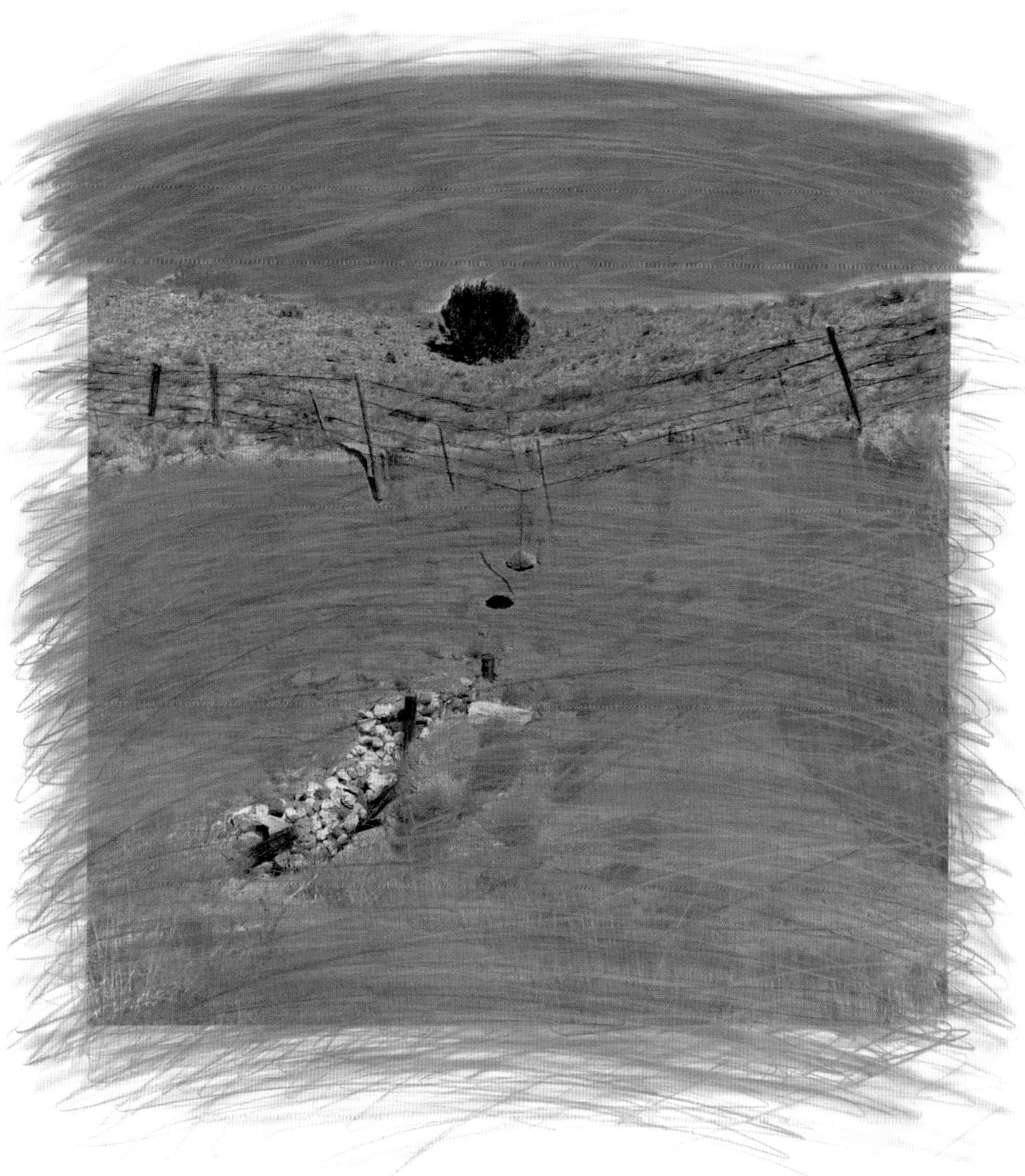

21. *Gravity Fence*, 1979.
Graphite and silver-colored pencil on gelatin silver print, 20 × 16 in.
In the collection of the Museum of Texas Tech University, Lubbock

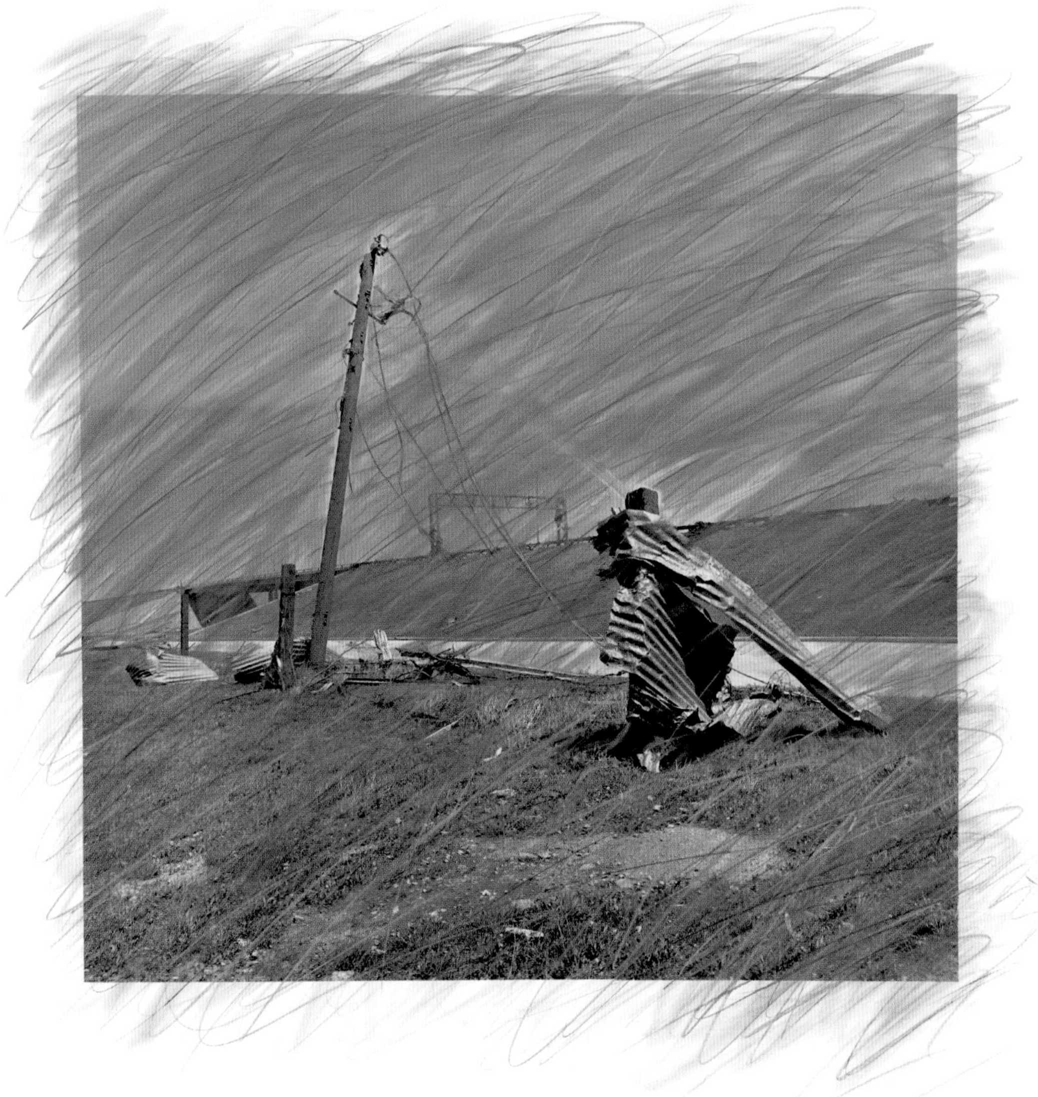

22. *After the Tornado at Wichita Falls*, 1979–82.
Graphite and silver-colored pencil on gelatin silver print, 20 × 16 in.
In the collection of the Museum of Texas Tech University, Lubbock

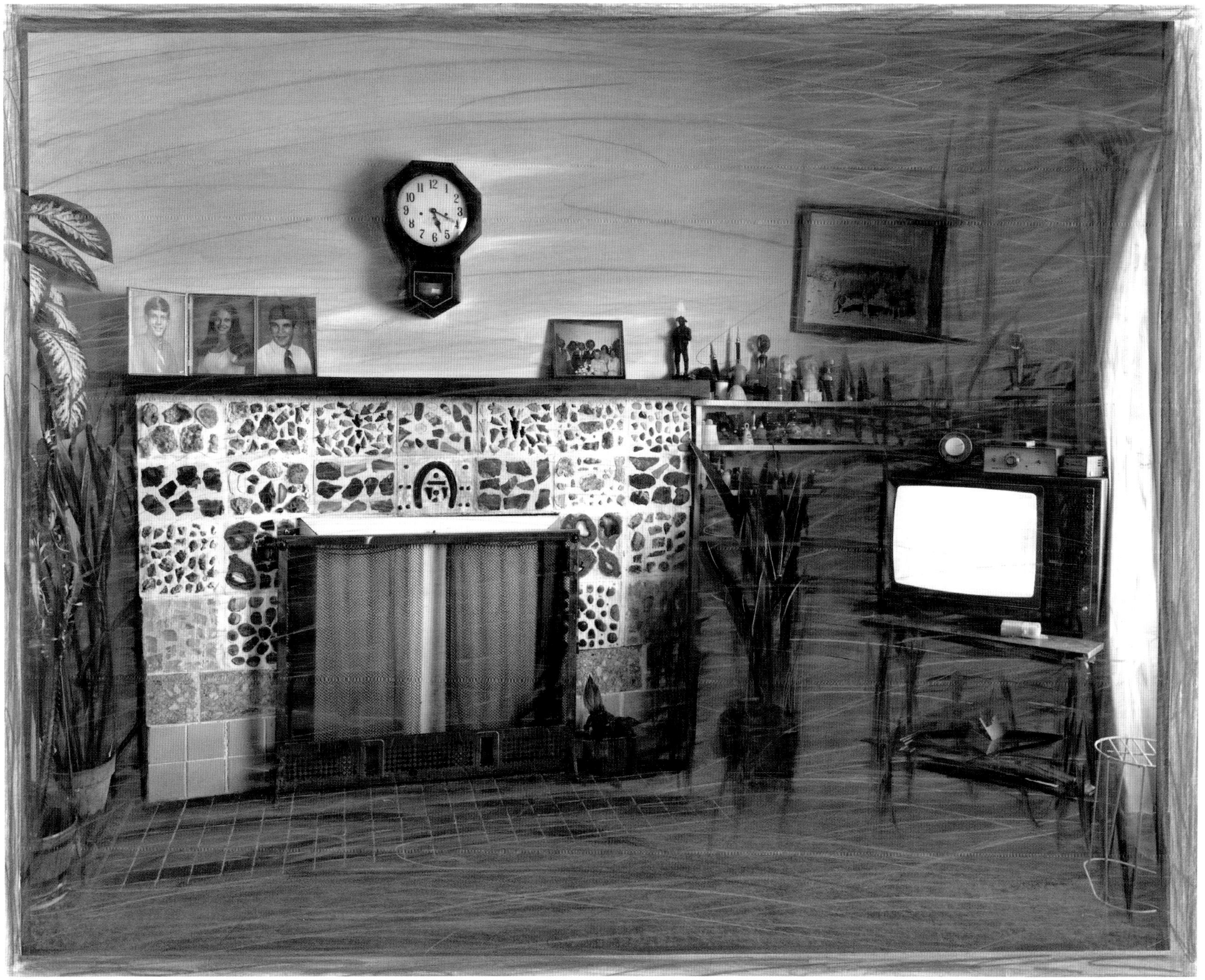

23. *Livingroom, Langtry, Texas*, 1984.
Graphite and silver-colored pencil on gelatin silver print, 16 × 20 in.
In the collection of the Museum of Texas Tech University, Lubbock

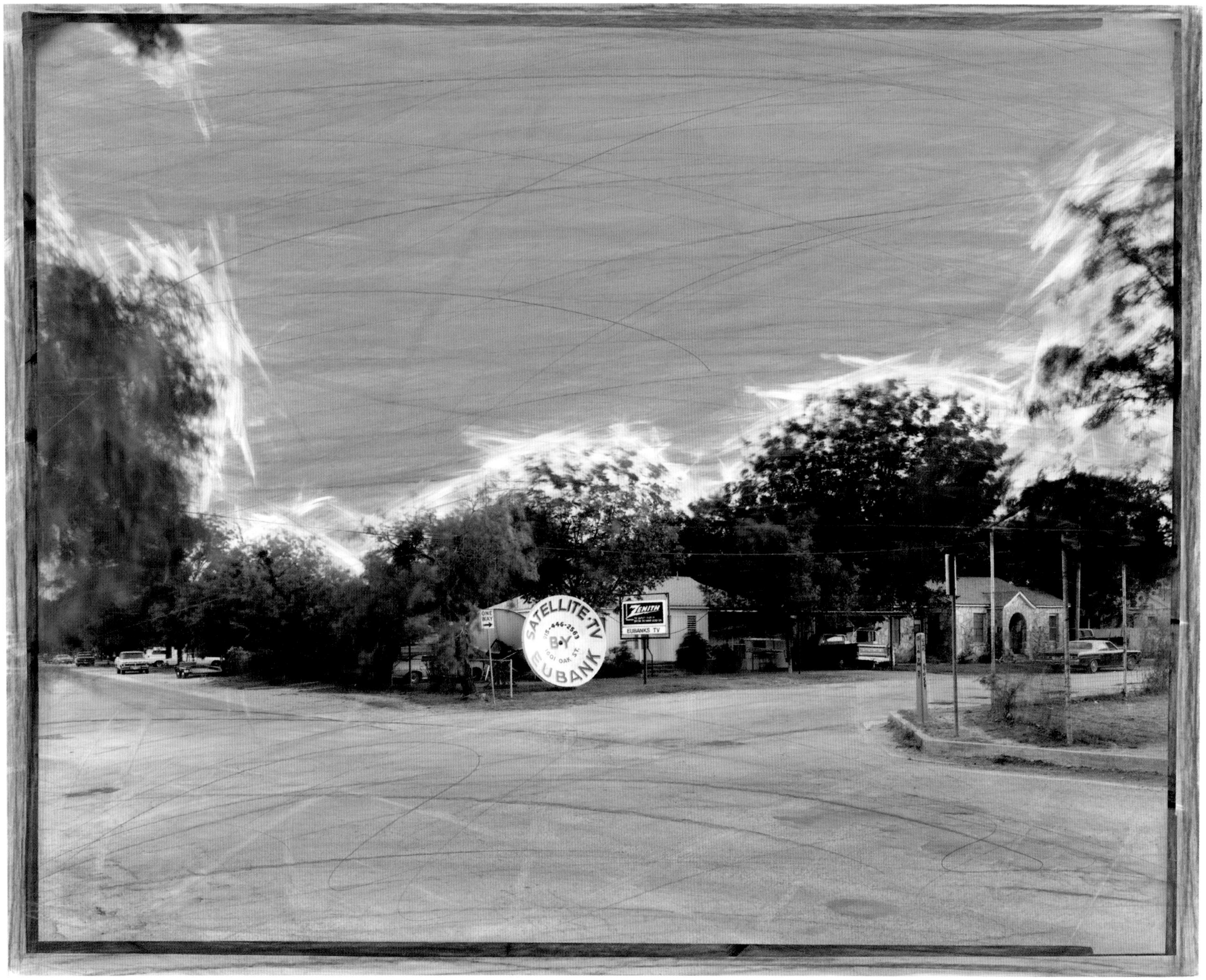

24. *Satellite TV, Junction, Texas*, 1984–85.
Graphite and silver-colored pencil on gelatin silver print, 16 × 20 in.
In the collection of the Museum of Texas Tech University, Lubbock

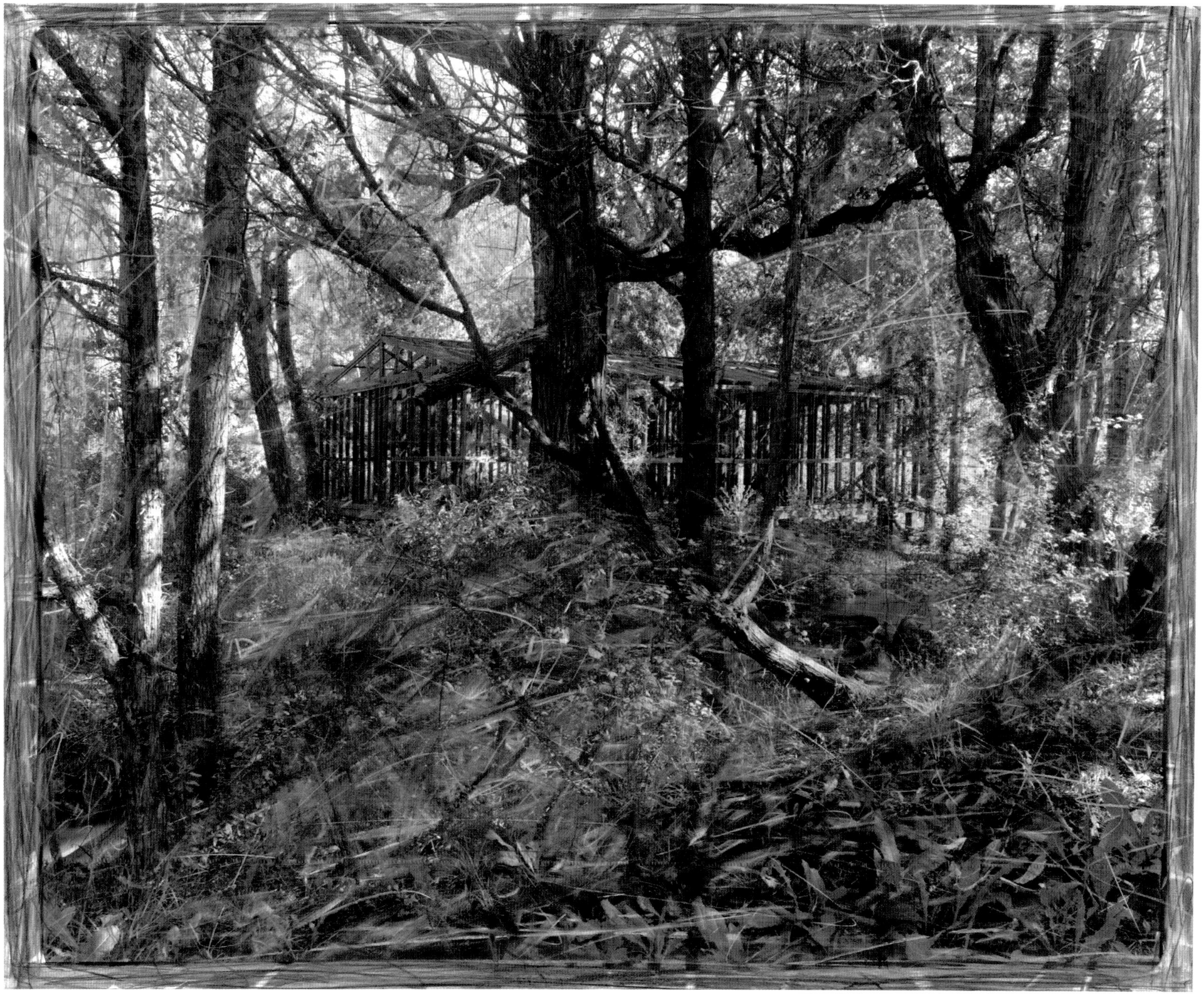

25. *Unfinished House in the Woods near Taos, New Mexico*, 1985–88.
Graphite and silver-colored pencil on gelatin silver print, 16 × 20 in.
In the collection of the Museum of Texas Tech University, Lubbock

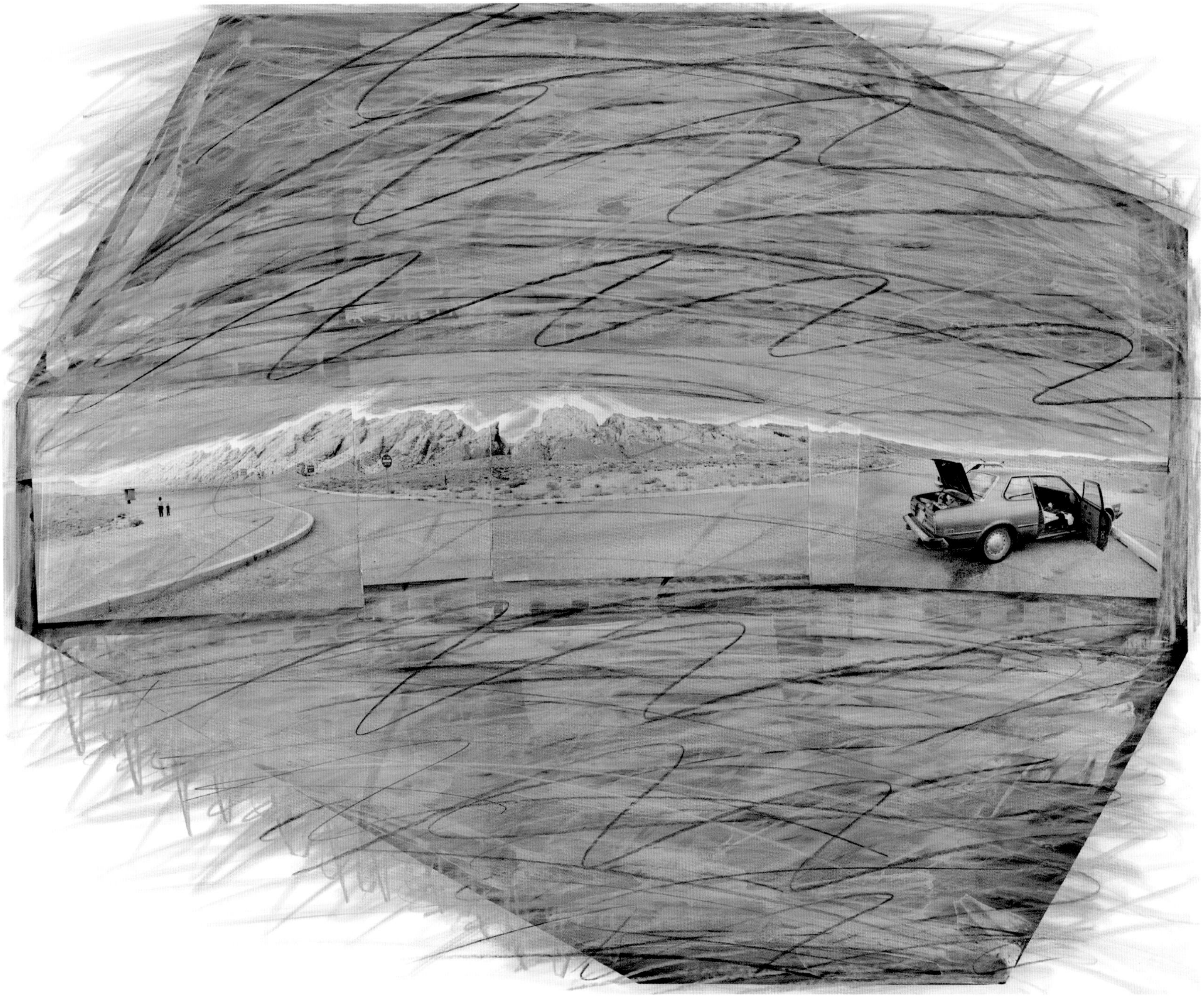

26. *Tilted Earth Shield: San Rafael Swell, Utah*, 1982–88.
Graphite and silver-colored pencil on gelatin silver print, 16 × 20 in.
In the collection of the Museum of Texas Tech University, Lubbock

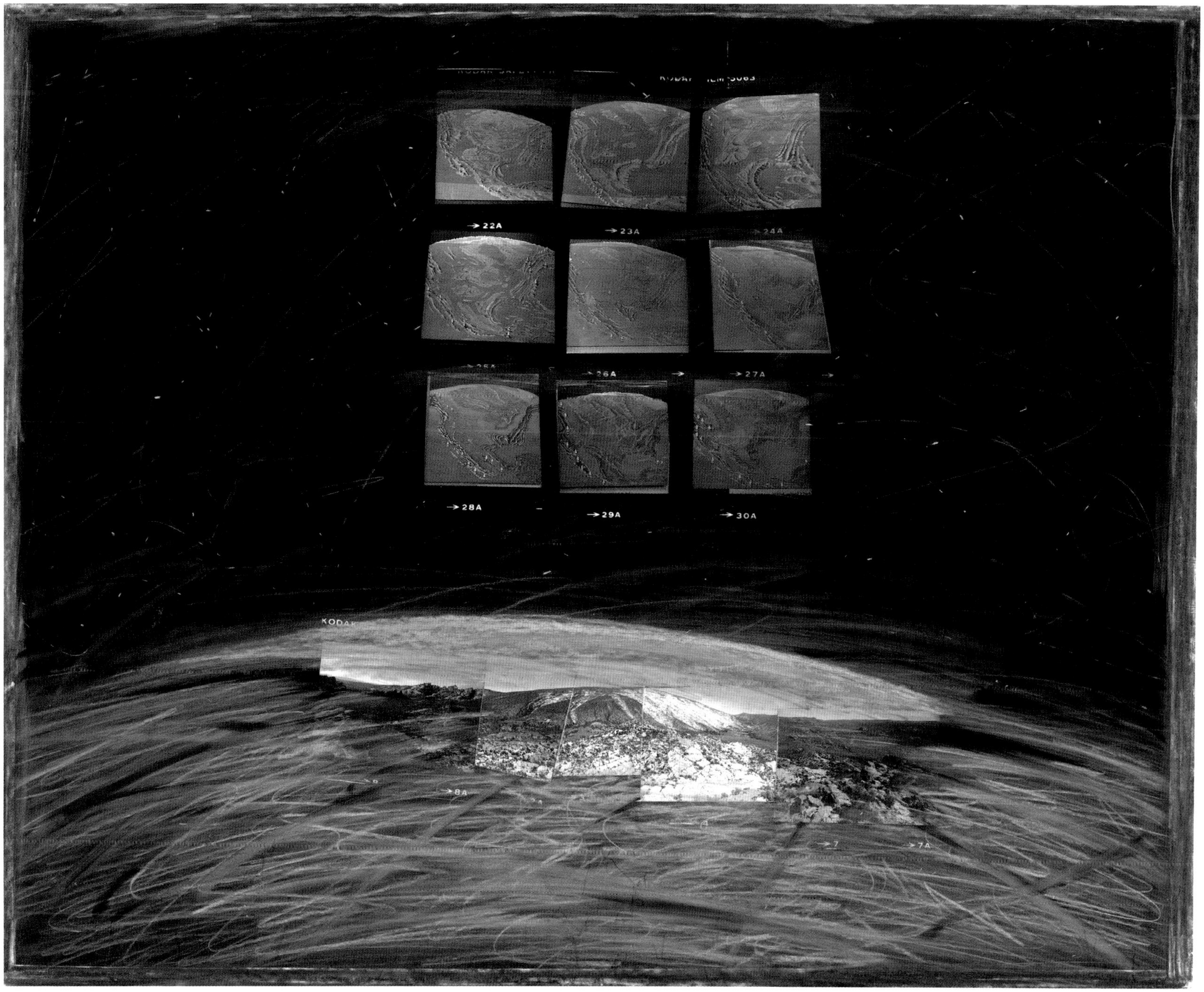

27. *Earth Changes: Past-Present-Future*, 1981–86.
Graphite and silver-colored pencil on gelatin silver print, 16 × 20 in.
In the collection of the Museum of Texas Tech University, Lubbock

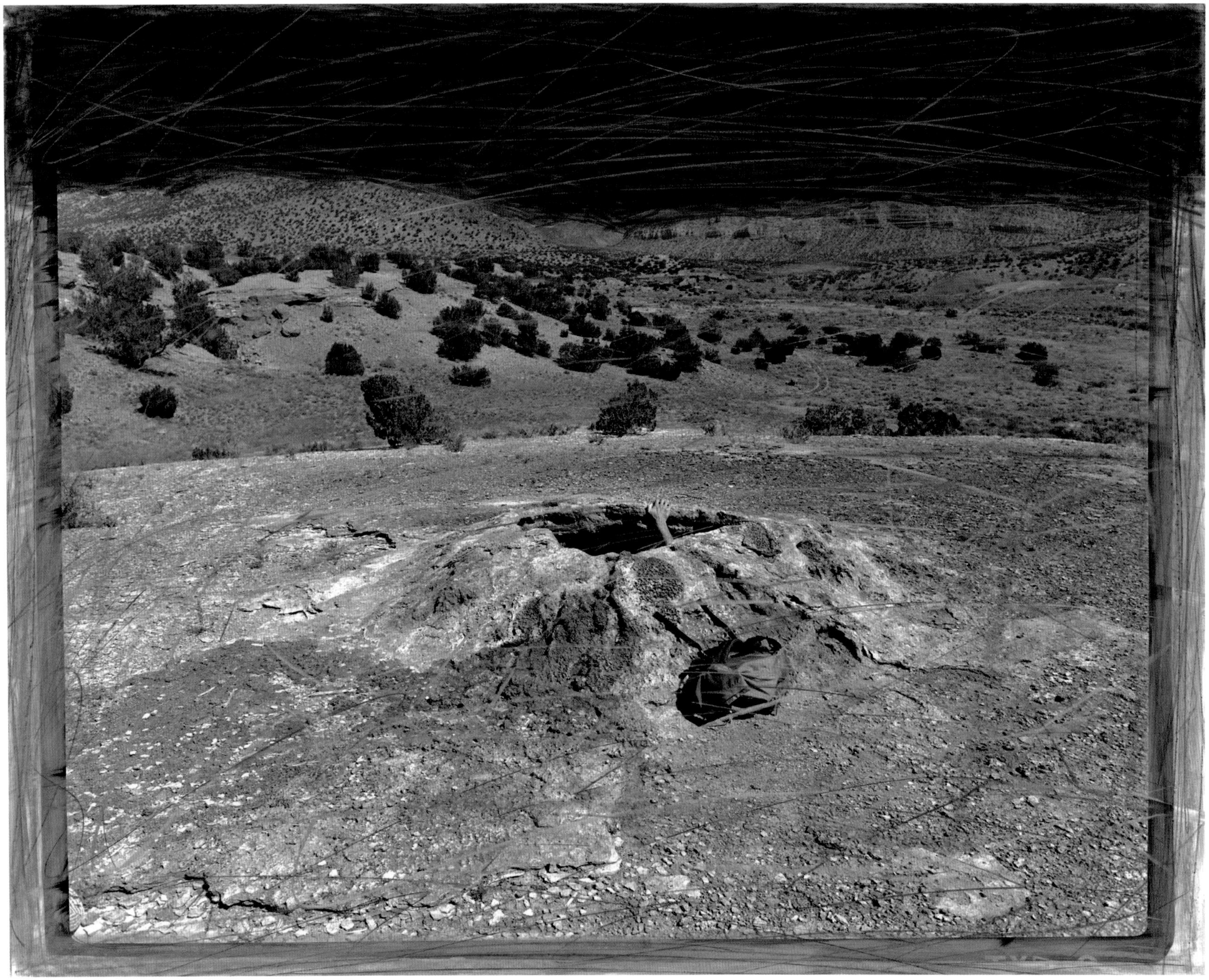

28. *Journey Within*, 1987–88.
Graphite and silver-colored pencil on gelatin silver print, 16 × 20 in.
In the collection of the Museum of Texas Tech University, Lubbock

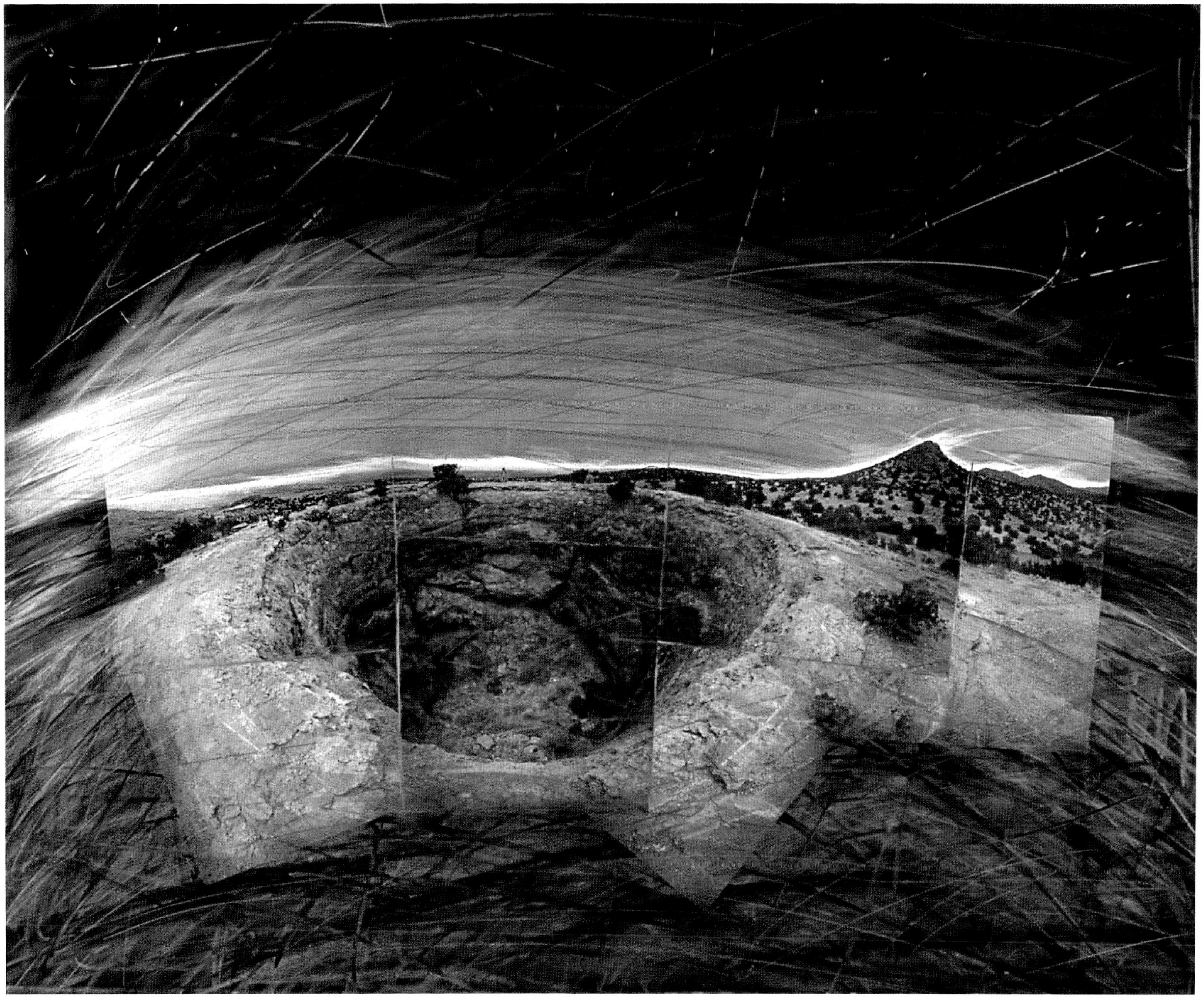

29. *Empty Soda Well near San Ysidro, New Mexico*, 1989.
Graphite and silver-colored pencil on gelatin silver print, 35 × 47 in.
In the collection of the Museum of Texas Tech University, Lubbock

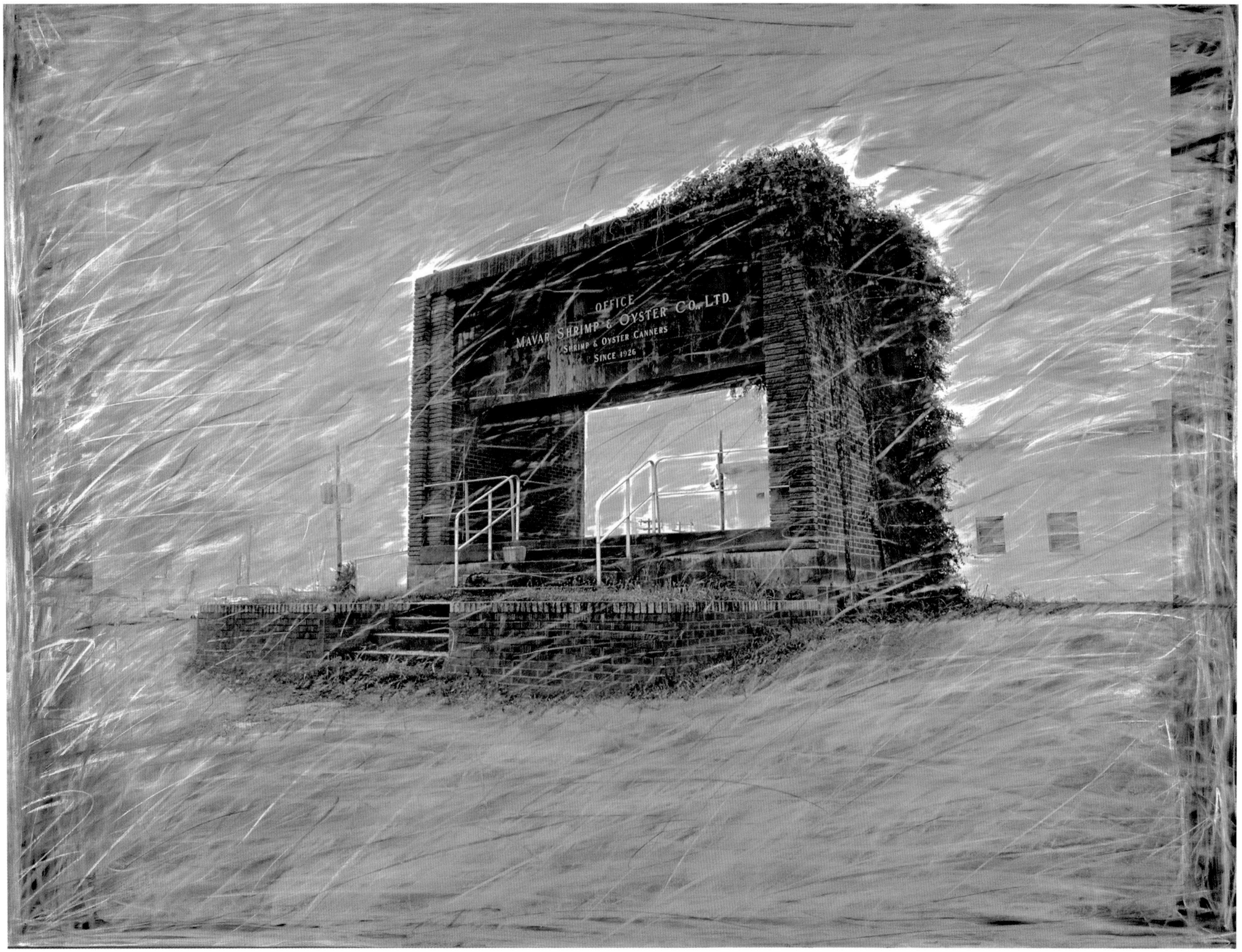

30. *Entrance, Gulf Coast, Mississippi*, 1988–90.
Graphite and silver-colored pencil on gelatin silver print, 35 × 47 in.
In the collection of the Museum of Texas Tech University, Lubbock

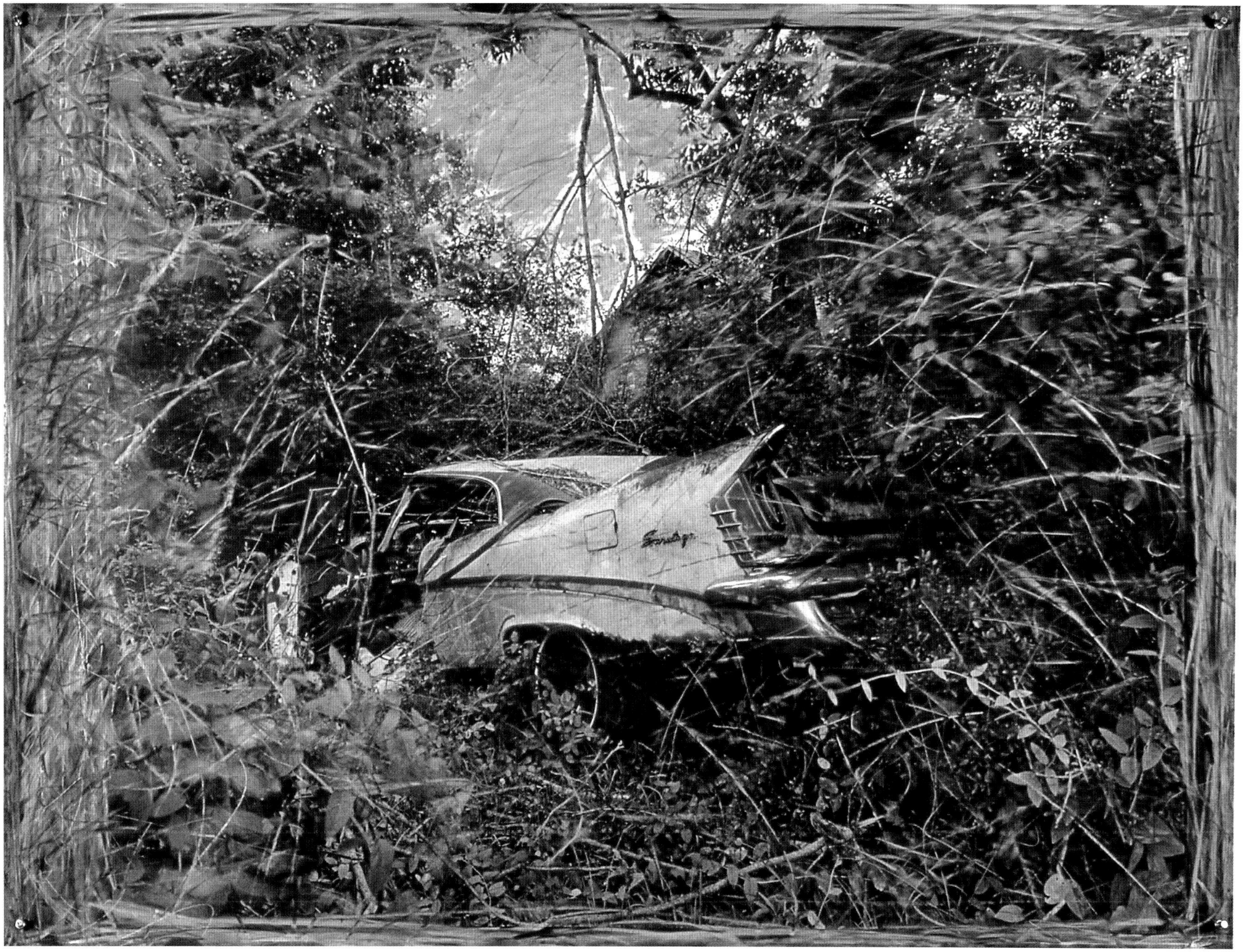

31. *Unfinished Business (Mississippi)*, 1989.
Graphite and silver-colored pencil on gelatin silver print, 35 × 47 in.
In the collection of the Museum of Texas Tech University, Lubbock

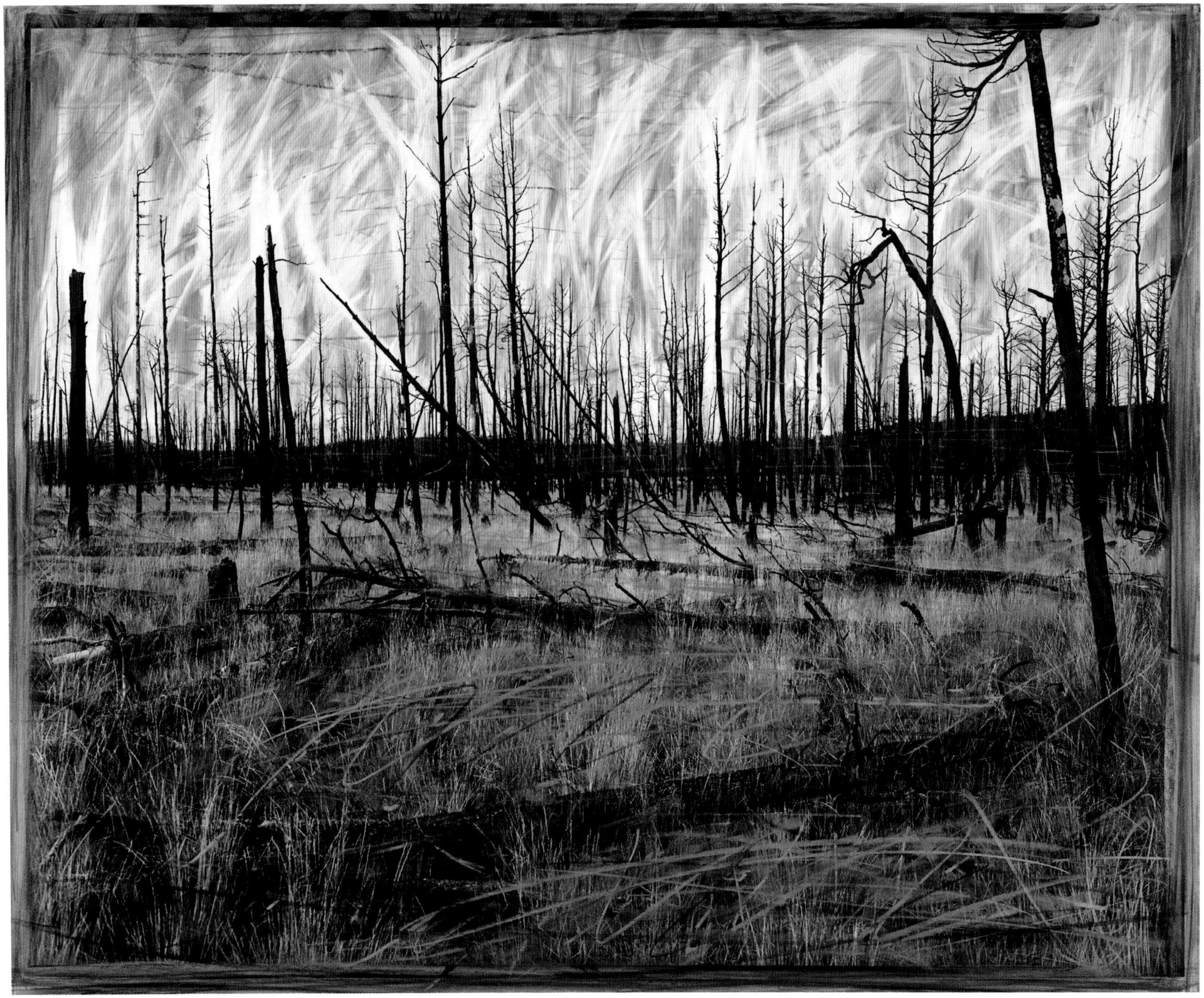

32. *Five Years after the Fire, Bandelier National Monument*, 1982–89.
Graphite and silver-colored pencil on gelatin silver print, 35 × 47 in.
In the collection of the Museum of Texas Tech University, Lubbock

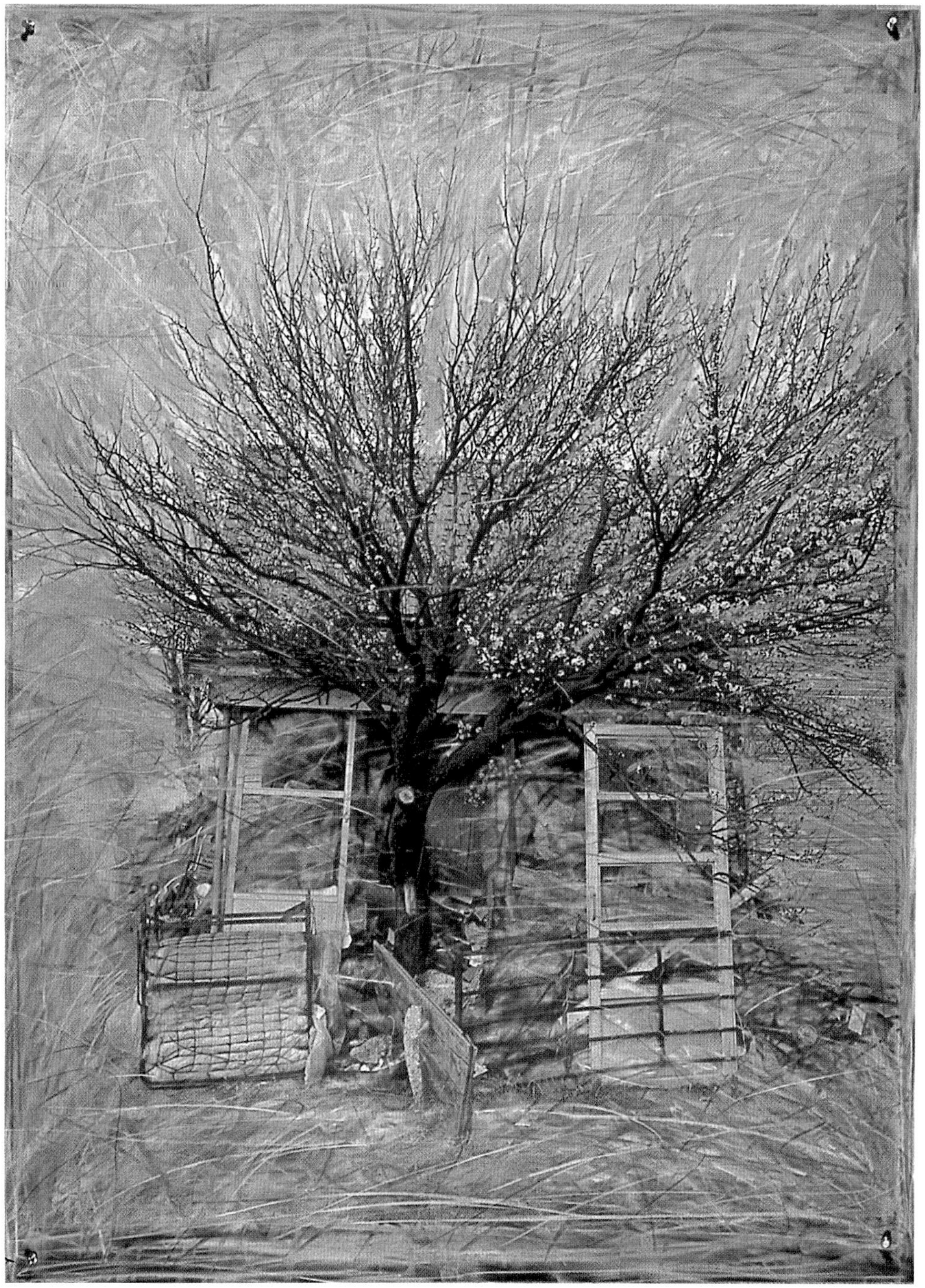

33. *Tree of Knowledge, Turkey, Texas*, 1988–89.
Graphite and silver-colored pencil on gelatin silver print, 47 × 35 in.

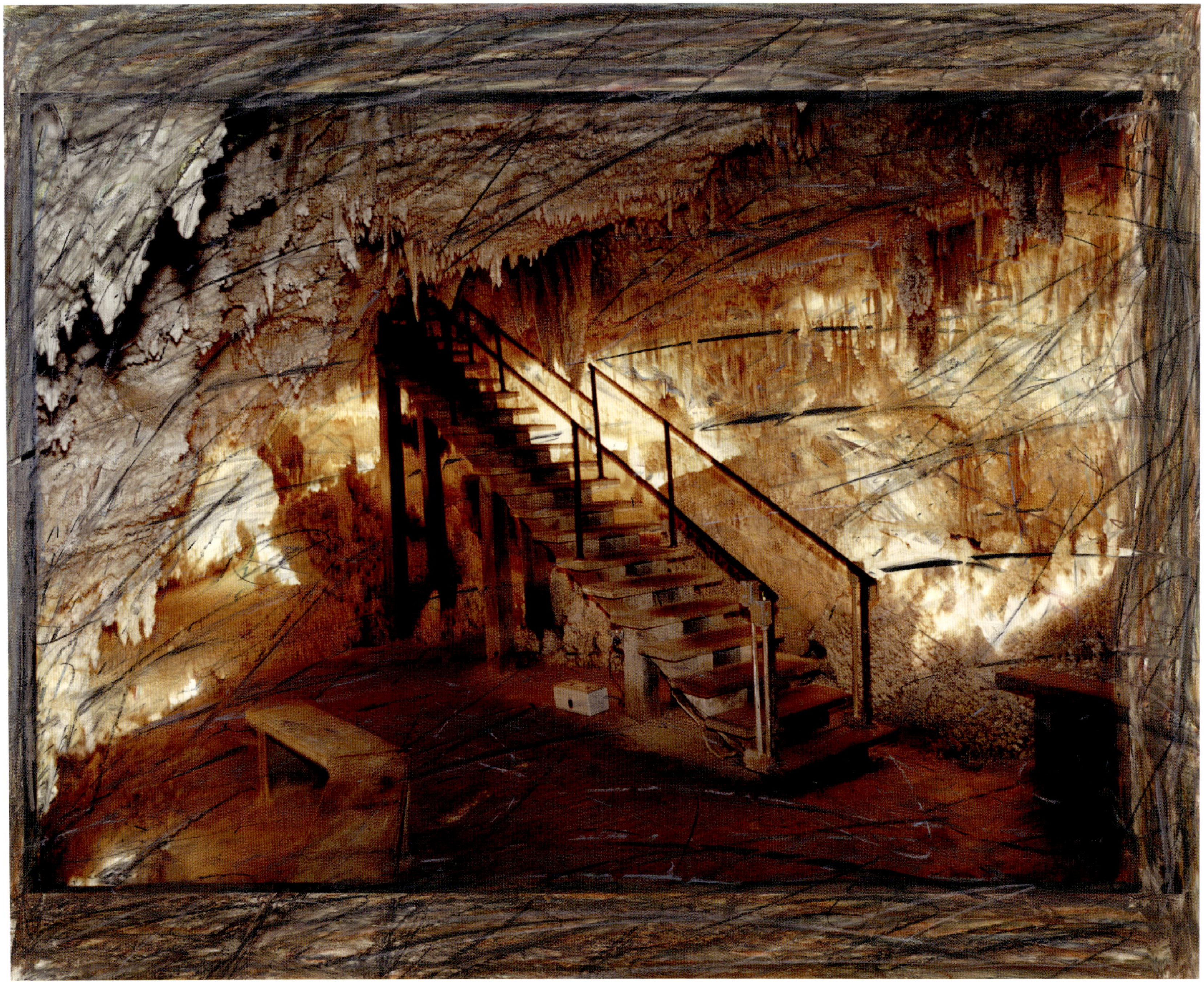

34. *Underground Stairway, Sonora Caverns, Texas*, 1993.
Crayon on chromogenic print, 16 × 20 in.
In the collection of the Museum of Texas Tech University, Lubbock

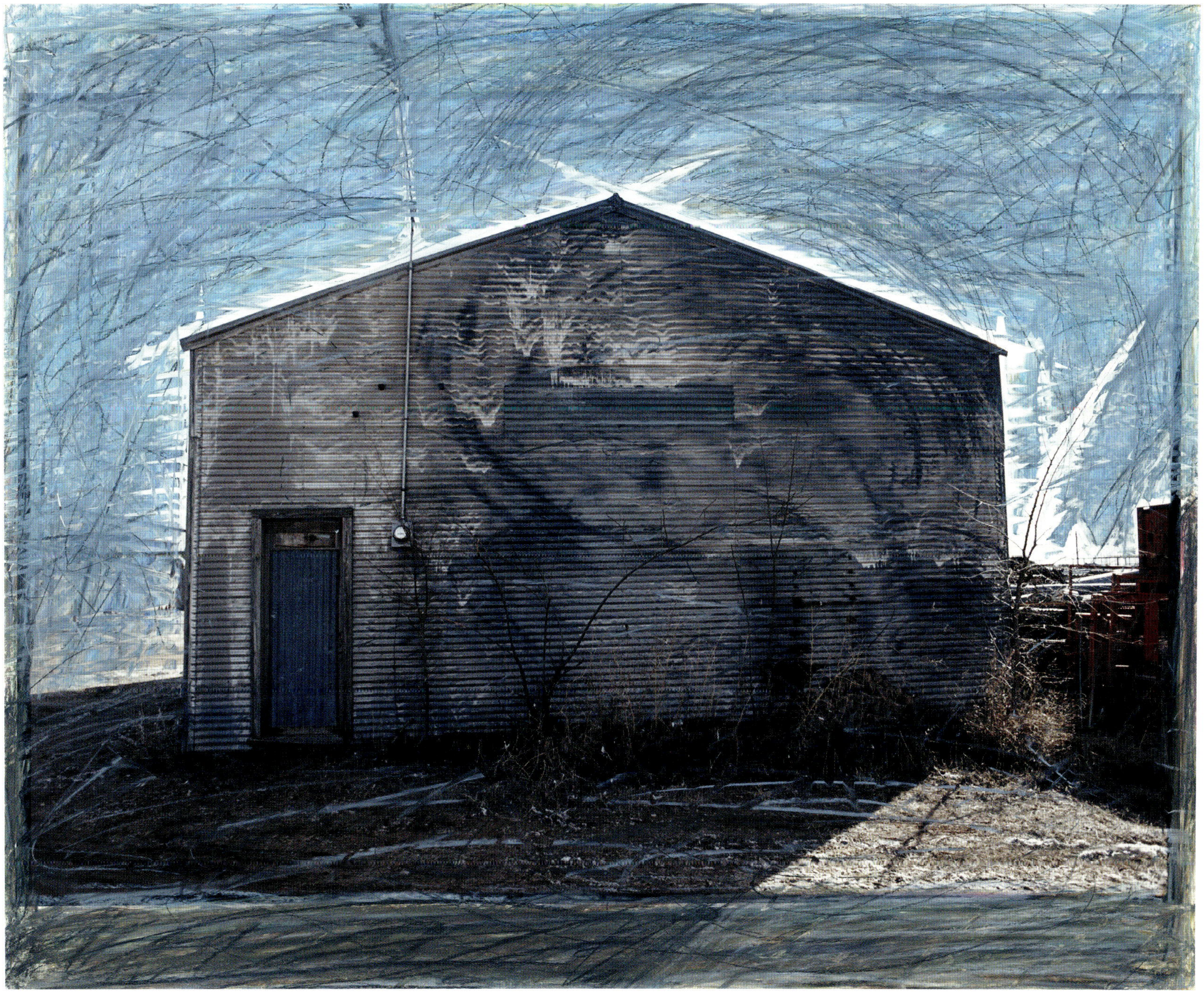

35. *Wind Scored Tin*, 1995.
Crayon on chromogenic print, 16 × 20 in.
In the collection of the Museum of Texas Tech University, Lubbock

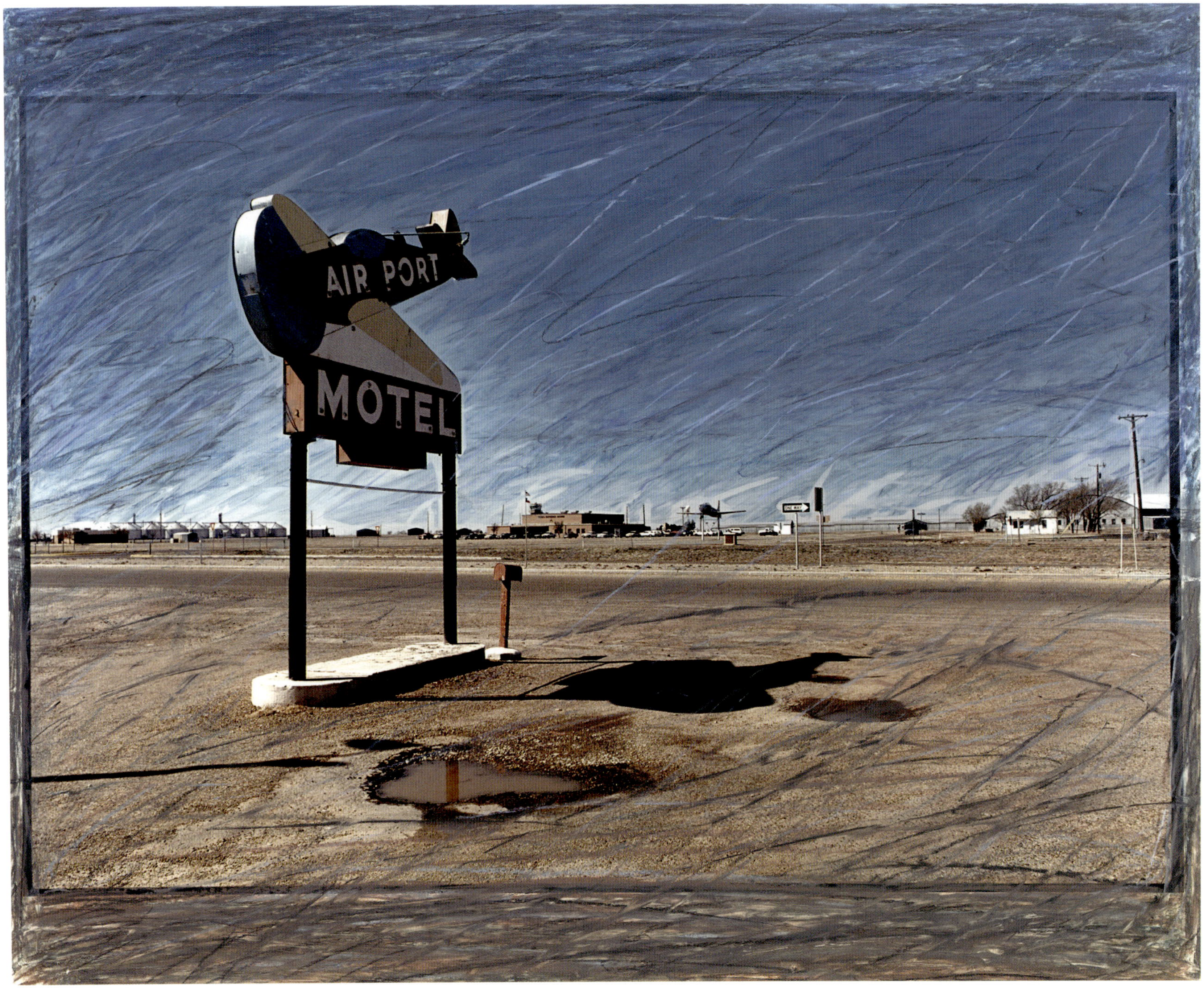

36. *Airport Motel, Plainview, Texas*, 1992.
Crayon on chromogenic print, 16 × 20 in.
In the collection of the Museum of Texas Tech University, Lubbock

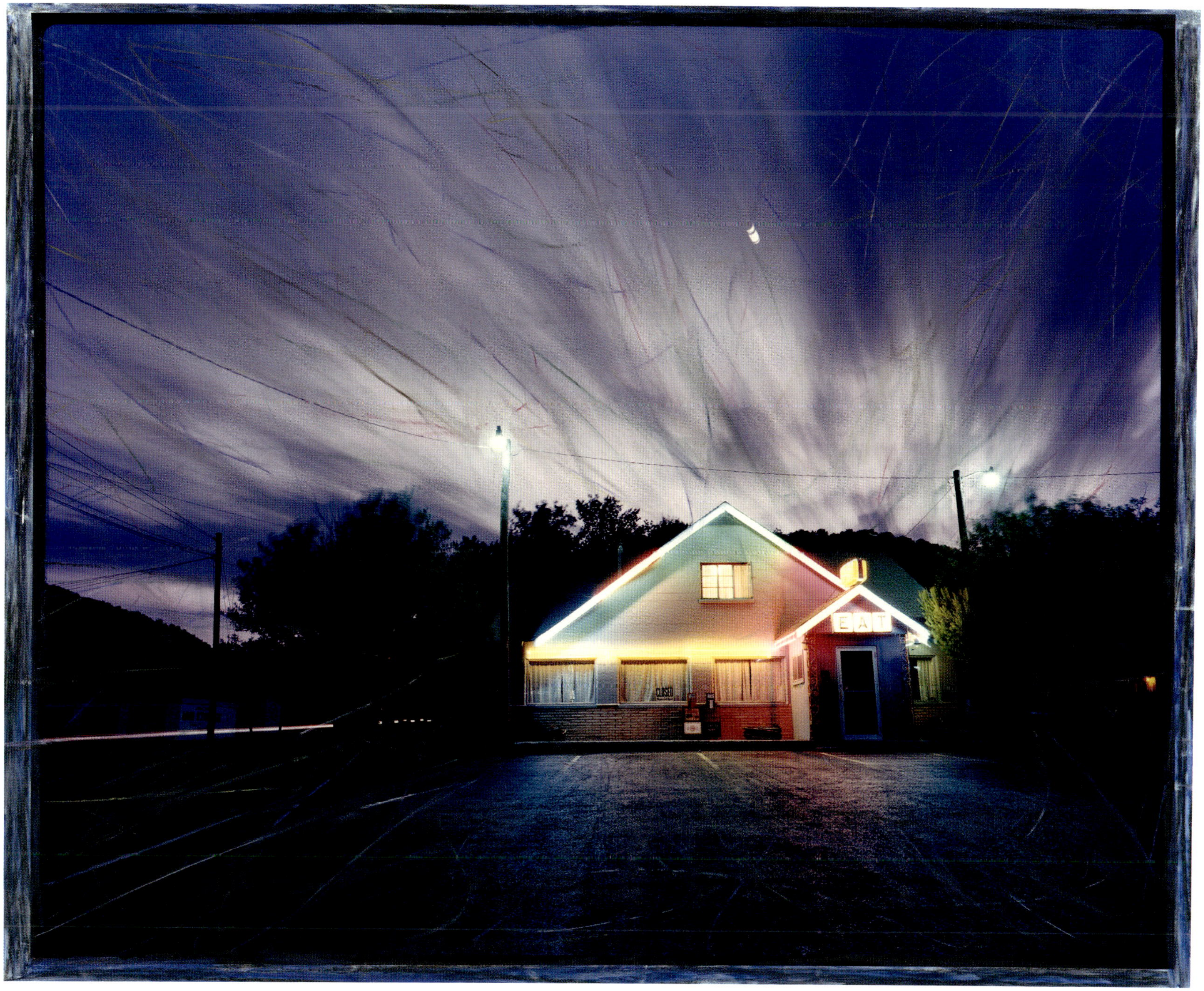

37. *Neon Motel, Junction, Texas*, 1992.
Crayon on chromogenic print, 16 × 20 in.
In the collection of the Museum of Texas Tech University, Lubbock

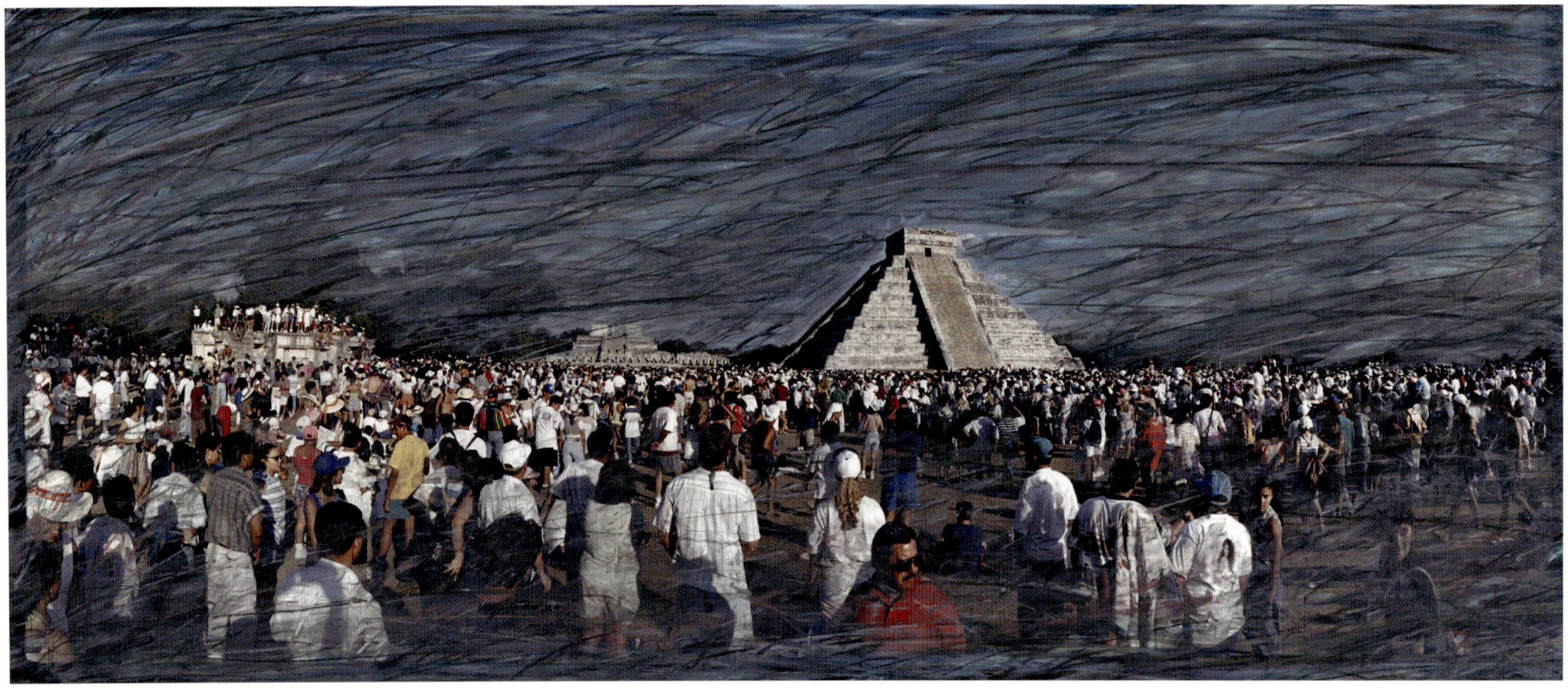

38. *Equinox Sunset Snake Creeps Down, Chichen Itza, Mexico*, 1995–96.
Crayon on chromogenic print, 16 × 38 in.
In the collection of the Museum of Texas Tech University, Lubbock

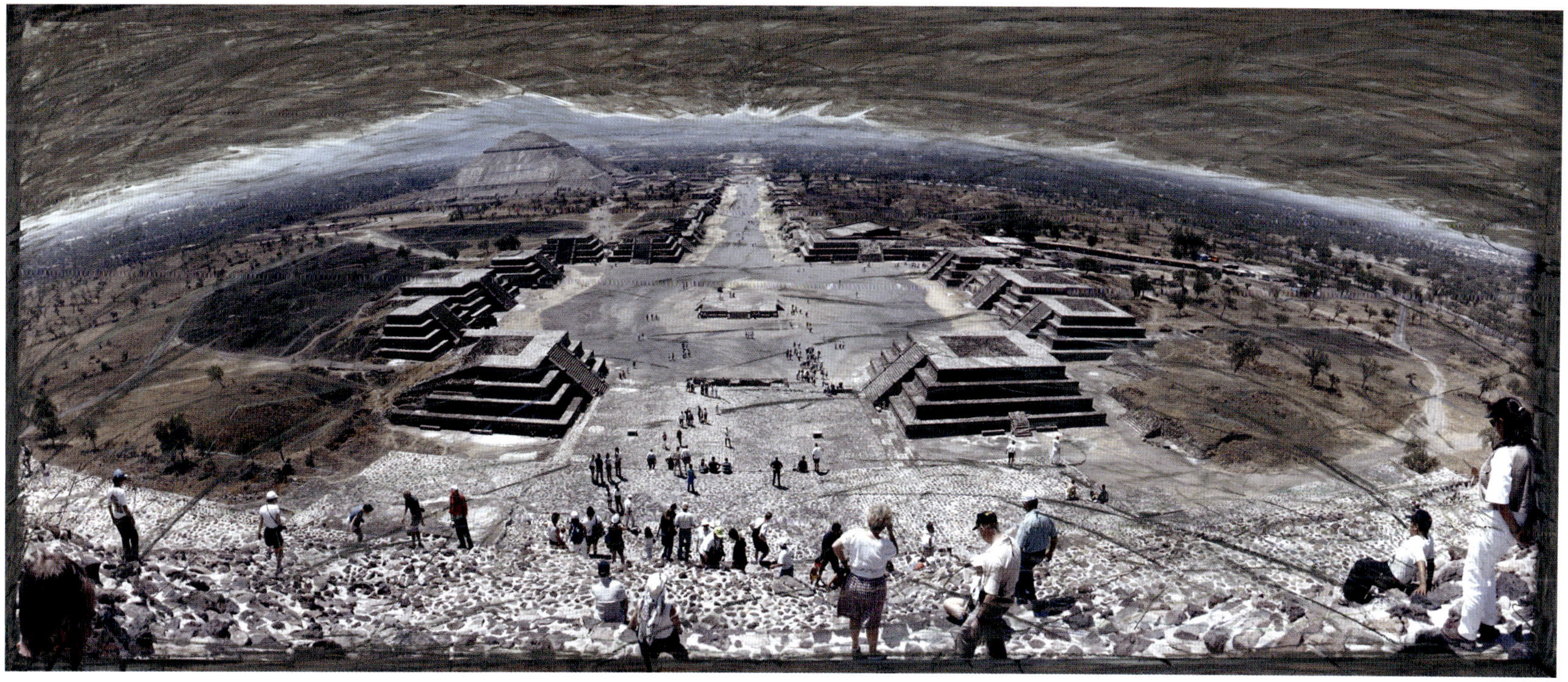

39. *Teotihuacan (From the Pyramid of the Moon)*, 1997–98.
Crayon on chromogenic print, 16 × 38 in.
In the collection of the Museum of Texas Tech University, Lubbock

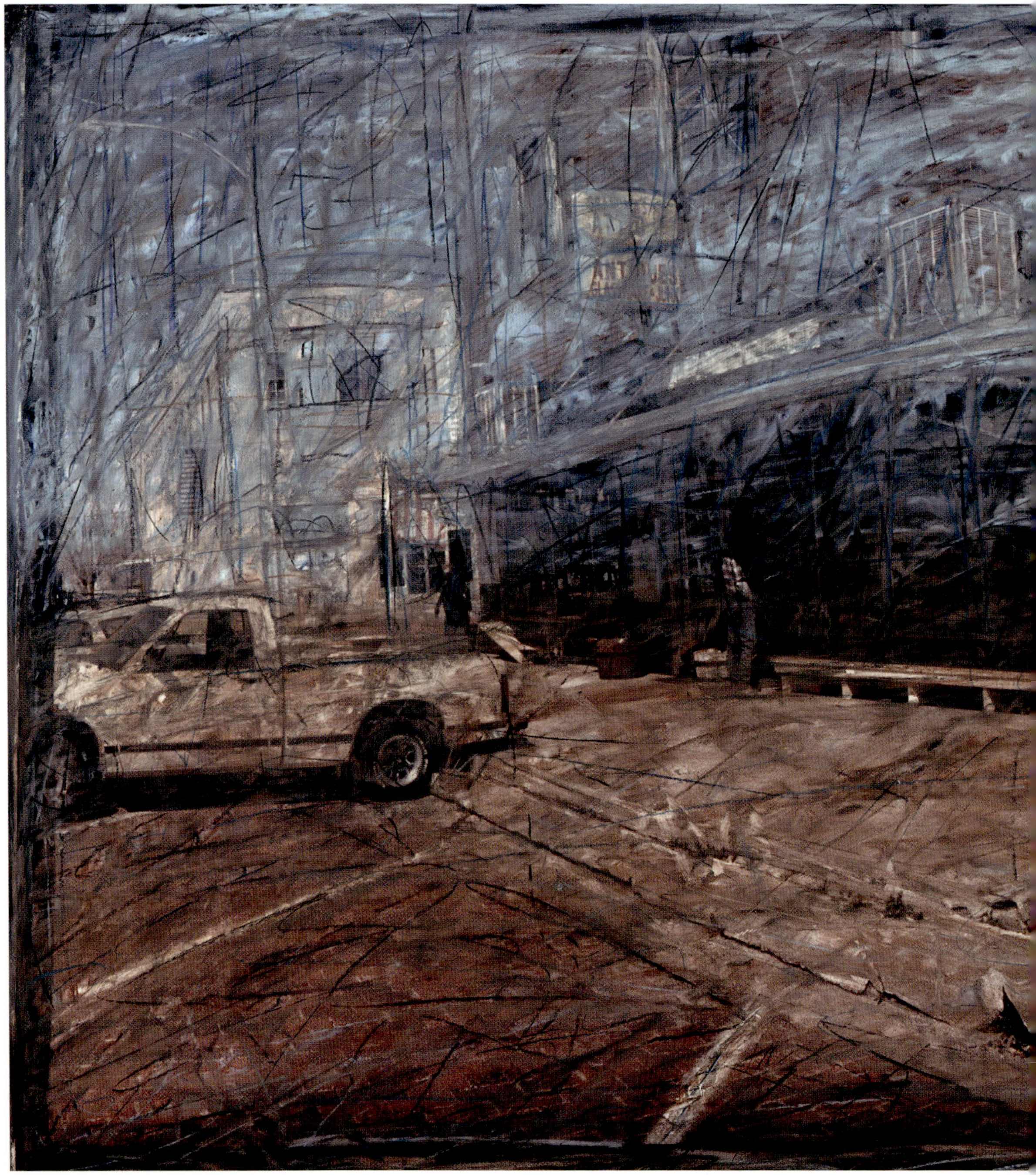

40. *Storefront Landscape, Texas Panhandle*, 1998.
Crayon on chromogenic print, 16 × 38 in.
In the collection of the Museum of Texas Tech University, Lubbock

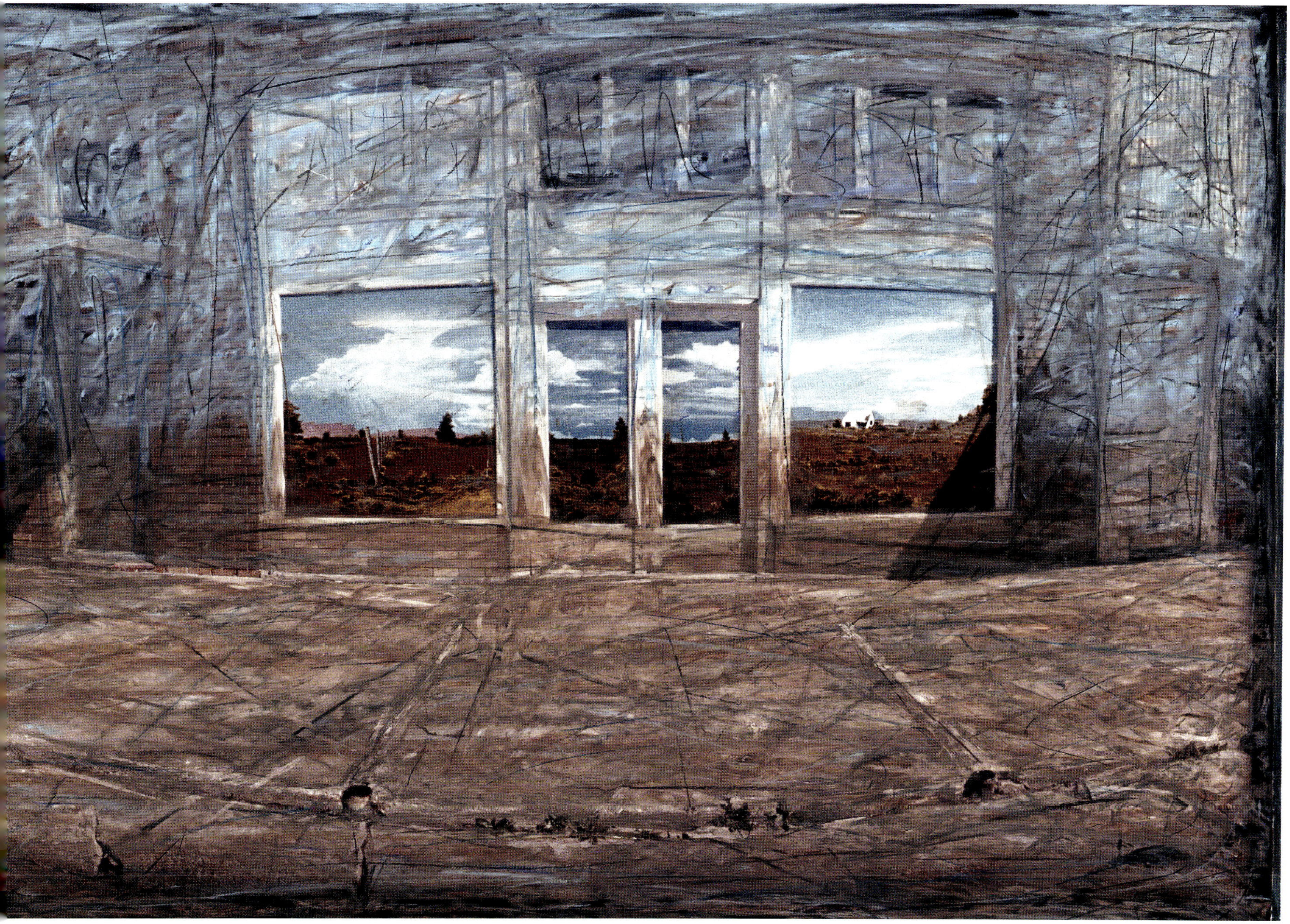

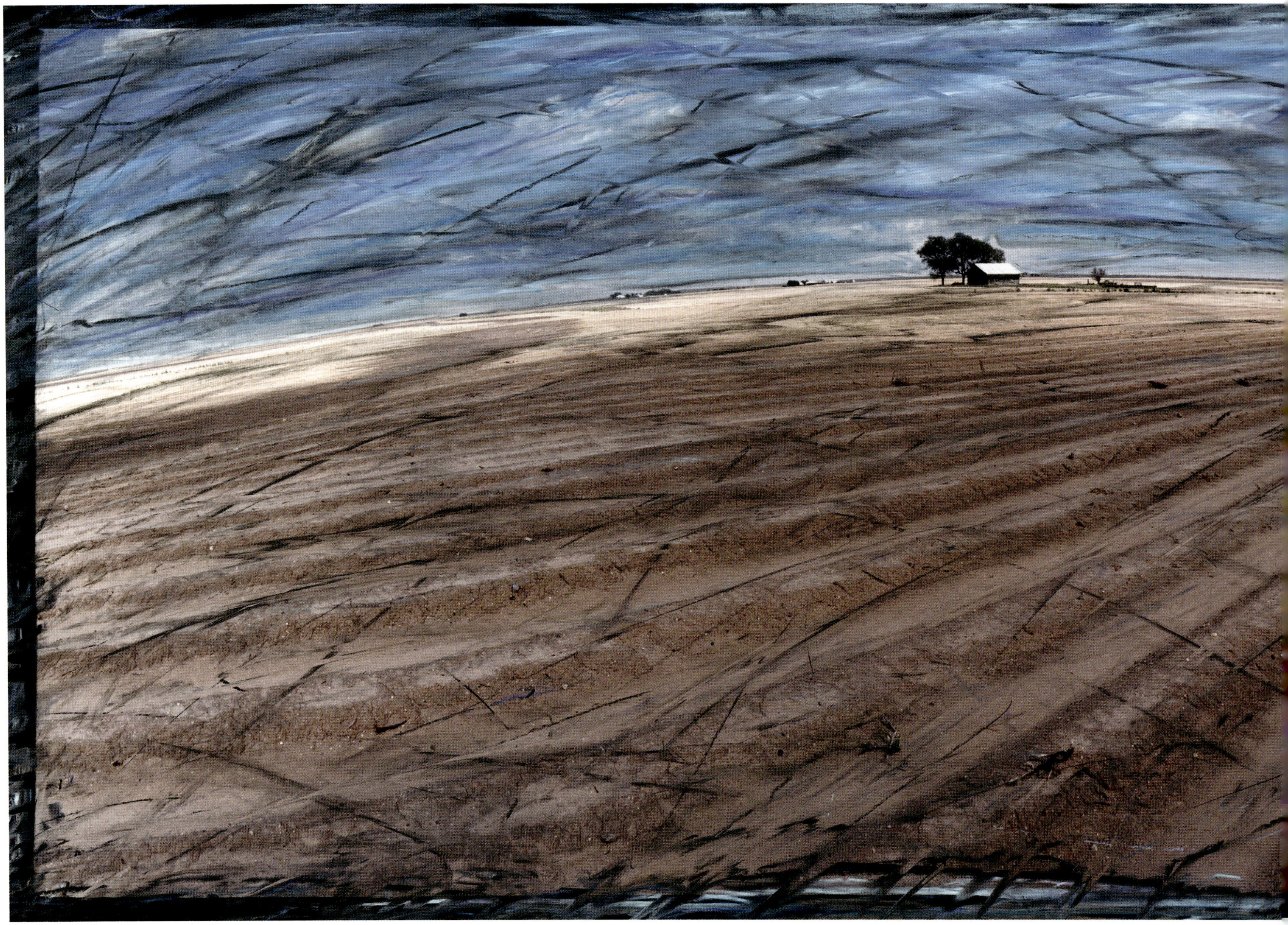

41. *Plowed Fields near Colorado City, Texas*, 1994–96.
Crayon on chromogenic print, 16 × 38 in.
In the collection of the Museum of Texas Tech University, Lubbock

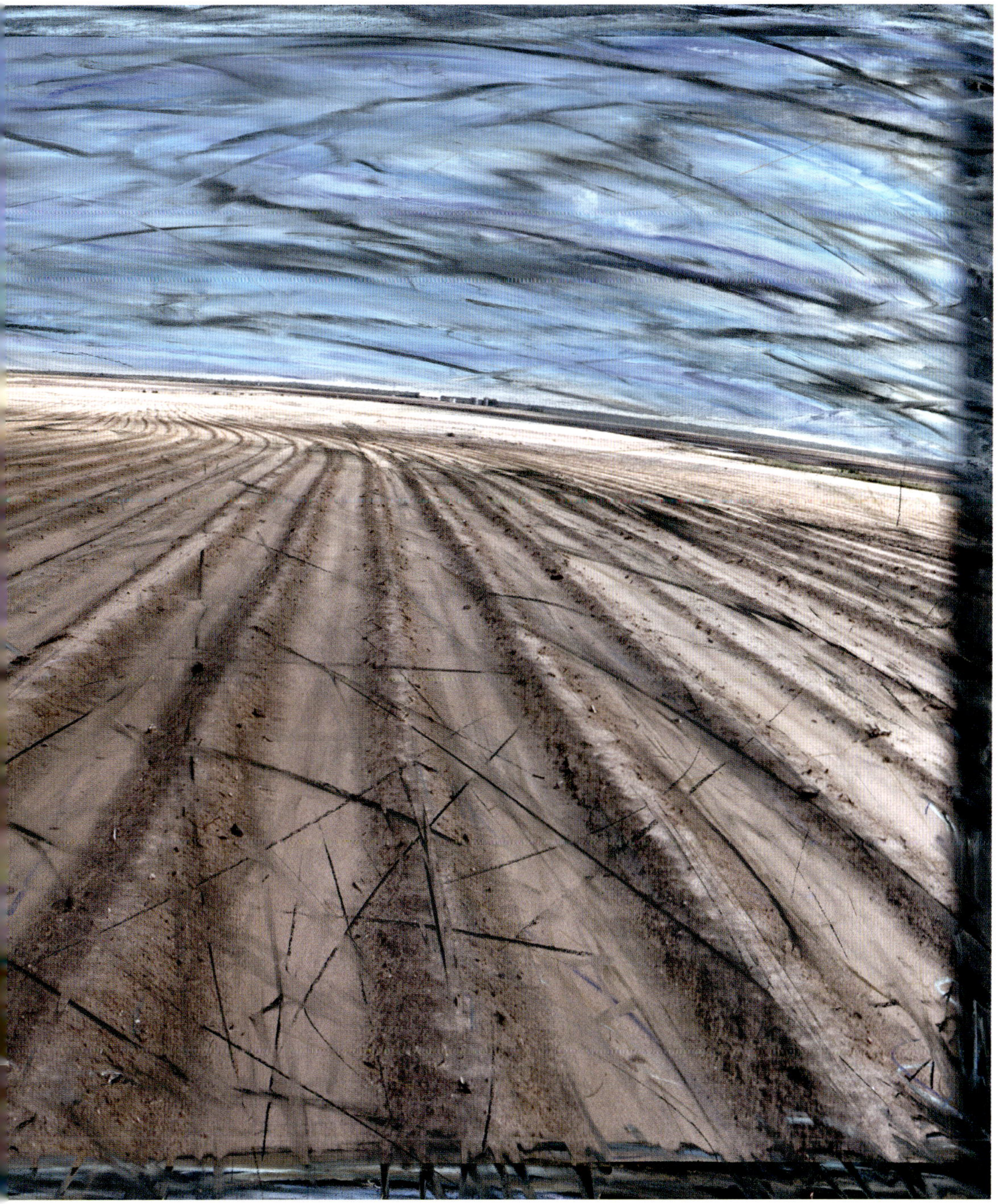

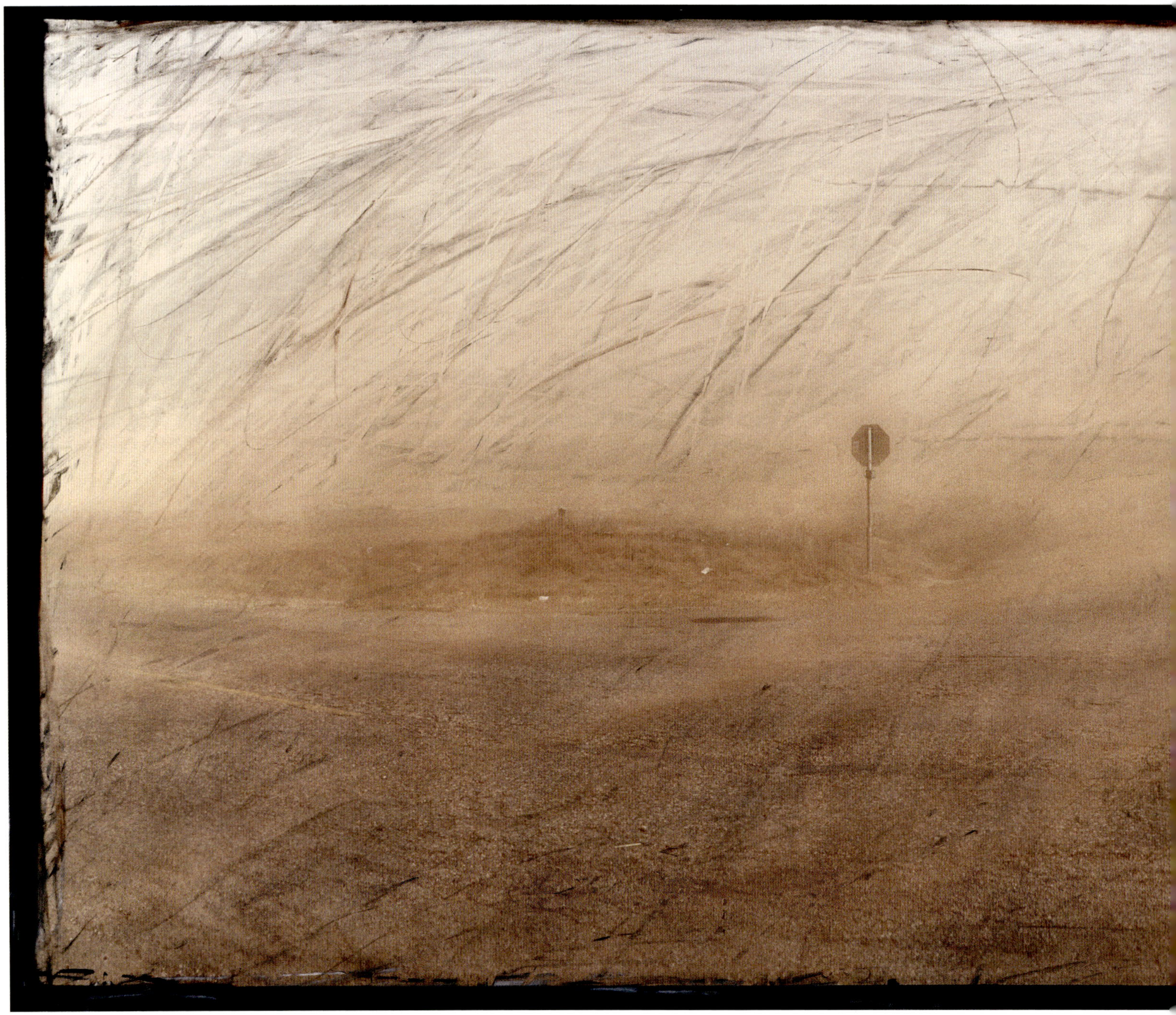

42. *Lubbock Dust Storm*, 1995.
Crayon on chromogenic print, 16 × 38 in.
In the collection of the Museum of Texas Tech University, Lubbock

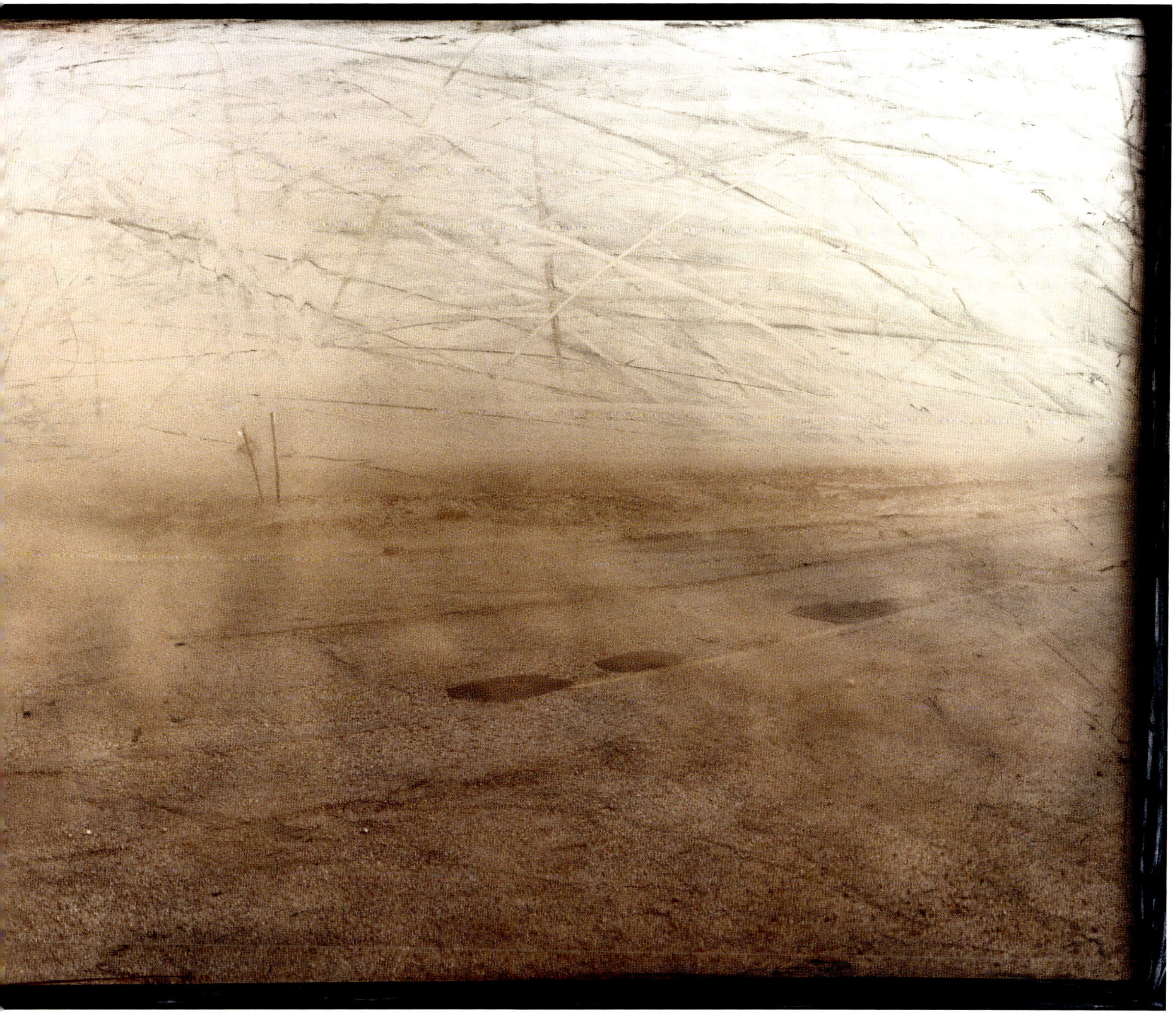

43. *Field House near Snyder, Texas*, 1994–96.
Crayon on chromogenic print, 16 × 38 in.
In the collection of the Museum of Texas Tech University, Lubbock

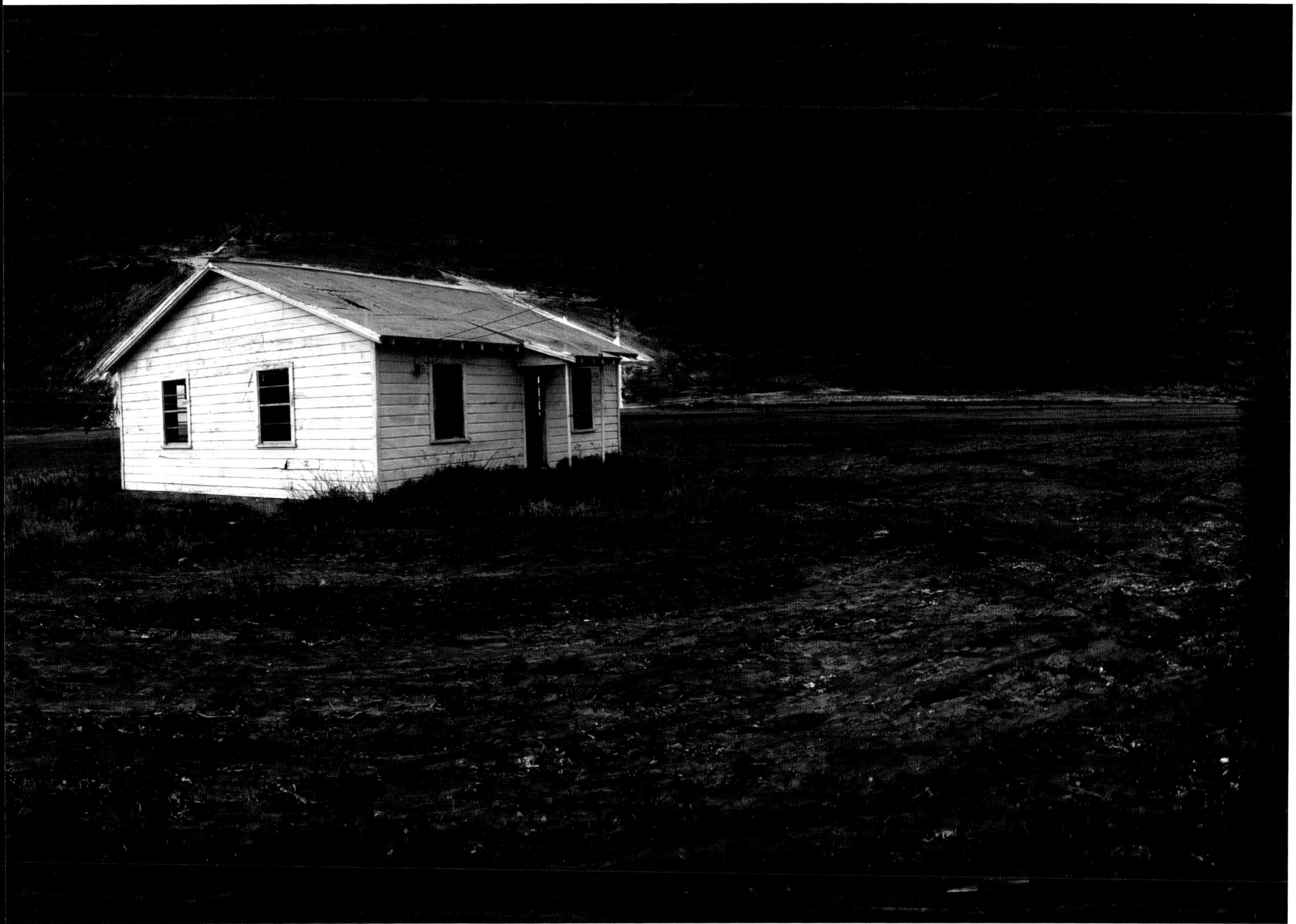

Marks in Place, 1982–1986

I spent several years working on another NEA-funded survey, Marks in Place: Contemporary Responses to Rock Art, with Linda Connor, Steve Fitch, John Pfahl, and Charles Roitz. This project involved photographing places in the American West that contained petroglyphs or pictographs made by Native Americans.*

* See Linda Connor, Rick Dingus, Steve Fitch, John Pfahl, and Charles Roitz, *Marks in Place: Contemporary Responses to Rock Art* (Albuquerque: University of New Mexico Press, 1988).

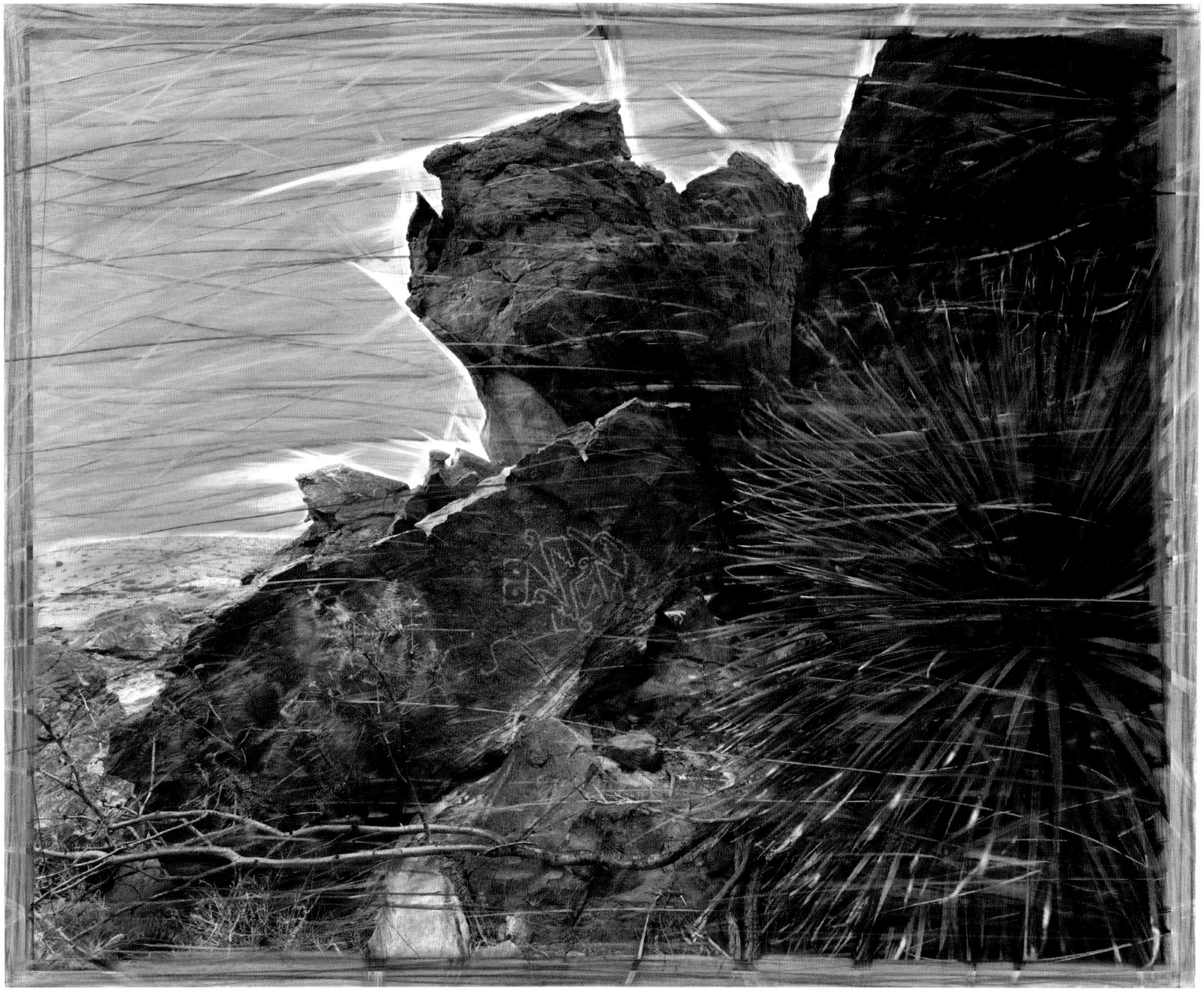

44. *"Tlaloc" Petroglyph near Cooks Peak, New Mexico*, 1984–88.
Graphite and silver-colored pencil on gelatin silver print, 16 × 20 in.
In the collection of the Museum of Texas Tech University, Lubbock

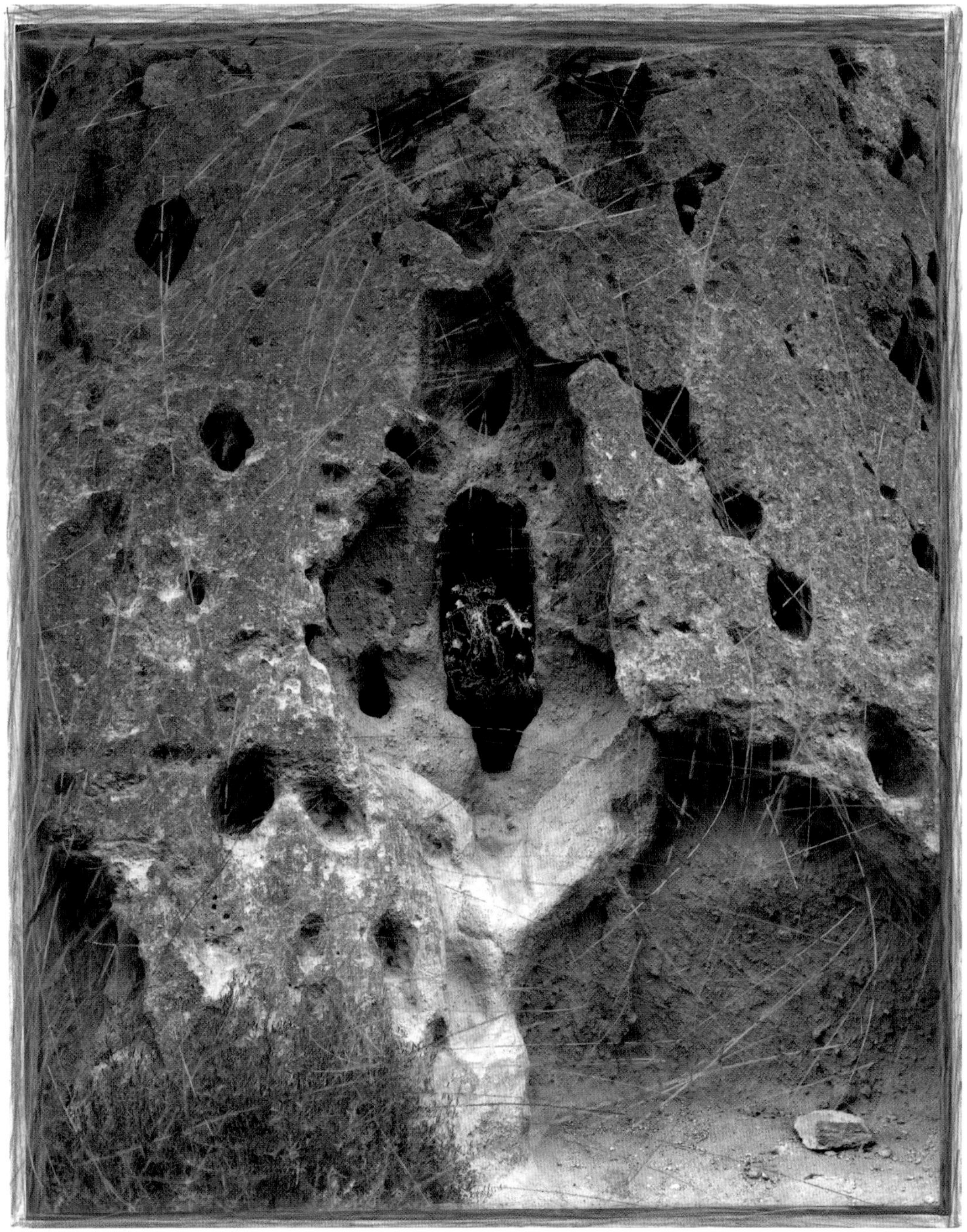

45. *Exterior: Cave Kiva near White Rock, New Mexico (Rebirth Place)*, 1982–86.
Graphite and silver-colored pencil on gelatin silver print, 20 × 16 in.
In the collection of the Museum of Texas Tech University, Lubbock

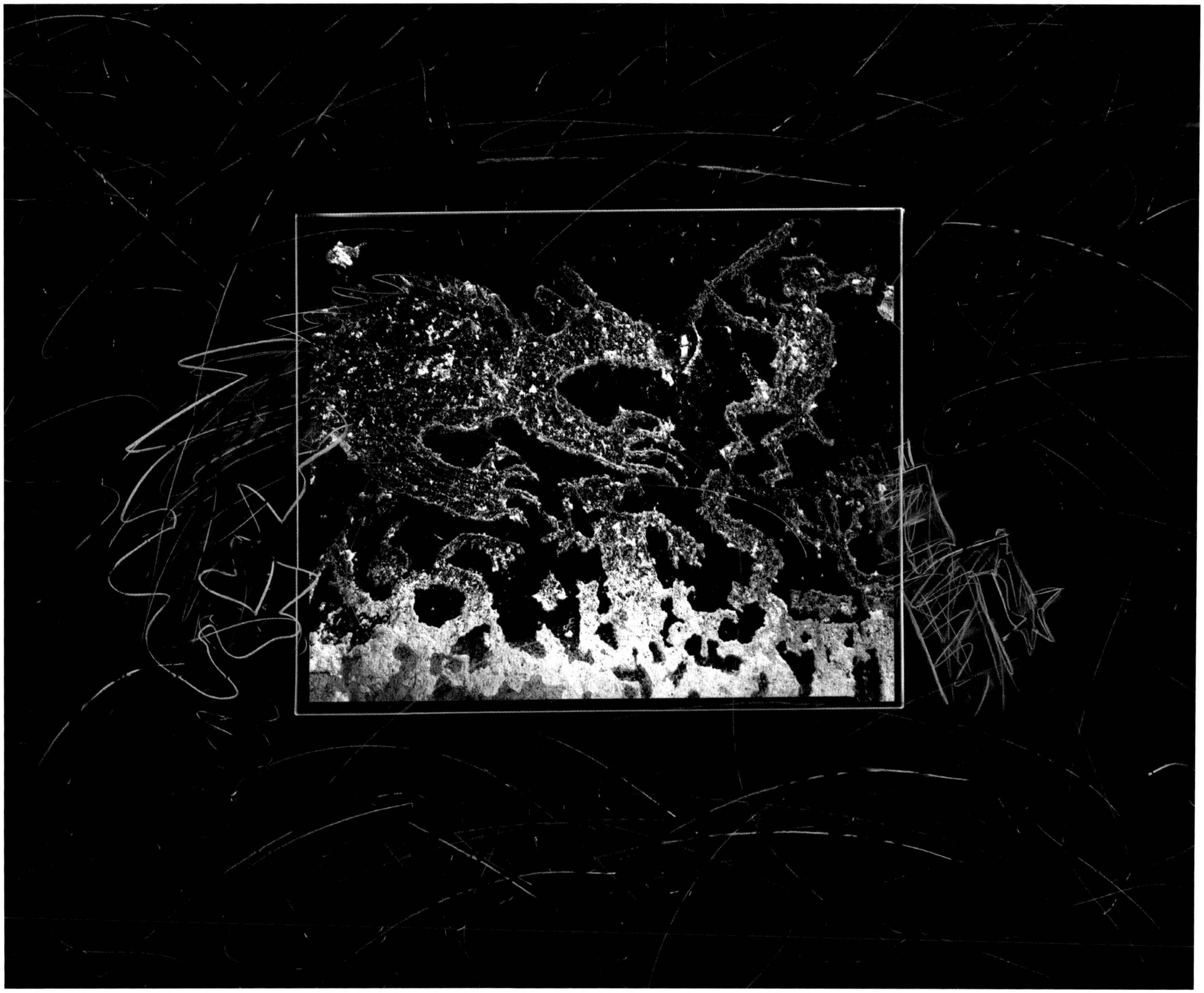

46. *Interior: Cave Kiva near White Rock, New Mexico (Mythical Fragments)*, 1984–86.
Graphite and silver-colored pencil on gelatin silver print, 16 × 20 in.
In the collection of the Museum of Texas Tech University, Lubbock

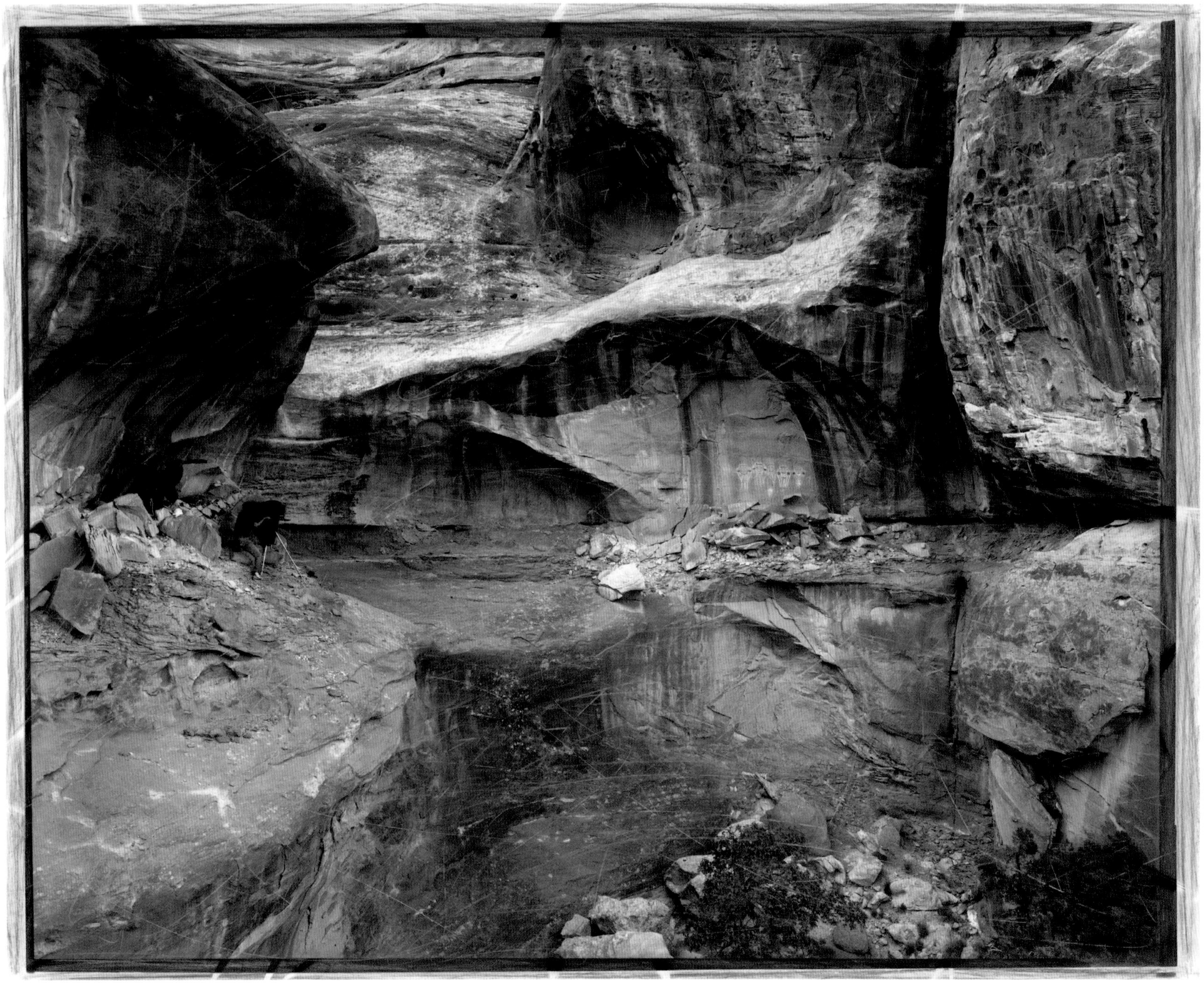

47. *"Five Portraits" Ceremonial, Davis Canyon, near Canyonlands, Utah (Proposed Nuclear Waste Disposal Site)*, 1982–85.
Graphite and silver-colored pencil on gelatin silver print, 16 × 20 in.
In the collection of the Museum of Texas Tech University, Lubbock

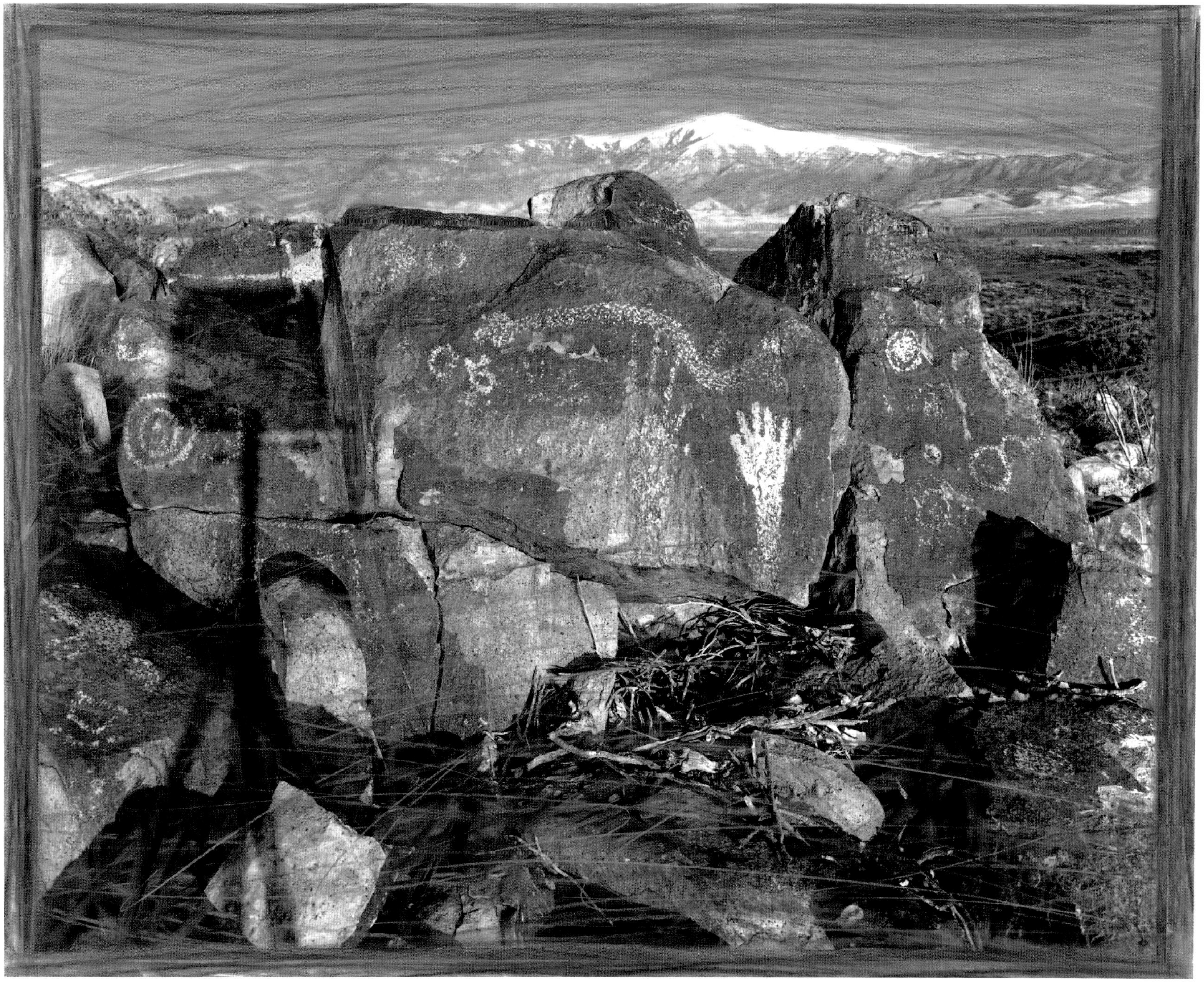

48. *Marking the Passage, Three Rivers, New Mexico*, 1983–86.
Graphite and silver-colored pencil on gelatin silver print, 16 × 20 in.
In the collection of the Museum of Texas Tech University, Lubbock

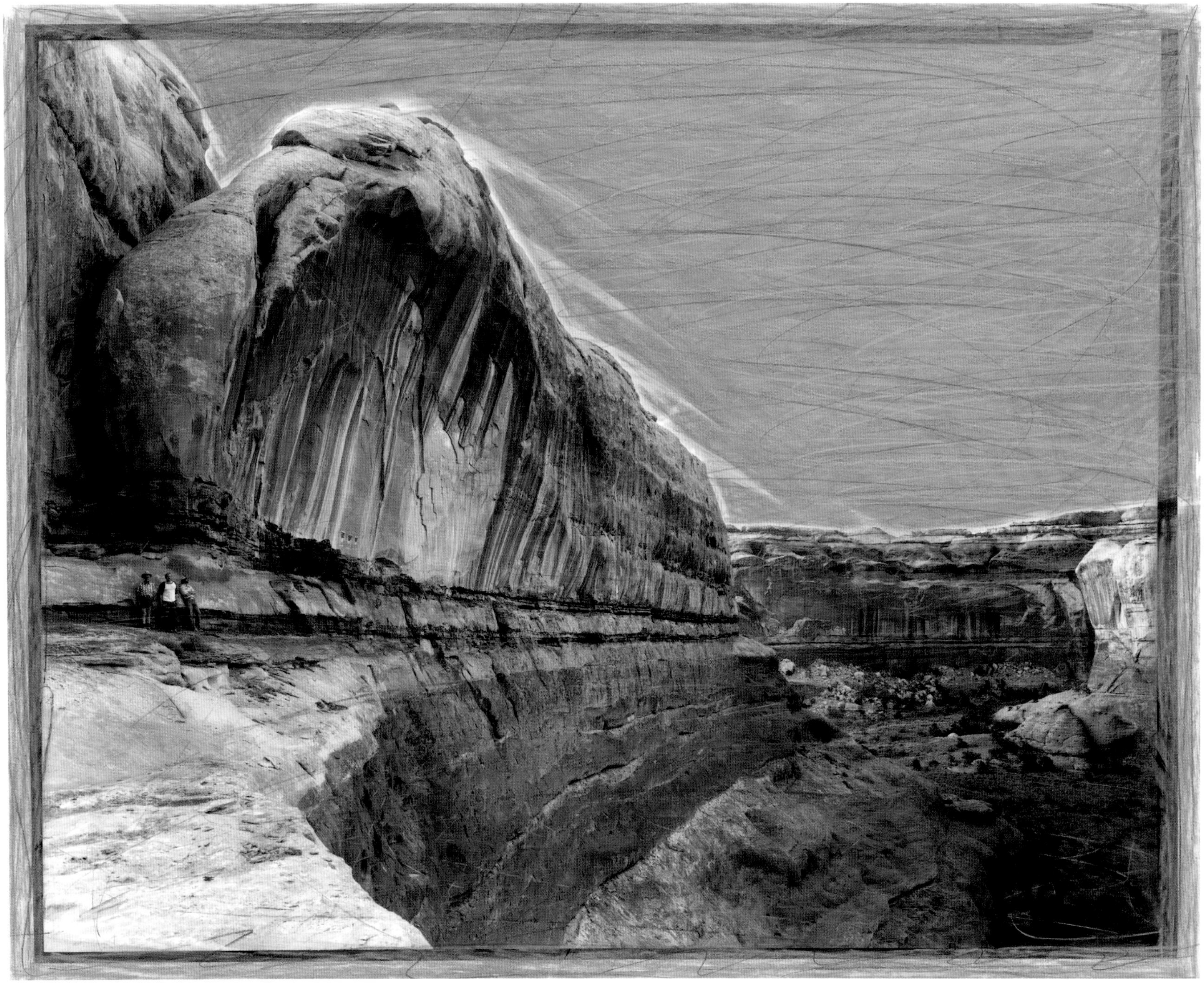

49. *Location of the "Sky Faces" Pictographs, Canyonlands, Utah*, 1982–84.
Graphite and silver-colored pencil on gelatin silver print, 16 × 20 in.
In the collection of the Museum of Texas Tech University, Lubbock

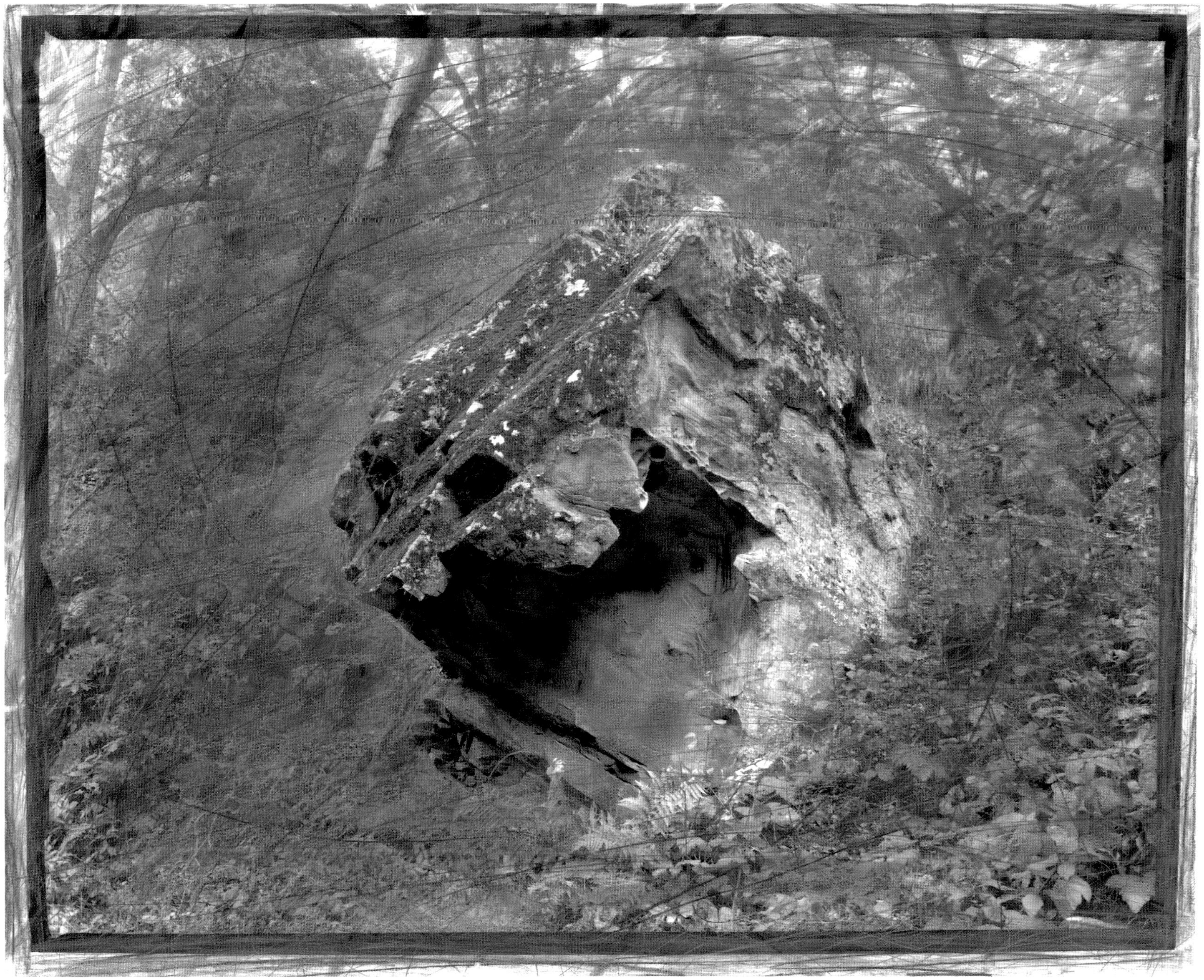

50. *Painted Rock, San Marcos Pass, California*, 1983–84.
Graphite and silver-colored pencil on gelatin silver print, 16 × 20 in.
In the collection of the Museum of Texas Tech University, Lubbock

Dinétah-Hajiinei: Place of Emergence, 1987–1988

I joined another rock art project, which was funded by the Arizona Commission on the Arts. With Lawrence McFarland, Linda Connor, Mark Klett, and graduate students from Arizona State University, I worked under the direction of Navajo elders to photograph the rock art in Dinétah-Hajiinei: Place of Emergence.

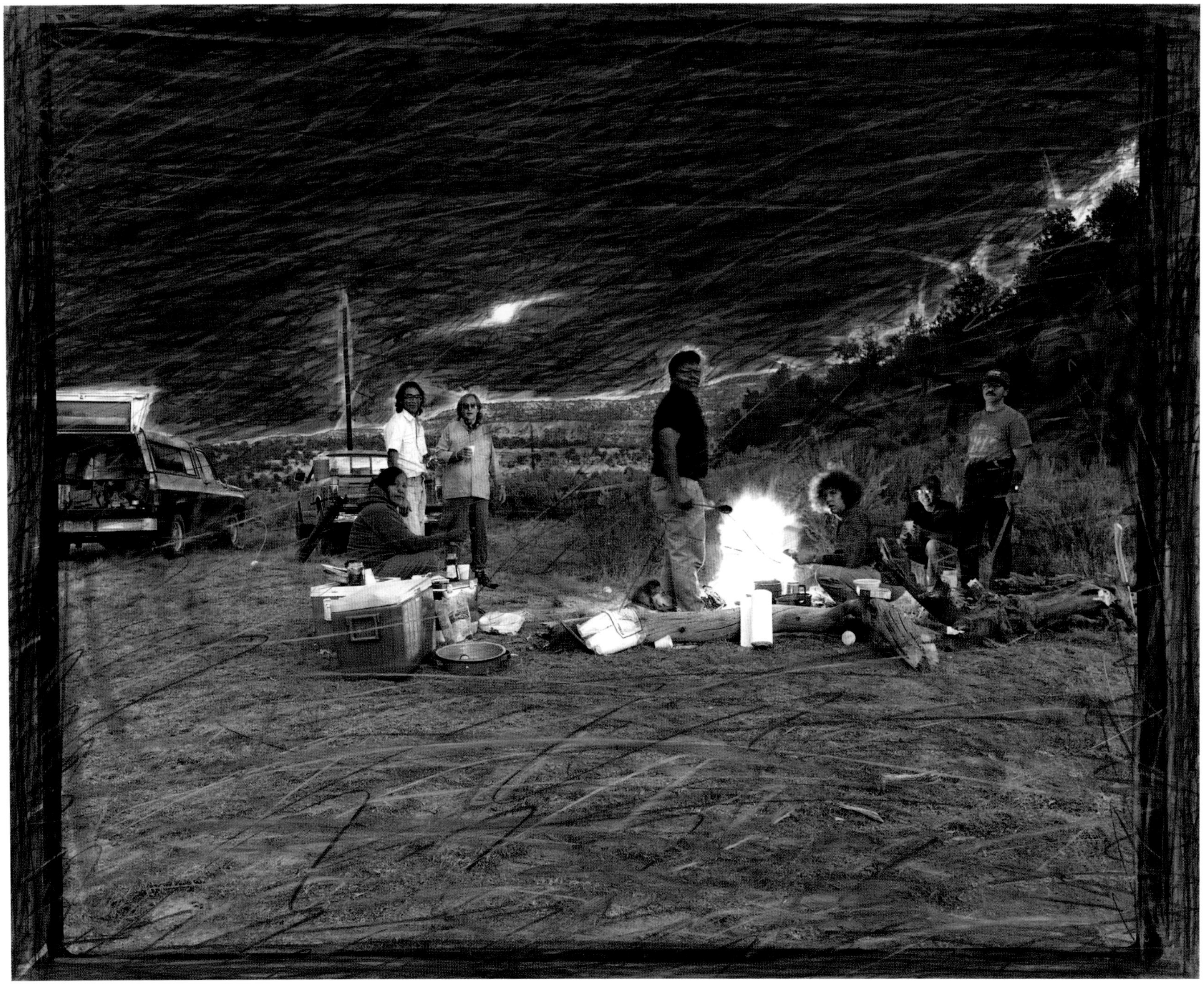

51. *Lessons by the Fire*, 1987–88.
Graphite and silver-colored pencil on gelatin silver print, 16 × 20 in.
In the collection of the Museum of Texas Tech University, Lubbock

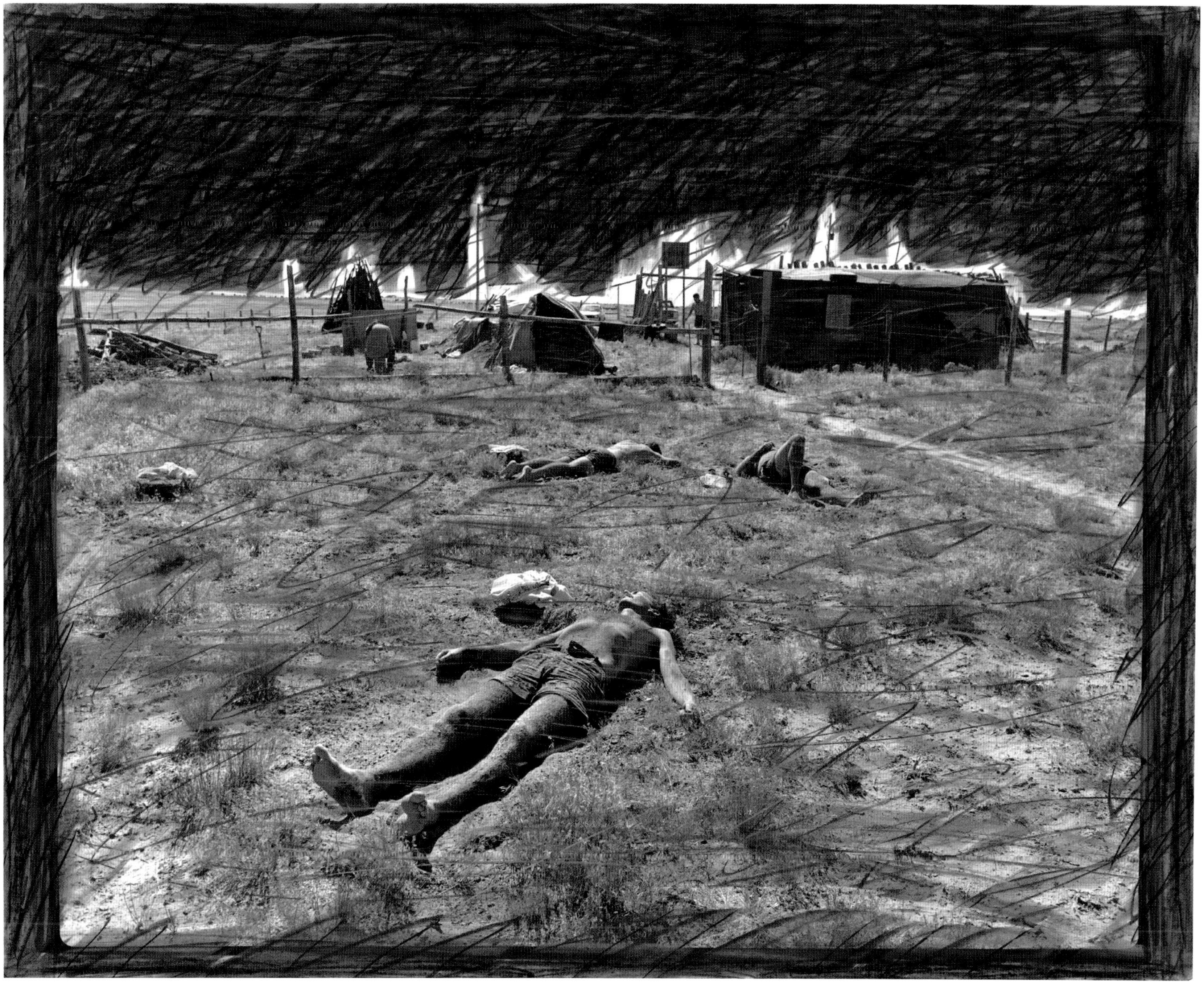

52. *After the Sweat, Lukachukai, Arizona*, 1987–88.
Graphite and silver-colored pencil on gelatin silver print, 16 × 20 in.
In the collection of the Museum of Texas Tech University, Lubbock

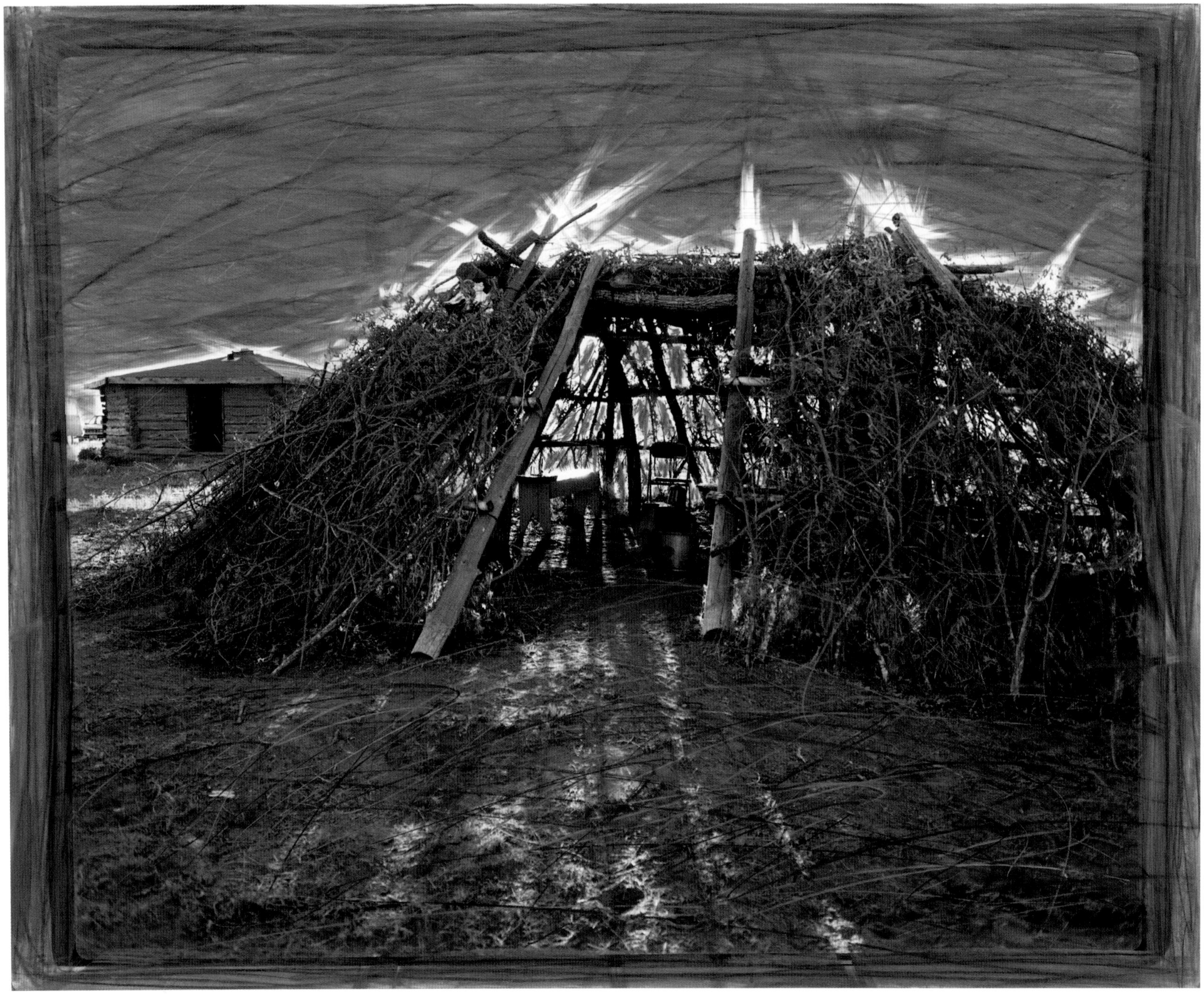

53. *Shade House Full of Light, Lukachukai, Arizona*, 1988.
Graphite and silver-colored pencil on gelatin silver print, 35 × 47 in.
In the collection of the Museum of Texas Tech University, Lubbock

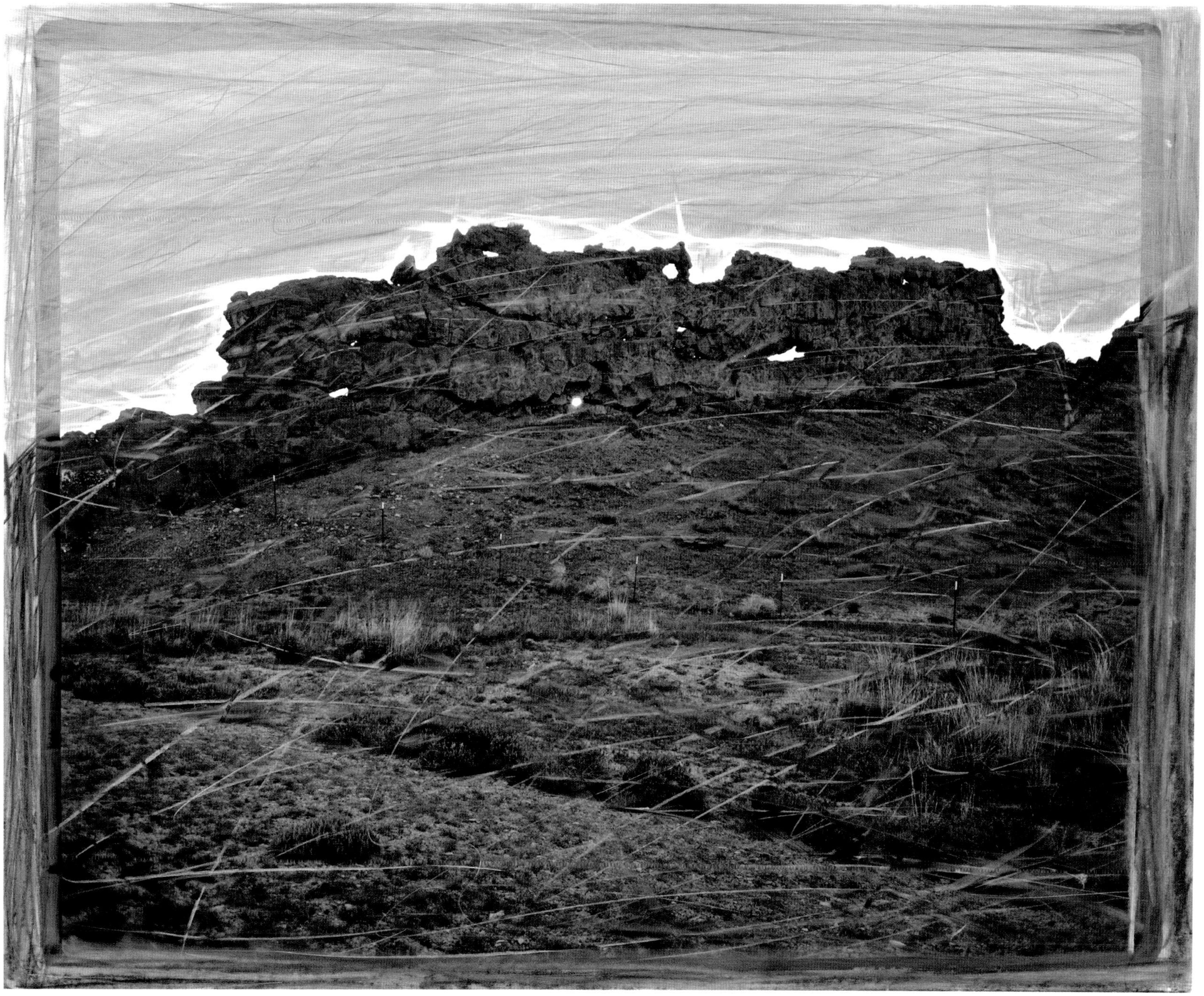

54. *Volcanic Wall near Shiprock, New Mexico (Wings of the Giant Bird in the Journey to the Father Story of the Navajos)*, 1987–88.
Graphite and silver-colored pencil on gelatin silver print, 16 × 20 in.
In the collection of the Museum of Texas Tech University, Lubbock

India, 1988–1990

With a grant from Art Matters, I traveled to India to photograph shrines, temples, and pilgrimage sites to study the relations and tensions between the sacred and the secular. This was an extension of photographing rock art sites, "trading places" by comparing different cultural points of view, and exploring connections between inner landscapes of the mind and the external world. I was studying not just how places change physically over time, but how places also change us. I was investigating how the places we visit, travel through, and live in affect and alter who we are and who we become by creating impressions we carry that inform our ongoing choices and actions.

When I was working on a project on the reservation, I asked a Navajo medicine woman if certain places were more sacred than others. She shook her head and said, "No, every place is equal; we may honor specific places because they represent certain things, but in the end, it is all the same. Everything is sacred, so no single place is really more sacred than another." And in one of the lectures I attended in India in 1987–88 about how particular places come to be regarded as sacred, an Indian guru said, to the best of my recollection, "A place becomes known as sacred only because we see it that way. Sacredness may be hidden, but it actually exists everywhere. When you approach a place as sacred, for healing or for spiritual transformation, you are merely seeking to invoke the sacred aspect that already exists inside of you that has not yet been brought into focus."

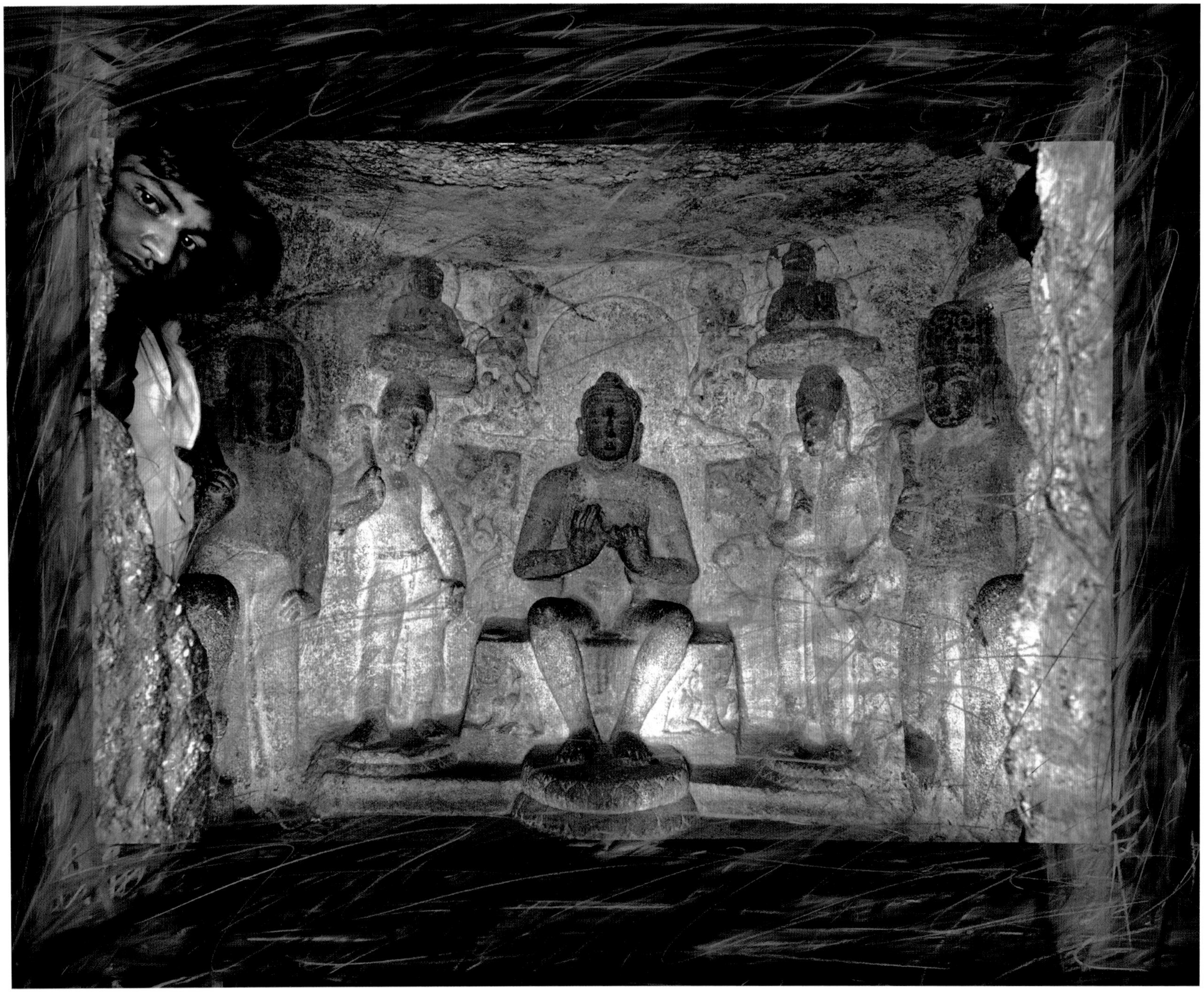

55. *Buddha with Onlookers, Pandu Lena Caves near Nasik, Maharashtra, India*, 1988–90.
Graphite and silver-colored pencil on gelatin silver print, 16 × 20 in.
In the collection of the Museum of Texas Tech University, Lubbock

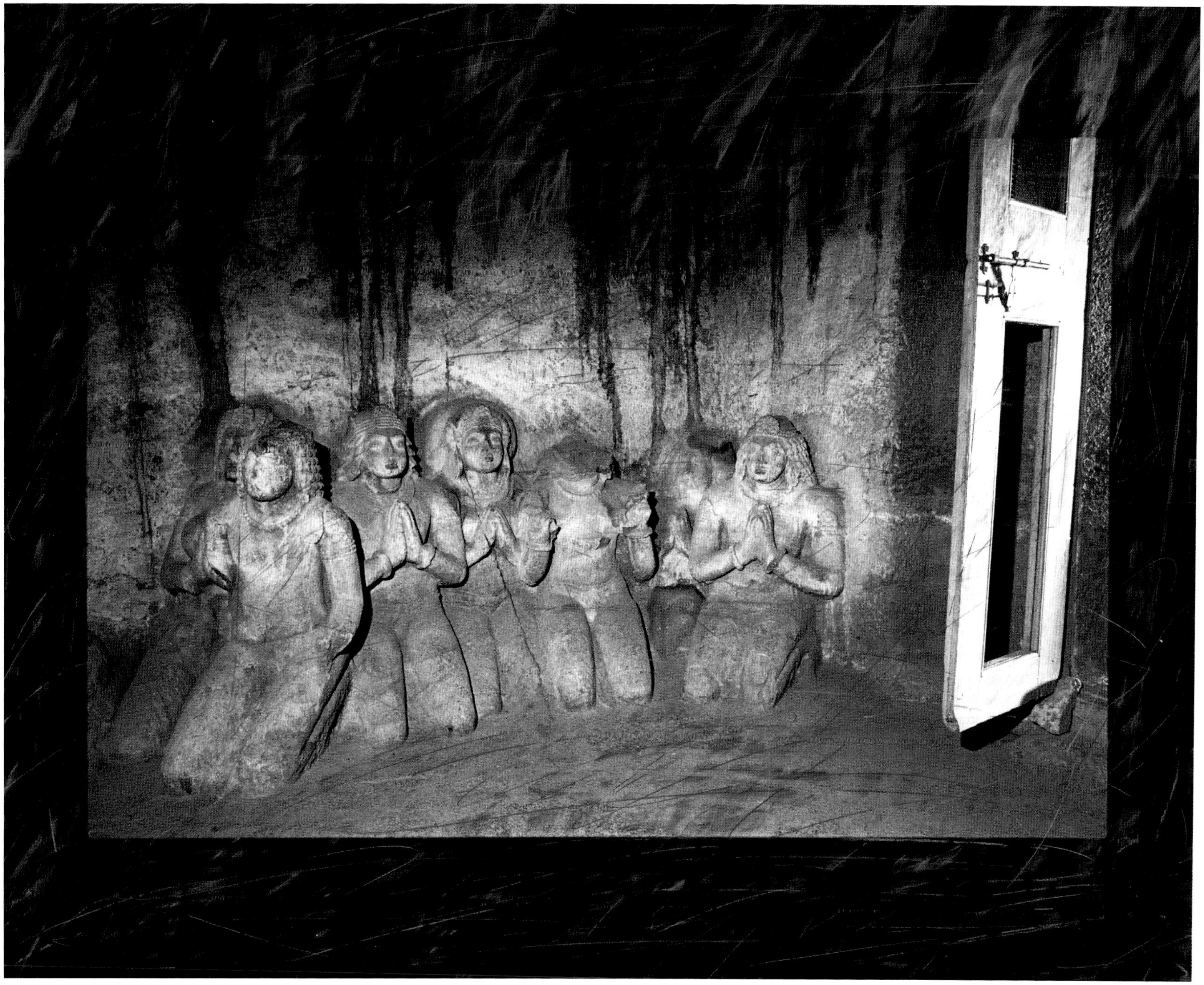

56. *Kneeling Figures, Buddhist Caves near Aurangabad, Maharashtra, India*, 1988–90.
Graphite and silver-colored pencil on gelatin silver print, 16 × 20 in.
In the collection of the Museum of Texas Tech University, Lubbock

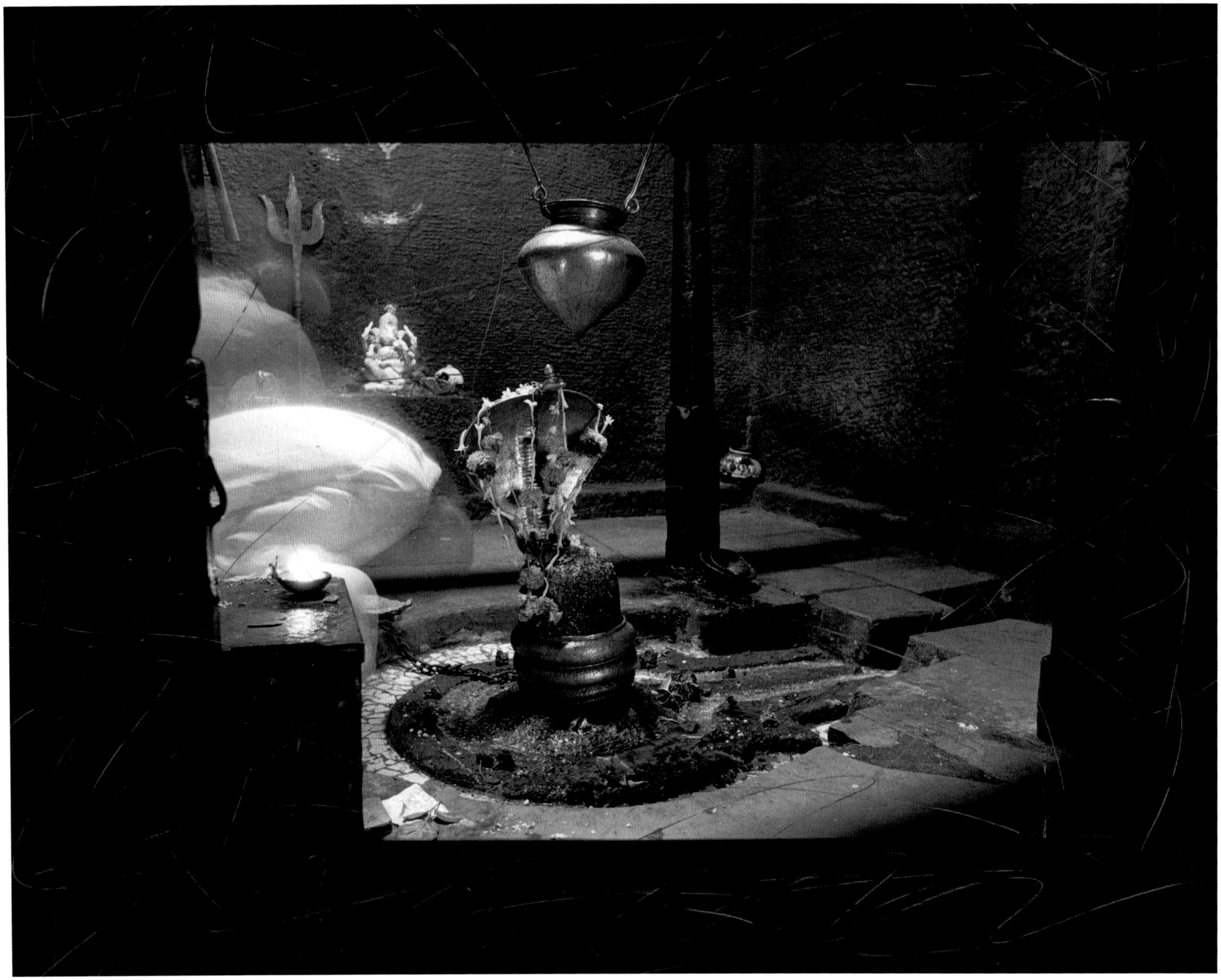

57. *Shiva Lingam, Panchaleshwar Temple, Poona, Maharashtra, India*, 1988–90.
Graphite and silver-colored pencil on gelatin silver print, 16 × 20 in.
In the collection of the Museum of Texas Tech University, Lubbock

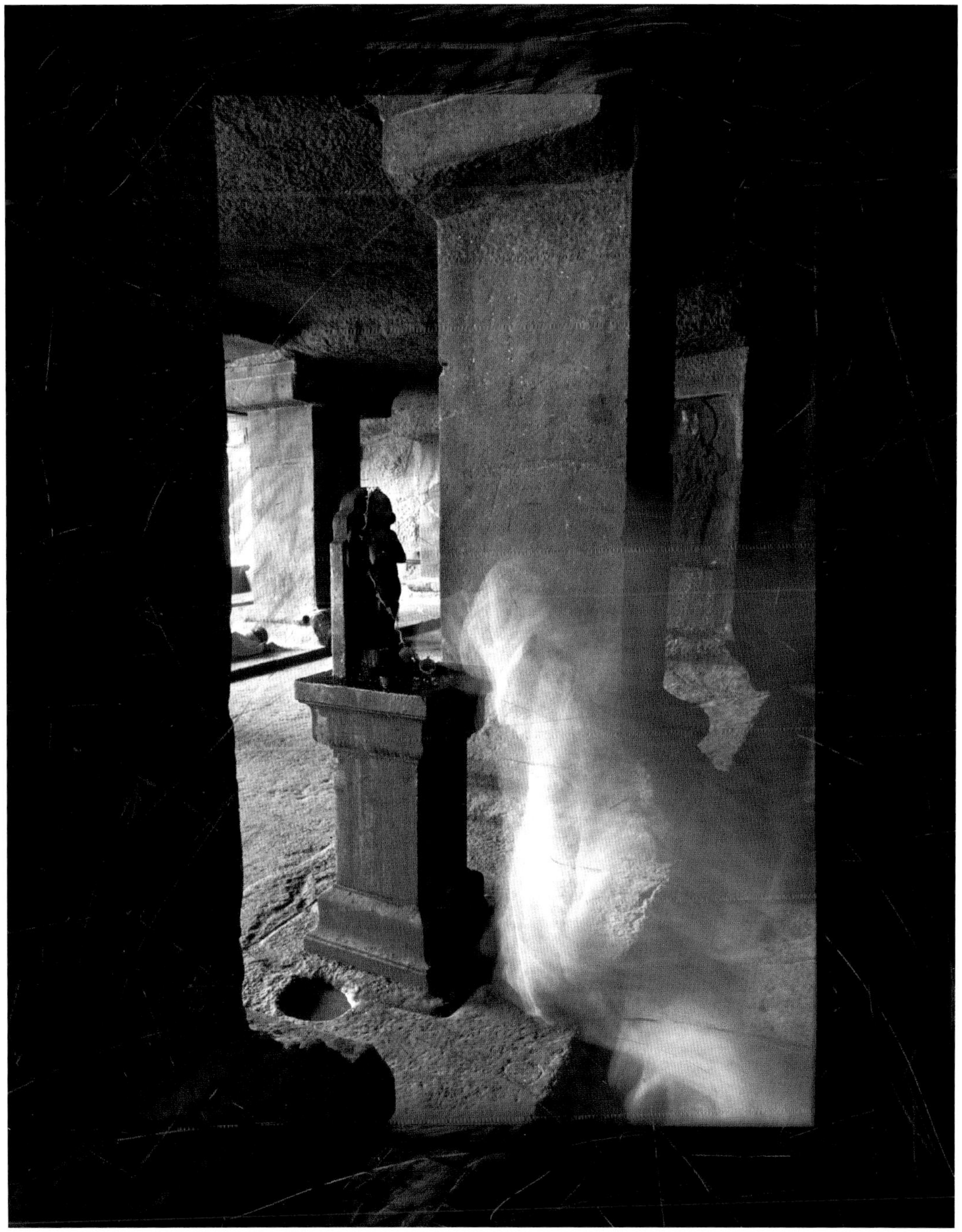

58. *Hanuman, Panchaleshwar Temple, Poona, Maharashtra, India*, 1988–90.
Graphite and silver-colored pencil on gelatin silver print, 20 × 16 in.
In the collection of the Museum of Texas Tech University, Lubbock

NAVAJO PLACES, 1989–1992

Will Tsosie invited me to return to the Navajo Nation to explore contemporary landscape as a continued investigation of connections between past and present and sacred and secular, as well as the relationships of stories, ceremonies, and identity to places.

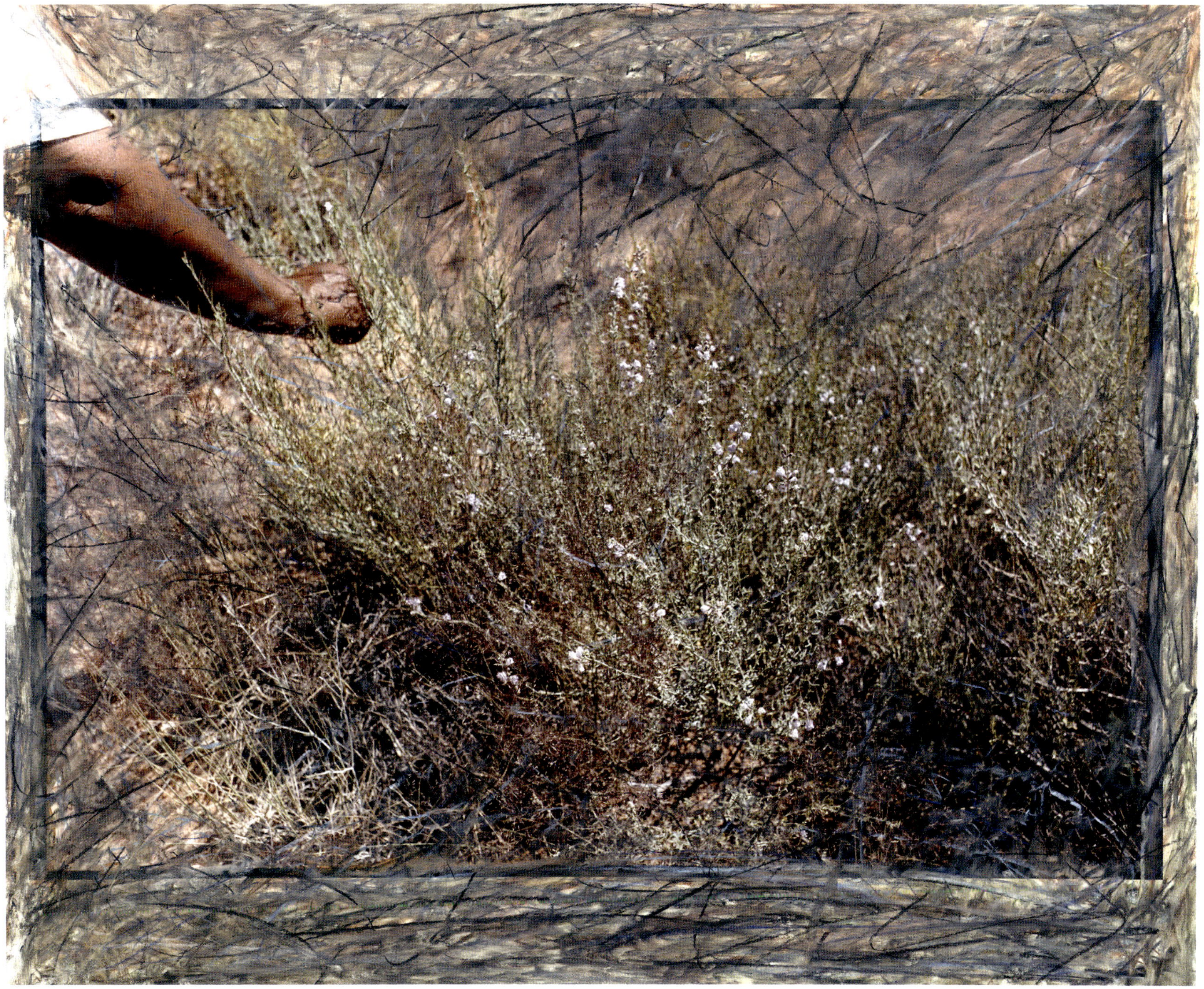

59. *Collecting Navajo Smoke*, 1992–93.
Crayon on chromogenic print, 16 × 20 in.
In the collection of the Museum of Texas Tech University, Lubbock

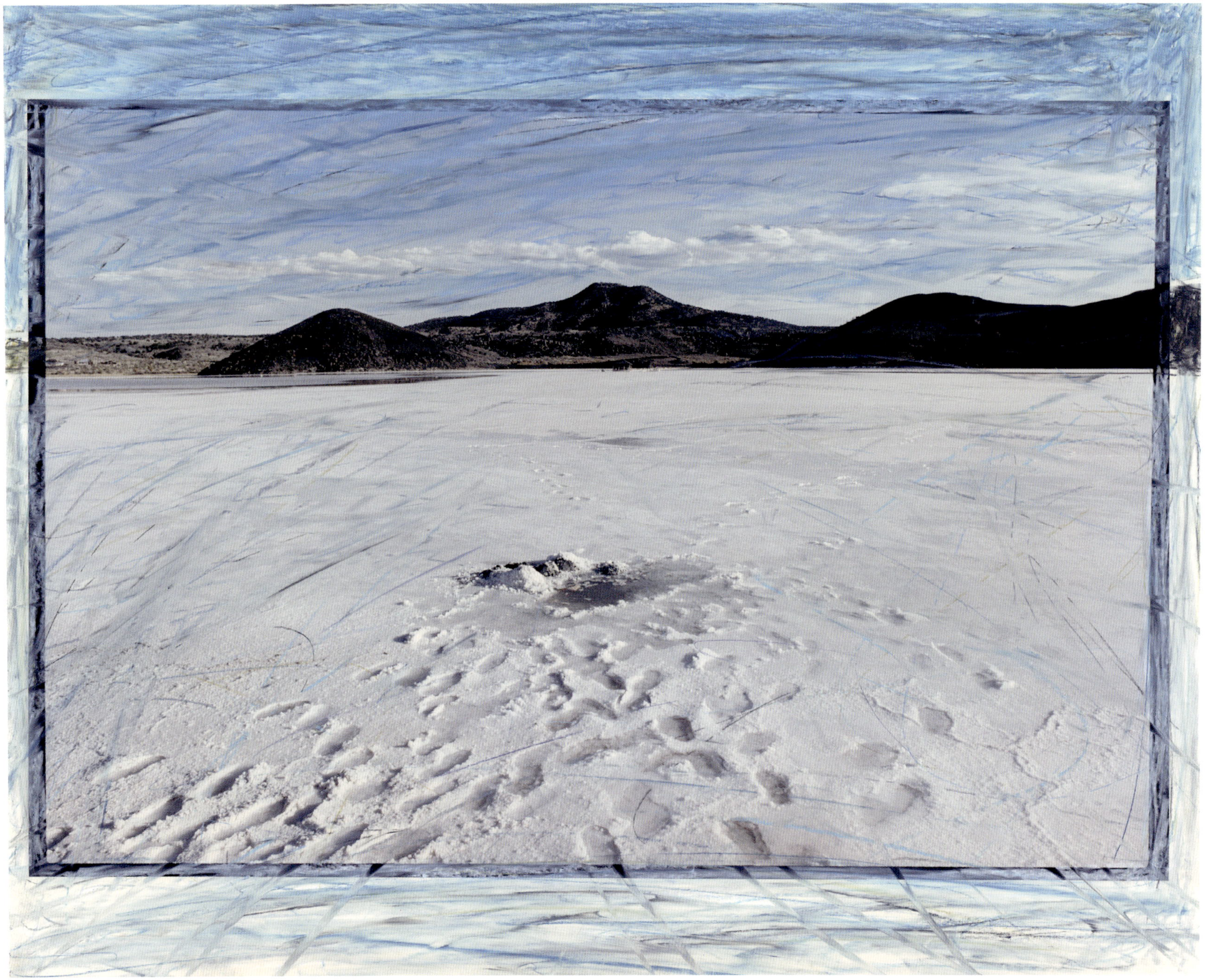

60. *Collecting Salt at Zuni Salt Lake*, 1991–92.
Crayon on chromogenic print, 16 × 20 in.
In the collection of the Museum of Texas Tech University, Lubbock

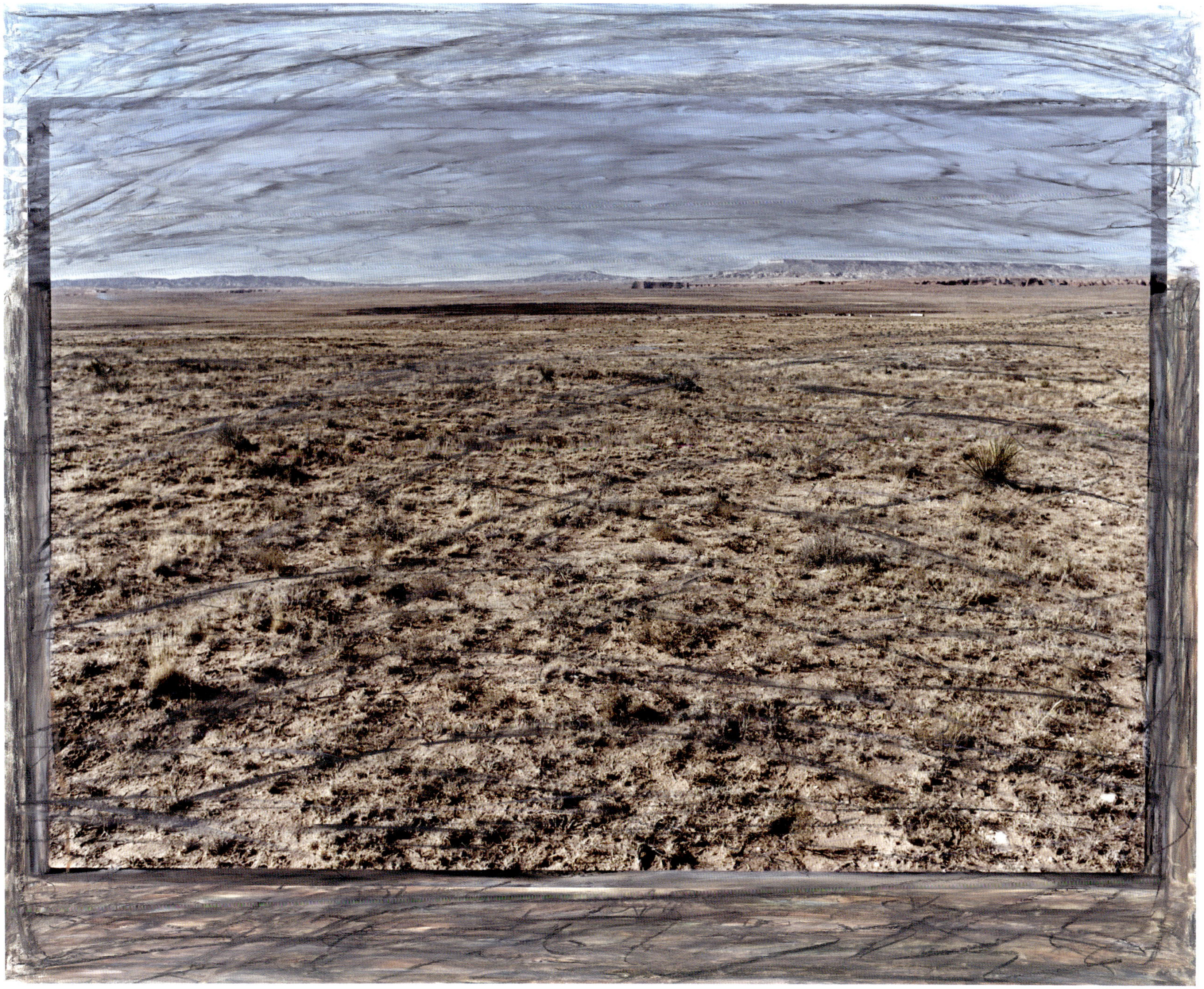

61. *Shadow over Moaning Lake*, 1991–92.
Crayon on chromogenic print, 16 × 20 in.
In the collection of the Museum of Texas Tech University, Lubbock

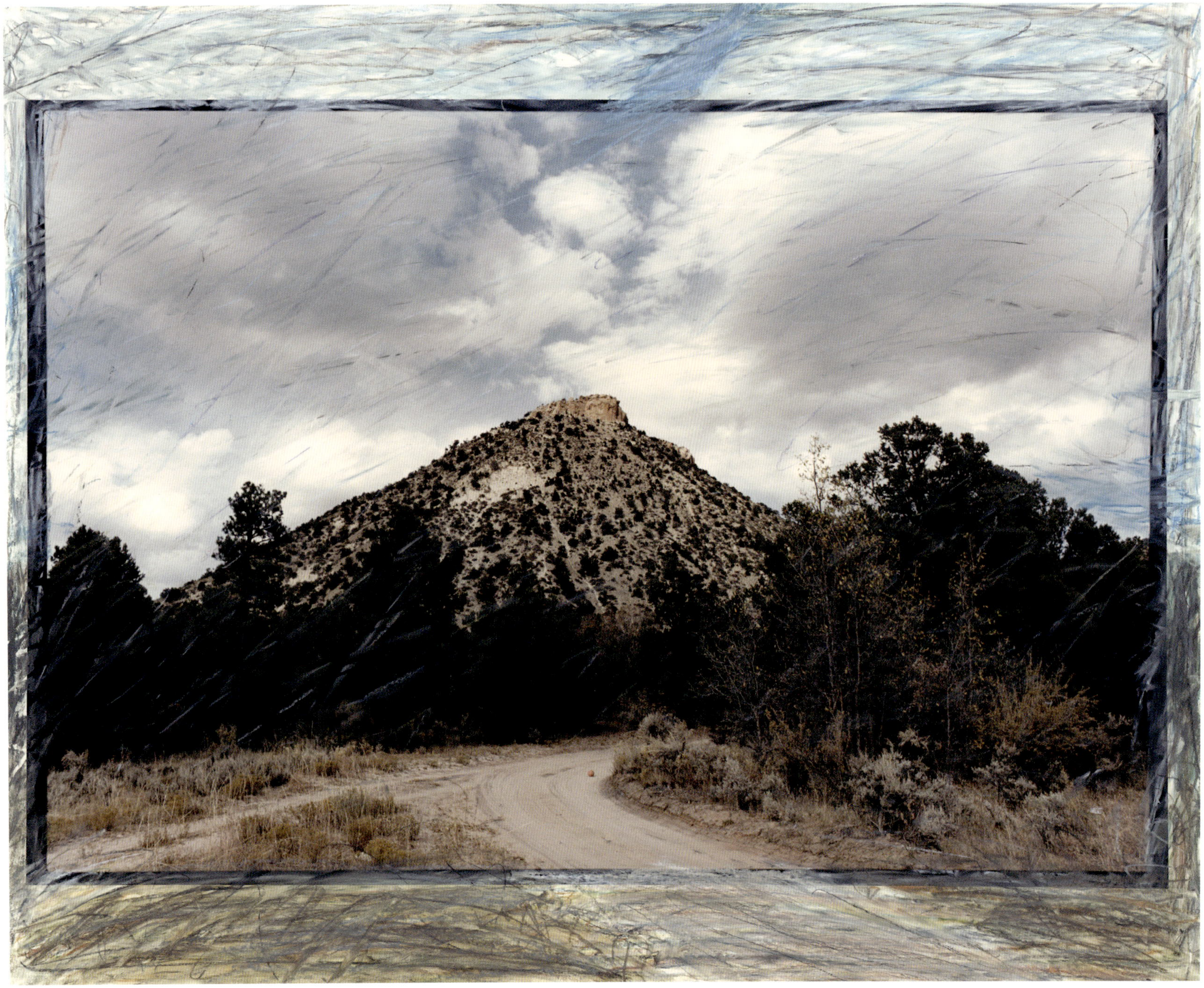

62. *White Cone*, 1991–92.
Crayon on chromogenic print, 16 × 20 in.
In the collection of the Museum of Texas Tech University, Lubbock

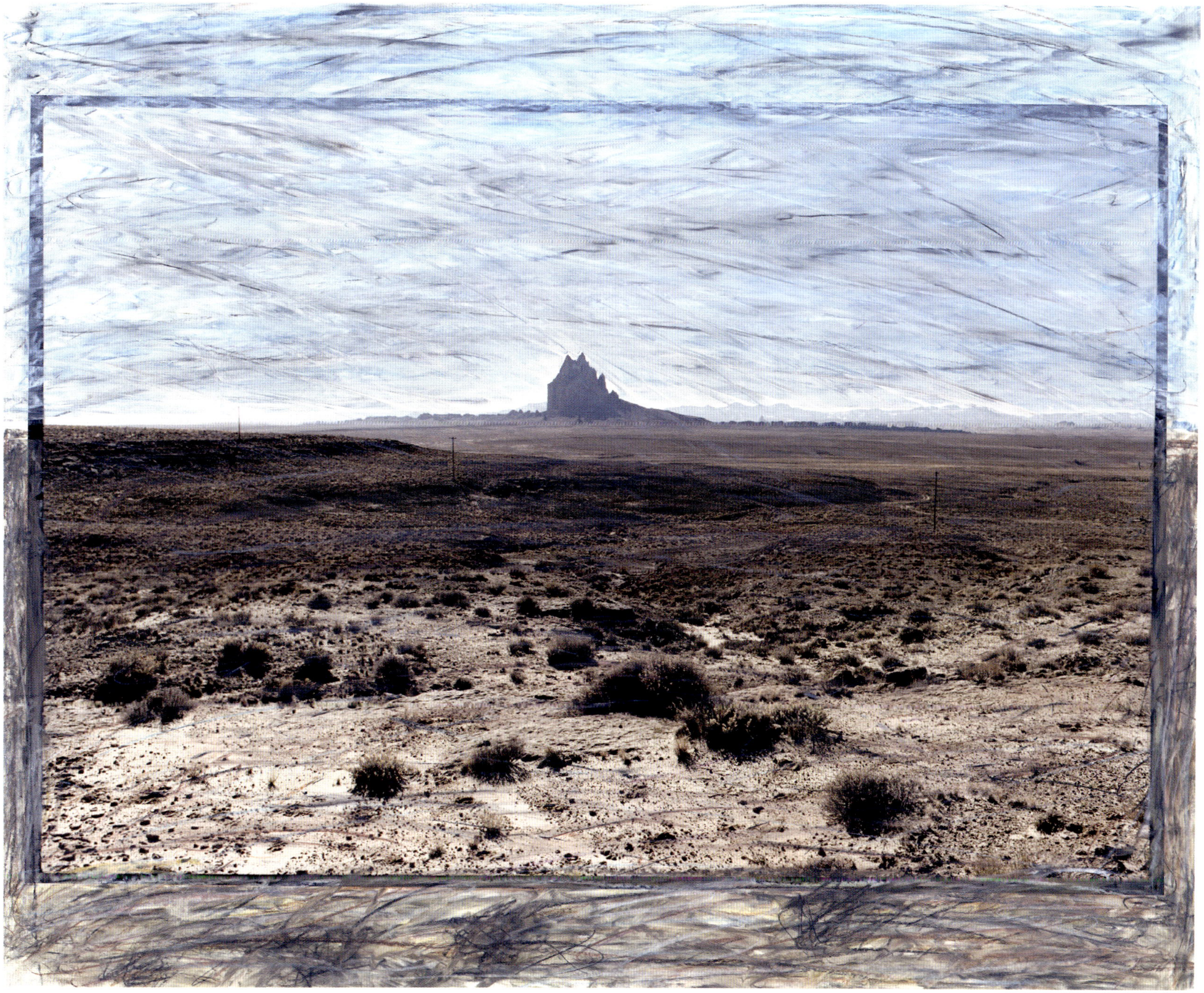

63. *Shiprock*, 1991–92.
Crayon on chromogenic print, 16 × 20 in.
In the collection of the Museum of Texas Tech University, Lubbock

Double Visions

Lucy R. Lippard

Rick Dingus's straight and altered photographs are conceived both as autonomous images/artifacts and as bridges between the photographer's experiences and those of the viewers. The shifting and changing that interests him takes place not only in his images but in the ways they are transmitted and received, as suggested in the title of this book, with its emphasis on transformation. He is concerned with *translating* information across visual borders, a process that demands a double focus, sometimes reflected in strategic juxtaposition, but more evident in the underlying meaning: the view shifts, the place changes . . . movement in time or space becomes the subject.

It is not easy to pin down a single focus for this body of work, since Dingus does not quite fit into the army of what I call "critical landscape photographers," who are shooting up land use in the West with overtly activist overtones, although some of his work lies comfortably in that category, such as the panoramic images of the oil industry in the Texas llano, and *Global Rescue Station* (figure 98), a Green Party installation within an old-growth forest in Tasmania threatened by clear-cutting (and other pictures of the done deed at nearby sites). Most of Dingus's work is more about undertones. The environment is a concern but his immersion in landscape is also personal—experiential and wide ranging. His deliberately erratic course reflects his habit of walking, which allows for independent stops and detours, and his fondness for noting places to go back to while driving around. On return, the place may have changed, and will change again, and perhaps be visited again, or not. Down on ground level, Dingus has described these vernacular landscapes as "localized symbol[s] of the Earth."[1] Far above, in *Earth Changes: Past-Present-Future*, 1981–86 (figure 27), the nine numbered rectangles (seen in a natural history museum) are an artist's conception of different stages of geologic time on one patch of place. "I was equating the illusion of a photograph stopping time," says Dingus, "with the illusion that the earth is not moving when viewed from the span of a human lifetime."[2] He often mentions science as an influence on his work, via his older brother, who worked at Los Alamos as a physicist. The artist was briefly a scientific photographer at Kirtland Air Force Base in Albuquerque in the late 1970s.

Dingus was in art school in the early 1970s, when a pseudoscientific approach to the everyday was popular with conceptual artists. In 1972, he conducted an experiment that echoed the prevalent minimal and conceptual concerns with permutation, time lapse, and repetition when he photographed minute alterations in a single view of a beach in Isla Vista, California, at exactly 5 P.M., for twenty-eight days in February (figure 3). The choice of black and white film that dominated most of Dingus's earlier work might have also been influenced by the conceptualist preference for the casual snapshot; color seemed too seductive, or professional. Unlike the conceptualists, however, Dingus perceived black and white as "less literal" than color, which "added more layers of information," when he was finally seduced by it in 1990.[3] He shared an interest in Eadweard Muybridge's motion studies with permutation master Sol LeWitt, and it is tempting to associate Dingus's *After the Fire, Bandelier National Monument, New Mexico (Topography Grid)*, 1977–78 (figure 6), constructed by ecologists studying the effects of fire, with LeWitt's "non-visual structures." When Dingus went on to graduate school at the University of New Mexico, he did his MFA dissertation on the great nineteenth-century western survey photographer T. H. O'Sullivan, whose work has continued to interest him. (See figure 67, *O'Sullivan's Fissure Vent with Camera*; and figure 69, *Dam and Viewing Platform,* both 1998–99.)

Once his course was set, Dingus did not veer in the direction of photo montage but chose a painterly approach. Drawing with silver-colored pencils, crayons, or graphite directly on black and white and then color prints, he made surfaces flicker, shift, and change. The scribbles in these photo drawings can electrify the images, endowing them with an otherworldly glow. (See figure 32, *Five Years after the Fire*; and figure 59, *Collecting Navajo Smoke*) In New Mexico, Dingus was struck by the "magical realism" of the clarity of light on the arid landscape. The state's "strange mix of time frames and cultures comingled in the present" made him "think differently about the landscape."[4] (I get it, having lived there for twenty-three years.) The rapidly changing West, old and new, remains a major player in Dingus's work, perhaps providing its underlying narrative, even when the images are taken elsewhere.

In the late 1970s, through some geologist friends, Dingus was invited to join a small group of photographers in the landmark Rephotographic Survey Project, which involved returning to the sites of a monumental nineteenth-century western survey a hundred years later and shooting them, when possible, from the same vantage point.[5] He had already been applying the repeat process, finding that it "tested the tolerances of photographic documentation as an objective tool."[6] It also echoed his *Every day at exactly 5 P.M. in February 1973* (figure 3). But the rapid momentum of ocean waves and student project are considerably slowed by this time. Rephotography reveals visible social change or the lack thereof. One pair of photographs—of Witches Rock, in Weber Valley, Utah—speaks less to change than to the unchanging, underlining the length of time certain places, left alone, remain almost the same. A century has not altered this nubbly hoodoo, but even the posture of the small figure at its base in the original photograph betrays its origin in another era (figures 15 and 16). Dingus also discovered that O'Sullivan had had his own fun with *Tertiary Conglomerates* (figure 18) at the same site, in 1869, when he framed the outcrop at an angle, slightly distorting the landscape.

On the other hand, when revisited after one hundred years, *Big Cottonwood Canyon* (an idyllic valley and unencumbered mountain view photographed in 1868 by T. H. O'Sullivan) is still "sublime," but it is now encumbered by an industrial site and pole in the foreground, disrupting any "pristine" experience of wilderness (figures 13 and 14). Similarly, in *Hanging Rock (and Pulpit Rock), Echo City, Utah Territory*, taken by A. J. Russell in 1868, the geologic monuments overwhelm a seated figure and a little farm; when W. H. Jackson was at the same site a year later, two telegraph poles appear (probably just omitted from Russell's image). And by 1978 Pulpit Rock has disappeared, and railway tracks run below Hanging Rock (figures 9–12).

Scrutinizing these "then and now" images, Dingus considered "the role played by each viewer of a photograph." He hopes to make images that "pose questions rather than confirm assumptions."[7] (Of course, what any viewer already knows and assumes is always a mystery; for one person, a photograph could be old hat or impossibly unfamiliar, for another, a revelation.) Always doubling around, Dingus fuses his mystical inclinations with the documentary impulse that remains at the heart of the photographic enterprise—the need to preserve a sight, a moment.

I first saw Dingus's work in the late 1980s, when he participated in the Marks in Place project—another formative experience, also based in collaboration. He coordinated the resultant book, *Marks in Place: Contemporary Responses to Rock Art*, for which I wrote the foreword. The subject was petroglyphs and pictographs in the American West. I was just being introduced to this field. My first trip into the Utah Canyonlands was with a University of Colorado photo class, courtesy of Charles Roitz (Marks in Place project director). It was a life changer. Little did I know that I too would soon become obsessed by rock art, history, and archaeology, and that I would move a few years later to the Galisteo Basin in New Mexico, where we are surrounded by images inspired by indigenous belief systems we will never fully understand. In *Marks in Place*, I wrote about five artists "trying to lose themselves in time, or about five artists finding themselves in place."[8] These secular photographers reinvested "rock art" with the respect given to "art" in the dominant culture (though many Pueblo people today refuse the Western label of "art" for their religious imagery).

The cultural landscapes revealed by the rock art offered foils to the artists' various styles and goals.[9] Dingus wanted to make "new images about old locations" (and his dreams about them)—a continuation rather than a break with the past, augmenting the work of anthropologists and archaeologists by responding "in an alternate manner to the same subject."[10] In my own experience—and his too, I suspect—I have found rock art an invaluable guide to broader senses of place. It is far more integrated with its contexts than any contemporary land art. Walking the land and looking for traces can be as satisfying as finding them.

In the late 1980s the search for rock art was an esoteric pastime. Archaeologists often avoided the subject, put off by the uncertainty of the glyphs' dates. These five artists were of course attracted precisely to this "timelessness" and often seemed less interested in the ancient meanings than in the present experience, wisely avoiding interpretation that was in a sense none of their business, given the ongoing significance for contemporary Puebloans.[11] Polly Schaafsma, whose work almost singlehandedly brought southwestern rock art into the scholarly canon, wrote that "when religion was abstracted and removed from its geographic place of origin and housed in man's architectural creations, the landscape became secularized, a resource available for exploitation merely, 'a land of many uses,'" photography being one of them.[12]

Dingus worked among these many uses, concentrating on the sites. The glyphs often revealed themselves under closer scrutiny, as they do in the landscape. In *"Five Portraits" Ceremonial, Davis Canyon, near Canyonlands, Utah (Proposed Nuclear Waste Disposal Site)*, 1982–85 (figure 47), contemporary issues combined with the ancient images. With his photo drawings, Dingus chose a personal, hands-on approach, scratching almost randomly on the surface of his prints in homage to the artists who had inscribed the rocks. Sometimes the collaboration between old and new took precedence, as in the powerful *Interior: Cave Kiva near White Rock, New Mexico (Mythical Fragments)*, 1984–86 (figure 46), in which the altered photograph brings to life a dynamic struggle between bear and human.

Marks in Place led Dingus farther afield, where he could test his "assumptions with alternatives offered by other cultures and disciplines."[13] He was invited to participate in another rock art project in Navajoland, under the direction of tribal elders, and was then called back by them to consider connections between past and present in the contemporary landscape. He studied Eastern thought: Yoga, Sufism, Hinduism, Buddhism, Taoism, Zen koans, Tai Chi, and Kashmir Saivism (which reminded him of quantum mechanics theories).[14] In the late 1980s, he received a grant to travel in India, where he photographed caves, shrines, and temples, variations on rock art. (Figure 58, *Hanuman, Panchaleshwar Temple, Poona, Maharashtra, India*, 1988–89, is a classically beautiful image from this series that might have been taken many decades ago.) In the *Marks in Place* book, Dingus had written: "Before we dismiss all myth as outmoded superstition, let us beware of our own mechanistic attitudes."[15] Although that was almost thirty years ago, his words are still relevant, especially to the ways we see land and landscape, a responsibility of photographers as much as of scientists and scholars. I have found in my own work in the Southwest the necessity of balancing my political pessimism about the effects of development and extraction industries on the future of the places I love with more optimistic belief systems that are in a sense foreign to me—those of the Native peoples with whom we coexist. The destruction, for instance, of Navajo lands and water over years of uranium mining introduced by major corporations (and warned against in ancient "myths") is illuminated by the belief that disaster was sparked by bad choices, out of harmony, out of balance, calling for healing ceremonies.[16]

Encounters of "nature" with human-made places and products is an underlying theme in this book, as is a certain melancholy about the erosion of culture and nature. For example, in *Unfinished House in the Woods near Taos, New Mexico*, 1985–88 (figure 25), and *Tree of Knowledge, Turkey, Texas*, 1988–89 (figure 33), abandoned or disintegrating structures are being swallowed up by "wild" nature; in *Unfinished Business (Mississippi)*, 1989 (figure 31), a vintage car with dramatic fins has come to rest in a thicket, its speed-oriented design halted for good. Yet humor nudges its way into some pictures. In *Recycled Beetle*, a VW Bug on spider legs adorns a local zoo (figure 71). The giant label of *Climate Controlled Storage, Lubbock, Texas*, 2005–2006 (figure 82), stretches across the horizon like a caption to the tire-tracked grass and power line.

Dingus has an eye for the peculiar, and for tweaking the ordinary with photographic technique and technology. One way he does this is by using wide-angle lenses or the swing lens of a panorama camera to show the curvature of the earth on distant horizons, evoking far more distance than is actually visible, as in *Old Home Place in a Plowed Field, Posey, Texas*, 2004–2006 (figure 90), where a vanished farmstead is survived only by its planted trees, adrift in a sea of dirt. Or he mimics the notion of "peephole" photography (figures 91–102), having invented a camera that makes circular images on a black ground, as though he (and we) are looking out through a spying device, emphasizing the fact that all photographers are voyeurs at heart.

He thinks about how and why we look as well as what we are looking at, thus his interest in tourism, where the "view" is manipulated—activated either by resonant histories and visual uniqueness or by marketing strategies. The best souvenirs are the creation of "new memories." His photographs of tourists or tourist sites are often layered, or doubled. *Merged Moments*, 1976 (figure 5) depicts a woman looking at two separate projections—urban and desert—or standing in two places at once, or holding two different images in her own mind. Three decades later a similarly doubled experience, combined with the concept of the portable landscape, appears in *Visitor Center, Monahans Sandhills State Park*, 2004–2006 (figure 88); a big interior screen features a filmed image of what is seen outside the adjacent picture window. Three empty chairs face out toward the actual view, turning their backs on its representation. Another color photo (figure 77) shows Mount St. Helens towering outside a visitor's center movie theater, or maybe it shows the film of the same view projected on the screen before it was rolled up, exposing the real thing, or another illusion?

Straddling aesthetics and documentation is the challenge many contemporary landscape photographers must meet. While for some, activism outweighs art, both goals depend on the visual strength of the image. Once achieved, it may be open to multiple readings, or offer multiple truths. Dingus has said that during his visits to India, trying to perceive and photograph "through the lens of another culture, . . . I tried to keep one foot grounded so I could remember where I came from; with the other I'd try to go as far as I could away from that grounding to see how things appeared from another angle."[17] Photography is often defined as stopping time in its tracks, but the sequential possibilities of the medium to define a place *and* a time are more important to those whose work, like Dingus's, has both an active and a contemplative side, sometimes simultaneously.

The world is so full of photographs that choice is the crucial aesthetic tool. And place is a heavy hand on the process of looking. Tourist destinations demand different frames, and frames of mind, than do home places. The photo of a monumental globe in Lubbock's International Cultural Center (figure 87) highlights the city where Dingus has lived for over thirty years, making it the center of the world. Yet Lubbock remains elusive in this collection, perhaps best defined by dust: *Lubbock Dust Storm*, 1995 (figure 42), and the *Crop Duster Mural*, 2005–2006 (figure 83), stretching across the wall of a Lubbock cafe. Dingus seems more at home on the broad flat plains of the Llano Estacado (or Staked Plain, which was so vast and featureless that early explorers planted stakes so they could find their way). The wide-angle horizontal format is perfect for that landscape. The curvature of the sky can be relocated to the earth, upended to become a terrestrial bowl, as in the wonderful *Horse, Wheatland, New Mexico*, 2004–2006 (figure 86).

In a sense all these images are teaching moments. Dingus is good at looking, and he encourages us to do the same. Good looking differs from looking good. He selects his landscapes not for their superficial beauty, and not for the moment, but for how they are affected by time, thus his interest in the continuous span of history from the past into the present and the future, which is, of course, gone today and here tomorrow. In line with the title of this book, he advocates images that are flexible (defined in my dictionary as "pliant, not rigid, adaptable, shifting"), but not ambiguous ("doubtful, indistinct, uncertain") despite the much-touted role of ambiguity in contemporary art and theory. Here too he shares responsibility with the viewer, who is not so much kept guessing as kept looking.

The two most recent series pull away from ground level, reaching up into aerial and astronomical ranges. The Star Party series—begun in 2011 when Dingus audited an observational astronomy class at Texas Tech University, where he teaches—might be considered a form of cosmic tourism, although it never leaves the ground, and the stars themselves are out of sight (figures 103–10). It was shot at night at an annual event in Oklahoma with a homemade infrared filter taped over his electronic flash to maintain the night vision necessary to participants. Inspired by how astronomers tease information from digital image files, he began to adopt some of their methods, modifying a DSLR camera to record visual information from any part of the full spectrum. In another departure, Star Party is photographed in a participatory proximity, with tents, telescopes, and generalized figures (some with no heads). An additional offshoot of this preoccupation is the artist's involvement in planning a public camera obscura structure in Lubbock—a communal photographic project with everyone as photographer.

The themes of distance and nearness, representation and reality, vertical and horizontal, conscious and unconscious, inside and outside, underground and celestial recur in Dingus's work over the years. The IR Aerials were shot from commercial planes in bright daylight with an infrared filter behind the lens (figures 111–22). The resultant images, identified by their flight paths from airport to airport, are understated but striking. They are all vertical, as though echoing the height of the photographer's vantage point. They focus on the abrupt encounter of dry mountains cracked by arroyos and perfectly circular irrigation units in a fertile valley, an interface that epitomizes the western landscape, marked as it is by the invisible force of water and lack thereof. Dingus's father used to tell him, "You can't put a row of stakes in a straight line without walking backwards." His recent return to black and white images is both an opportunity to rethink his own past and a "new twist." Everything is still shifting and changing.

Notes

1. Rick Dingus, in Peter S. Briggs, "Ground Level: An Interview with Rick Dingus," this book.

2. Dingus, e-mail message to the author, May 10, 2015.

3. Ibid.

4. Dingus, in Briggs, "Ground Level."

5. Mark Klett, Ellen Manchester, and JoAnn Verburg, *Second View: The Rephotographic Survey Project* (Albuquerque: University of New Mexico Press, 1984).

6. Dingus, "Places, Dreams, and Journeys: Long Term Contexts for Now and Later," in *Marks in Place: Contemporary Responses to Rock Art*, by Linda Connor, Rick Dingus, Steve Fitch, John Pfahl, and Charles Roitz (Albuquerque: University of New Mexico Press, 1987), 34.

7. Dingus, in Peter Briggs, "Way West: A Conversation with Rick Dingus," *AFTERimage* (September/October 2014), 16.

8. Lucy R. Lippard, foreword, in Connor et al., *Marks in Place*, ix.

9. Roitz and Linda Connor concentrated on the indigenous images and their immediate contexts. Steve Fitch lit fires near the panels so the light would be shimmering and unfamiliar, harking back to the era in which they were made; he was later excoriated by archaeologists for endangering the sites. John Pfahl's elegiac, conceptual strategy showed only the reservoirs beneath which many rock art sites had been "drowned" in favor of modern needs.

10. Dingus, "Places, Dreams, and Journeys," 33.

11. There was some danger of the work being seen as blasphemy rather than homage. Appropriation was popular in the art world but destined to irritate and anger living heirs to the indigenous cultural images depicted and then "borrowed."

12. Polly Schaafsma, "Rock Art: Ideas in Time and Space," in Connor et al., *Marks in Place*, 3.

13. Dingus, in Briggs, "Way West," 16.

14. Ibid., 18.

15. Dingus, "Places, Dreams, and Journeys," 38.

16. In "The Shadow of Death," in his book *If You Poison Us* (Santa Fe, N.Mex.: Red Crane, 1994), Peter Eichstaedt relates a Diné story: When the people emerged into the fourth world they were given a choice between two yellow powders—one dust from the rock, the other corn pollen. They chose the pollen, and the gods nodded, warning them to leave the yellow dust in the ground, or it would bring evil.

17. Dingus, in Briggs, "Way West," 17.

REGARDING TECHNOLOGY, 1998–2002

THIS SERIES RECOGNIZES TECHNOLOGY NOT ONLY as a mechanical process, but as "a thing behind the thing" that reflects cultural attitudes and understandings. Questions of credibility, reliability, and objectivity that vex any informed approach to photographs are also present in science and technology. I photographed technology (using technology: a camera) to examine who we are as humans—individually and collectively—focusing on our changing attitudes and understandings about natural processes and our role within the natural scheme.

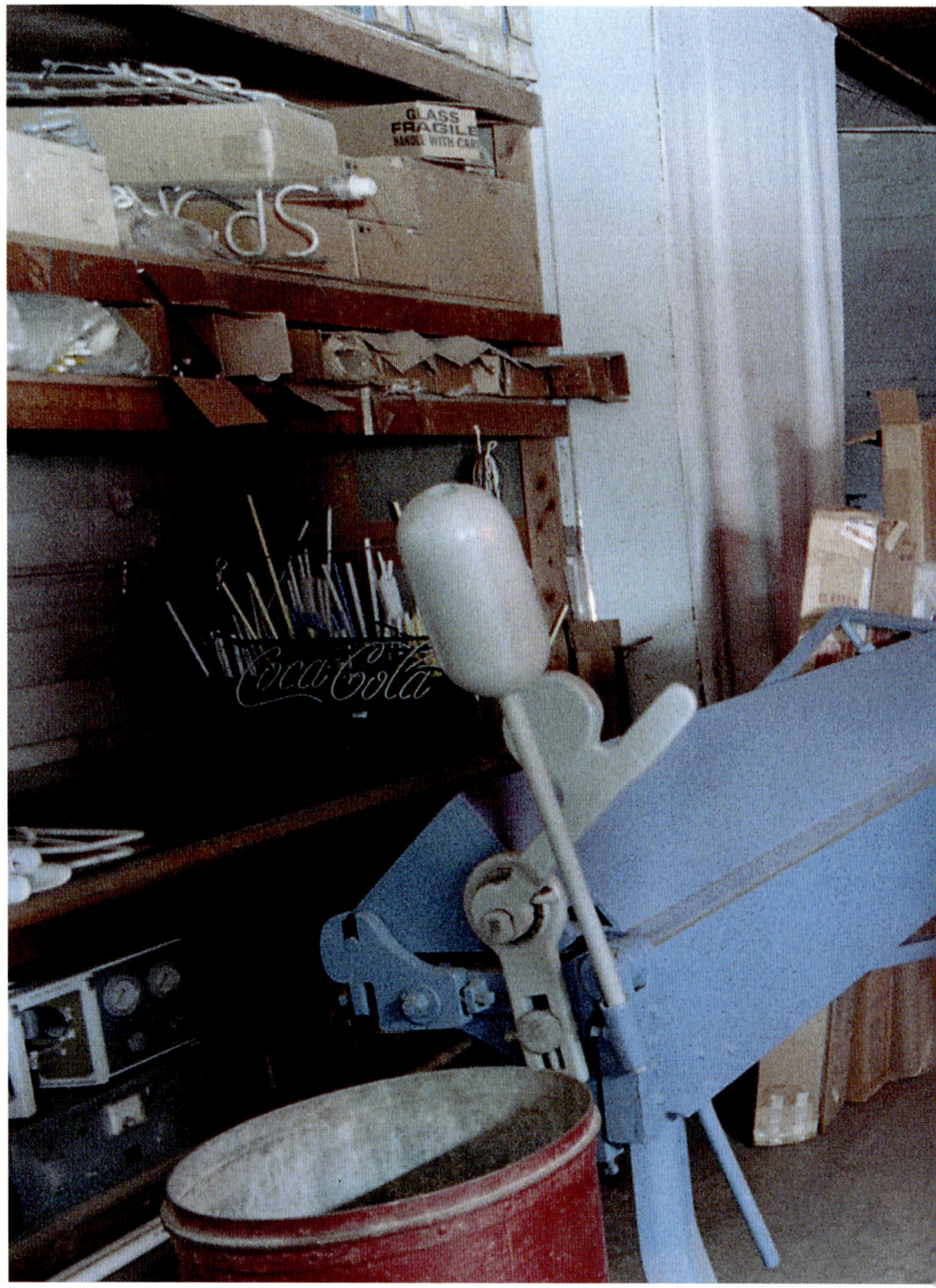

64. *Tony Greer's Tesla Coil, Lubbock, Texas*, 2000–2002.
Chromogenic print, 10 × 24 in.
In the collection of the Museum of Texas Tech University, Lubbock

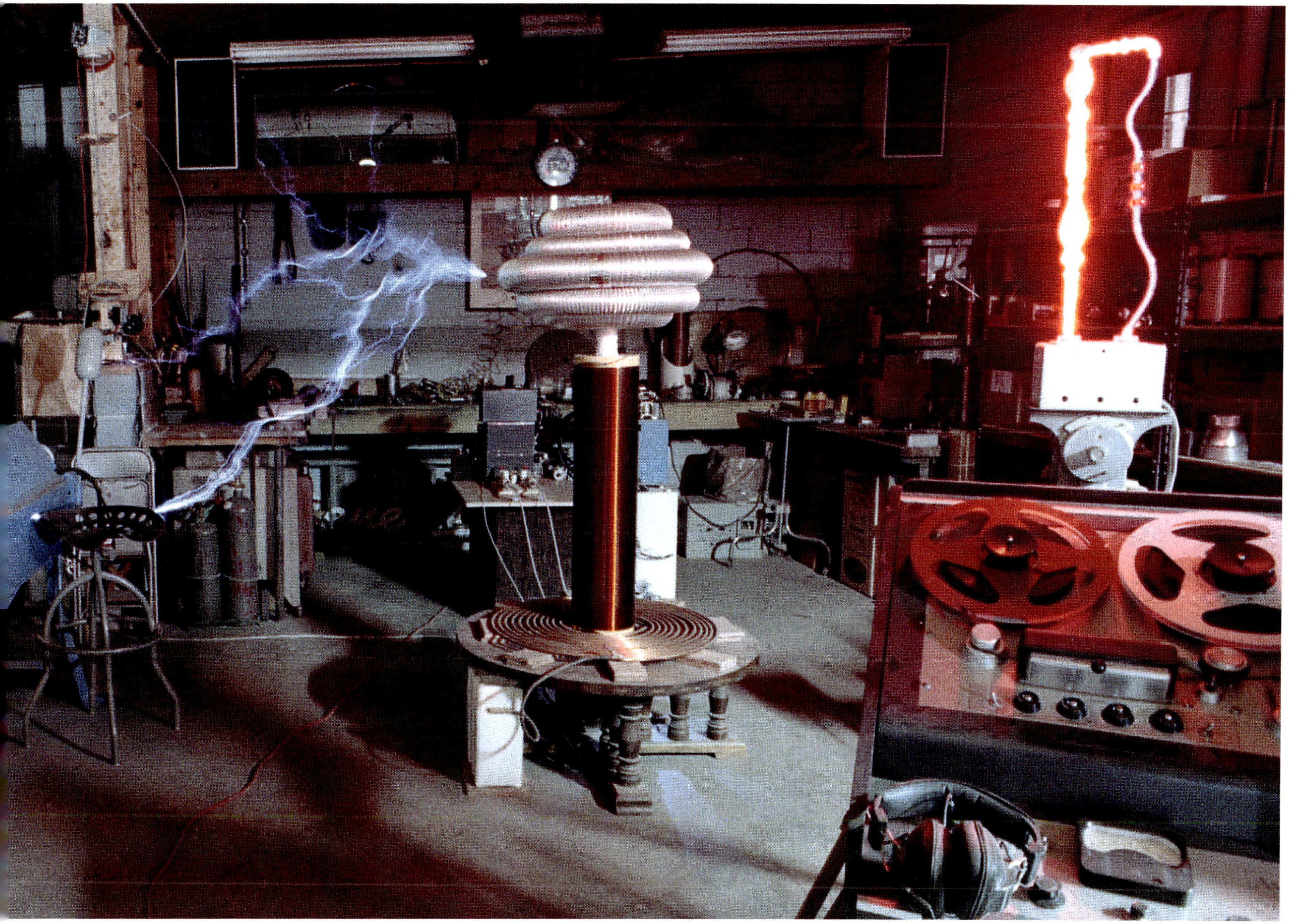

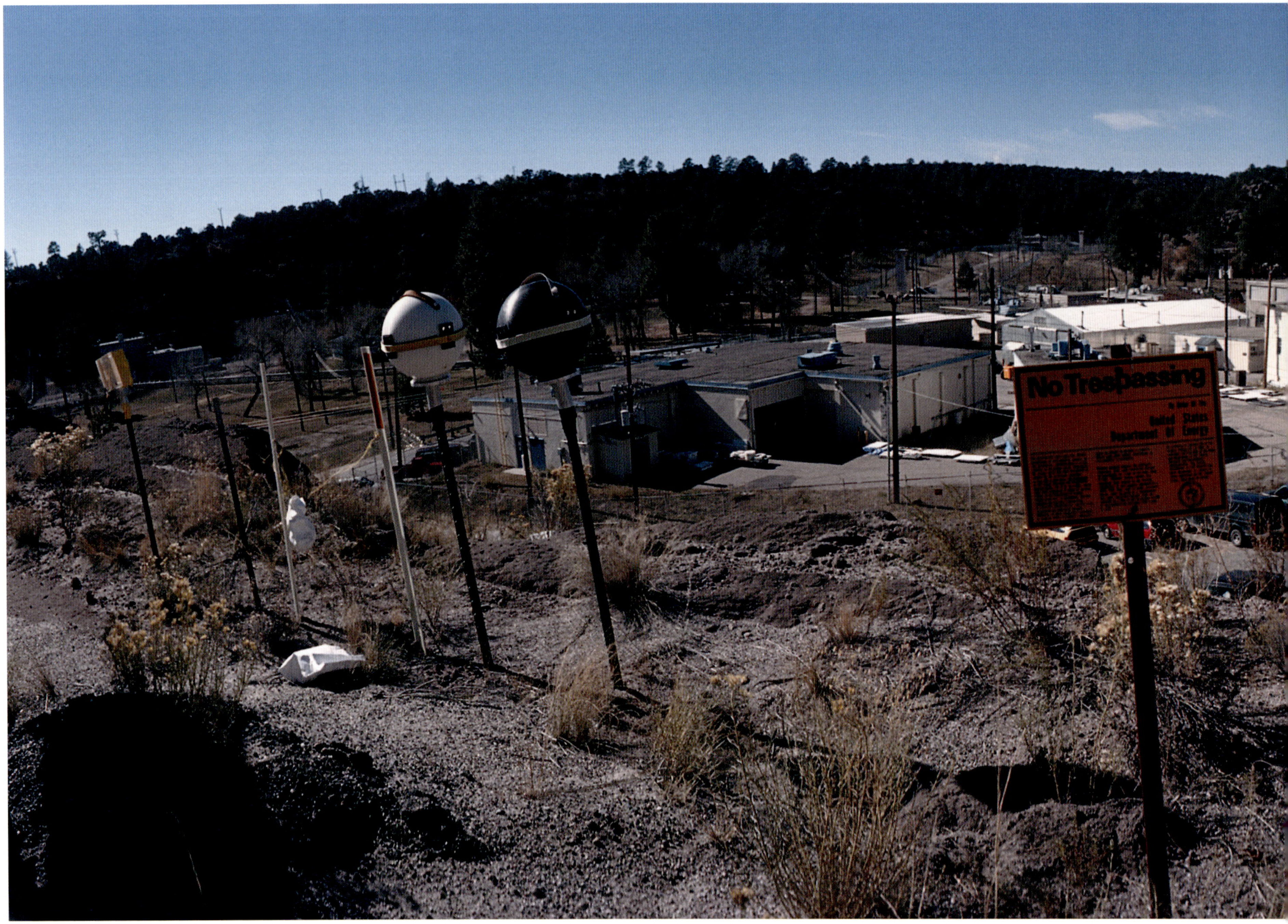

65. *Unmarked Sensors, Los Alamos, New Mexico*, 1998–99.
Chromogenic print, 16 × 38 in.
In the collection of the Museum of Texas Tech University, Lubbock

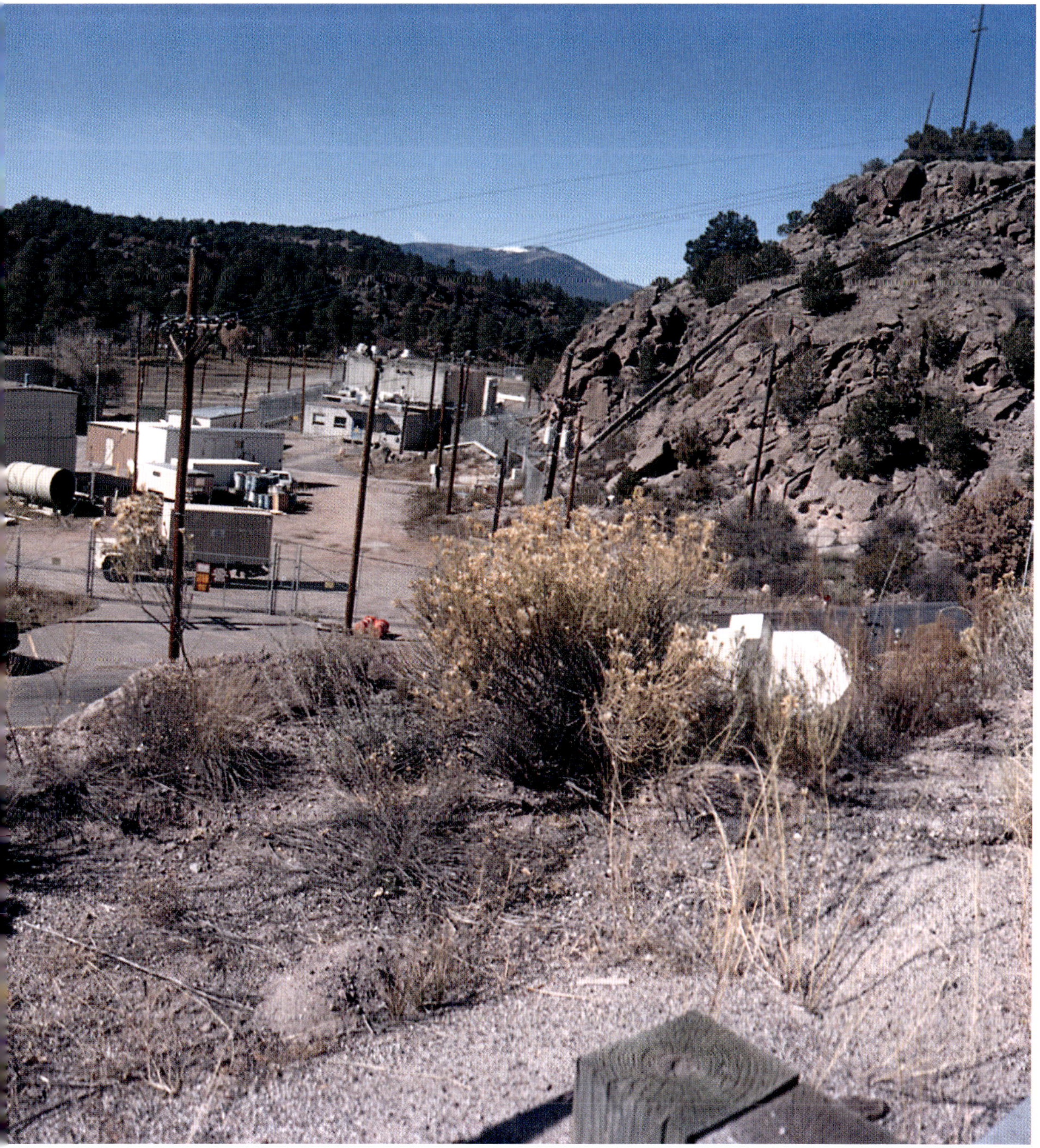

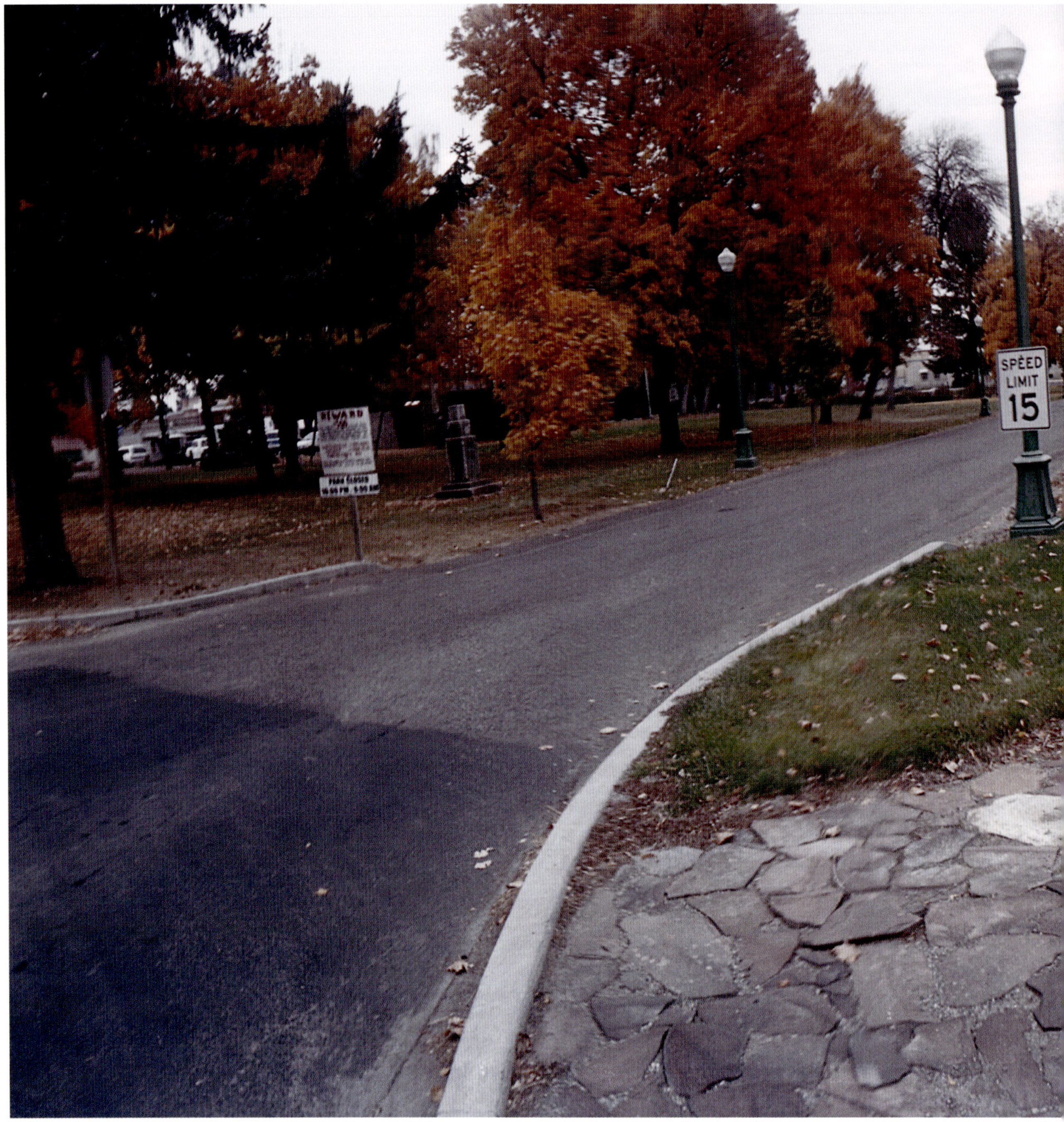

66. *Statue of a Water Witcher, Waterville, Washington*, 1998–99.
Chromogenic print, 16 × 38 in.

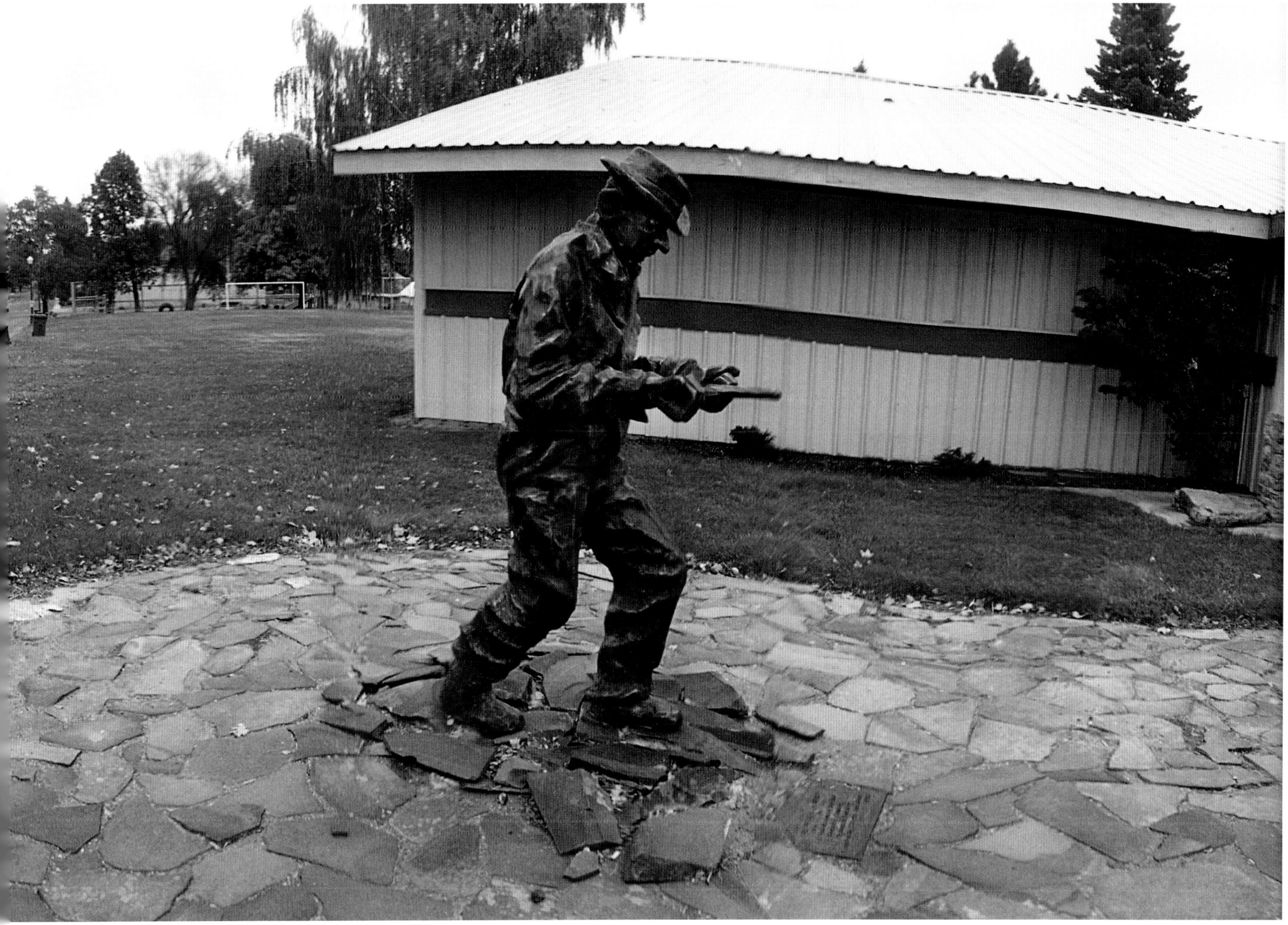

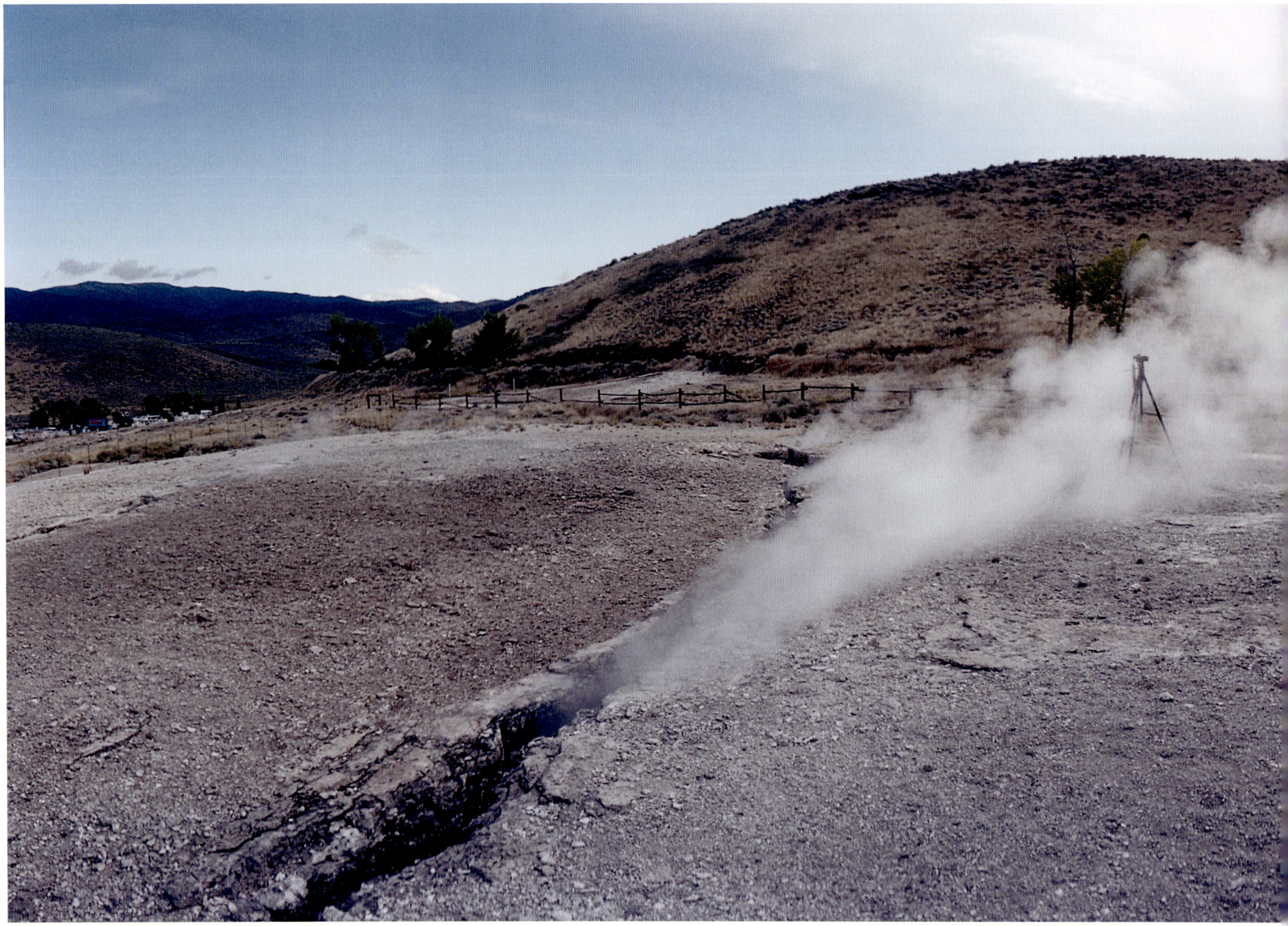

67. *O'Sullivan's Fissure Vent with Camera, near Reno, Nevada*, 1998–99.
Chromogenic print, 16 × 38 in.
In the collection of the Museum of Texas Tech University, Lubbock

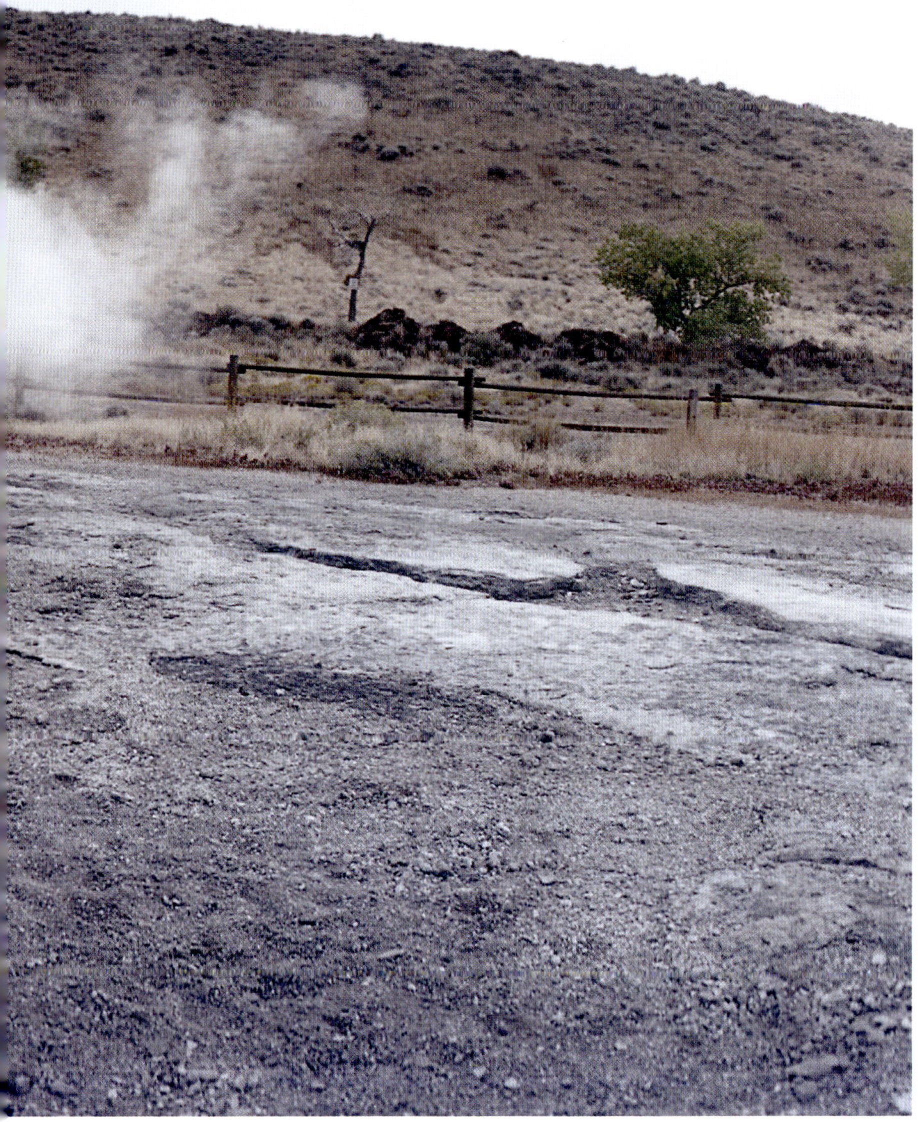

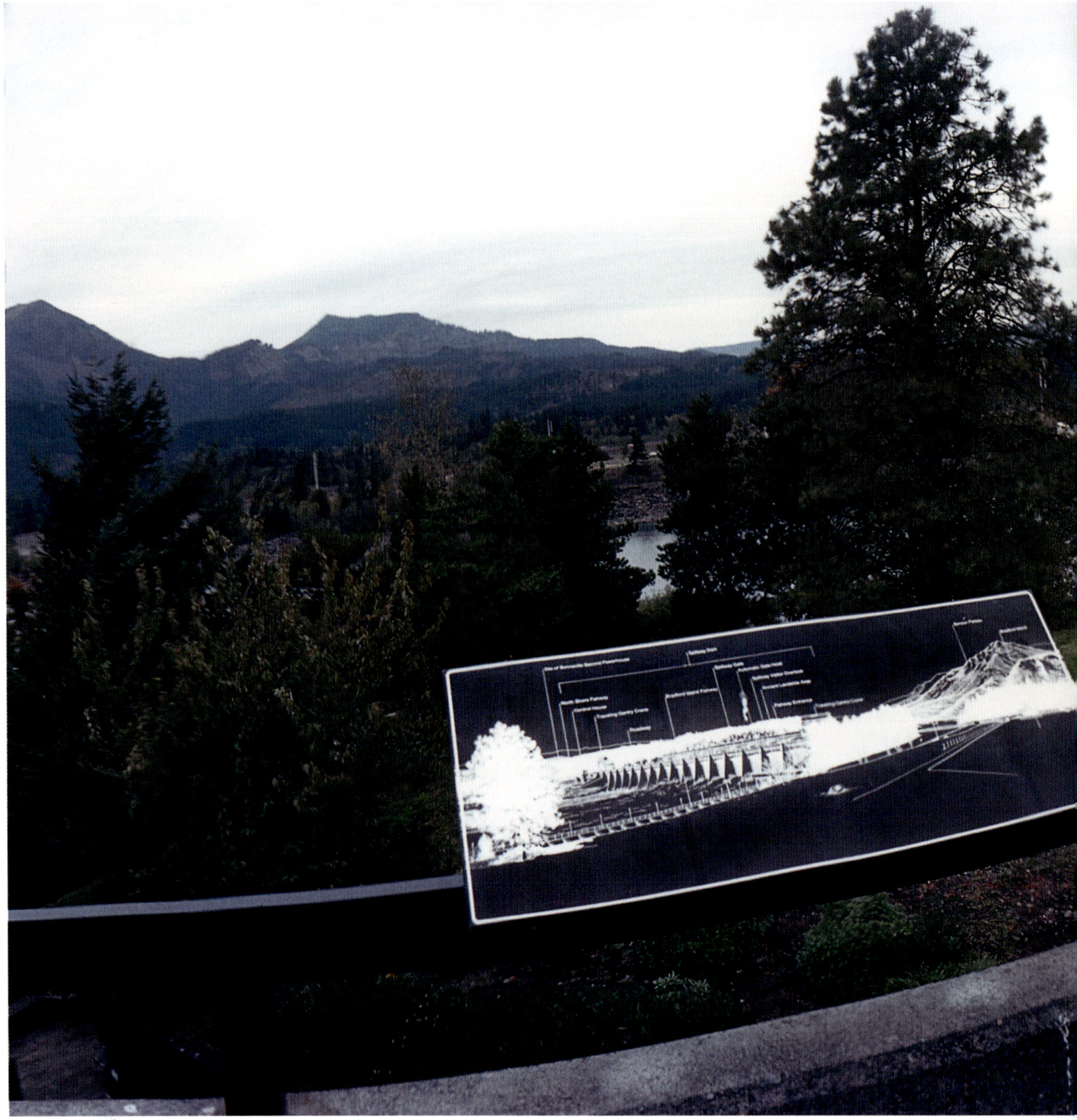

68. *Tourists at Bonneville Dam, Columbia River, Oregon*, 1998–99.
Chromogenic print, 16 × 38 in.
In the collection of the Museum of Texas Tech University, Lubbock

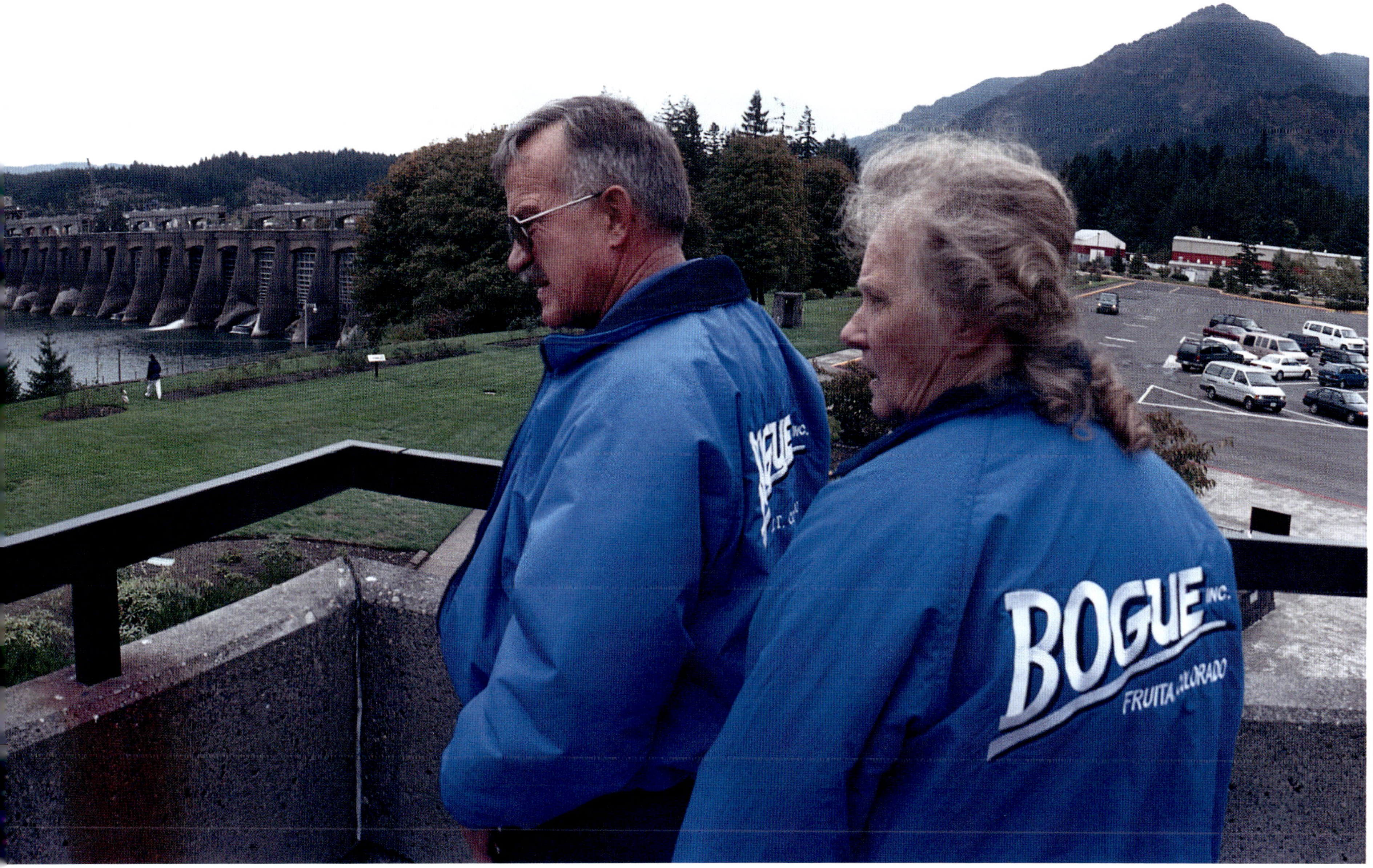
BOGUE INC.
FRUITA

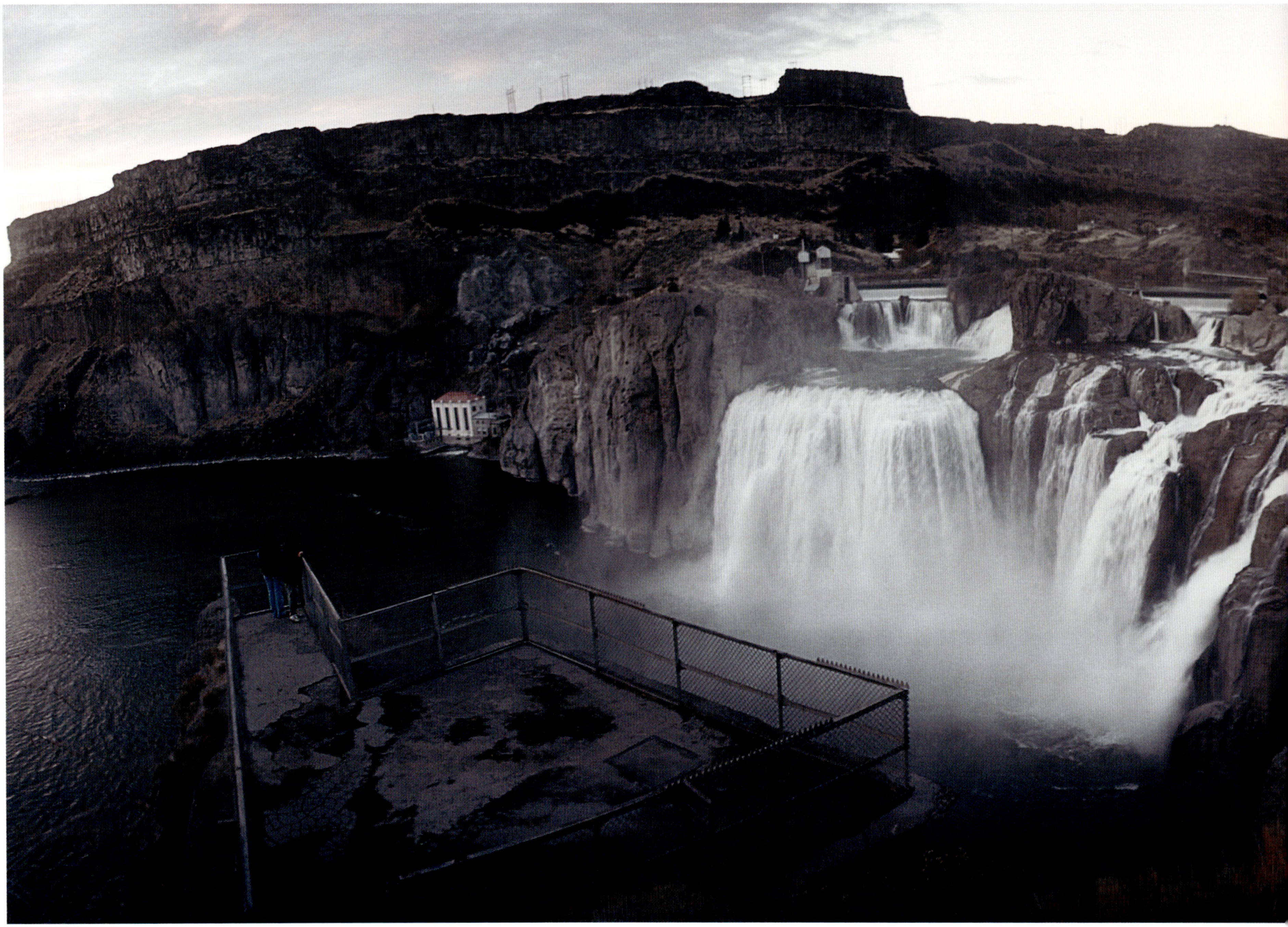

69. *Dam and Viewing Platform, Shoshone Falls, Idaho (After T. H. O'Sullivan)*, 1998–99.
Chromogenic print, 16 × 38 in.
In the collection of the Museum of Texas Tech University, Lubbock

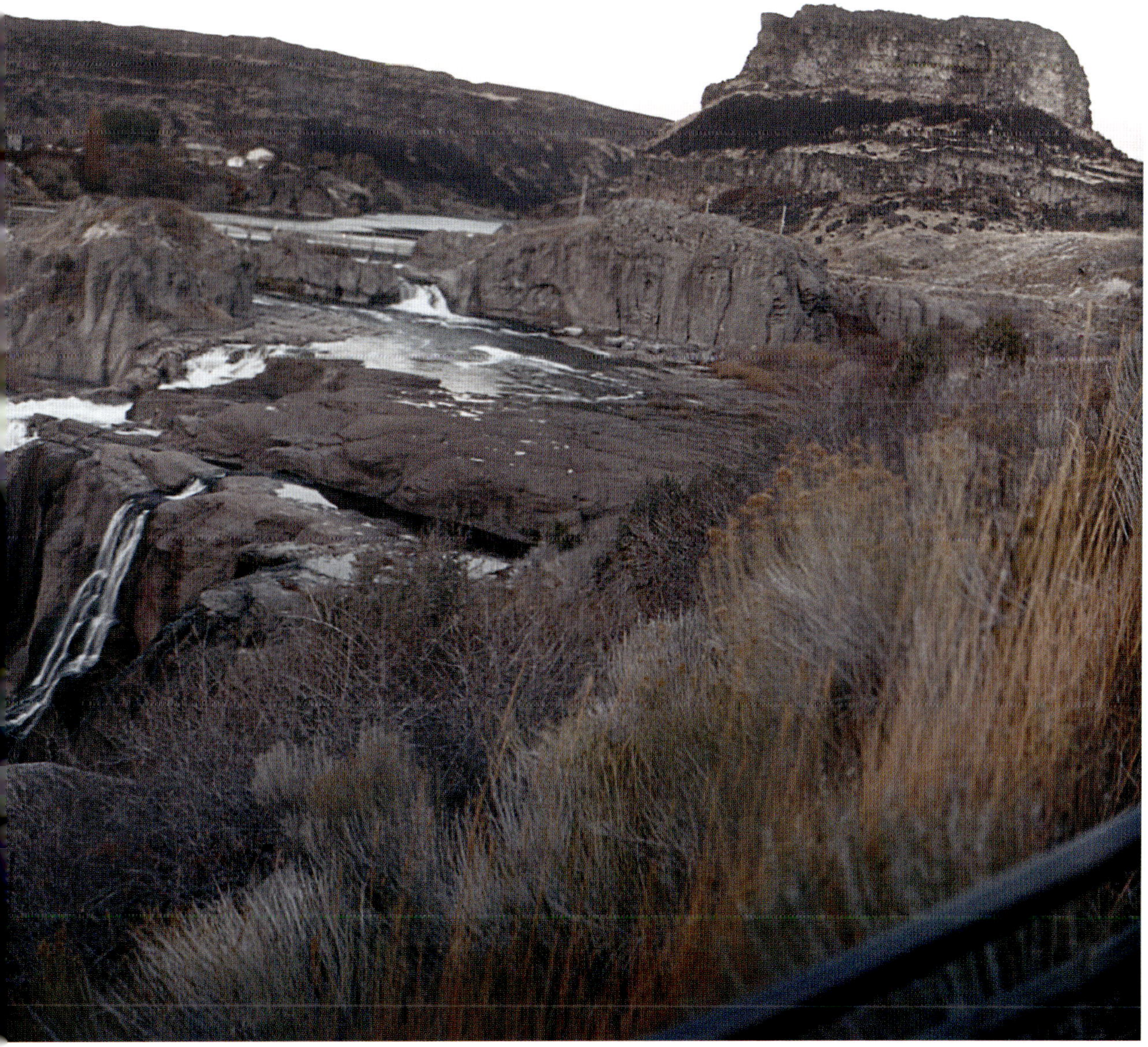

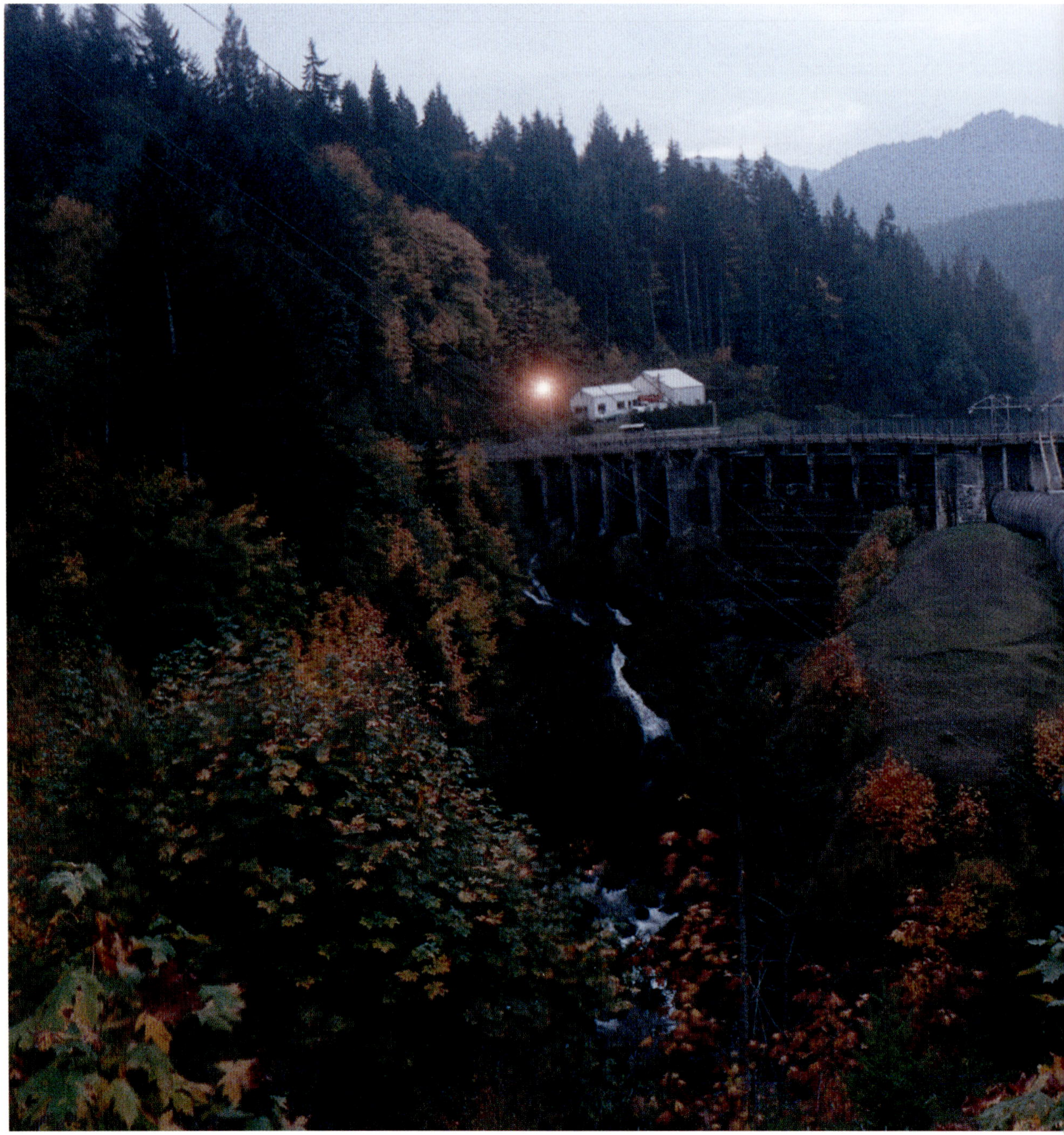

70. *Scheduled for Removal: Lower Elwa River Dam, Washington*, 1998–99.
Chromogenic print, 16 × 38 in.
In the collection of the Museum of Texas Tech University, Lubbock

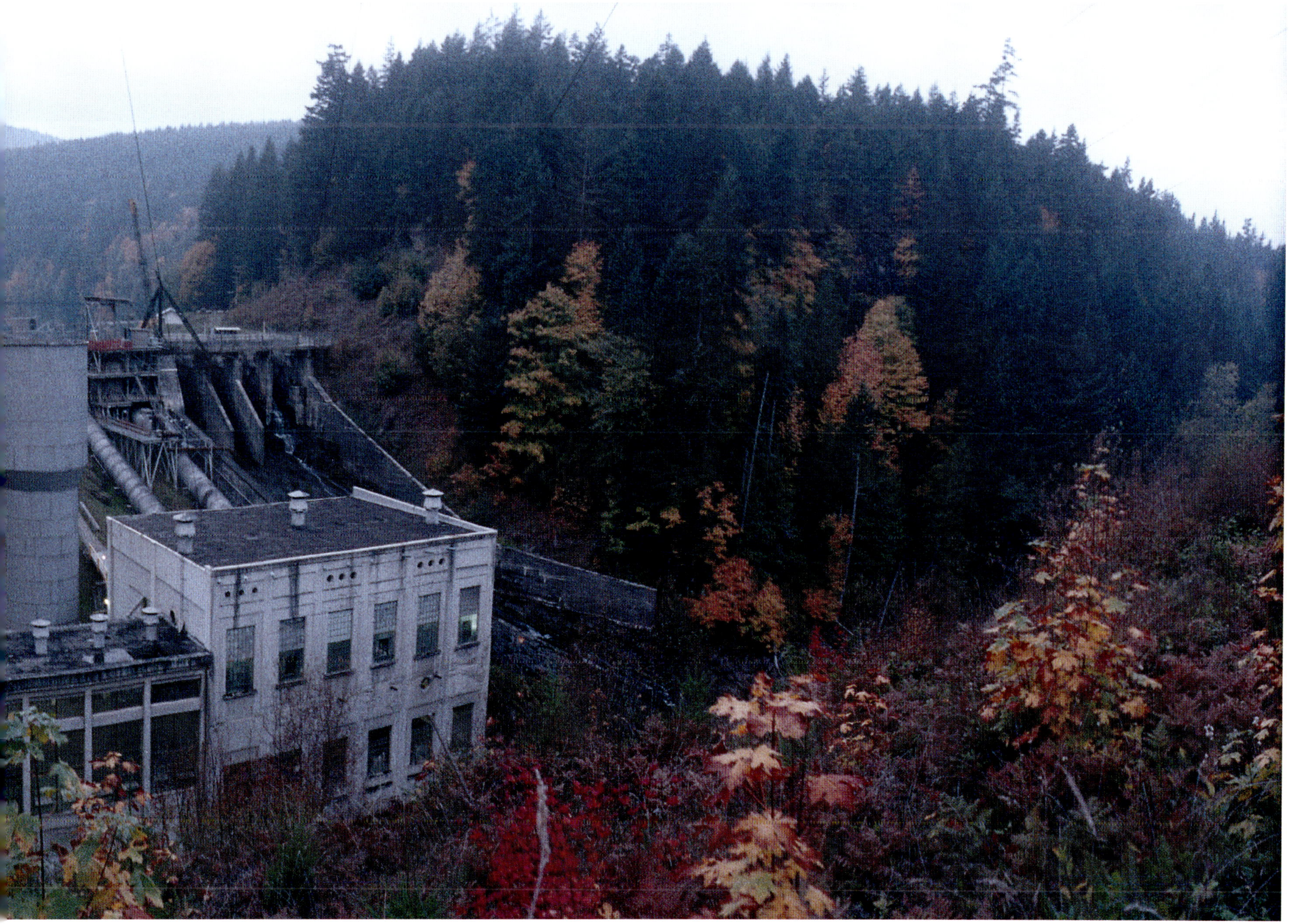

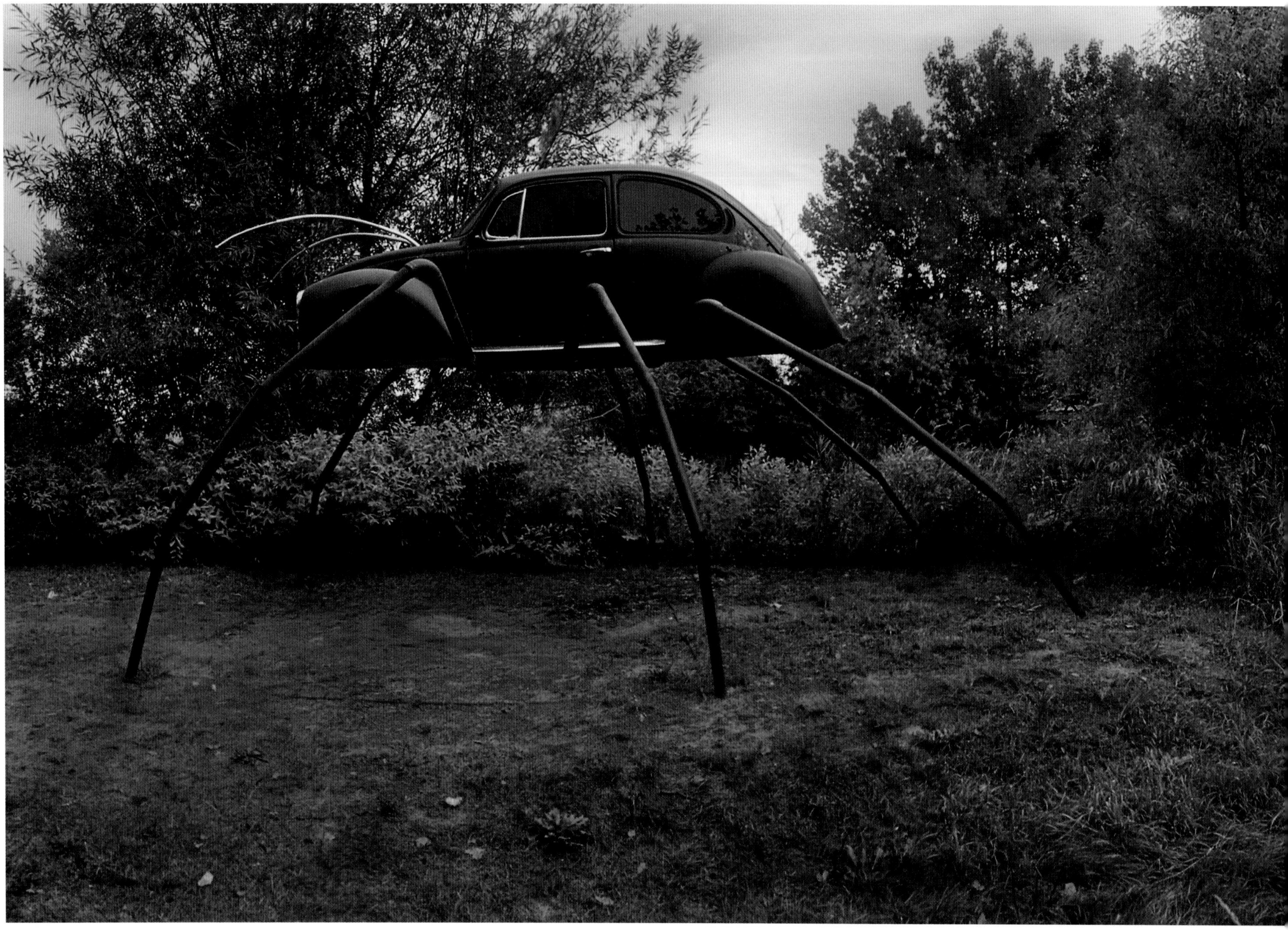

71. *Recycled Beetle, Swetsville Zoo, Fort Collins, Colorado,* 1998–99.
Chromogenic print, 16 × 38 in.

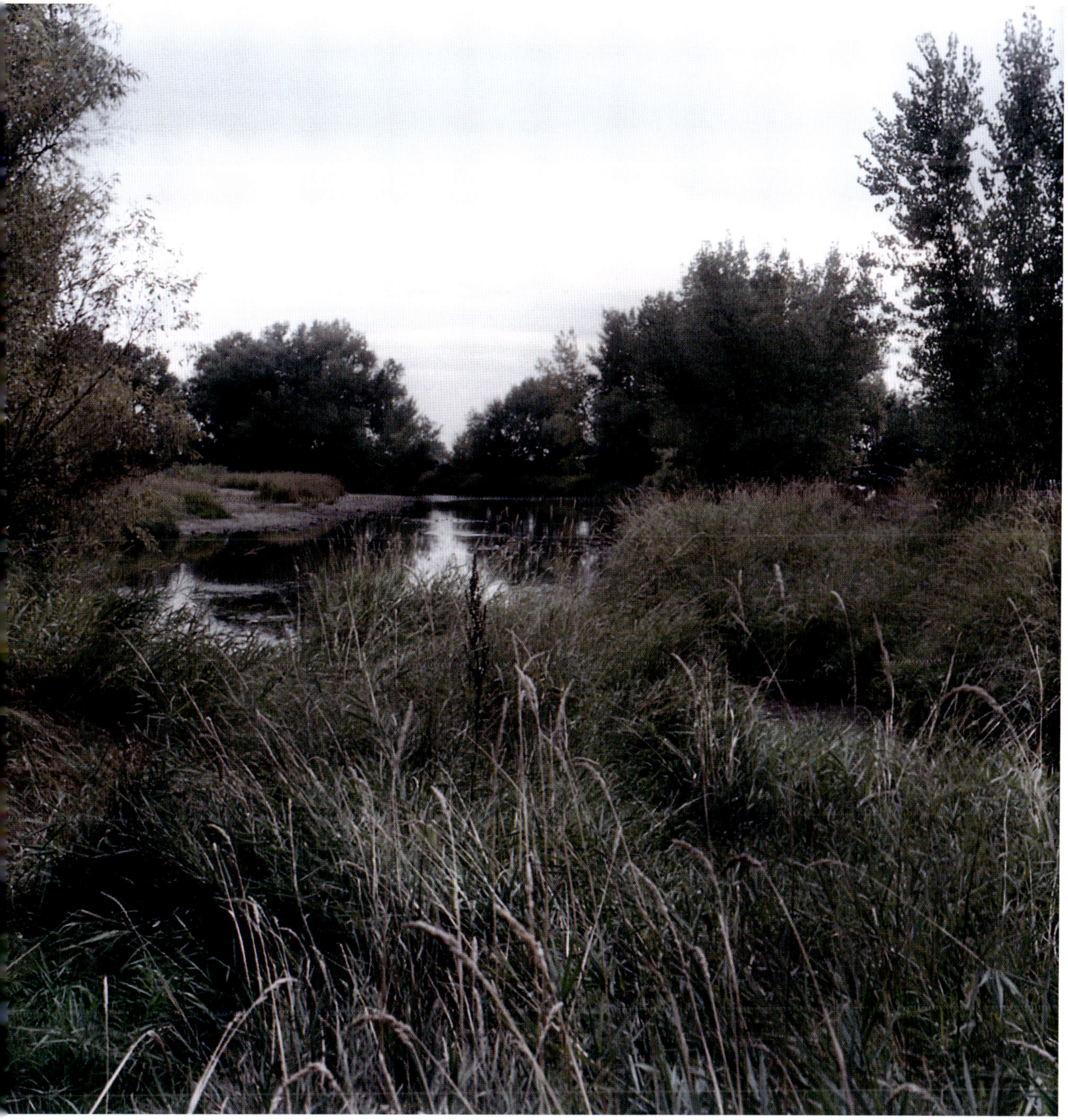

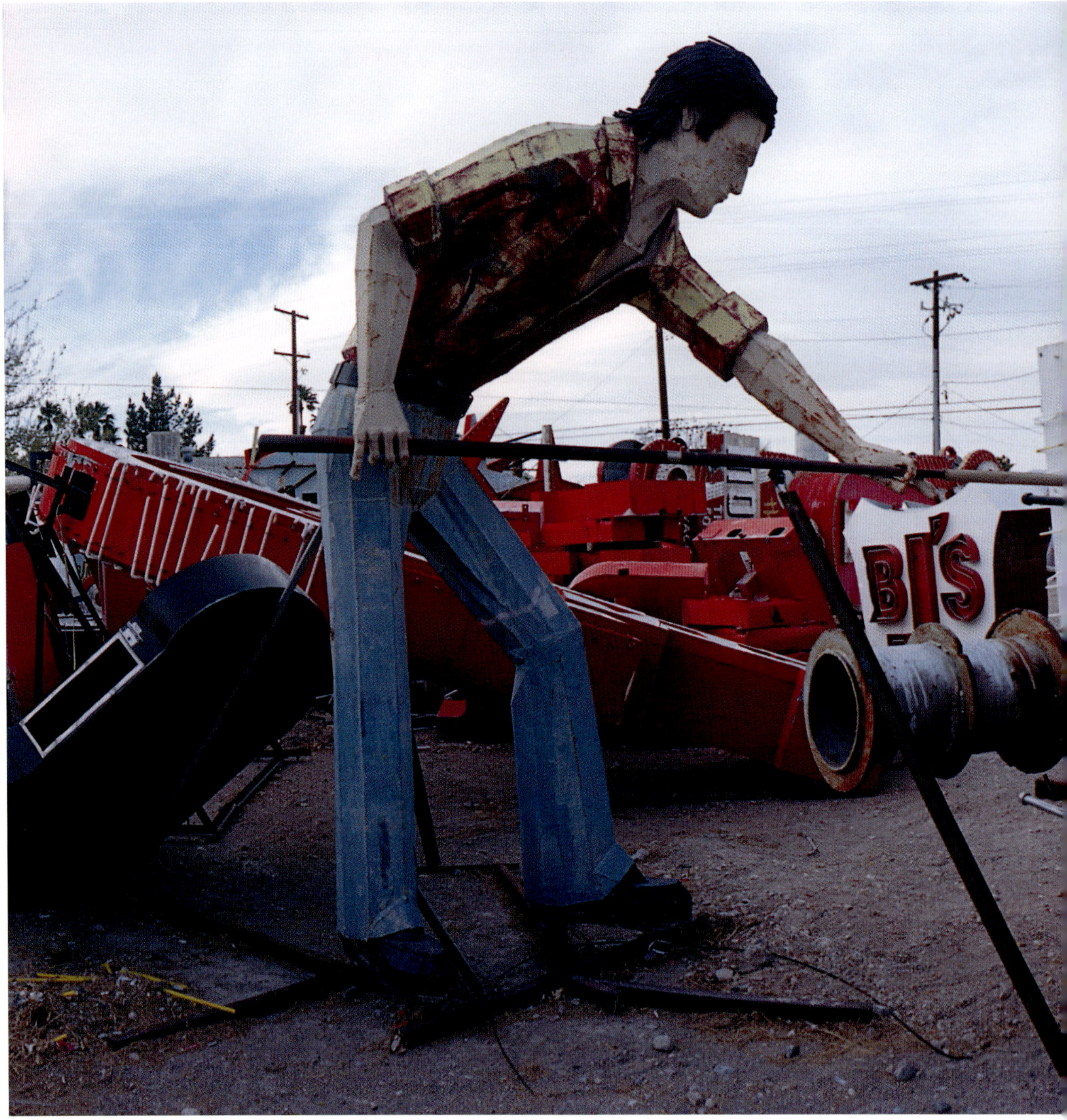

72. *Neon Boneyard, Las Vegas, Nevada*, 2002.
Chromogenic print, 10 × 24 in.
In the collection of the Museum of Texas Tech University, Lubbock

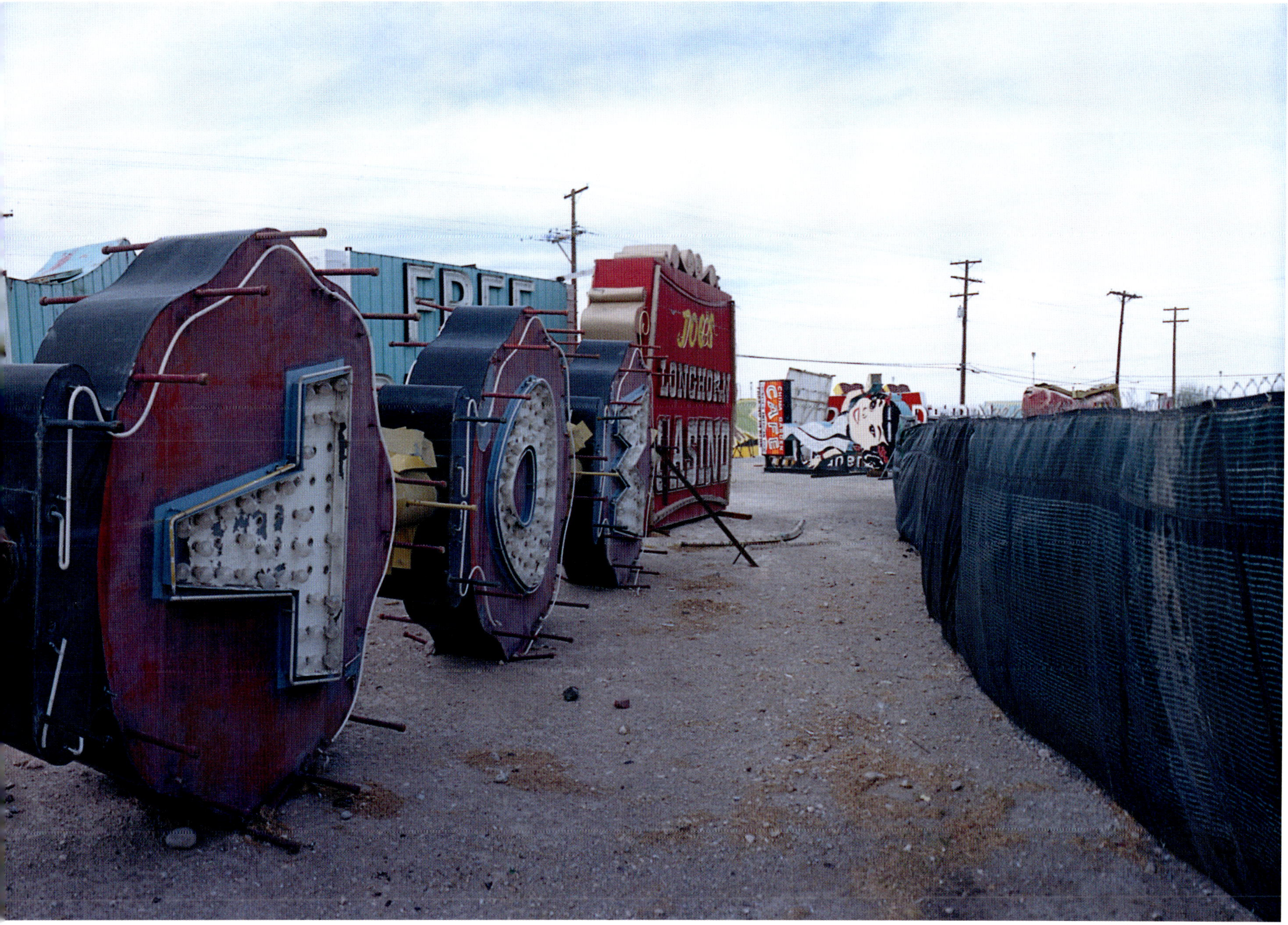
FREE
JOE'S
LONGHORN
CASINO
CAFE

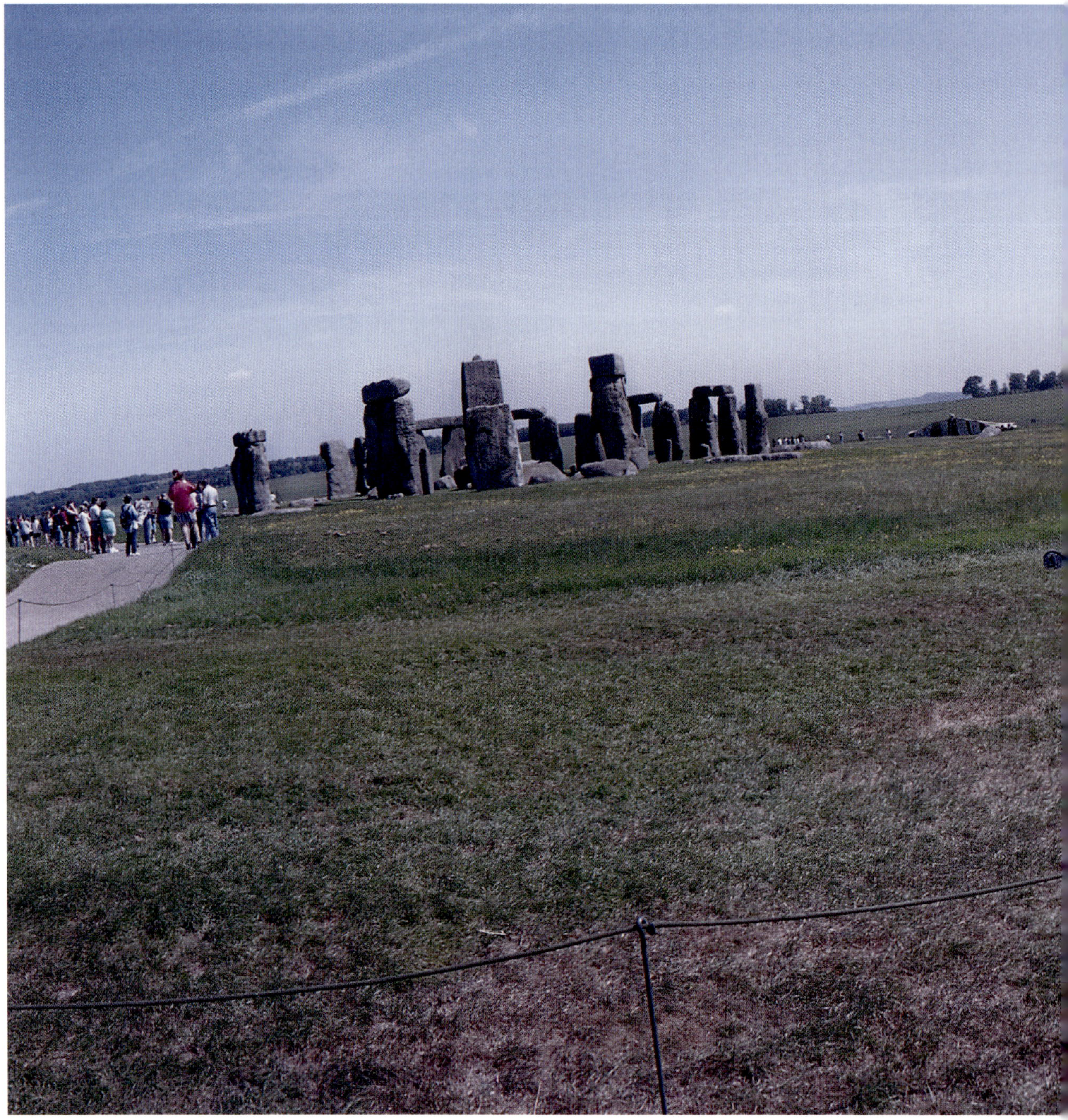

73. *Listening to Stonehenge (Audio Tour), Wessex, England*, 1998–2002.
Chromogenic print, 10 × 24 in.

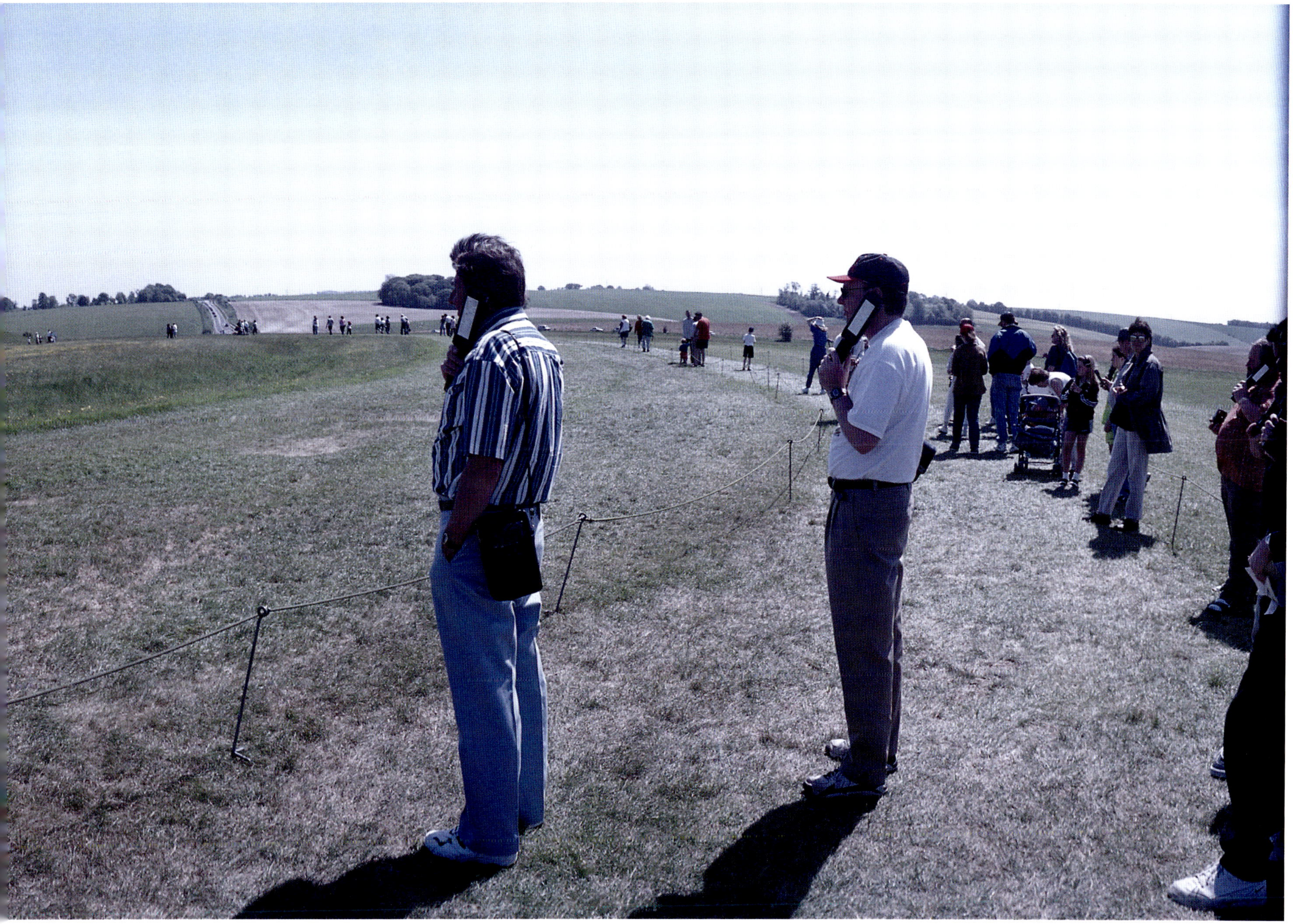

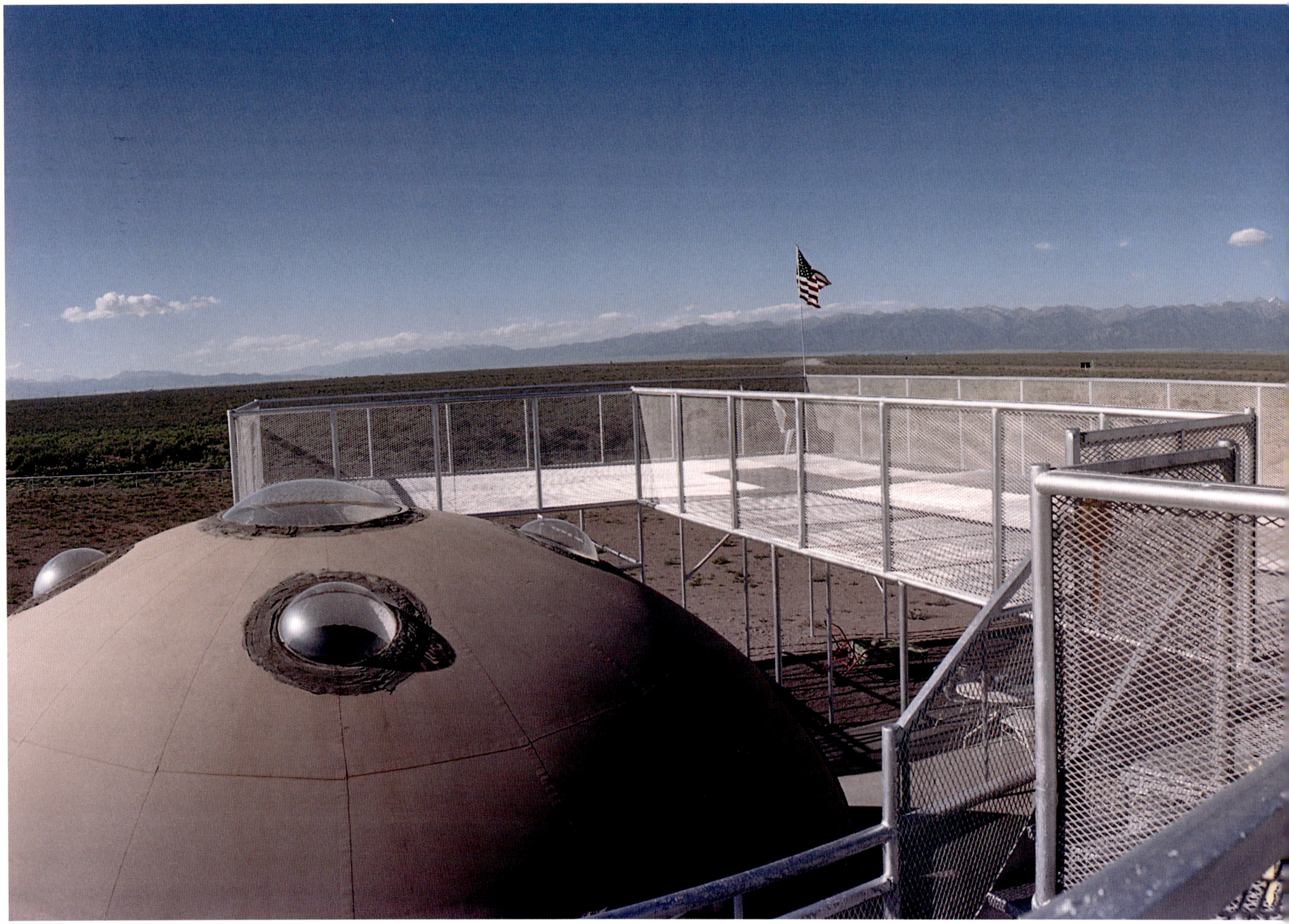

74. *UFO Watchtower near Hooper, Colorado*, 2001–2002.
Chromogenic print, 10 × 24 in.
In the collection of the Museum of Texas Tech University, Lubbock

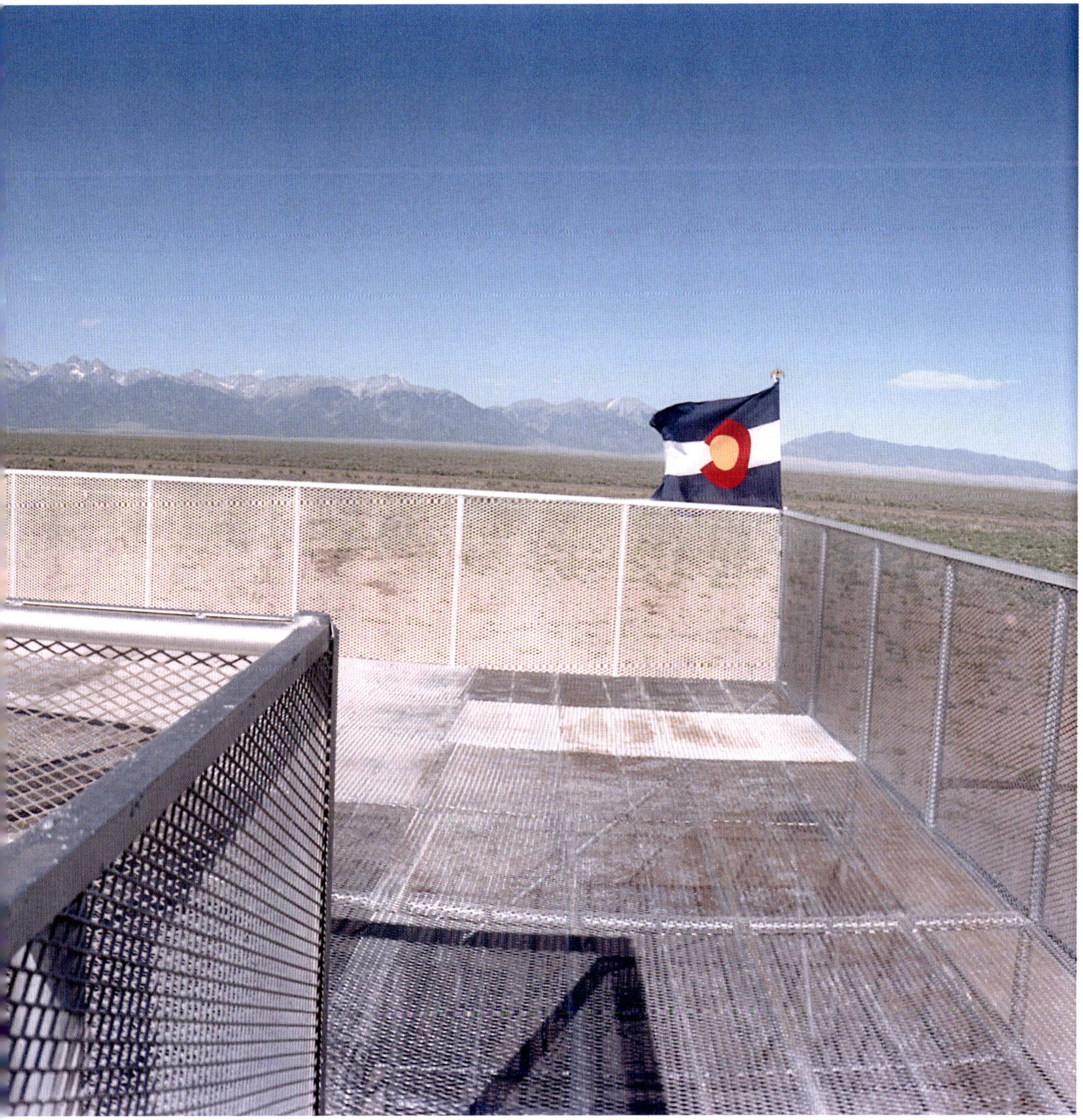

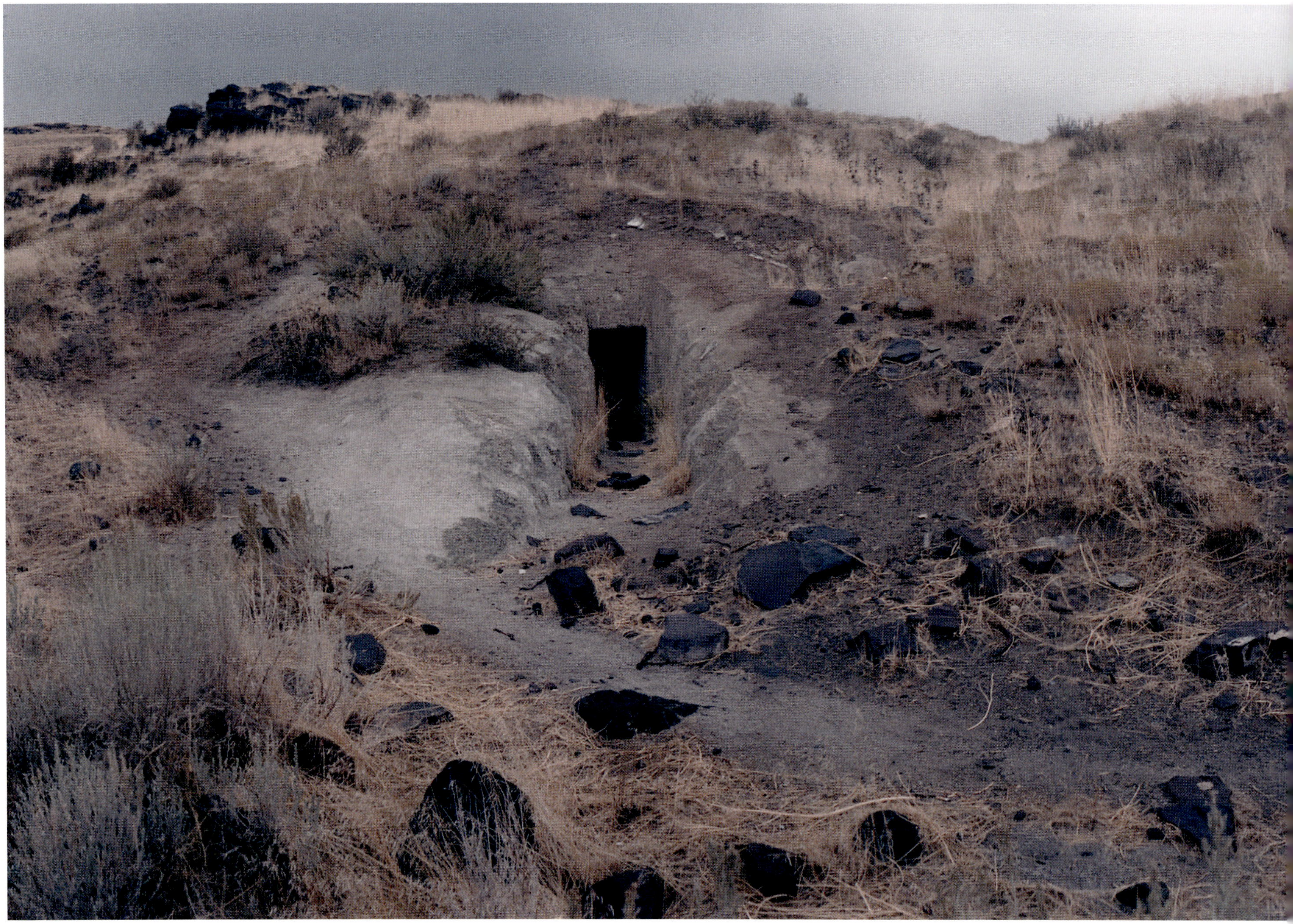

75. *Supposed Hermit's Dugout near Twin Falls, Idaho*, 1998–99.
Chromogenic print, 16 × 38 in.
In the collection of the Museum of Texas Tech University, Lubbock

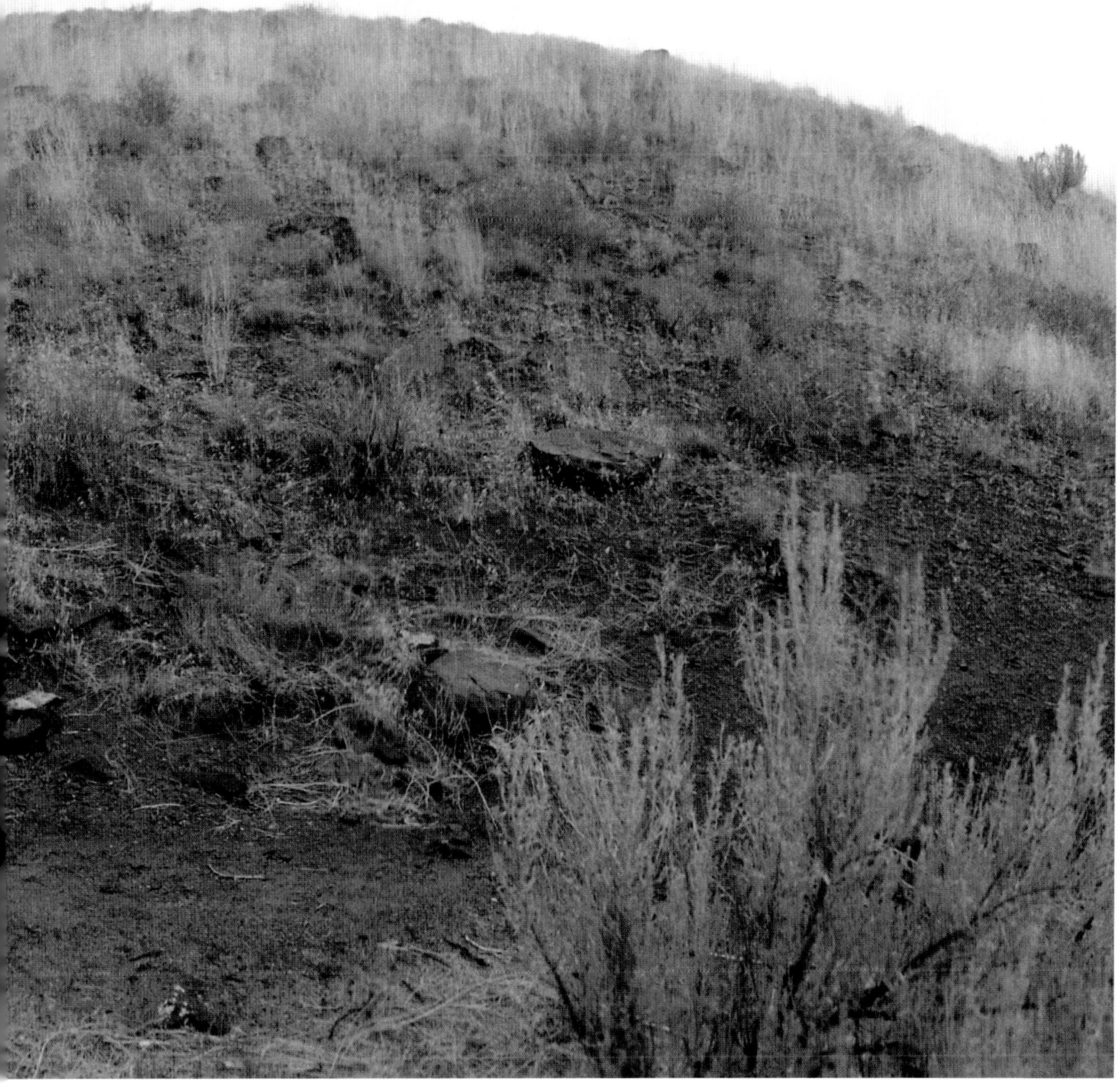

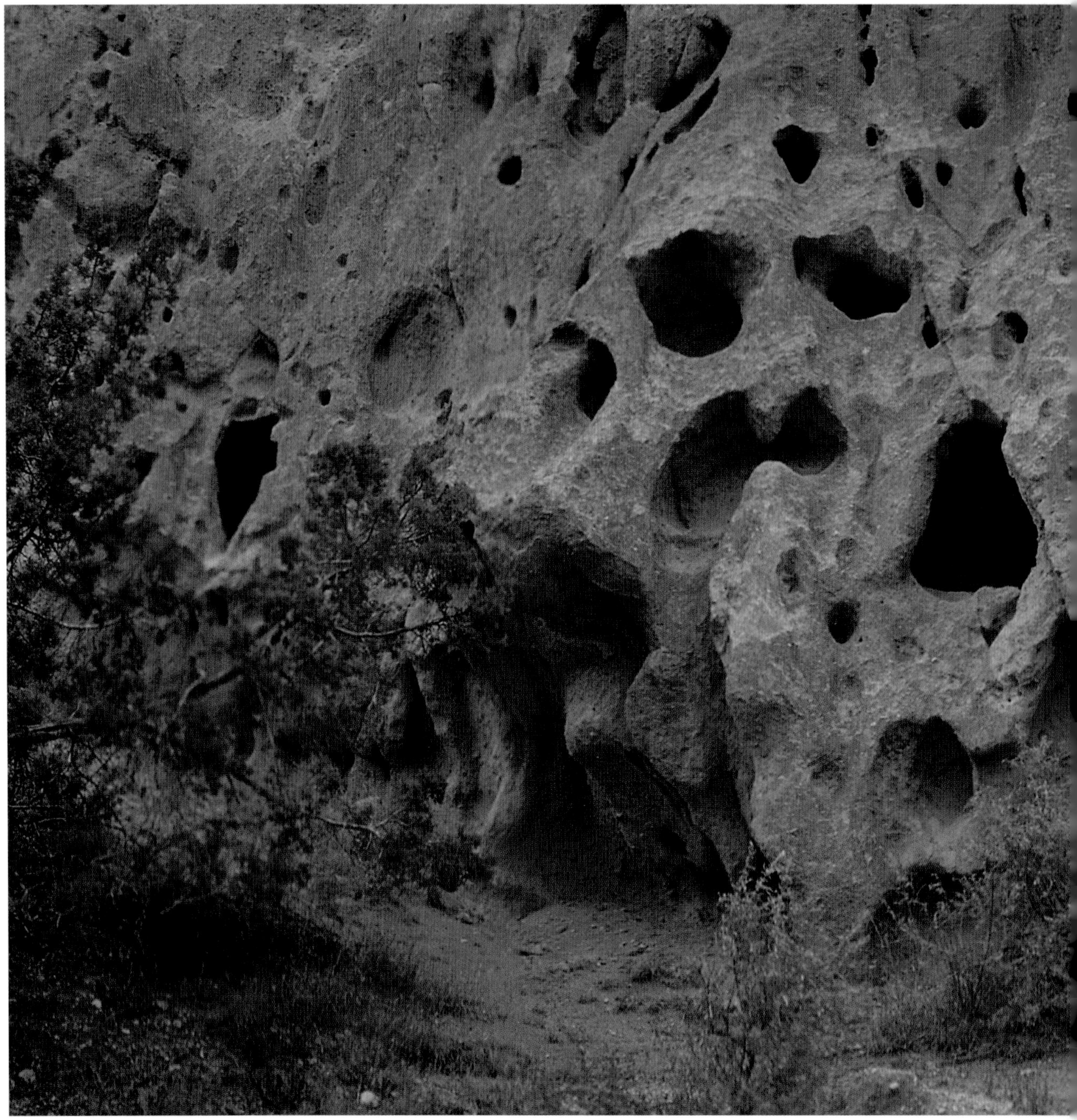

76. *Caged Cave Kiva near Los Alamos, New Mexico*, 1998–99.
Chromogenic print, 16 × 38 in.
In the collection of the Museum of Texas Tech University, Lubbock

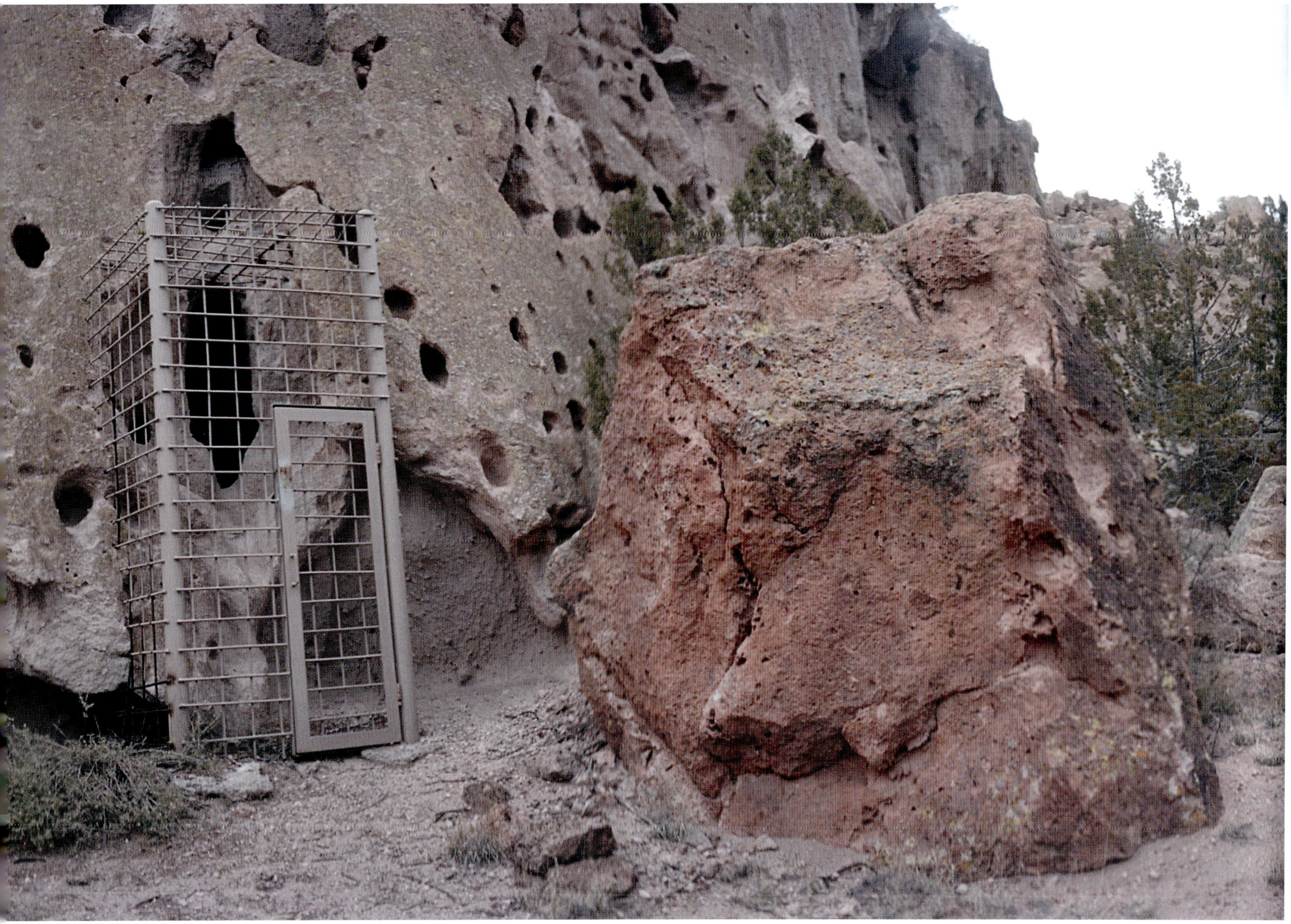

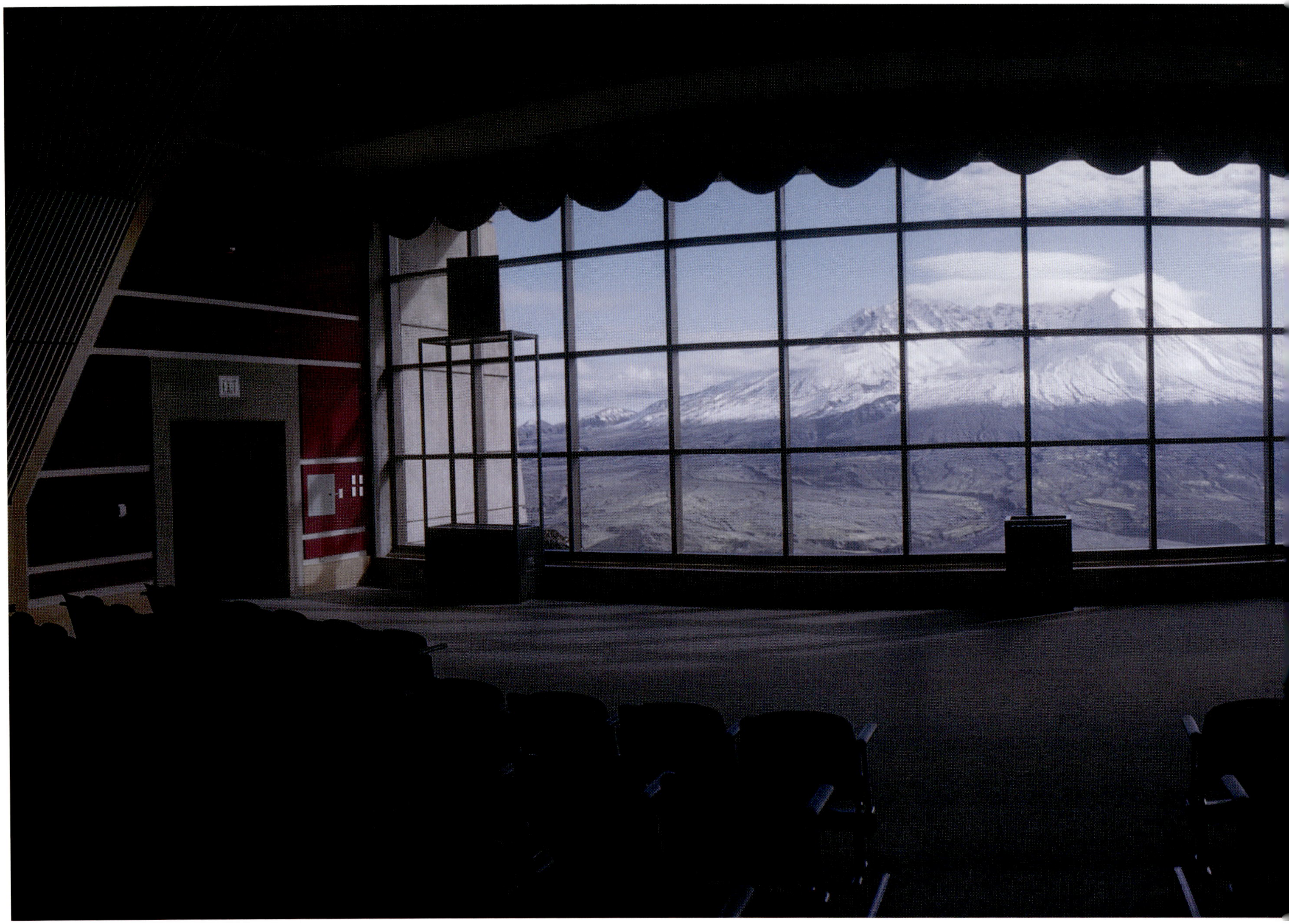

77. *Movie Theater, Mt. St. Helens Visitor Center, Washington*, 1998–99.
Chromogenic print, 16 × 38 in.
In the collection of the Museum of Texas Tech University, Lubbock

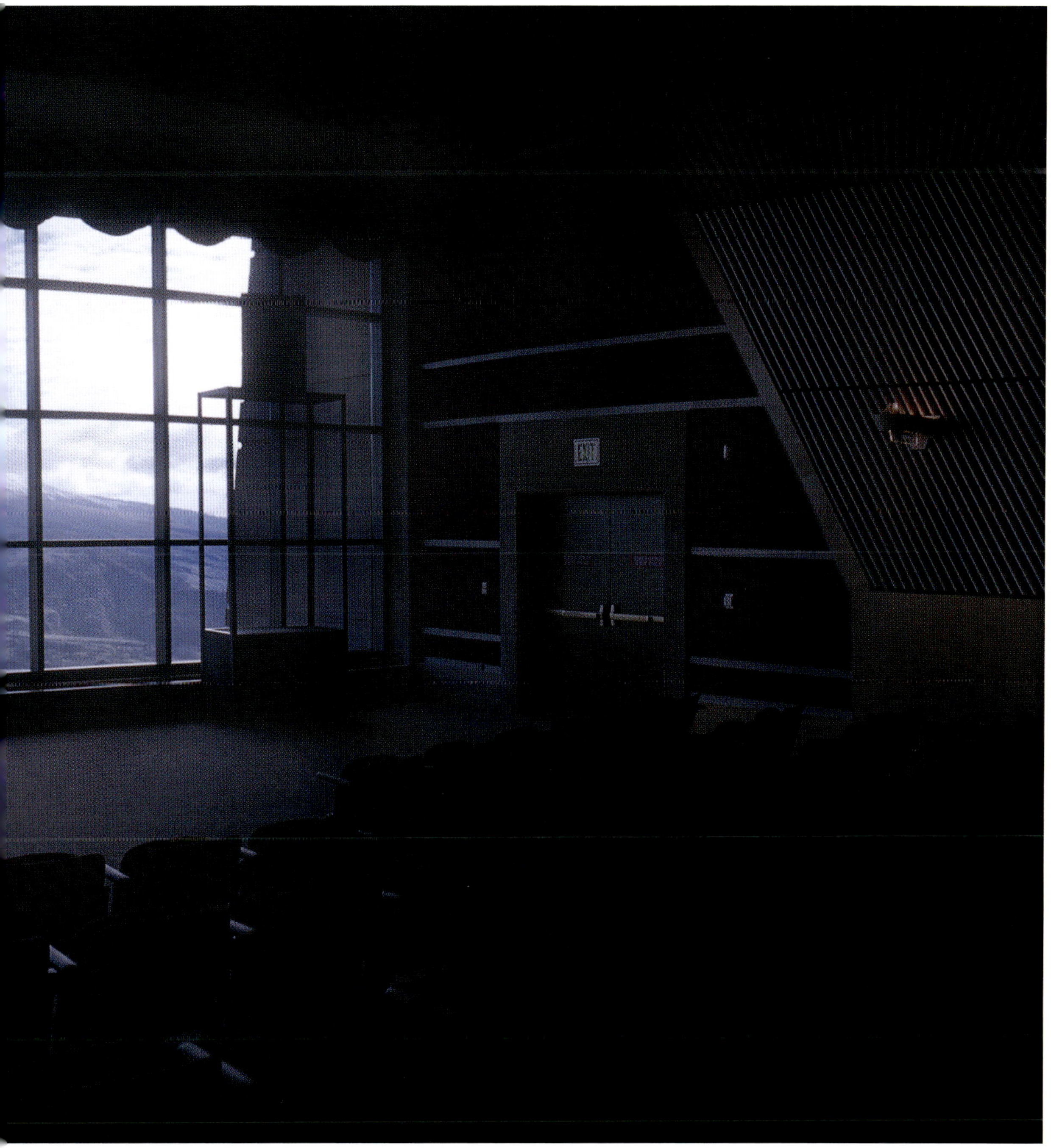
EXIT

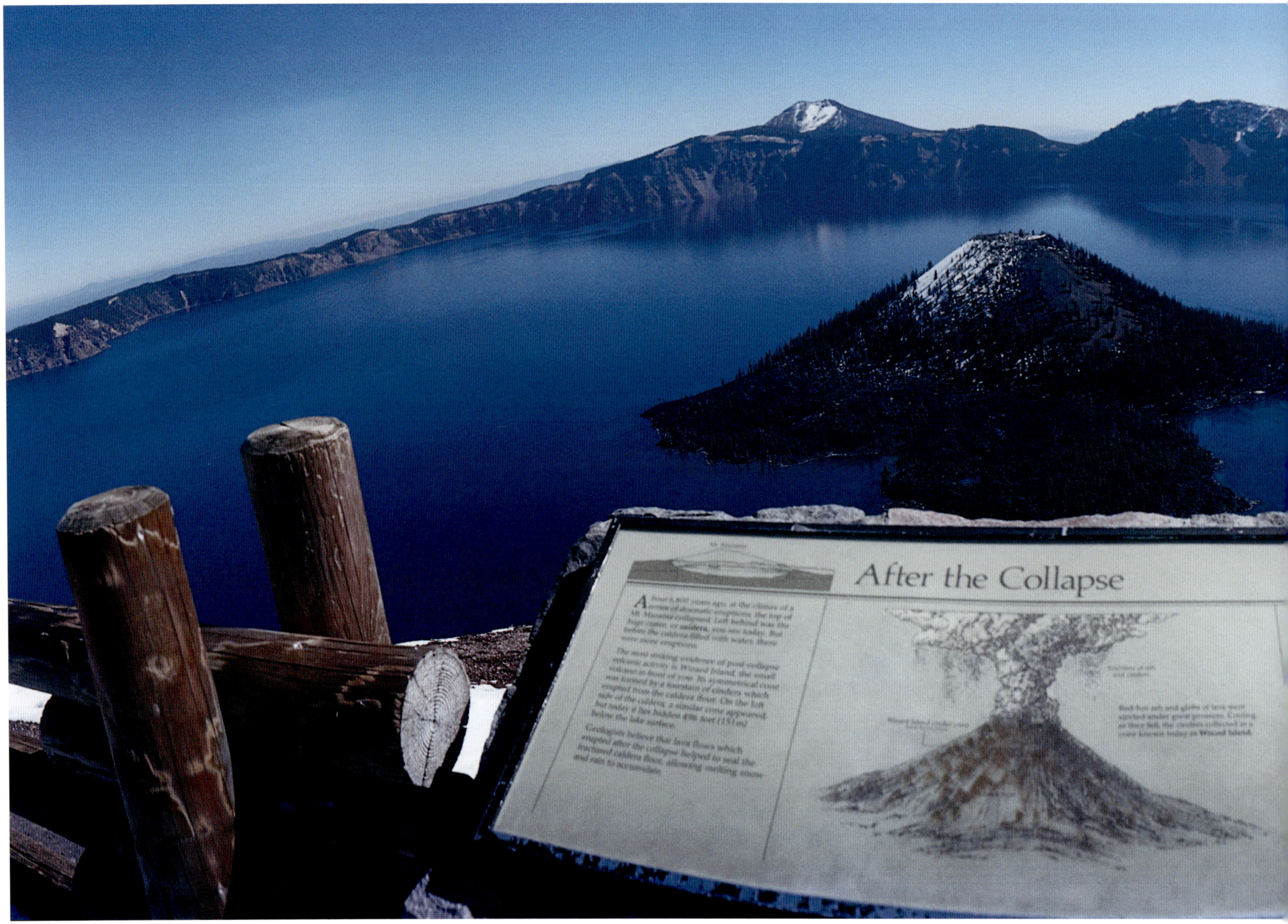

78. *After the Collapse, Crater Lake, Oregon*, 1998–99.
Chromogenic print, 16 × 38 in.

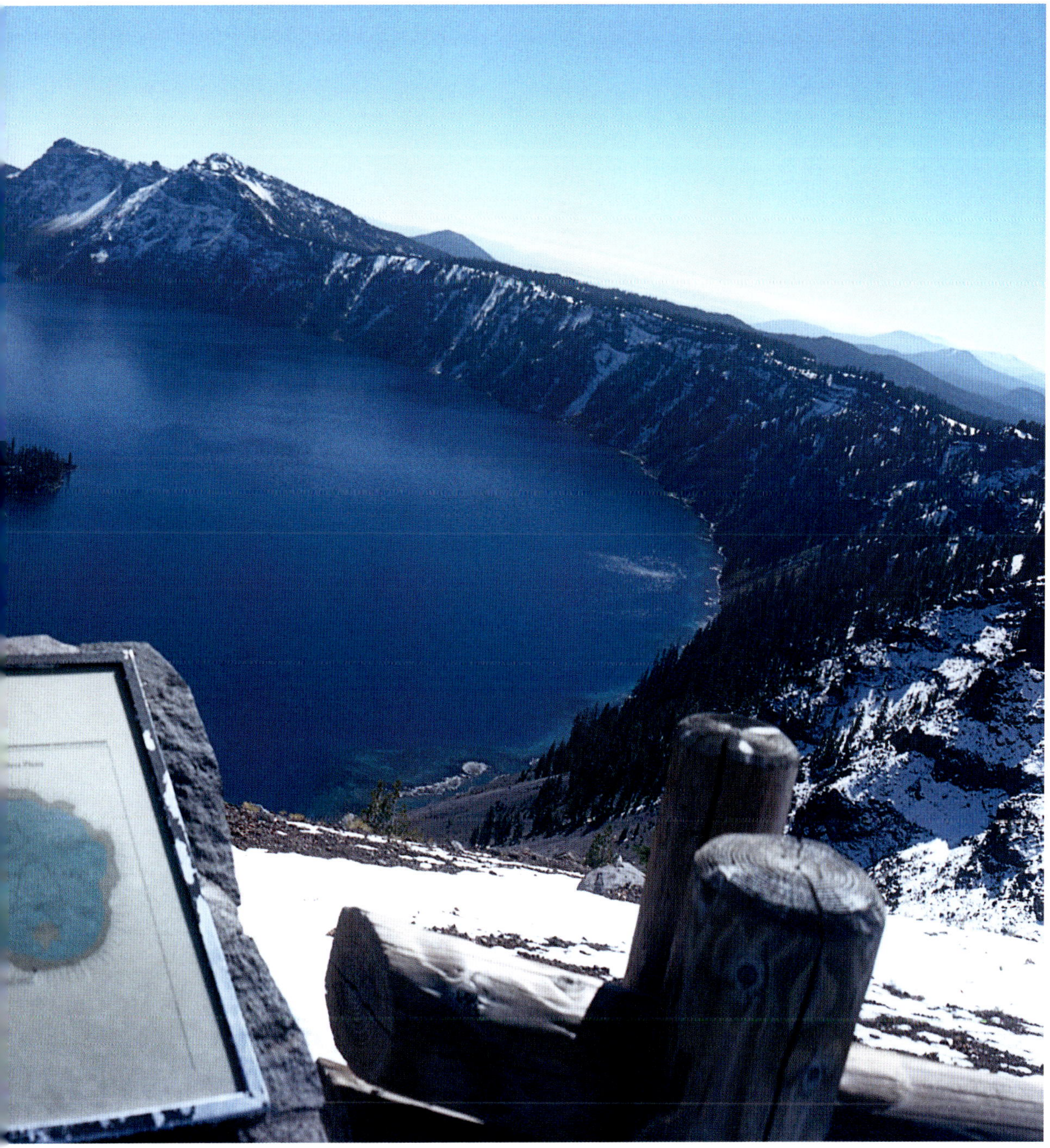

Llano Estacado

An Island in the Sky, 2004–2006

In 1999 I created the Millennial Collection at the Southwest Collection/Special Collections Library at Texas Tech University. This archive of more than 1,500 photographs, films, and artists' books recorded varied responses by different people to the region I lived in. The Llano Estacado project developed from the Millennial Collection.* A grant from the Helen Jones Foundation supported six photographers (Steve Fitch, Miguel Gandert, Tony Gleaton, Peter Brown, Andrew Liccardo, and me) to photograph the High Plains region (the llano) in western Texas and eastern New Mexico. I looked for vernacular markers of conflict and unresolved issues.

* See Stephen Bogener and William Tydeman, eds., *Llano Estacado: An Island in the Sky* (Lubbock: Texas Tech University Press, 2011).

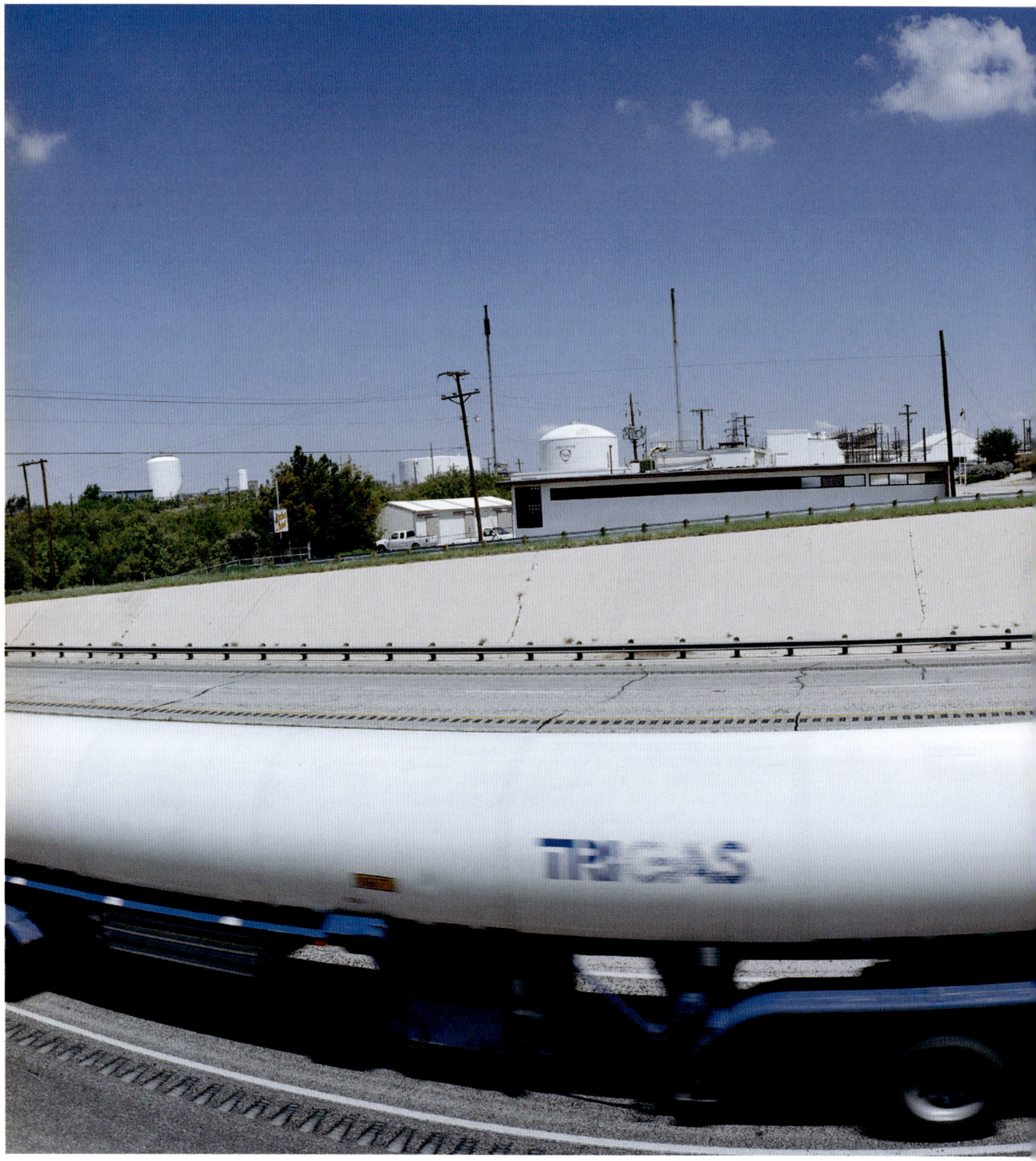

79. *Oil Refinery, Big Spring, Texas*, 2004–2006.
Archival pigment print, 22 × 49 in.
In the collection of the Museum of Texas Tech University, Lubbock

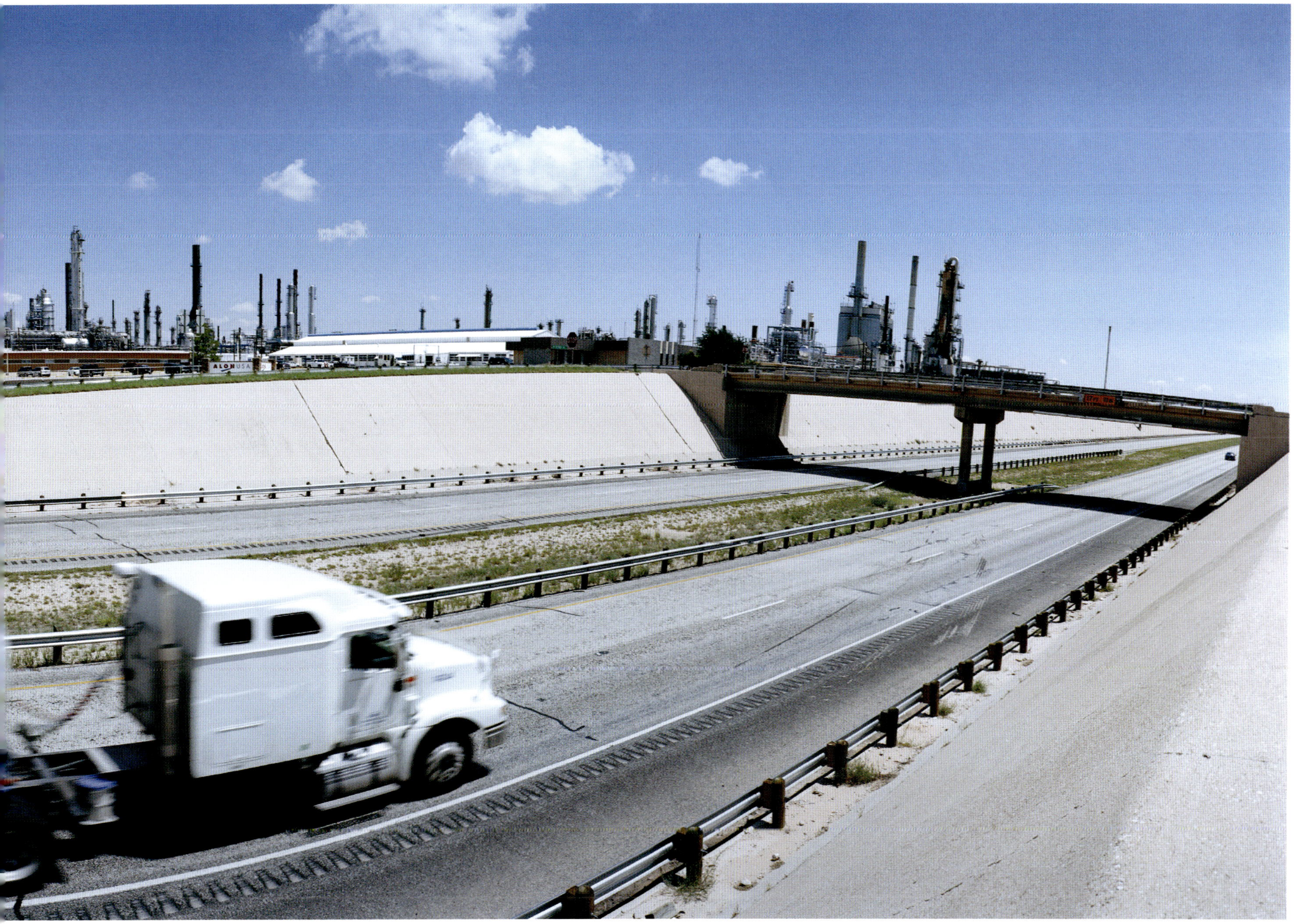

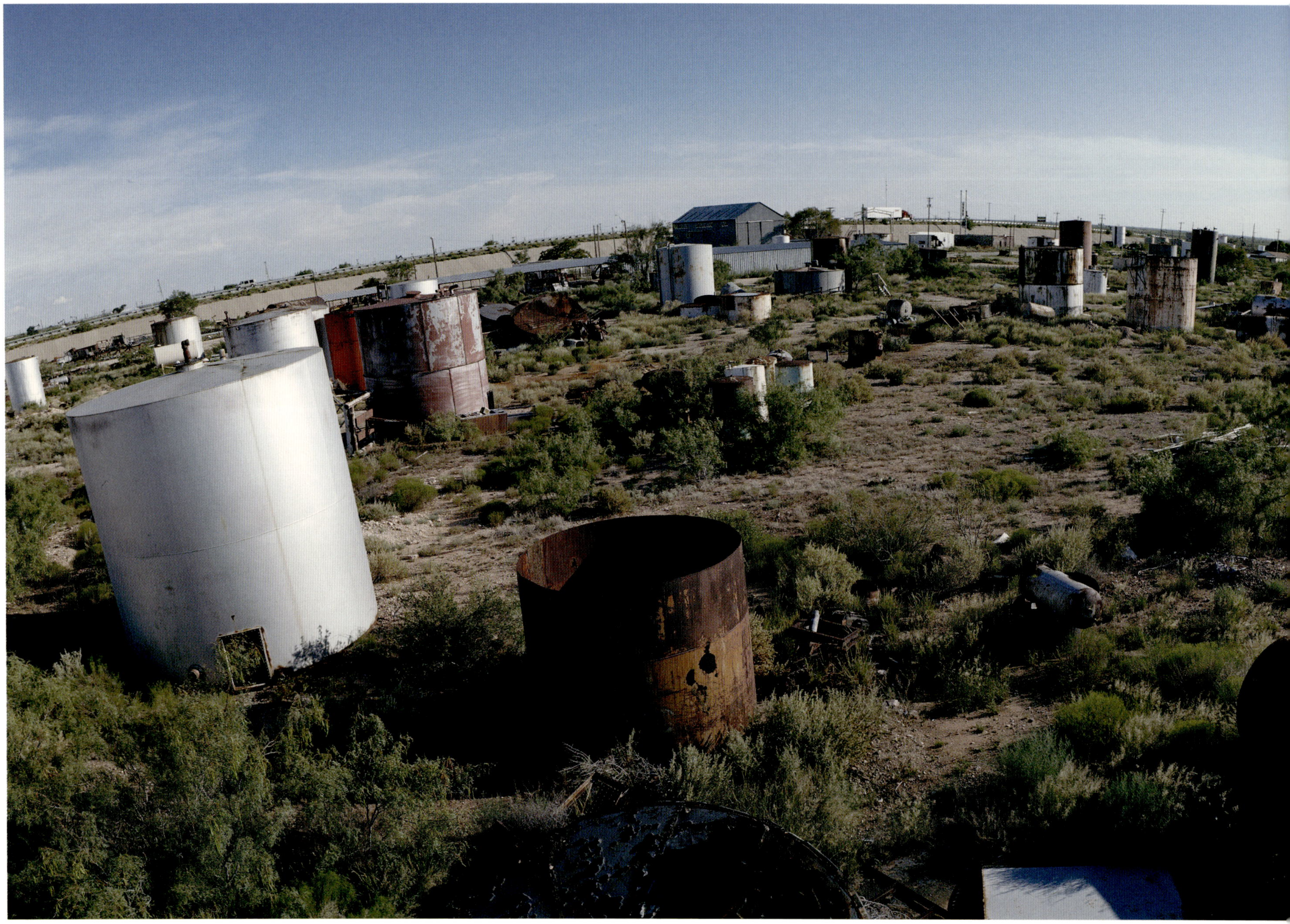

80. *Oilfield Trash, Penwell, Texas*, 2004–2006.
Archival pigment print, 22 × 49 in.
In the collection of the Museum of Texas Tech University, Lubbock

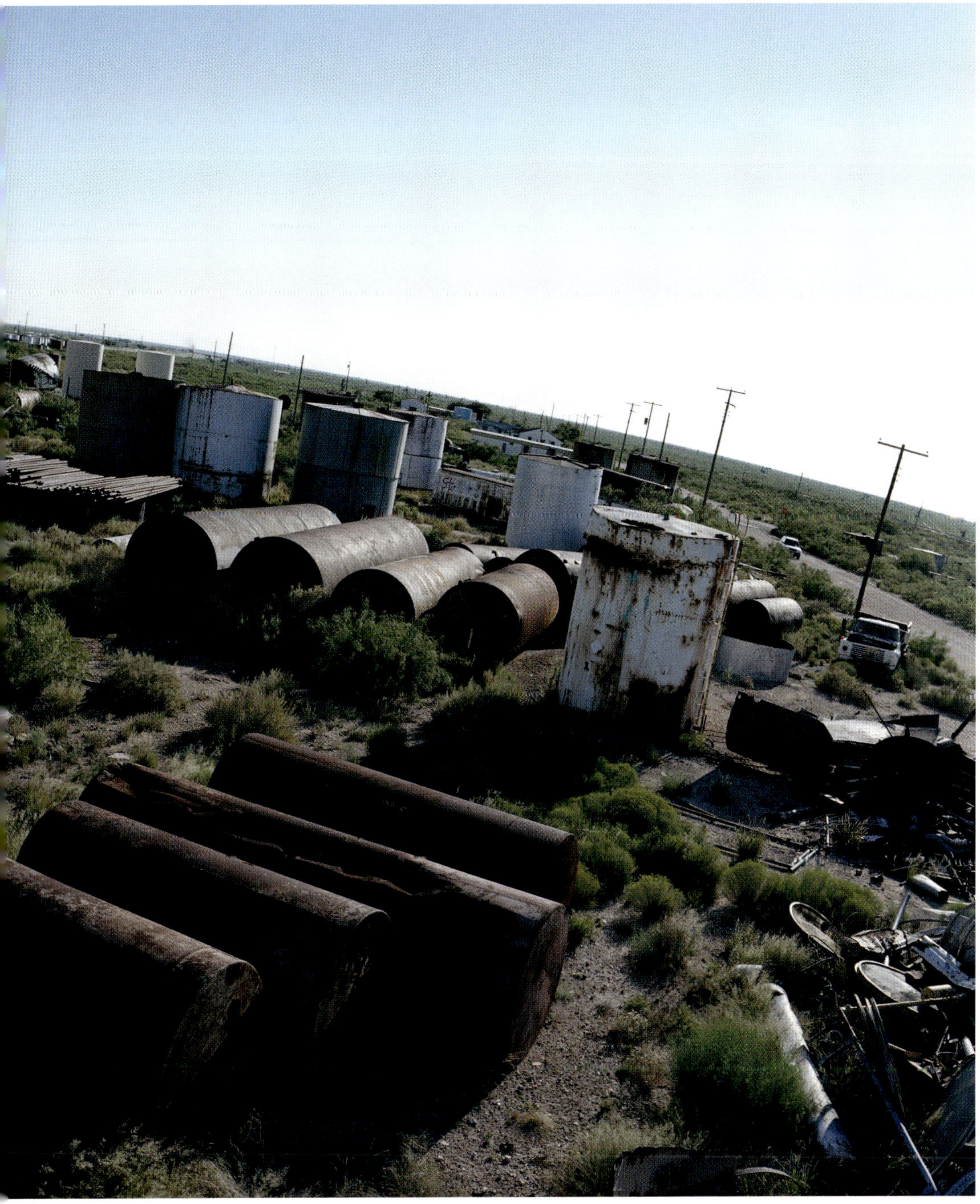

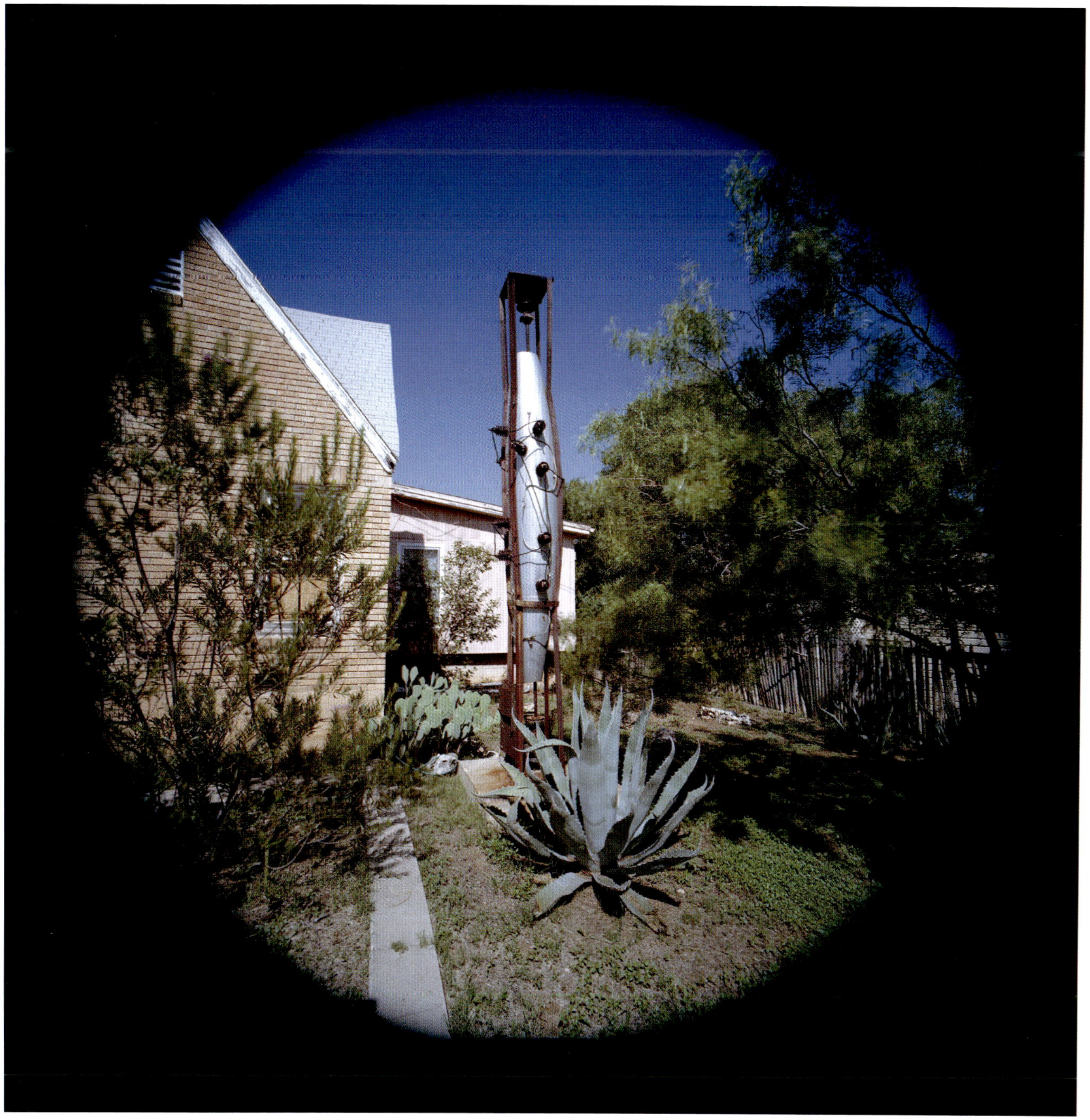

81. *Lamesa's "Rainmaker Rocket," Now in Big Spring, Texas*, 2004–2006.
Archival pigment print, 22 × 22 in.
In the collection of the Museum of Texas Tech University, Lubbock

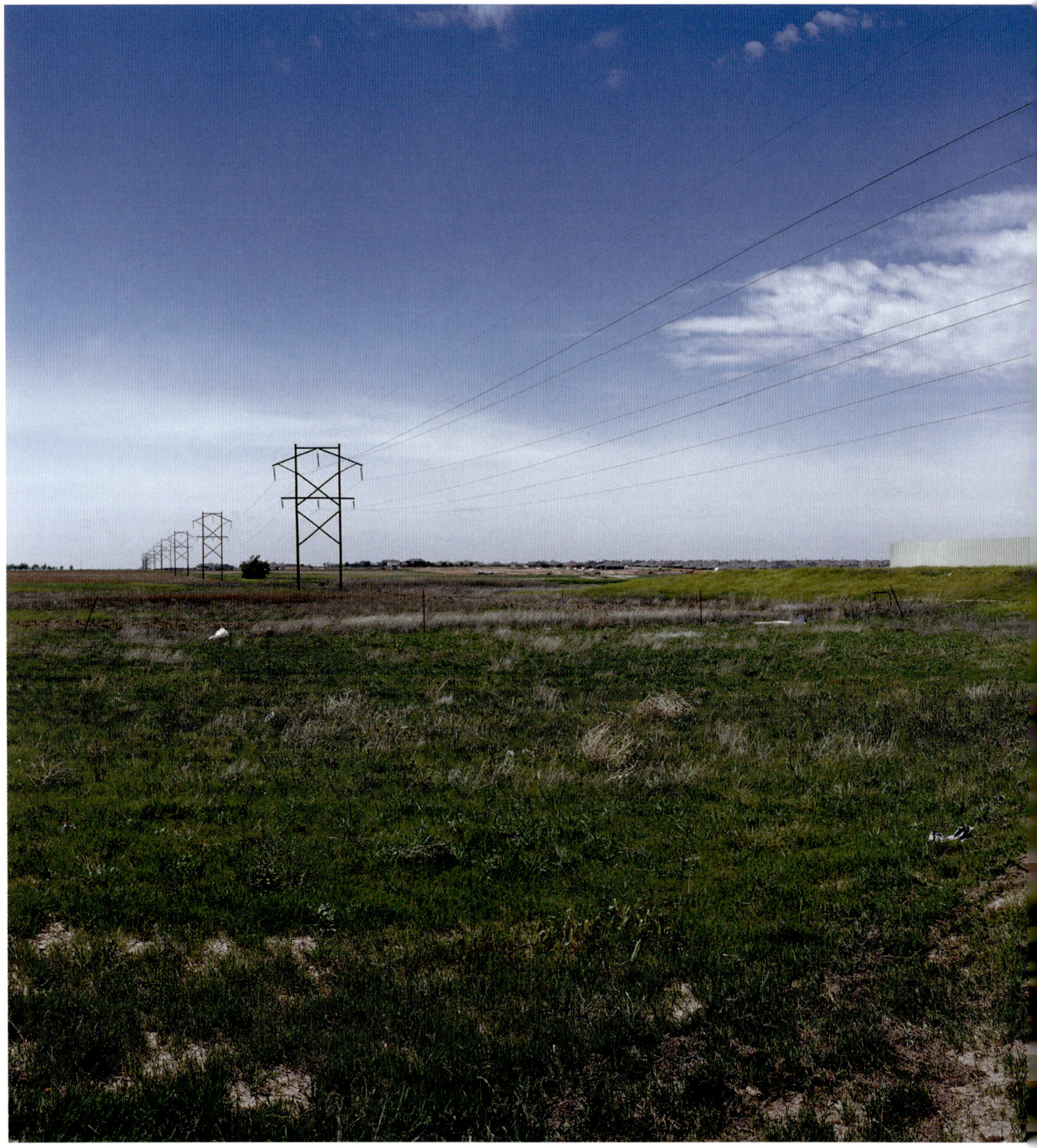

82. *Climate Controlled Storage, Lubbock, Texas,* 2005–2006.
Archival pigment print, 22 × 49 in.

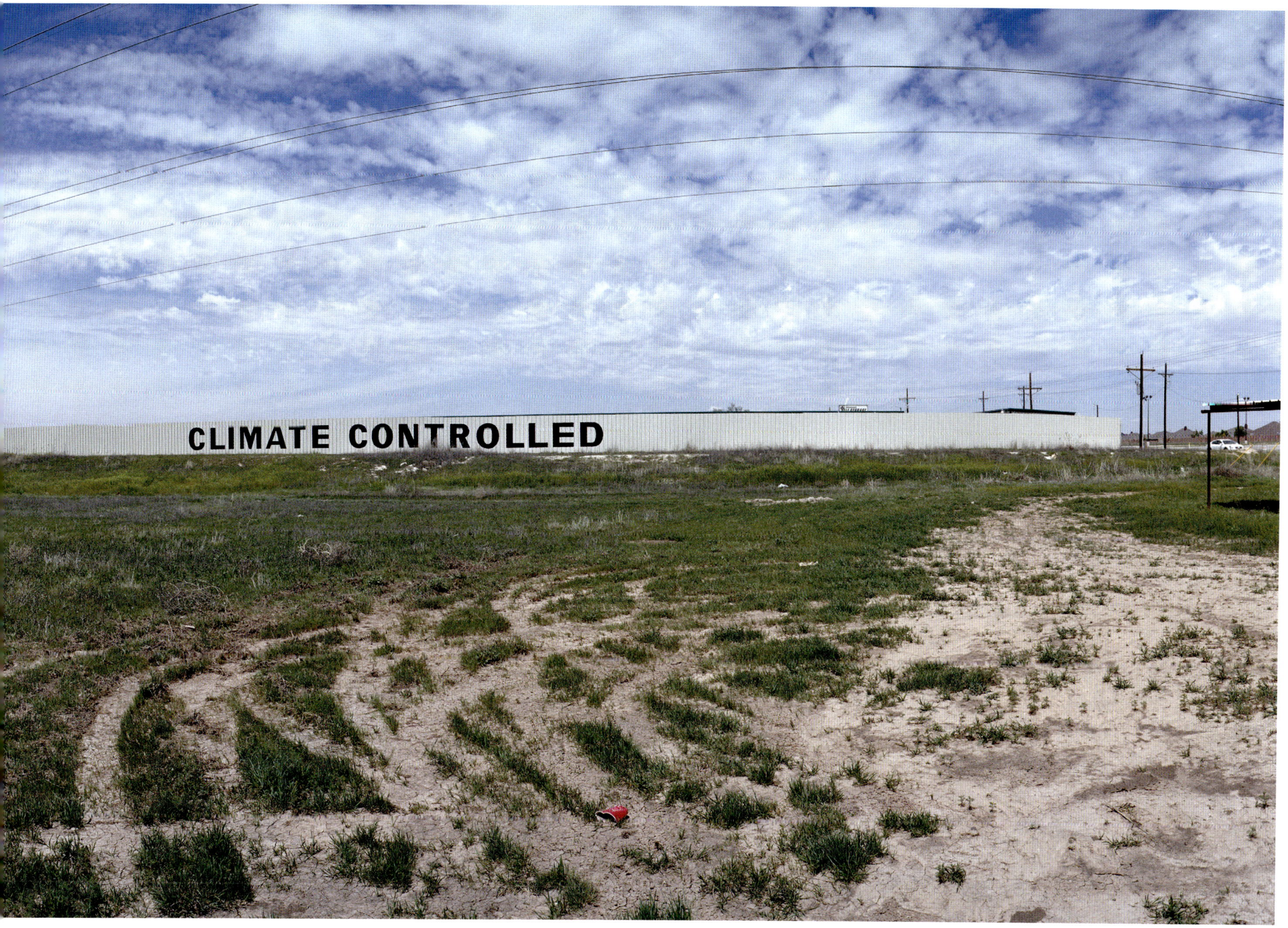
CLIMATE CONTROLLED

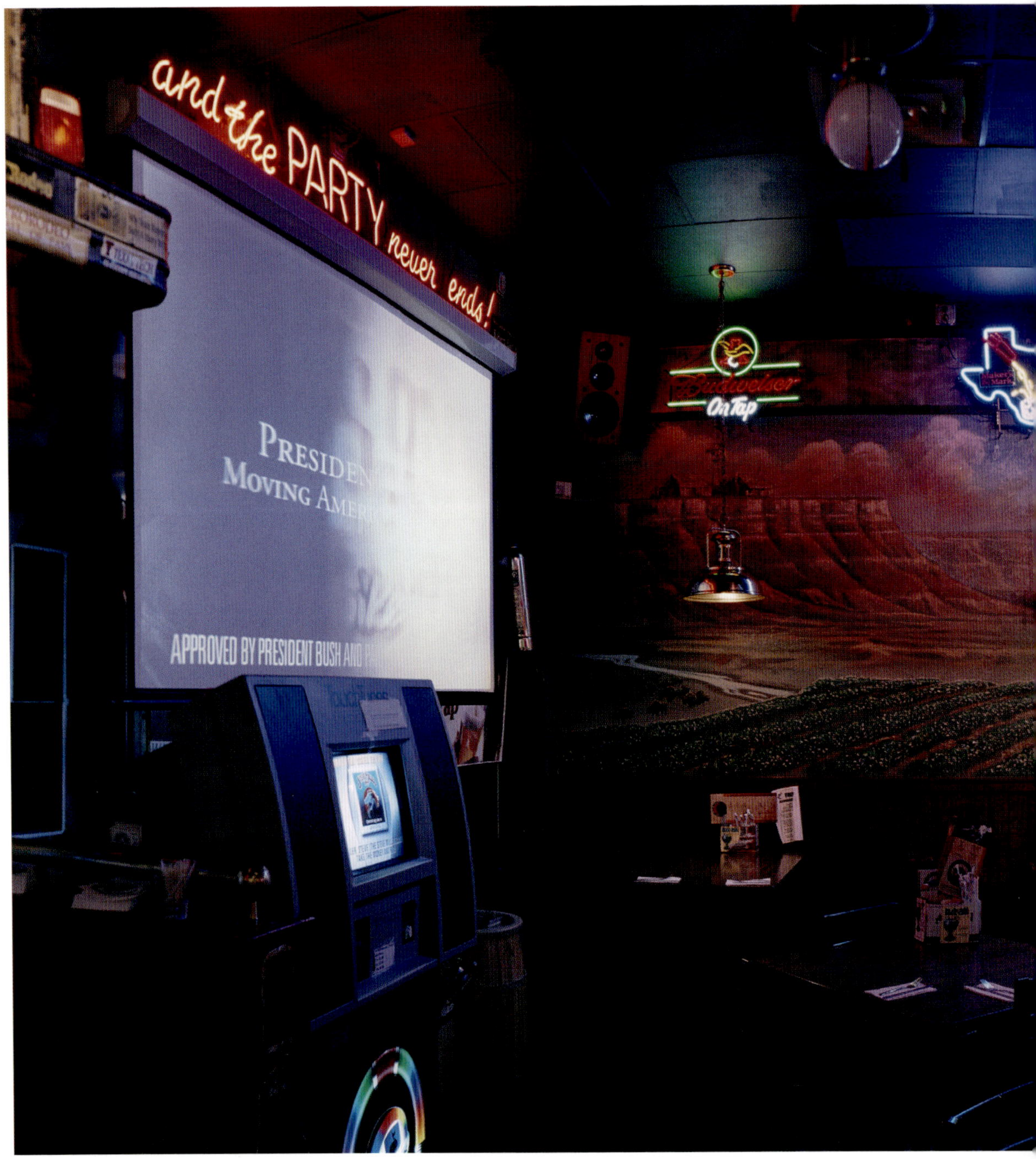

83. *Crop Duster Mural, Caprock Cafe, Lubbock, Texas*, 2005–2006.
Archival pigment print, 22 × 49 in.
In the collection of the Museum of Texas Tech University, Lubbock

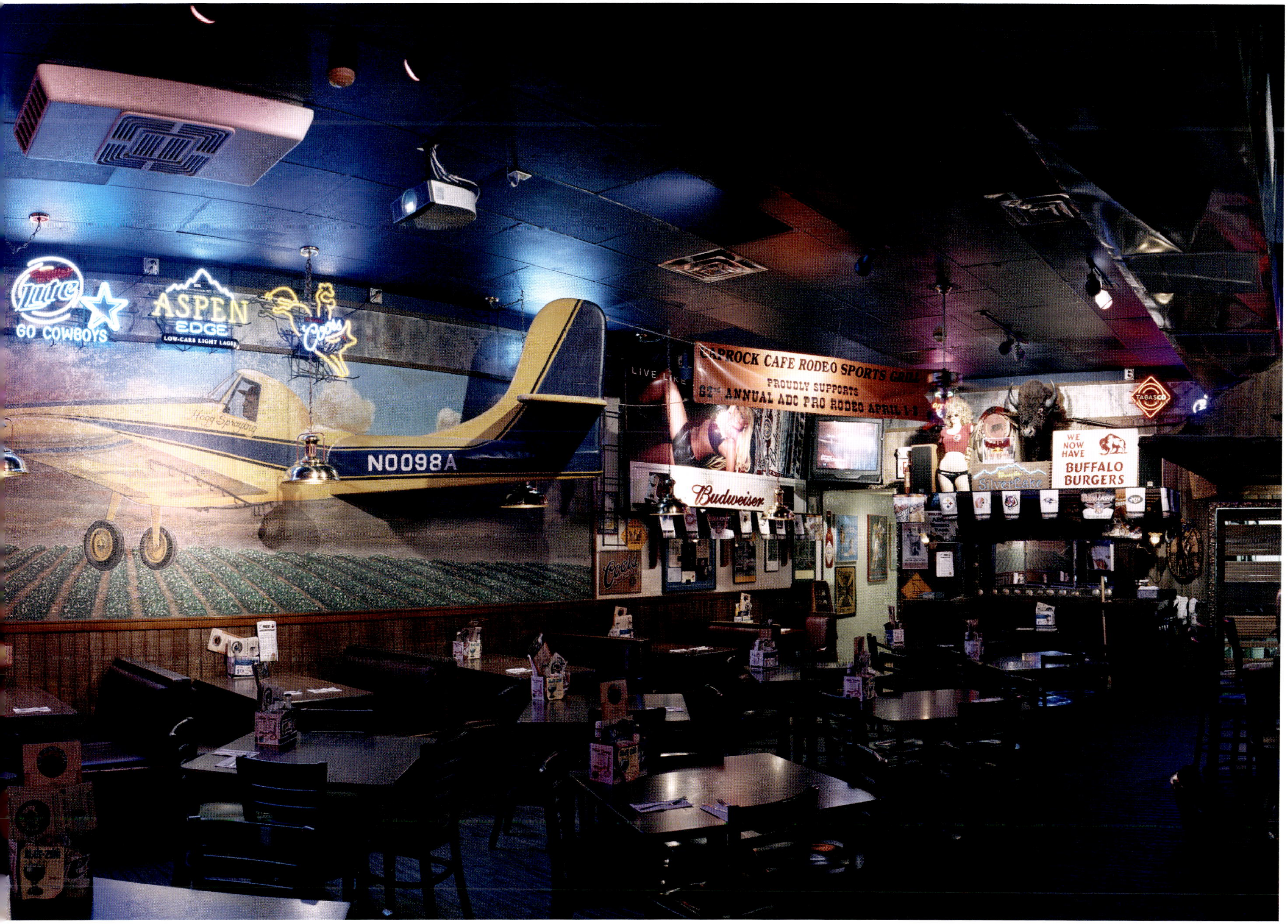
Lite
GO COWBOYS
ASPEN
EDGE
LOW-CARB LIGHT LAGER
N0098A
LIVE LIKE
PROUDLY SUPPORTS
Budweiser
WE
NOW
HAVE
BUFFALO
BURGERS
TABASCO

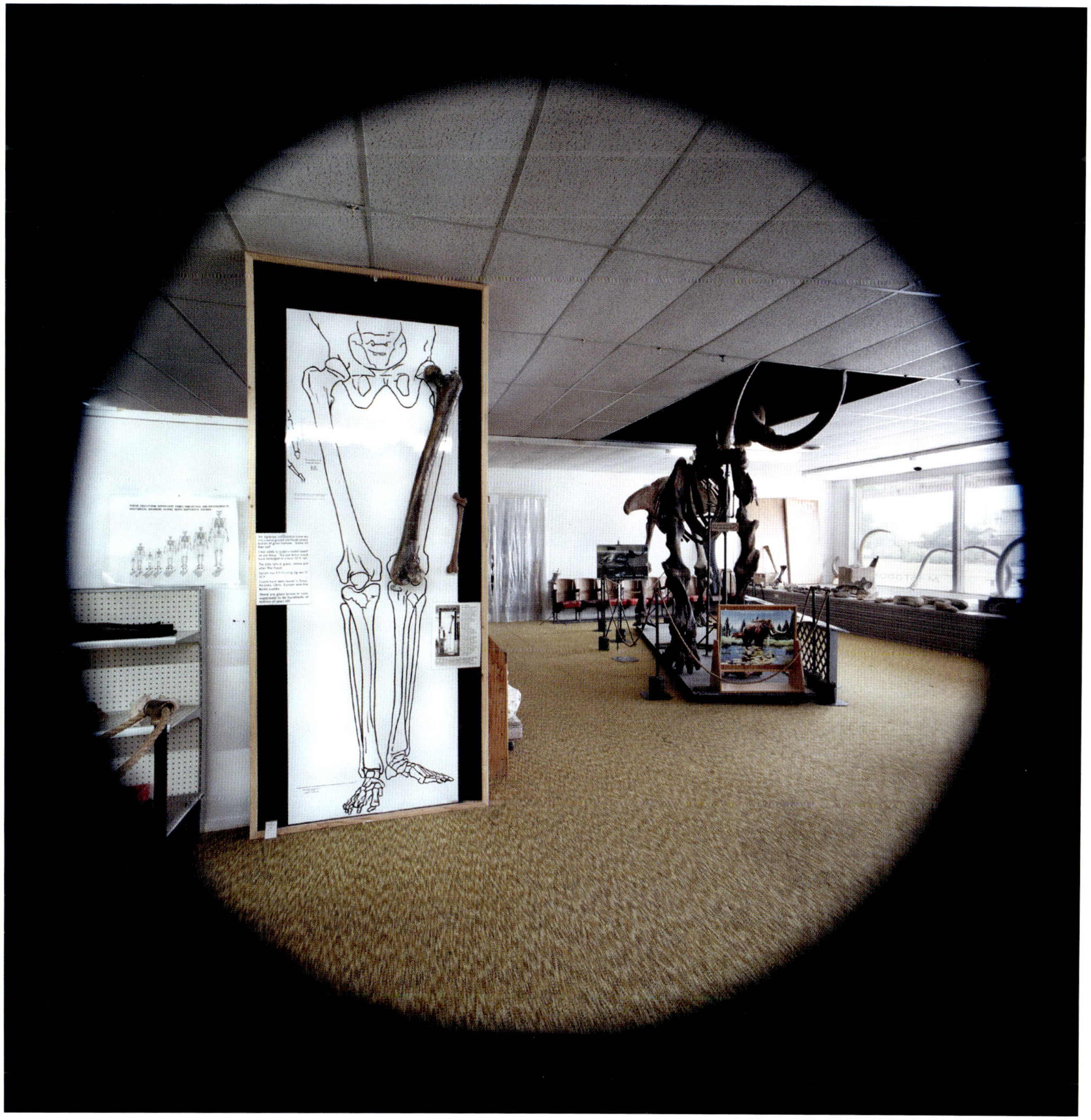

84. *Giant Femur, Mt. Blanco Fossil Museum, Crosbyton, Texas*, 2005–2006.
Archival pigment print, 22 × 22 in.
In the collection of the Museum of Texas Tech University, Lubbock

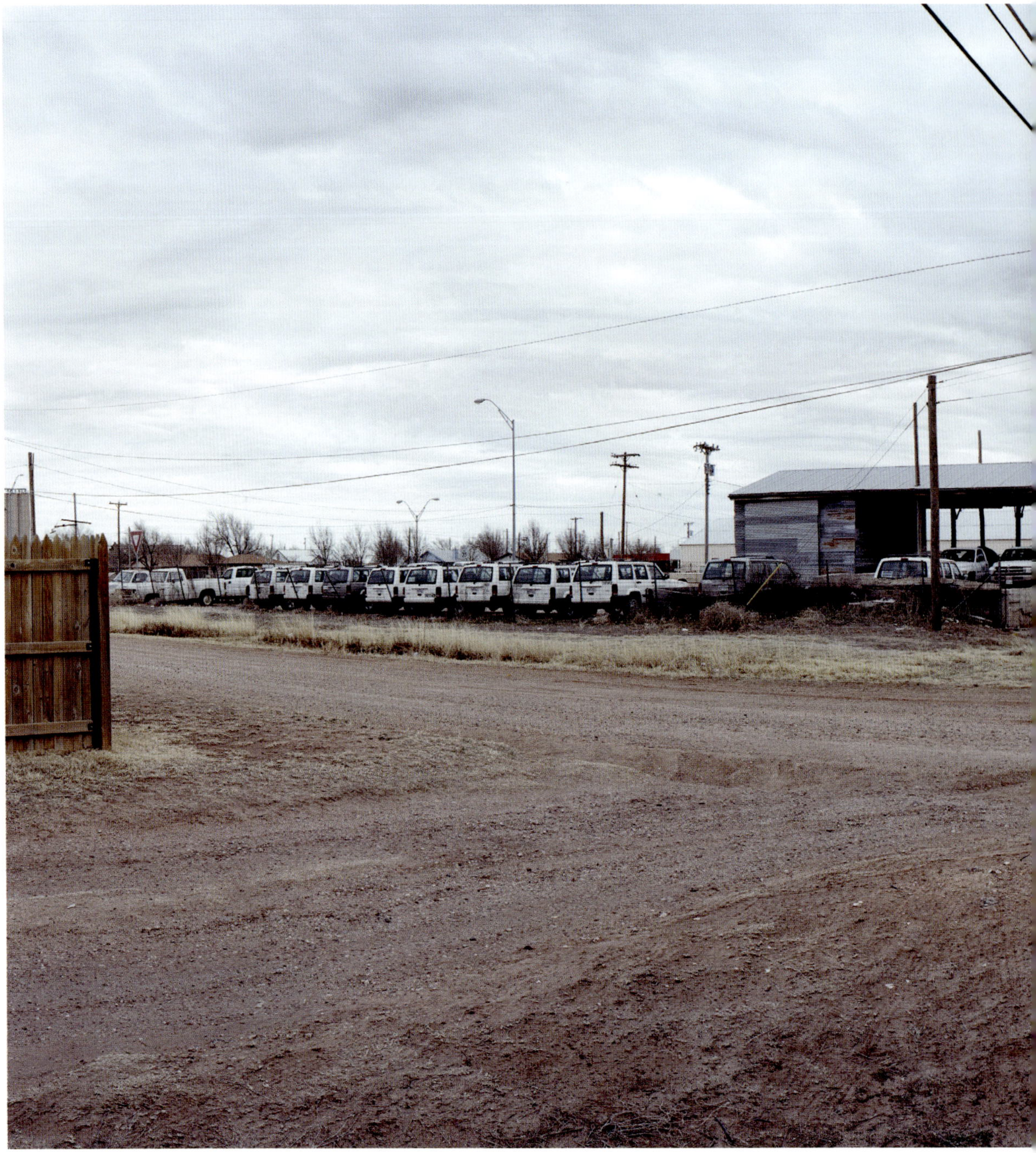

85. *Buffalo Mural, Hale Center, Texas*, 2004–2006.
Archival pigment print, 22 × 49 in.
In the collection of the Museum of Texas Tech University, Lubbock

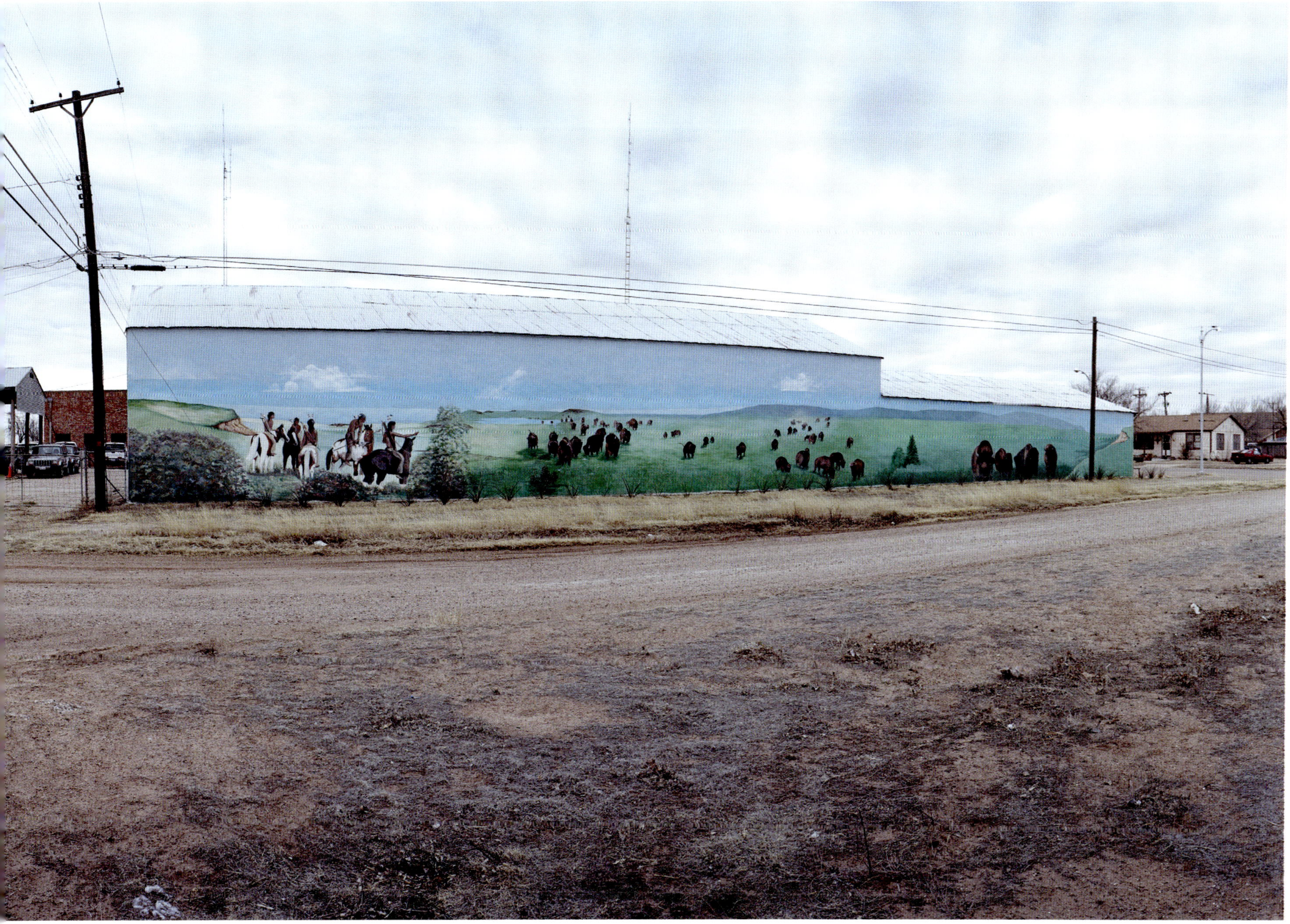

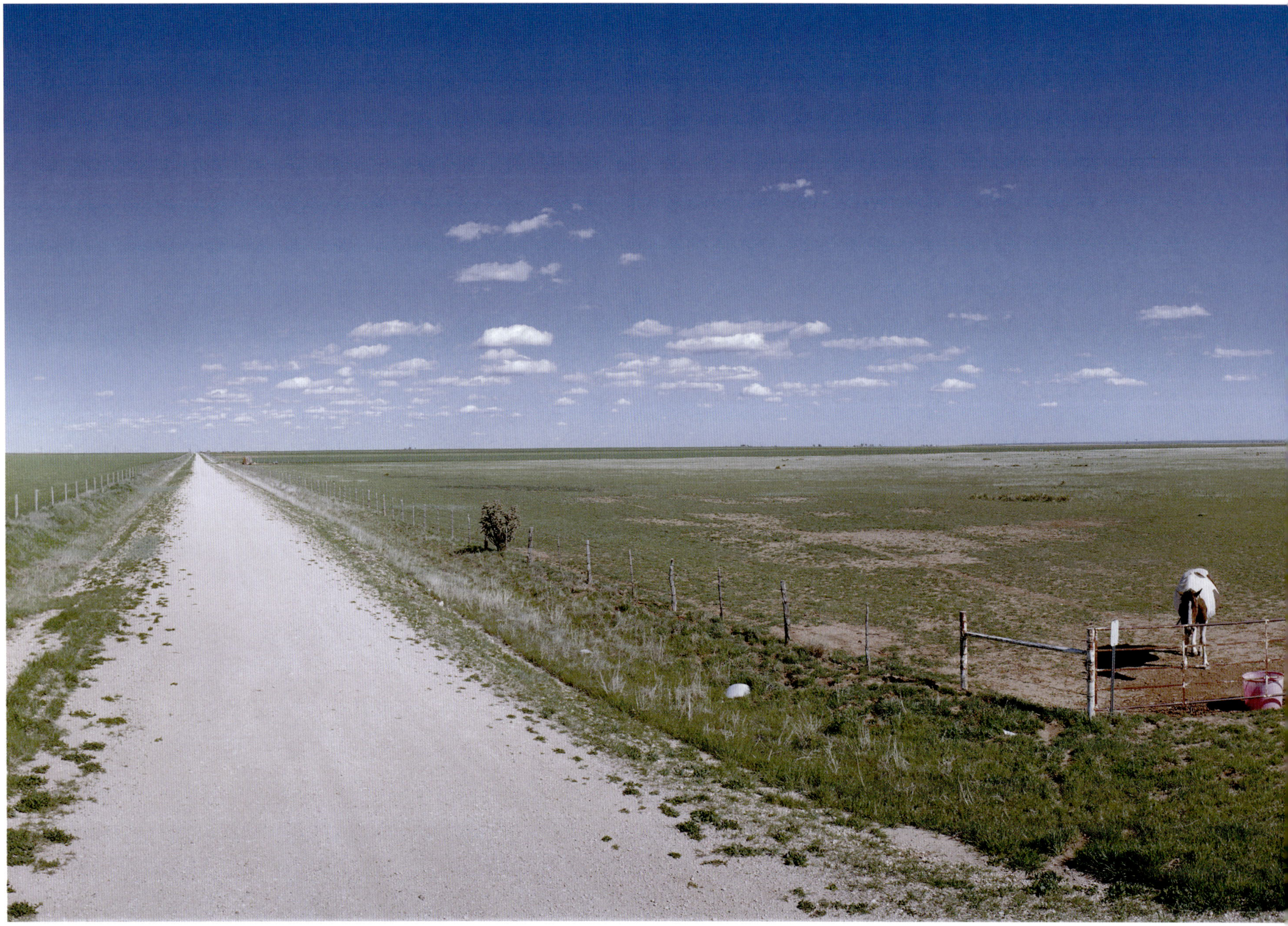

86. *Horse, Wheatland, New Mexico*, 2004–2006.
Archival pigment print, 22 × 49 in.
In the collection of the Museum of Texas Tech University, Lubbock

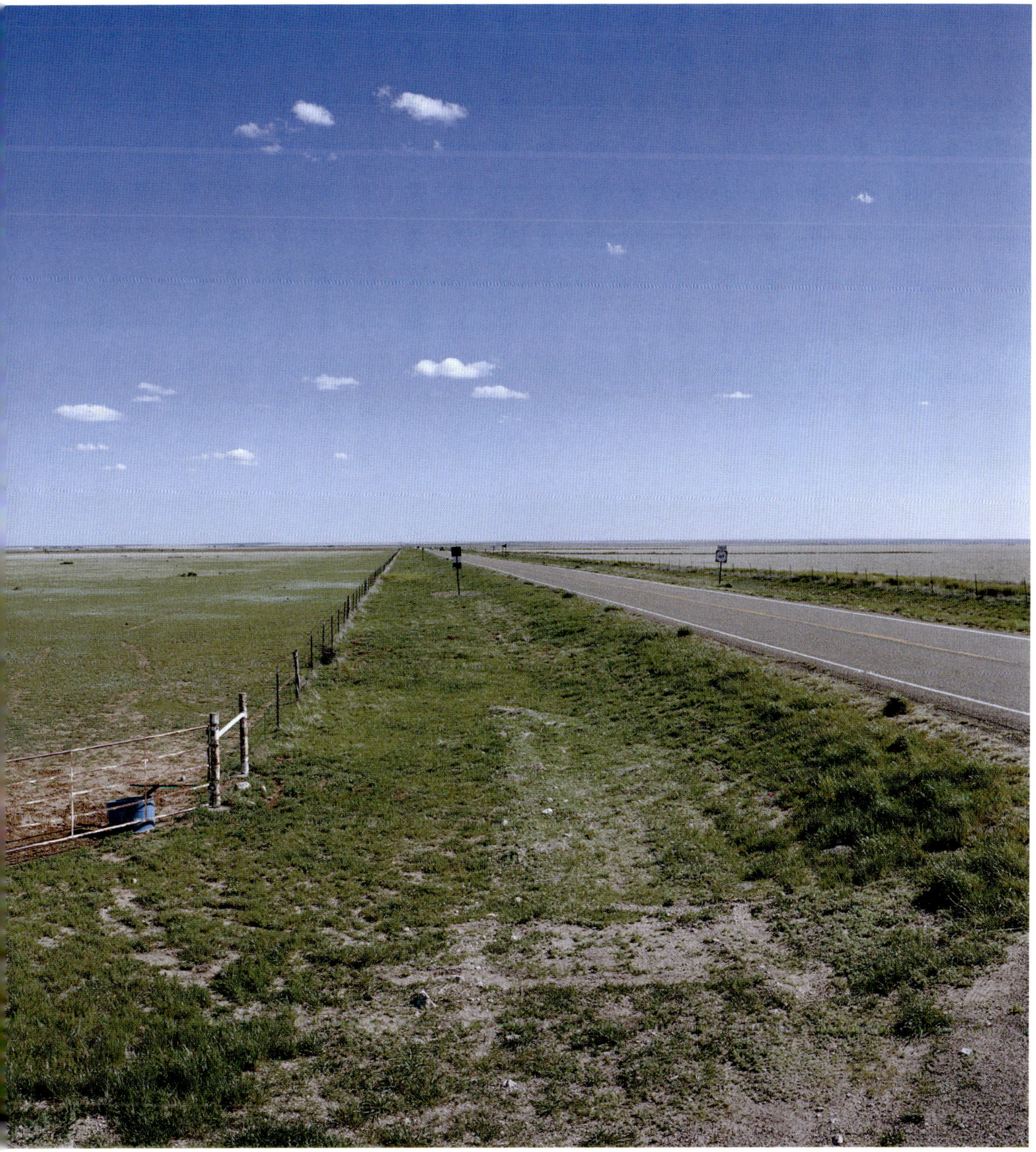

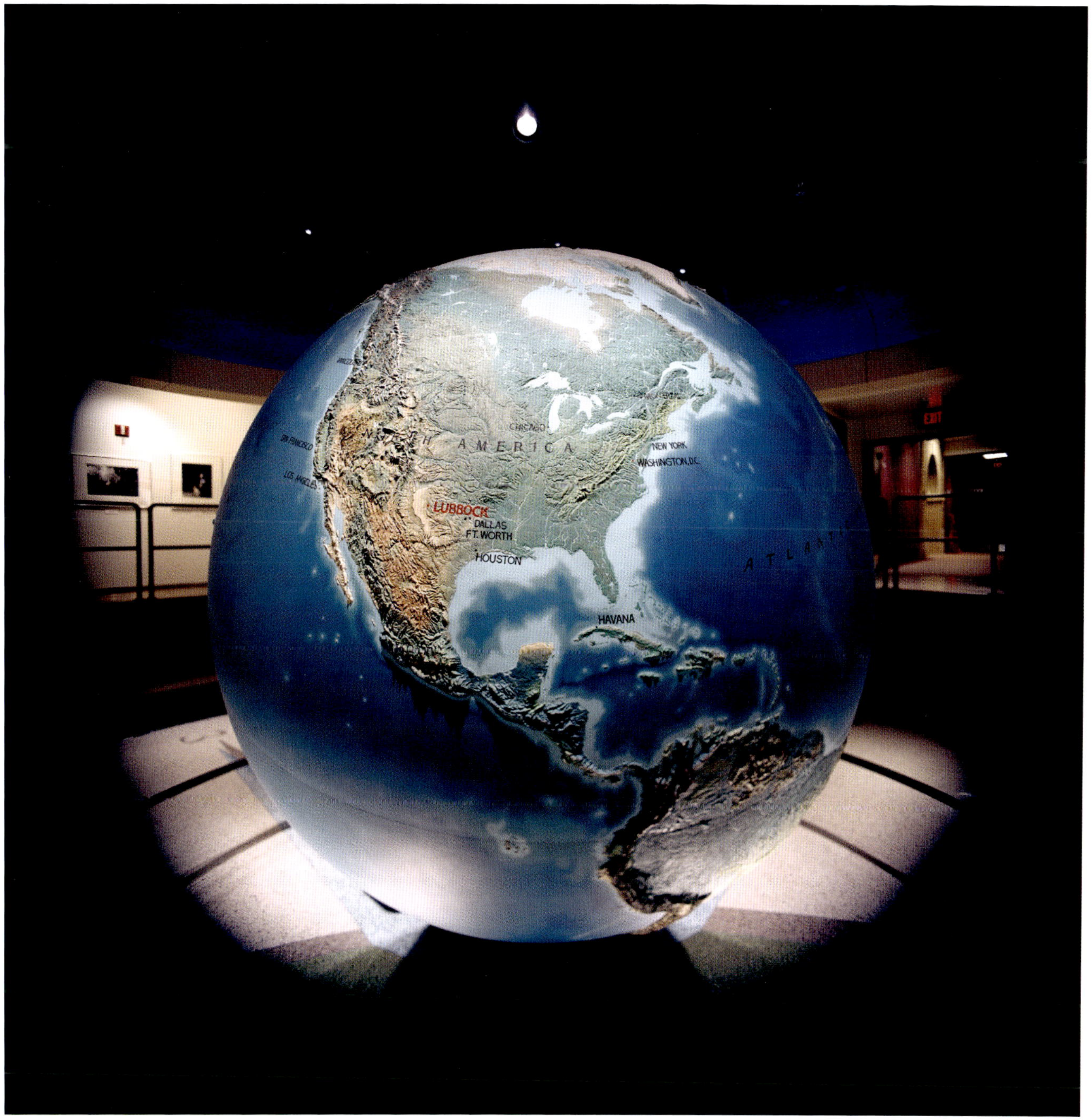

87. *Lubbock-Marked Globe, International Cultural Center, Lubbock, Texas*, 2004–2006.
Archival pigment print, 22 × 22 in.

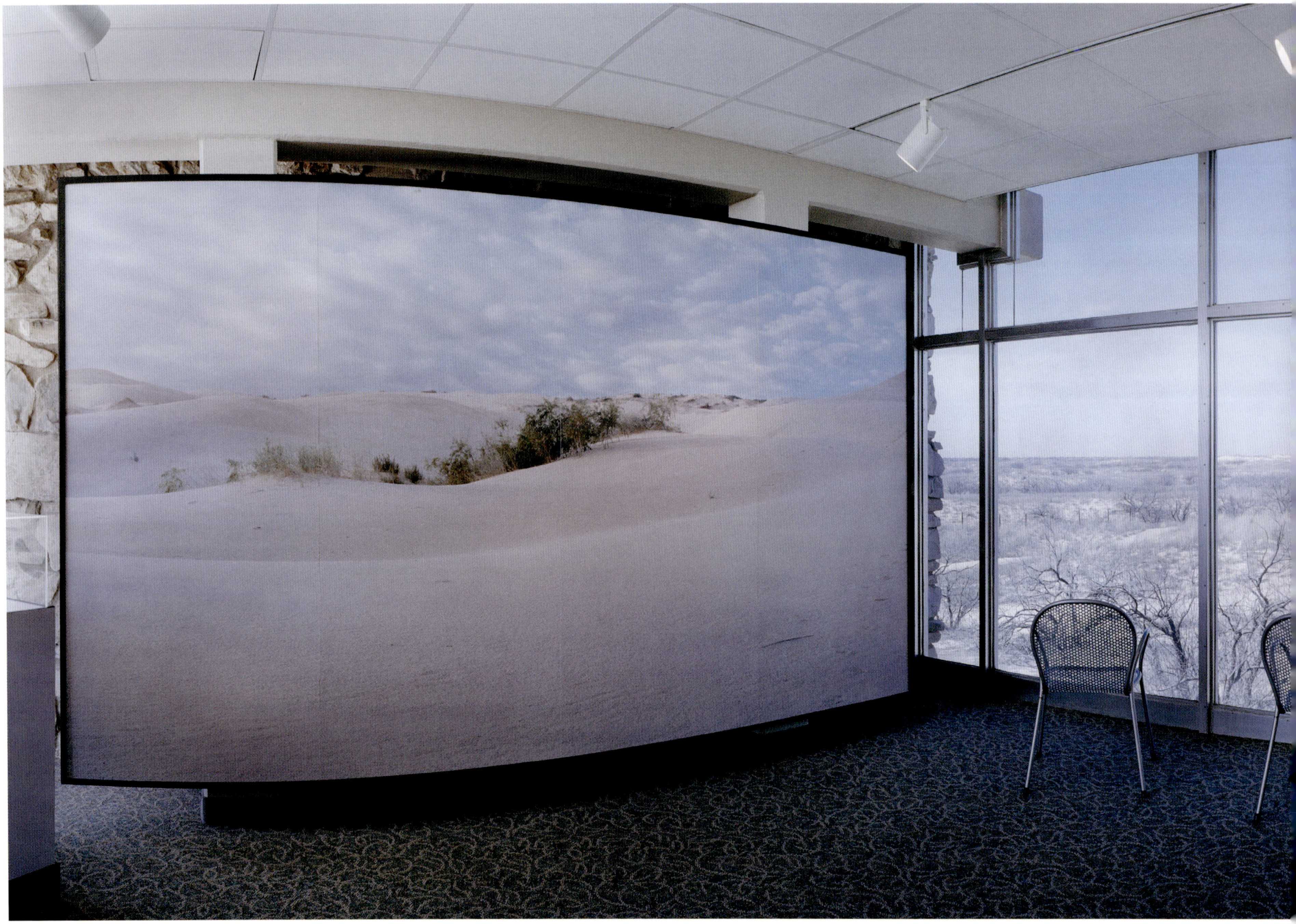

88. *Visitor Center, Monahans Sandhills State Park*, 2004–2006.
Archival pigment print, 22 × 49 in.
In the collection of the Museum of Texas Tech University, Lubbock

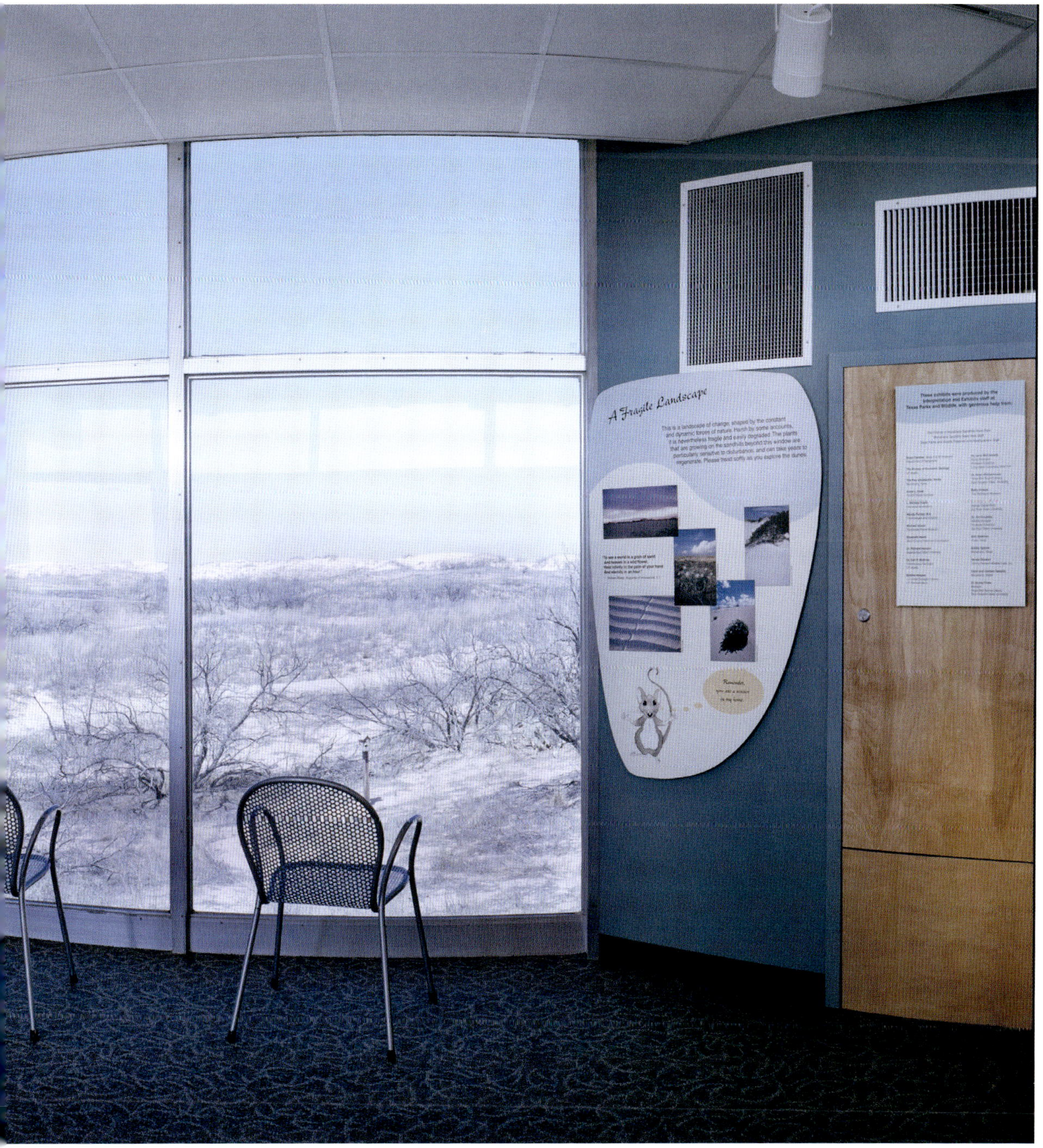
A Fragile Landscape

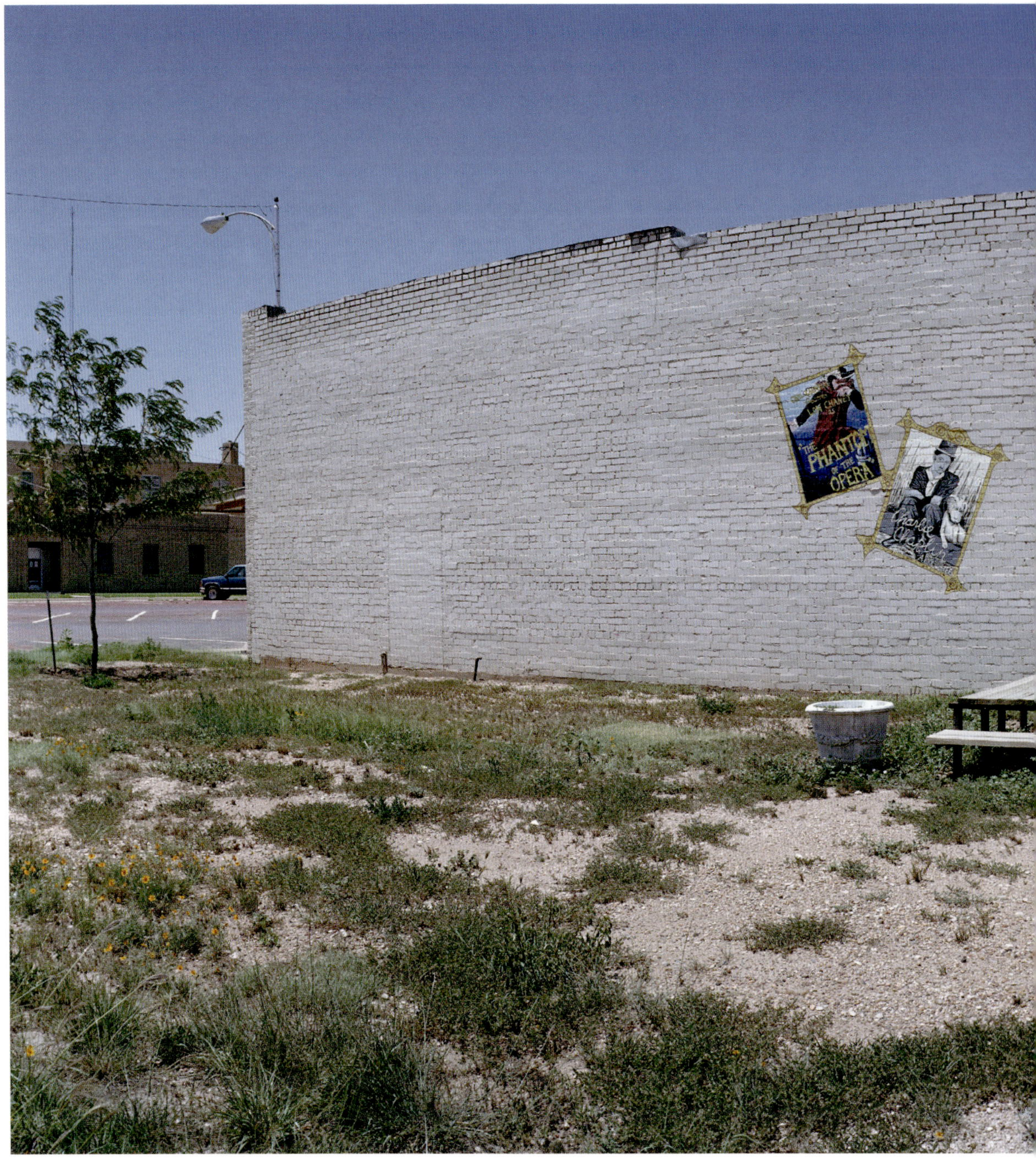

89. *Theater Mural, Floydada, Texas*, 2005–2006.
Archival pigment print, 22 × 49 in.

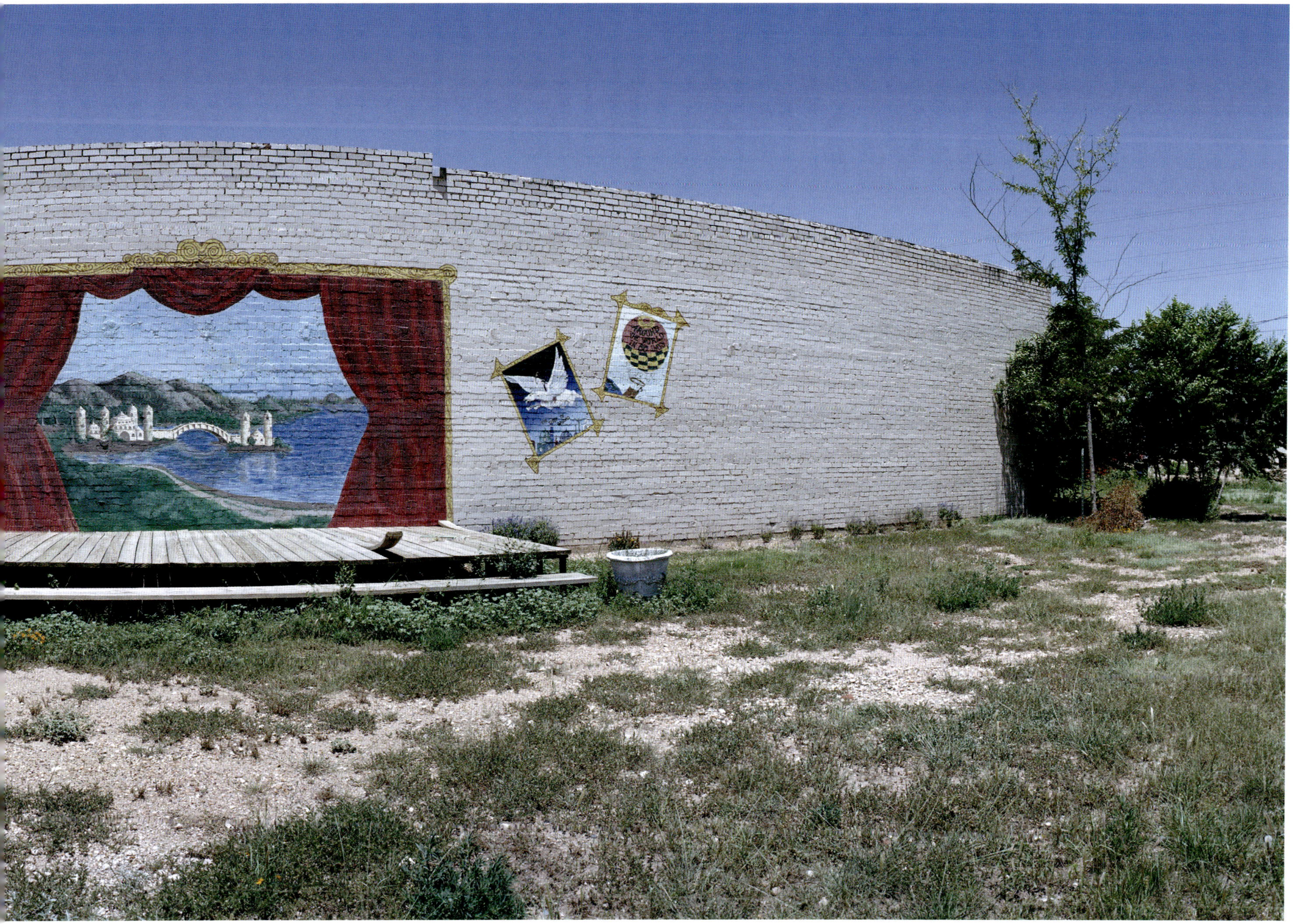

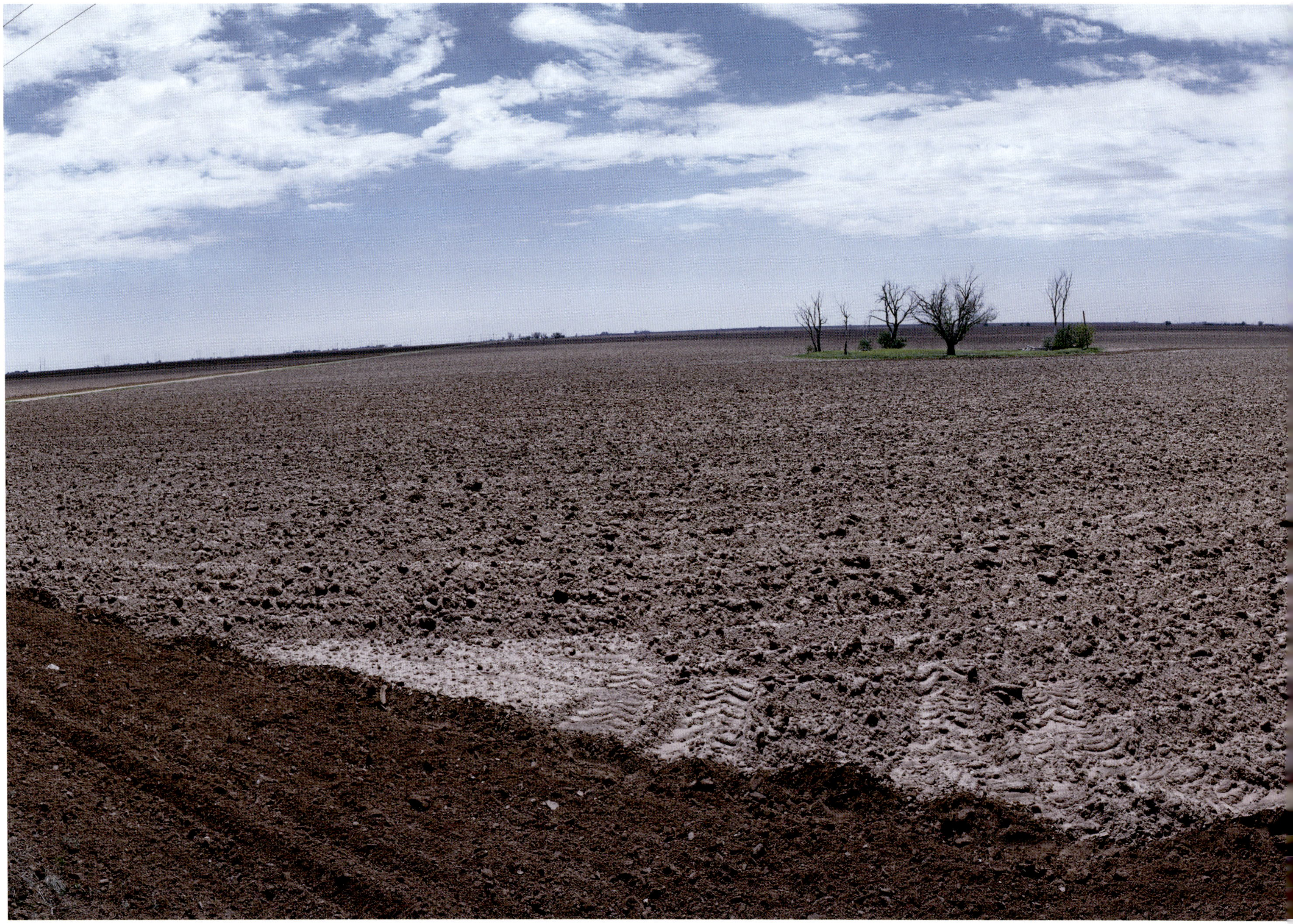

90. *Old Home Place in a Plowed Field, Posey, Texas*, 2004–2006.
Archival pigment print, 22 × 49 in.

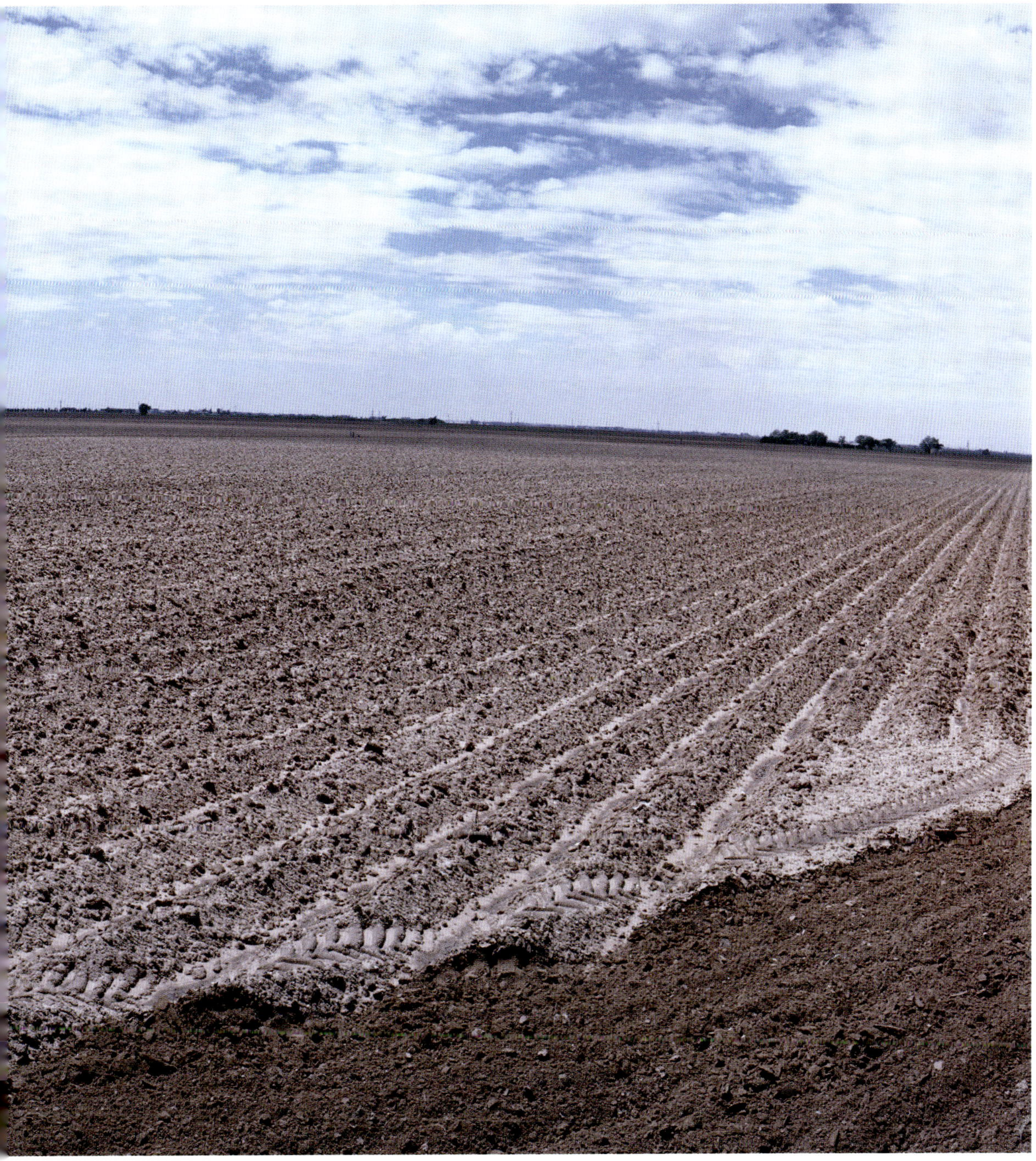

On Being Redacted

Finding Place

Shelley Armitage

THE BAR IS EMPTY. MAYBE IT'S BEFORE HAPPY HOUR or the late night crowd. For us, it's early afternoon, right after lunch. Tables gleam a reflected vacancy of the colors of the mural that covers the back wall. Depicting the Llano Estacado, the storied south plains flatlands and the canyonlands that border that plateau, it's a compressed sweep of time and space. Cotton fields form the settled foreground; there are signs, roads. Jutting from the mural itself—already impossible to take in in one look—the bright yellow tail of a crop-dusting airplane breaks the mural's plane: *coming at you.*

I'm looking at a photograph. Rick Dingus and I don't sidle up to the bar. Or do we? The photographer is taking me through sheaves of his single prints, this one titled *Crop Duster Mural, Caprock Cafe, Lubbock, Texas*, 2005–2006 (figure 83). Drawers below his large worktable hold layer after layer of other prints you can almost step into, challenging one's eye to dwell on the swell of information. There's the inevitable trail here, too: the sequencing of photographic projects through time—his explorations as an artist.

What I'm most struck by initially is how you enter these images yet stand outside them. *The here, the there.* Among the projects, the places—the rephotography, petroglyphs, Navajo sacred sites, India shrines, landscapes of the Great Plains, Australian frontiers, the llano, and most recently, planet earth—I recognize places I've been and others that seem familiar, even though I've not been there. No, I've not traveled in Tasmania, but the frontier aspects, images of settling practices, depictions of the environment and uses of it remind me of a common vernacular. Yet I am not *in* these places, and hardly anyone else is either. These landscapes are distinguished not by a nineteenth-century sense of awe or a twentieth-century notion of topophilia, but a feeling of *being redacted*—of human presence more obvious in its absence, prompting a consciousness of the complexities of our relationship to the natural world. Such vacancies suggest abandonment, the practices of uneasy use, then moving on. But as we experience the work of the camera, what Dingus calls "a viewing system," examining vacancy encourages the straddling of the here and there, of realizing human presence, like geography, as a feature of landscape in terms of its subject, the maker, and the viewer. As Leslie Marmon Silko reminds us that viewers are as much a part of the landscape as the boulders they stand on, Dingus's photographs invite us to question these relationships and facile assumptions about landscape and photography.[1]

This realization came home to me when I viewed my adoption records, which I had requested from the State of Texas Archives a few years ago. Warned that the records I received would be *redacted* to protect the privacy of those involved, I looked up that word.

At first the definition didn't seem to match the documents ("to draw up or frame"; "to collect, drive back"). But then I got to the relevant part of the definition, "to edit, to revise." I received about thirty pages of records, and thick black lines obscured certain pieces of information. Absence piques curiosity. I held the documents up to the light. *Couldn't see through the lines.* Then I spread the documents out to see them all at once on the table, to survey the blacked-out markings—where my history and my birth parents appeared as strike-throughs. Like holes in old IBM computer punch cards, the enforced absences invited me to look even more particularly at the environment, the context, seeking a pattern in the absence of clear meaning. I tried to read between the lines. Later, I discovered another frame of reference—a videotape, converted from the 16 mm film that my adoptive dad had taken on the day my family picked me up from the adoption cottage. Instantly, some interpretive record was reinscribed. My little bald head snuggled near my mother's pert 1940s hat as she carried me from the green two-story house in the country somewhere on the outskirts of Fort Worth, Texas, to an awaiting shiny beetle-backed Chevy. I had an odd feeling looking at the "I" who seemed simultaneously "other." And so I wonder: by what means are we led to reconsider the relationship of self and environment, of people and places, in terms of "viewing systems"? And, if so aware, how do we sense our feet on that inclusive boulder Leslie Marmon Silko speaks of?

Dingus's landscape photographs appear to reinforce or revisit the trope of vacancy or emptiness that countless observers and inhabitants of the Great Plains, the llano, the frontiers, the desert, or derelict places have emphasized. Yet, the residuals of human occupancy trump such conventional readings and invite us to view anew physical places as projections and interpretations—how they are constructed technically and in our imaginations. Problematizing the notion of optics, Dingus's work connects us with actual places and their human projects by drawing on photographs, building special viewing lenses and cameras, reminding us that the photograph has a foot in the actual world and in the world of image making. And that it operates through private and cultural symbols. I look at his work: flat barren fields, open farmland, vacated industrial projects, paint-peeling murals of mythical or forgotten places, faded petroglyphs, signs long abandoned. These places—framed, revised, or drawn—are brimming.

Being redacted removes the hierarchical "I" to briefly replace it with a horizontal consciousness of ourselves and places. But by initially seeing human projects and places as "other," we may notice ironies, consider new meanings ignored or unrealized. Human geography, like the landforms, altered or seemingly natural, is not static. Stepping out, stepping back from what we may think we know or have experienced, is a kind of focus. Our working imaginations and memories reengage. We note this in Dingus's stereograph photographs, for example, which locate a gap between images, like a third eye. What are our assumptions? these photographs ask. And how may shifting points of view challenge and change them?

Some of Dingus's images work through wry juxtaposition. To smile knowingly at them is to respond to a tone, an edge, a protracted and echoing irony. When we see "Climate Controlled" signed in black on a white building meeting the horizon line in a patch of arid plains (figure 82), we smile and muse over human "control." The folly of controlling or dominating or improving nature is a theme here, echoing a kind of Dorothea Lange *Tractored Out, Texas*. Dingus manages a kind of inside joke, at least a kind of whimsicality. As a recurring theme, he pictures what he calls "weird science"—the skewing of formal, time-honored knowledge and precepts about scientific information. As with science, a healthy skepticism marks these images. They invite more questions than conclusions. The joke turns sardonic in some photos as we note the remains of abandoned industrial waste, the redundancy of uses of the land (mines, water projects, forest destruction, extravagant pipelines), which, briefly plumbed, are relics of "progress." Indeed, the tropes of relic, ruin, and nostalgia that may replace actual loss are suggested in contemporary industrial and technological landscapes. Likewise, in another image of vacated development,

Oilfield Trash, Penwell, Texas, 2004–2006 (figure 80)— a ghost town of oil boom and bust—steel drums stand like a sculpture garden, reminding us of a predominant aesthetic of our commercial world. Culture and topography intertwine as omnivorous destinies.

Dingus comments on how his looking at photographs has shaped his sense of the endless dynamics of place as reflected in image making. In his early work on the rephotography projects, he valued what Timothy O'Sullivan's treatment of the western landscape taught him about the possibilities of the photographic image. The effect of the camera, a "box in the wilderness"—the photographic recording of the American West by O'Sullivan and other expeditionary photographers—was to forever alter the notion of "wilderness," or nature. For him, O'Sullivan's subtle method was at once cool, geographic, documentary, and incredibly layered, what Dingus calls "double-edged," containing its own referential symbols that also challenged conventional interpretation. What declared itself as documentary—scientific facts or information—was often canted or staged. During the process of repeat photography, Dingus learned, yes, that certain locales have changed through time, but more important, he discovered the impact of the "box"—how image making is necessarily an act of symbol making and how landscape is a reflection of our connection to but also our ongoing construction of the world.

Boxes suggest frames and categories, another kind of redaction. And they seem so very "western," don't they? Categories, rectangles. Peter Gay observed of Sigmund Freud that he lived more on his couch than in Vienna, suggesting that Freud failed to realize the full effect of environment on the psyche. One of Dingus's boxes opened up the entire field of photography to him. Discovering at his parents' house a cache of old photographs stored away in a wooden box in their attic, he was intrigued, as a young student, with the questions of anonymity these family photographs posed. Who were these unidentified people? Where were they? Searching, he discovered most were old family members, and his curiosity led him to track down specific places, names, and dates. Once anonymous images, these family "records" called for reassembling, making speculations that prompted contemplation, storytelling, myth making. In his own photography, the absence of people, the presence of anonymous places, prompt the desire to know, opening up possibilities about sight, sites, insight.

The box has long been a metaphor for the workings of the human brain. Recent studies by psychologists and neurologists investigate the seats of perception and imagination and posit how we think of their function and interaction. Comparing the brain to a camera, these researchers suggest that the front part of the brain is the locus of perception, while the back area is the site of the imagination. Speculation suggests that the rear of the brain may originate a "view" that challenges simple perception. And this gives rise to questions about the relationships among what we think we see, the influence of cultural conventions, and imagination. When Dingus builds cameras, makes his own viewing systems, we are reminded of how the box may be altered, specialized, and thus provide ground for the interaction of perception and imagination. Using a 35 mm camera lens on a medium format camera he built for his Here : There series, he accomplished a kind of fish-eye view, one he has described alternately as possibly voyeuristic or encouraging a dreamlike experience or fantasy. Such photographs invite an awareness of how we see through a manipulation of the technology that allows it: viewing equals an act of symbol making, of construction. One way in which we are invited by the viewing process to more closely investigate the subject is in the disjunctive articulation of space in these photographs. There is a disruption of the framing we've come to expect as characteristic of landscape photography. The photos play with the indexing of conventional meanings. In the Llano Estacado series, the apparent curve created by the use of a swing lens panoramic camera suggests the curvature of the eye itself, so that the landscape looks back. Is nature the transparent eyeball Emerson advocated? *The hierarchy of the "I" is supplanted by "the other."* Place and space and human residues look back, unblinkingly. And in the wide-angle shots, the edges appear curved. They seem to embrace us.

Such effects drawing our attention to the photographic subject are a result of the encounters of a physical and an intellectual connection to place. Dingus's work habits, such as walking, which he describes as essential to getting into a place he may photograph, remind us of the method of expeditionary photographers before him—traveling, searching, spending time on the ground, as in fieldwork. Here mobility means not flashing by, as in the case of traffic on a crowded thoroughfare, but looking. One must linger to look, spend time, dawdle, or as Rainer Maria Rilke said about the discovery of a poem—essential creative waiting. Walking and looking encourage an expectant serendipity. A common response to vernacular landscapes is to pass through them and quickly or essentially ignore them—they seem insignificant or too familiar. Whether of subjects familiar or exotic, Dingus's images call for physical engagement.

Can looking be this physical engagement, a kind of subversive walking? We may become aware intellectually of how the camera encourages new ideas. We may recognize that the camera reveals patterns of change that we've not perceived nor remembered. We surely will see the camera as posing questions about time, space, culture, place. But may "walking" these photographs also restore the experiential, an actual physical articulation that shapes out of space a sense of place?

There's a concept I think fits Dingus's work well, and I know this from years of walking my own family farm, certainly not an exotic place—a familiar place easy to take for granted. It lies on the northern edge of the llano, grassy plains with a few relieving draws, all buffalo grass, side oats grama, and sky. It resembles some of Dingus's llano photographs, both in geography and in use. Drought, overharvesting, and grazing mark it as a place where technology and nature chase one another, forever mixed. I walk it, have for some sixty years, for the pleasure of its company, for discoveries within something pedestrian, as a kind of meditation. But to really do this, the mind needs to be blank, perhaps an impossibility but worth trying. The senses need first to be primarily engaged. The communications scholar Brian Massumi describes this activity as "aspect"—the way vernacular experiences call up feelings before we name them.[2] Or, put another way, image reception may precede the assumed concepts based on sociolinguistic meanings. Massumi understands that images may prompt conventional associations. But affect, he says, operates in the gap between content and effect, as an intensity of surfaces—not of language or naming but of autonomic reactions, most directly manifest in the skin. So if I can bodily feel the farm's environment—the ceaseless wind, the toe-stumping rocks, the sensation of the shifting horizon line—such experiences exist outside theory.

An intensity of surfaces distinguishes Dingus's black and white and color photo drawings. Hand-built work, like his signature lens and camera, extends to these multimedia series in which he draws on the surface of the work. Intensity is created with silver-colored pencil and graphite—lines, layers, and markings that inscribe landscape forms, bushes, boulders, sky. The sensation is one not only of drawing but of sculpture, shaping space so that the subject seems to shift as we view it from different angles, allowing for varying depths of field and points of view. Standing before my own Dingus print of a pictograph and environs from the Marks in Place project, I feel this movement prompting a fresh awareness. The already mysterious image, itself a product of another culture's making and marking, appears and disappears just as if I were approaching it on foot. A Mexican dagger plant stands in the foreground etched with silver light; other details like the sky seem to move. These markings are palpable, their highlighting enabling us to sense the scene. They reflect and invite feeling, have a rhythm and almost a sound—vibrations. To me, they are like music. I'm engaged by the intensity of these photographic surfaces—the skin of the subject.

The idea of aspect may function in a different way, too. The sculptural qualities of certain pictures are like excavations, as if the artist is probing the surface for something below. Do we merely scratch the surface when we categorize work? In the mock documentary approach to photographing in his Regarding Technology or Llano Estacado series, Dingus explores unresolved issues of documentary, the effects of technology on how we view natural processes, and what he calls "mythical histories."

The spatial practices connected to aspect may be inseparable from a dreamed place or an imagined place, a storied place or an expressive one. In Here : There, we are drawn to a reconsideration of relationships. An Australian landscape bears the scars of mining expeditions; a grass soccer field originally denuded from toxic impacts of nearby mining operations remains gravel out of a sense of pride for the home team's advantage (figure 100). Industrial projects mirror one another's structure, as giant wooden pipes of an early hydroelectric system (figure 101) echo the pattern of a newer giant metal water relay, enormous pipes stretching into a wilderness, a metallic contour of the landscape. With gnome-like hope, Green Party members peek out from a mauled stump amid soon-to-be-felled trees in a dream of reclamation (figure 98). Dreams and imagination convene in the image of a south plains museum where (in a weird science encounter) a Mastodon skeleton is juxtaposed with a human femur, substantiating a claim for a mysterious race of men as archaeological science (figure 84). In a picture from Wyoming, the *Trail Head, Devil's Tower National Monument, Wyoming*, 2005–2007 (figure 94), parallels inform its natural namesake. An arriving truck at a Tasmanian art museum is painted with a reproduction of a romanticized nineteenth-century landscape (figure 97). The "facts" of these photos beg contemplation, questioning, looking below—or beyond—the surfaces.

This activity is perhaps most difficult yet essential when we encounter places and peoples we may find exotic or different. The Navajo and India landscapes may be unfamiliar, for example. But the pristine and unreachable essence of these sites is tempered by human presence. In *After the Sweat*, 1987–88 (figure 52), we see Navajos but also Anglos lying on the ground, absorbed in private reflections after a sweat lodge ceremony. In *Buddha with Onlookers*, 1988–90 (figure 55), several faces look directly into the camera, entering the frame and shrine. The exotic is humanized, the pristine challenged. In the Navajo series, everyday and exceptional coincide. For example, the hogan has a special meaning culturally. It is a living space but may also be the site of ritual, in which sand paintings created on the floor are part of a sacred healing ceremony. The sacred and profane may be one.

The Navajo, like any originally oral culture, value the highly participatory nature of sound that relies on memory. Mary Austin, the Southwest writer and philosopher, theorized what she called "the landscape line"—the way in which chants, stories, songs echoed the shape of the environment.[3] Memory was bound up in place. To be moved by stories is to give oneself to their life-changing influence, not simply to "memorize" them. Memorization and retelling, like ceremony, have to do with being properly placed, achieving a balance between interior and exterior states. Memory may be thought of as an internalization of aspect, a remembered intensity. Dingus's excavated lyrics invite us to value and care about the vernacular and the sacred, sometimes the same place—and more: to see ourselves in others' stories.

In his most recent work, Dingus tests the topographic experiments of his early work by taking to the sky. Interested initially in astrophotography, he attended star parties to get a sense of how professional and amateur astronomers view and photograph the heavens. He bought several telescopes and experimented with photographing the moon and stars. A breakthrough came when he traveled by air cross-country and began photographing the earth through airplane windows. Created by infrared photography, these images altered the common view from above: "The camera revealed things I could not see," he says, noting that infrared photography cuts through haze and fuzziness, revealing features not available to the human eye.[4] Making visible the invisible, these photos invite us again to question our relationship to place, to become aware of things we cannot see. Looking from such a great distance through this kind of filter—the ultimate redaction—human impact (and context) can be seen. Cultural and natural processes collide and intersect. This cosmic context mirrors earlier topographic fascination, bringing us full circle. We view the boulders that we also stand on.

I would like to think that photographing from space interrupts notions of photography merely stopping, freezing, or stilling time, providing instead a dramatic example of breaking the boundaries between photograph and subject space. Dingus defines the photograph as a "quotation," "an altered memory," an "artifact," suggesting the exploratory gaps his work creates.[5] Through these redactions, we learn that "being placed" means yielding our attention—that is, caring. His work offers us what John Berger called the gift of the artist in the face of indifference: "Poetry makes language care because it renders everything intimate. This intimacy is the result of the poem's labor, the result of the bringing together into intimacy of every act and noun and event and perspective to which the poem refers. There is often nothing more substantial to place against the cruelty and indifference of the world than this caring."[6] Or as these photographs show us, the land holds it all.

Notes

1. Leslie Marmon Silko, "Language and Landscape from a Pueblo Perspective," in *Yellow Woman and a Beauty of the Spirit* (New York: Touchstone Press, 1966), 53.
2. Brian Massumi, "The Autonomy of Affect," in "The Politics of Systems and Environments, Part II," special issue, *Cultural Critique* 31 (Autumn 1995): 86.
3. Mary Austin, *The American Rhythm* (New York: Houghton Mifflin, 1930), 55.
4. Unpublished interview with Shelley Armitage, 2013, n.p.
5. Unpublished interview with Peter Briggs, 2006-2007, n.p.
6. John Berger, "The Hour of Poetry," in *Selected Essays of John Berger*, ed. Geoff Dyer (New York: Pantheon Press, 2001), 451.

HERE : THERE

TASMANIA/NORTHERN U.S. PLAINS, 2005–2007

HERE : THERE EXAMINES CONTINUITIES BETWEEN the seemingly unrelated places of Tasmania, Australia, and the North American Great Plains. I photographed situations or places that represented evolving attitudes and relations between people and the natural world, with the recurring themes of ecology, settlement, and displacements of old technologies by new ones. To make these photographs, I created a camera body that used lenses from old 35mm cameras on medium format film to record the complete image circle cast by the lens.* The negatives were scanned and printed digitally to combine old and new photographic technologies.

* See Robert Hirsch's interview in *Transformational Imagemaking: Handmade Photography Since 1960* (New York: Focal Press, 2014), 148–51.

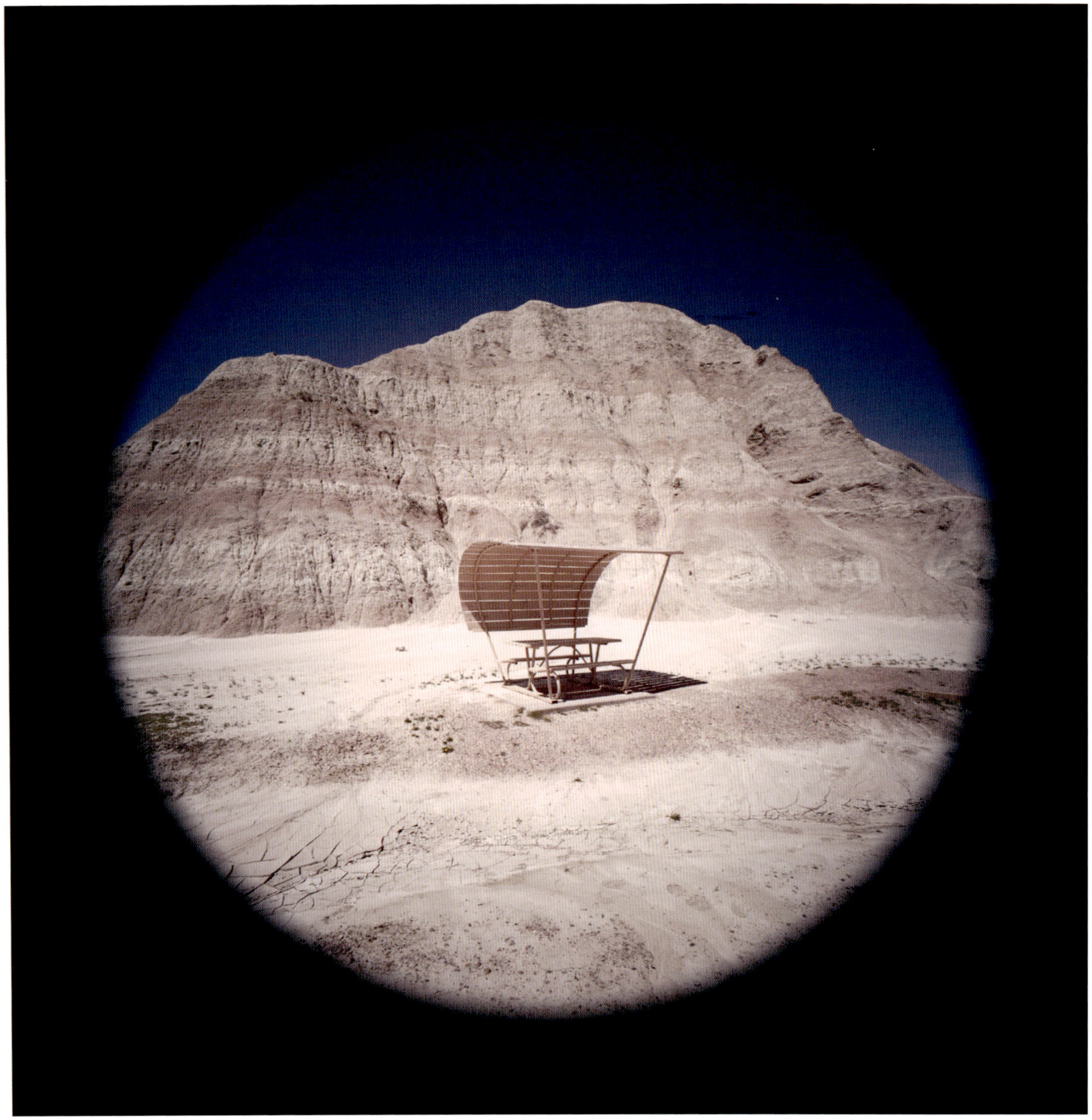

91. *Picnic Table, Badlands National Park, South Dakota*, 2005–2007.
Archival pigment print, 22 × 22 in.
In the collection of the Museum of Texas Tech University, Lubbock

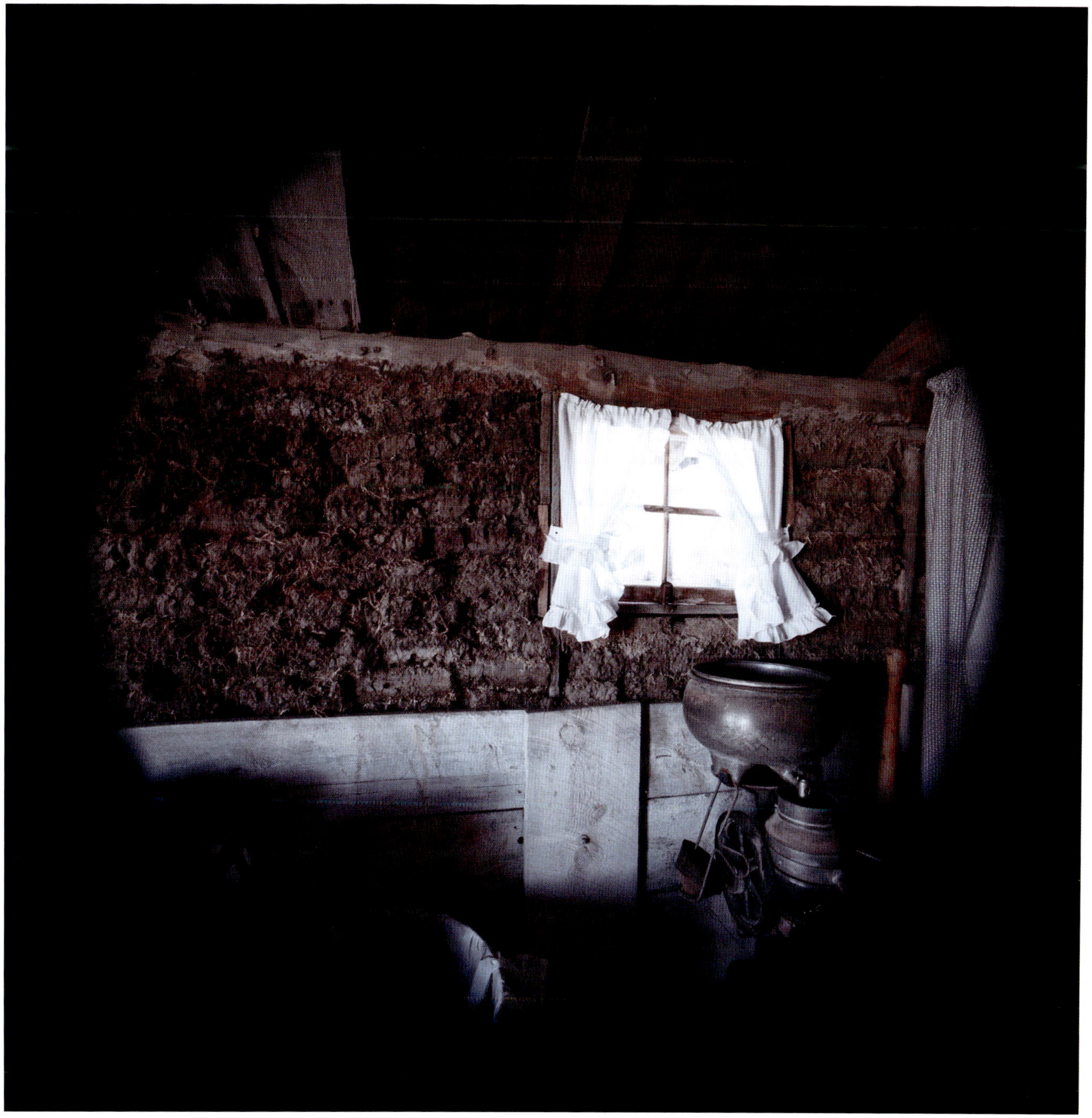

92. *Curtained Window in a Sod House, Prairie Homestead, Philip, South Dakota*, 2005–2007.
Archival pigment print, 22 × 22 in.
In the collection of the Museum of Texas Tech University, Lubbock

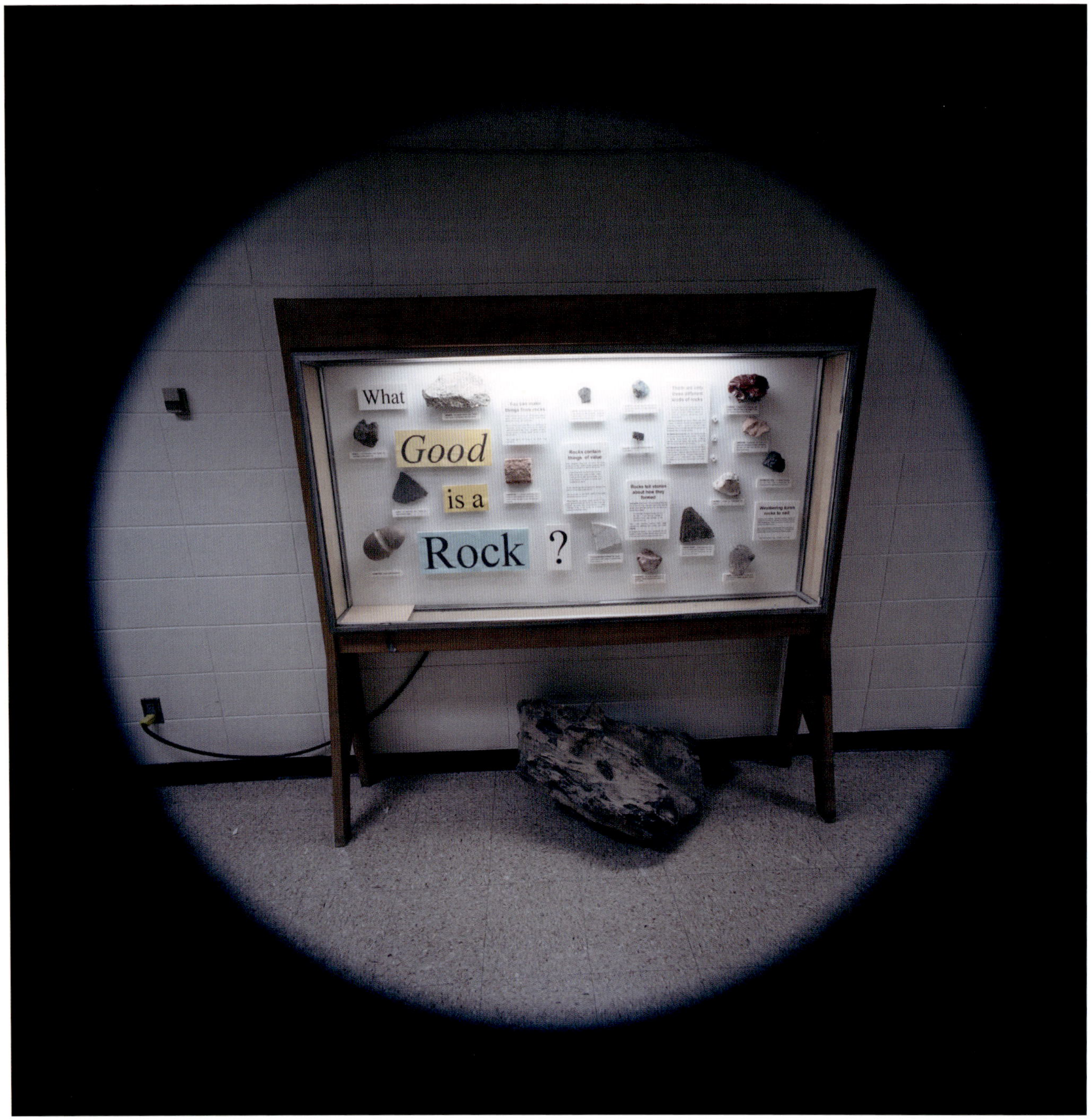

93. *Rock Display, Chadron State College, Chadron, Nebraska*, 2005–2007.
Archival pigment print, 22 × 22 in.
In the collection of the Museum of Texas Tech University, Lubbock

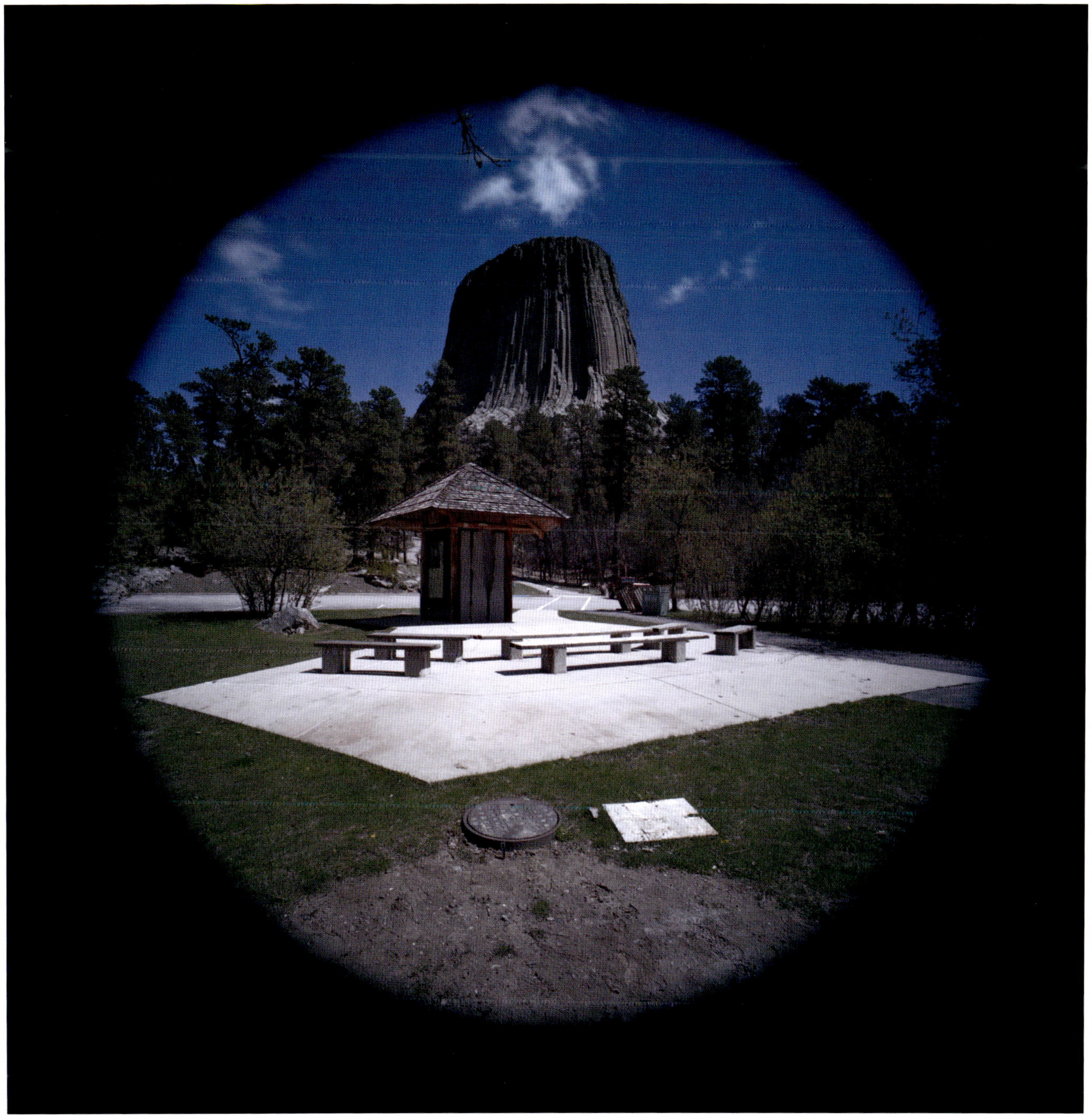

94. *Trail Head, Devil's Tower National Monument, Wyoming*, 2005–2007.
Archival pigment print, 22 × 22 in.
In the collection of the Museum of Texas Tech University, Lubbock

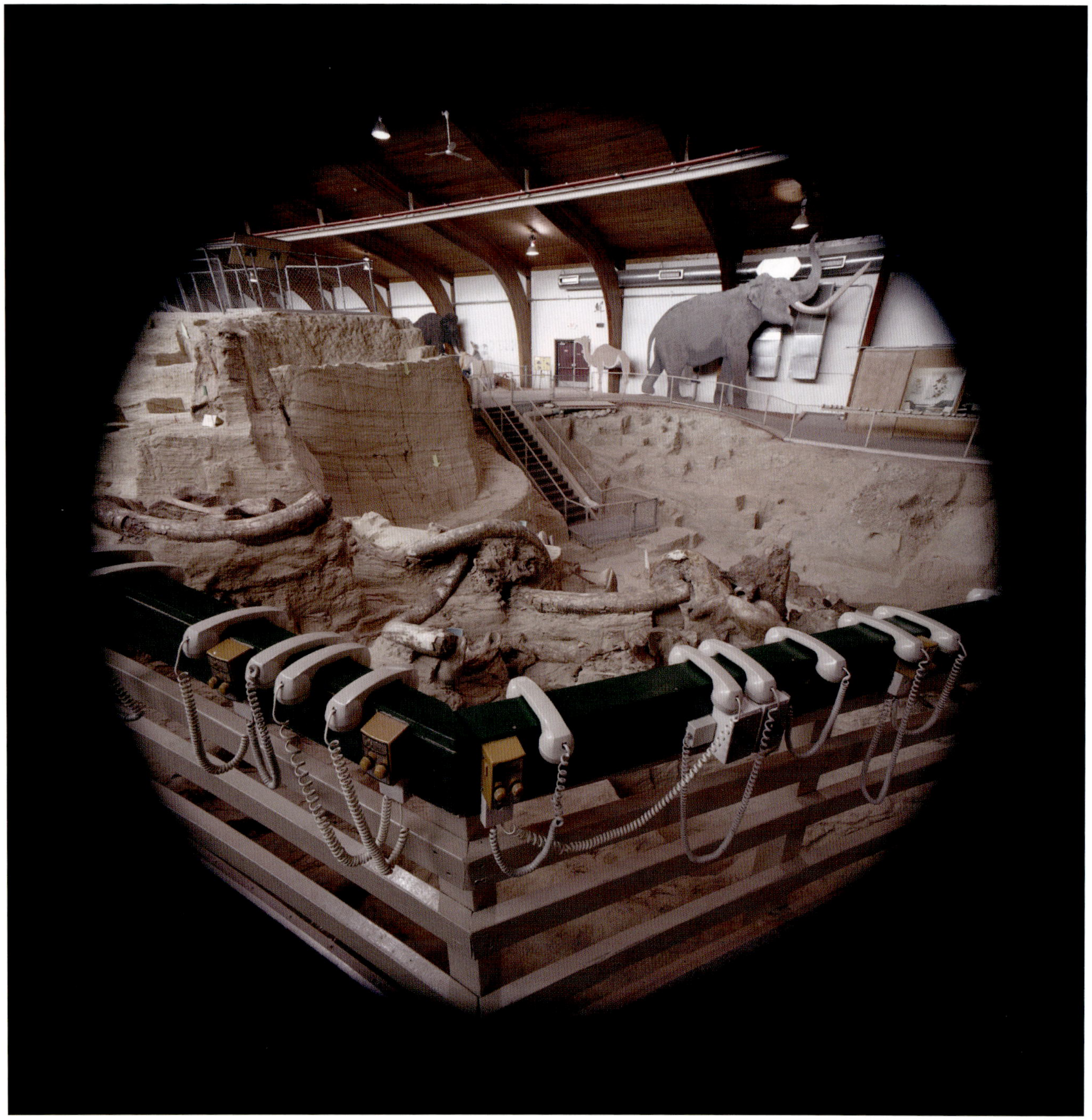

95. *Mammoth Site, Hot Springs, South Dakota*, 2005–2007.
Archival pigment print, 22 × 22 in.
In the collection of the Museum of Texas Tech University, Lubbock

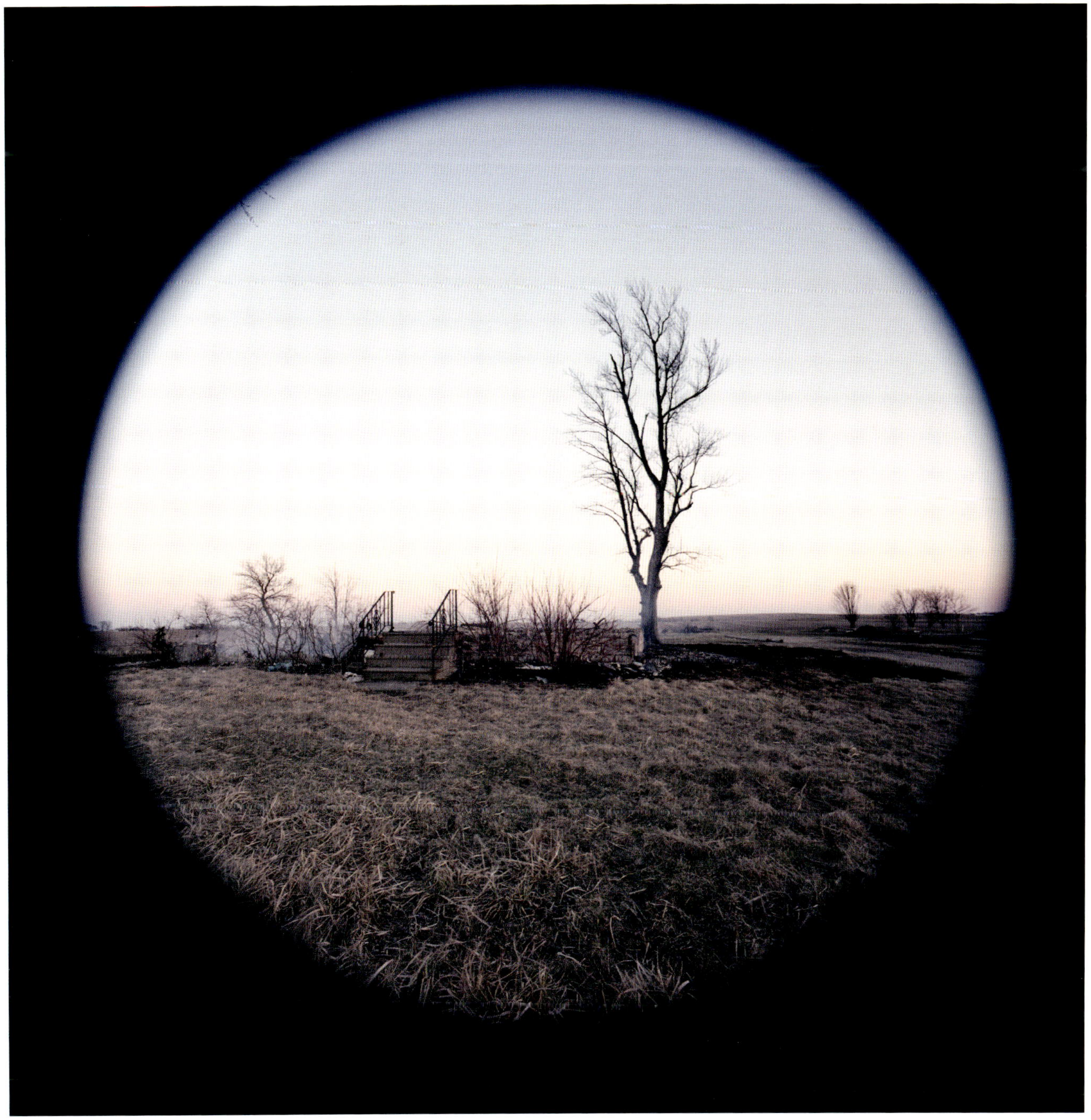

96. *Smoking Foundation near DeKalb, Illinois*, 2005–2007.
Archival pigment print, 22 × 22 in.
In the collection of the Museum of Texas Tech University, Lubbock

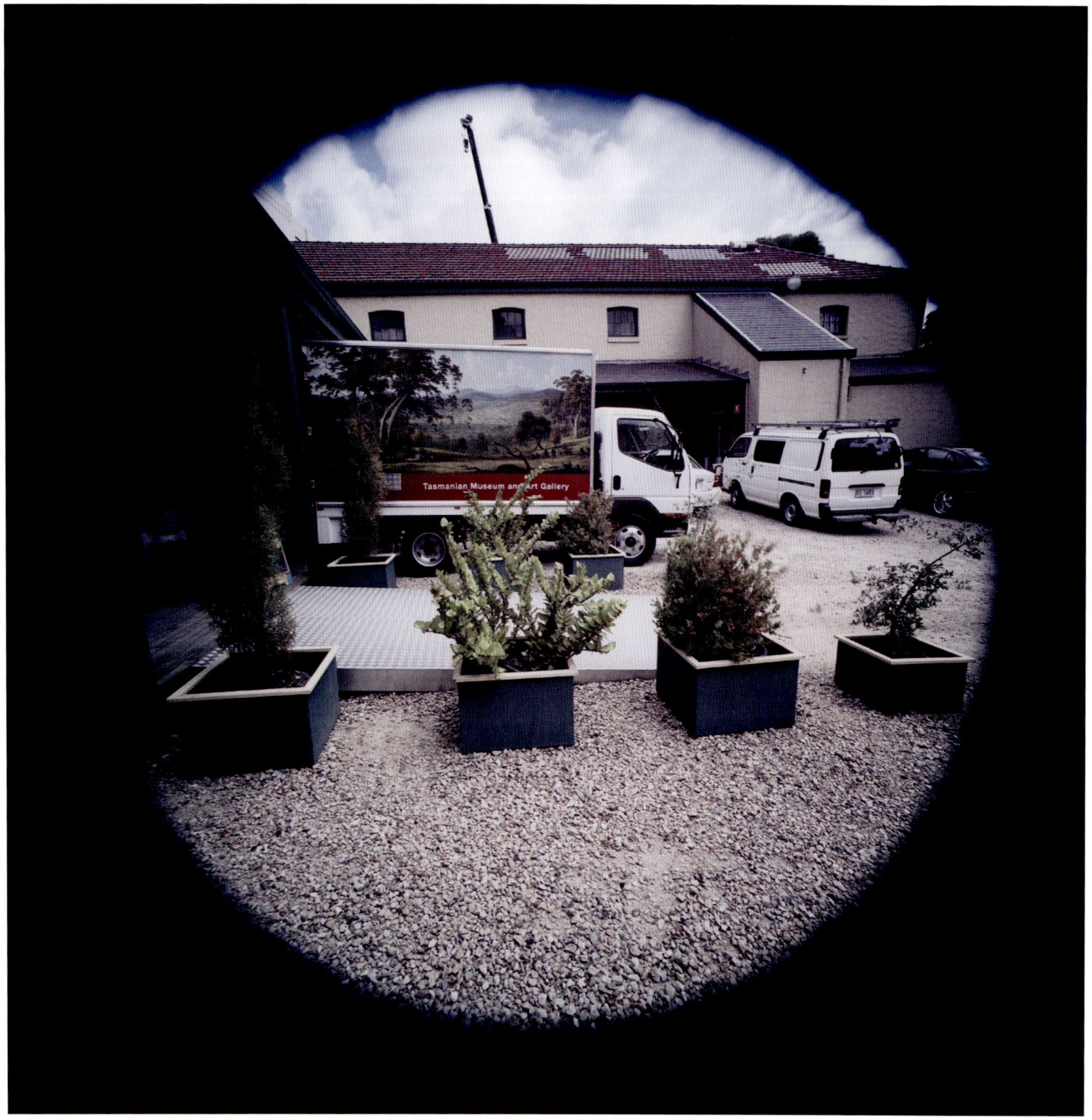

97. *Museum Courtyard, Tasmanian Museum and Art Gallery, Hobart, Tasmania, Australia*, 2005–2007.
Archival pigment print, 22 × 22 in.
In the collection of the Museum of Texas Tech University, Lubbock

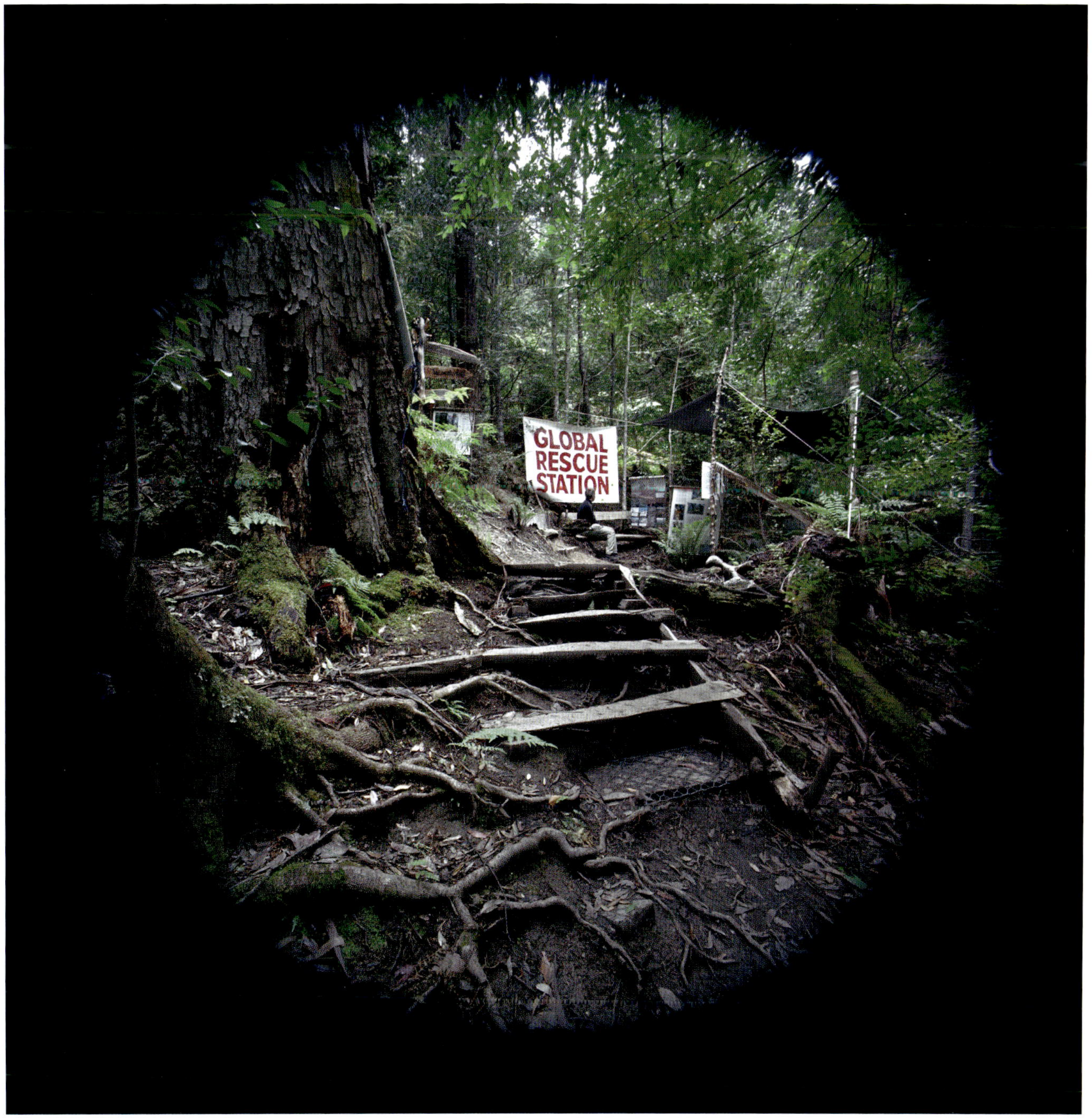

98. *Global Rescue Station (Old Growth Forest Scheduled for Clear-Cutting), The Styx Valley of the Giants, Tasmania, Australia*, 2005–2007.
Archival pigment print, 22 × 22 in.
In the collection of the Museum of Texas Tech University, Lubbock

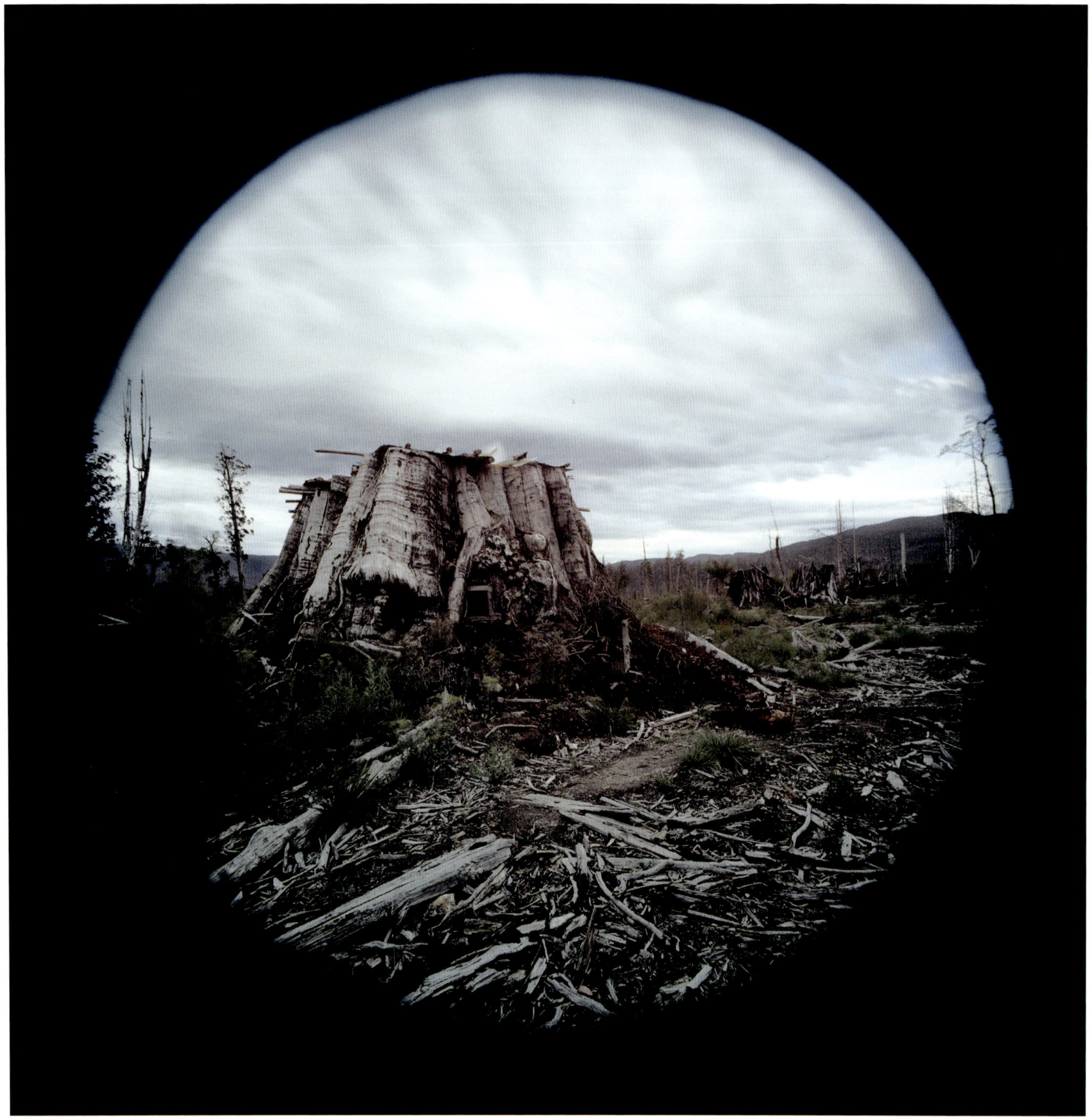

99. *Stump Shelter in a Clear-Cut Area of Old Growth Forest, The Styx Valley of the Giants, Tasmania, Australia*, 2005–2007.
Archival pigment print, 22 × 22 in.
In the collection of the Museum of Texas Tech University, Lubbock

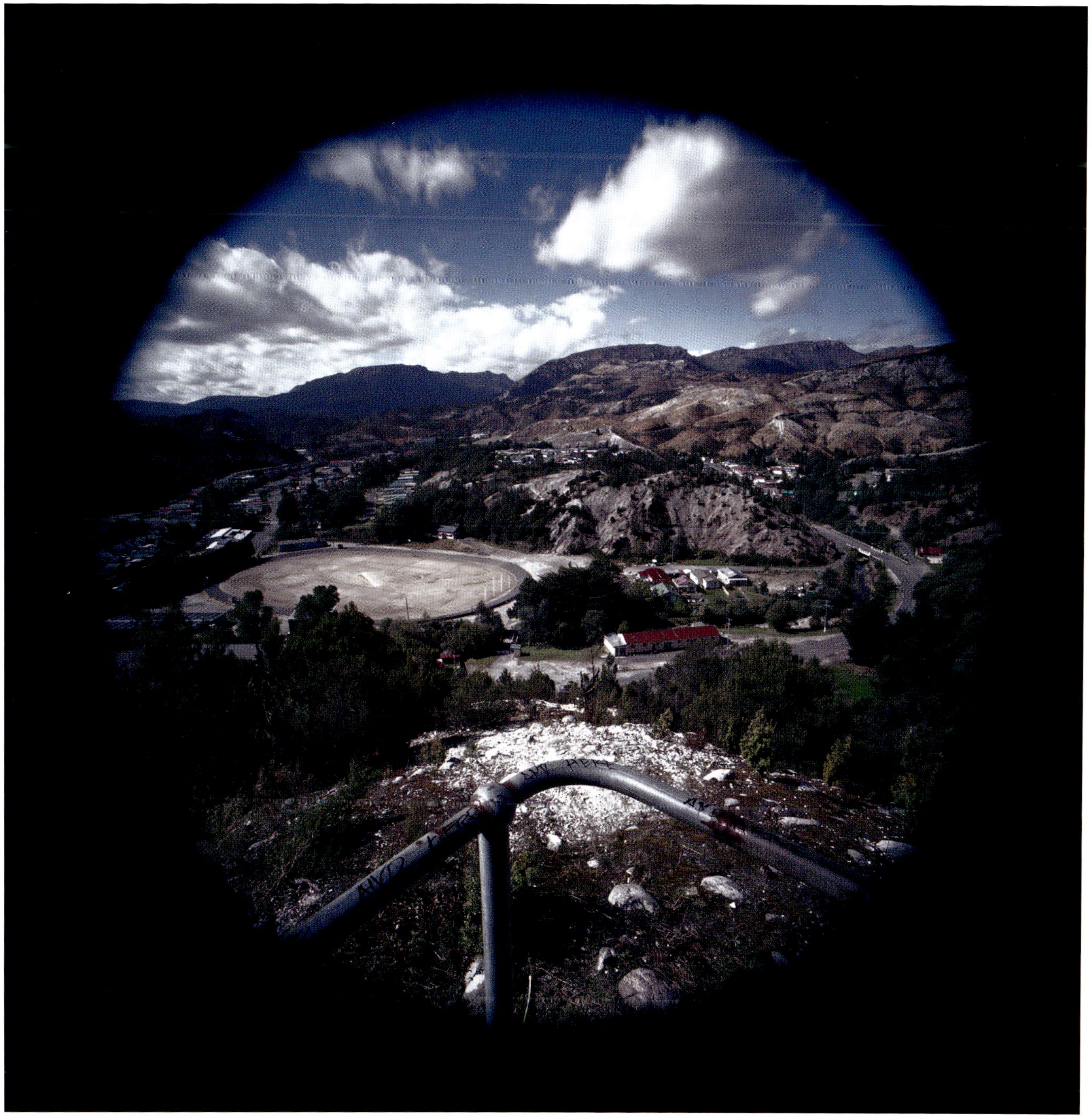

100. *Queenstown Overlook (Gravel Soccer Field near Landscape Denuded by the Mt. Lyell Mine), Queenstown, Tasmania, Australia*, 2005–2007. Archival pigment print, 22 × 22 in.

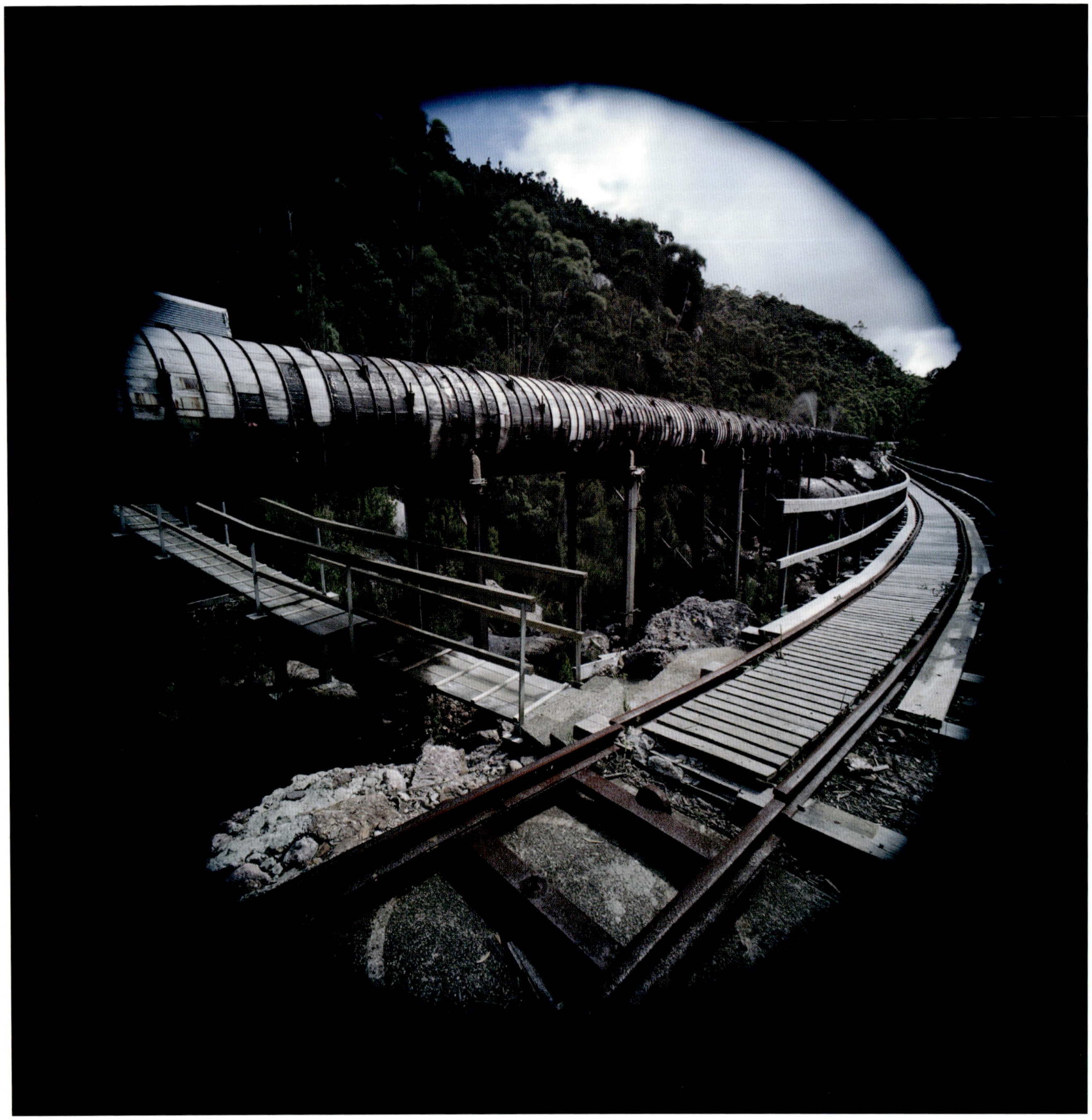

101. *Hydroelectric Water Transportation, Lake Margaret Dam, Tasmania, Australia*, 2005–2007.
Archival pigment print, 22 × 22 in.
In the collection of the Museum of Texas Tech University, Lubbock

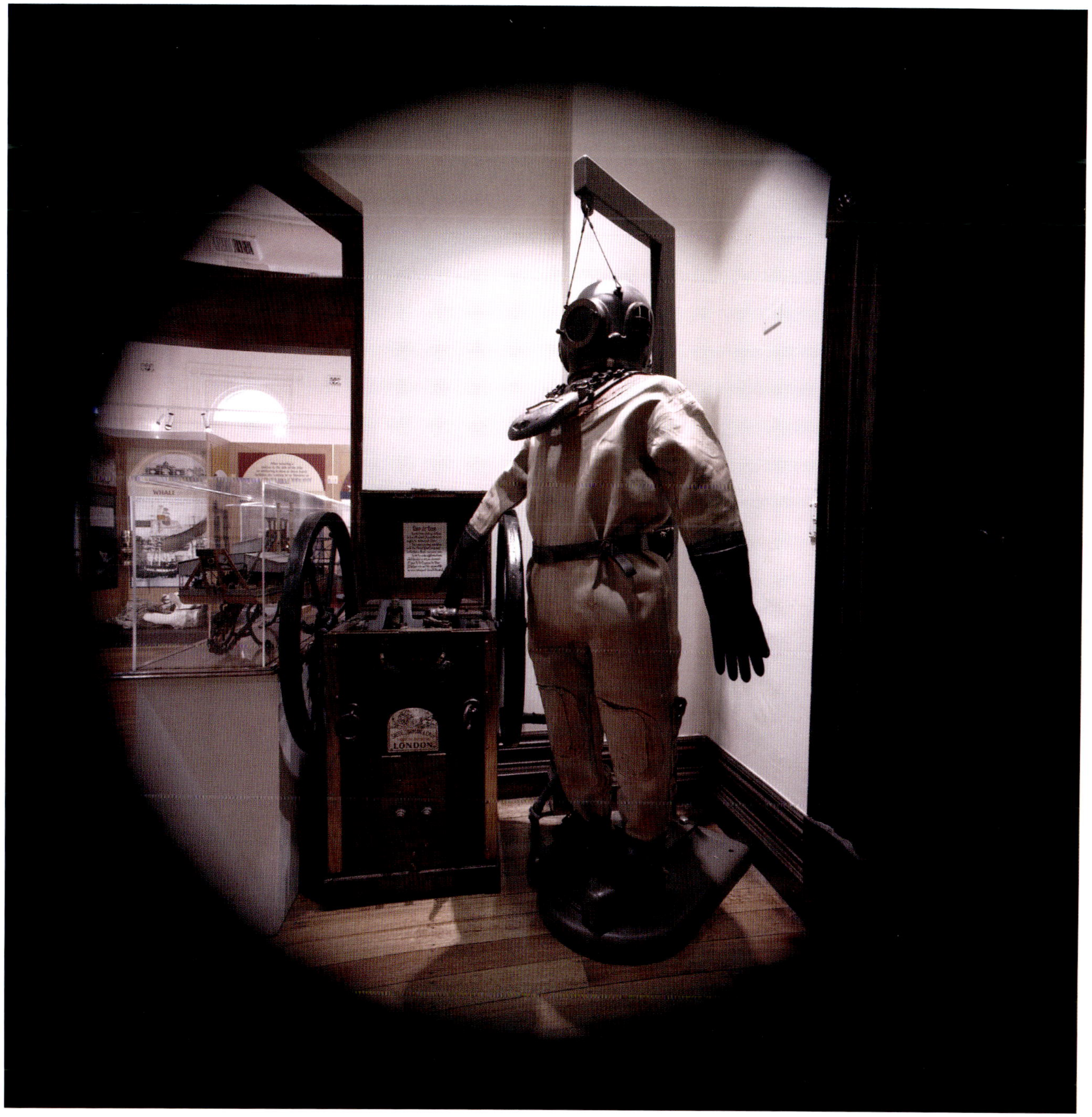

102. *Deep Sea Diver, Maritime Museum of Tasmania, Hobart, Tasmania, Australia*, 2005–2007.
Archival pigment print, 22 × 22 in.
In the collection of the Museum of Texas Tech University, Lubbock

Star Party & Infrared Aerials, 2012–2015

Inspired by what I learned about how amateur and professional astronomers tease information from digital image files, I began to experiment with shooting and creating images by adapting some of their methods. I modified a DSLR camera to record visual information from any part of the full spectrum. For both the Star Party and the IR Aerials series, I shot infrared images that looked back and forth between the heavens and the earth.

STAR PARTY

The Star Party photographs were made by taping a homemade infrared filter over my electronic flash so that I could invisibly photograph people in the dark without disturbing them. The infrared flash is invisible and does not disrupt the night vision needed by astronomers.

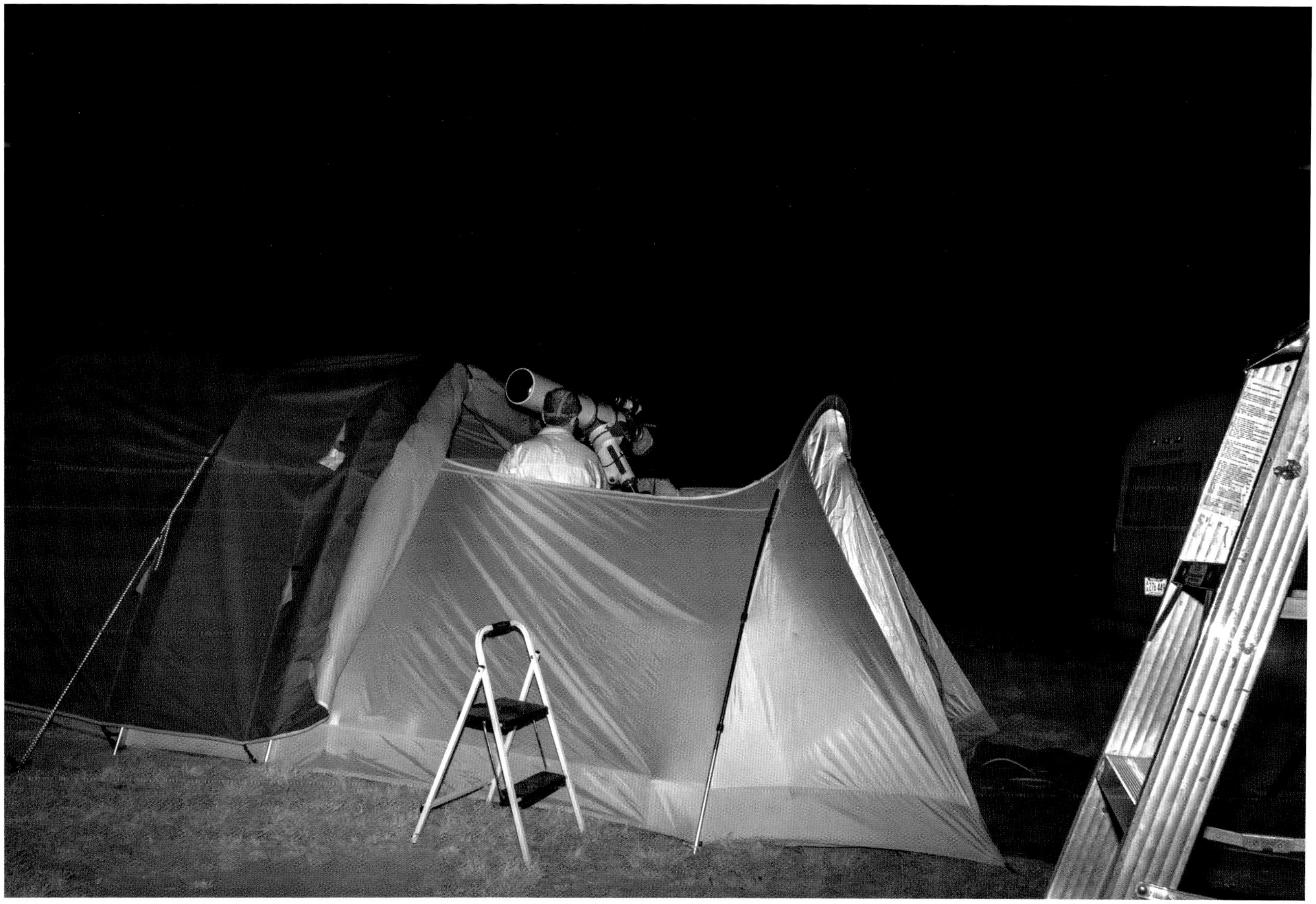

103. *Observatory Tent, Okie-Tex Star Party, Kenton, Oklahoma*, 2013–15.
Archival pigment print, 13⅓ × 20 in.
In the collection of the Museum of Texas Tech University, Lubbock

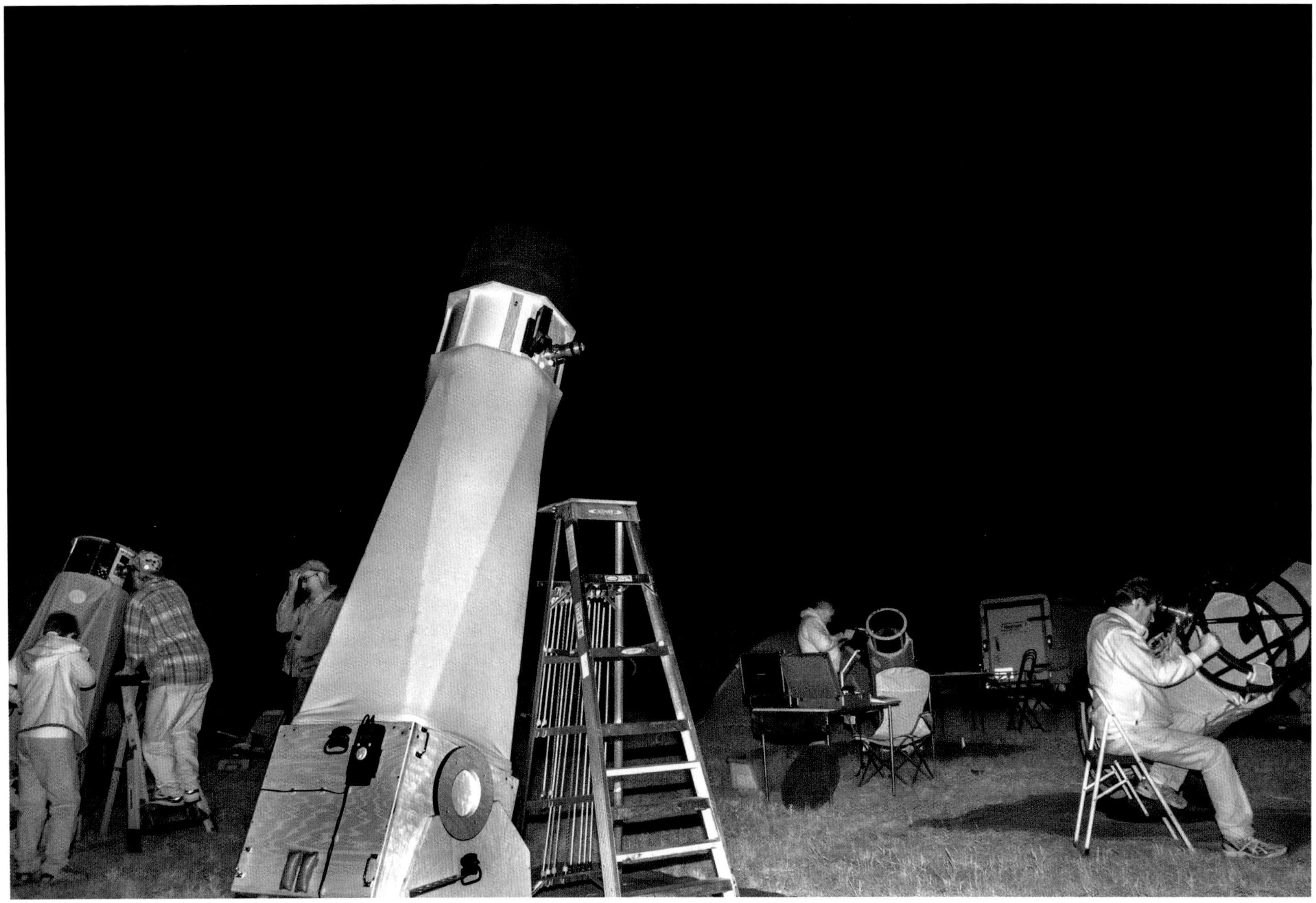

104. *Many Views, Okie-Tex Star Party, Kenton, Oklahoma*, 2013–15.
Archival pigment print, 13⅓ × 20 in.
In the collection of the Museum of Texas Tech University, Lubbock

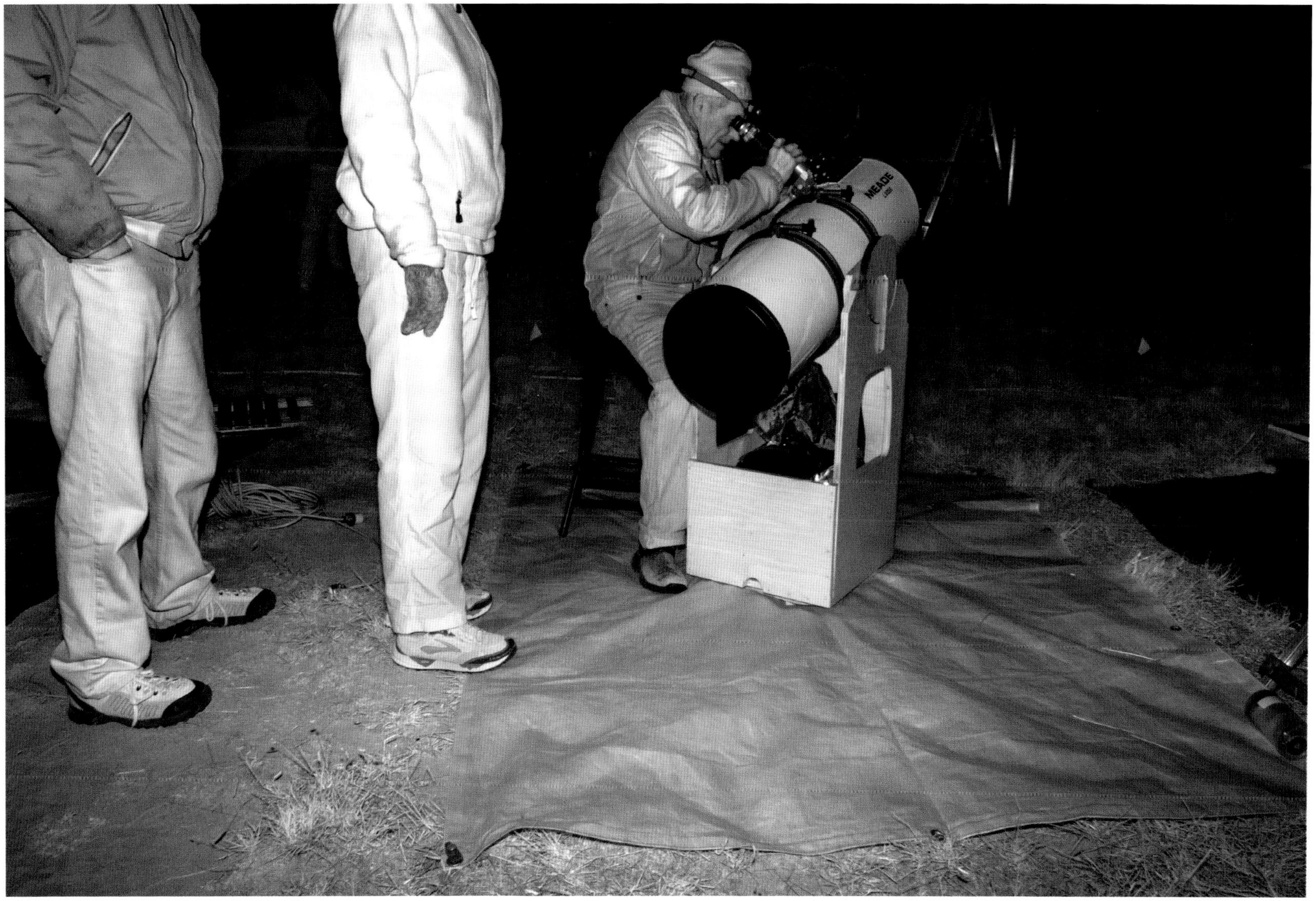

105. *Queue for a View, Okie-Tex Star Party, Kenton, Oklahoma*, 2013–15.
Archival pigment print, 13⅓ × 20 in.
In the collection of the Museum of Texas Tech University, Lubbock

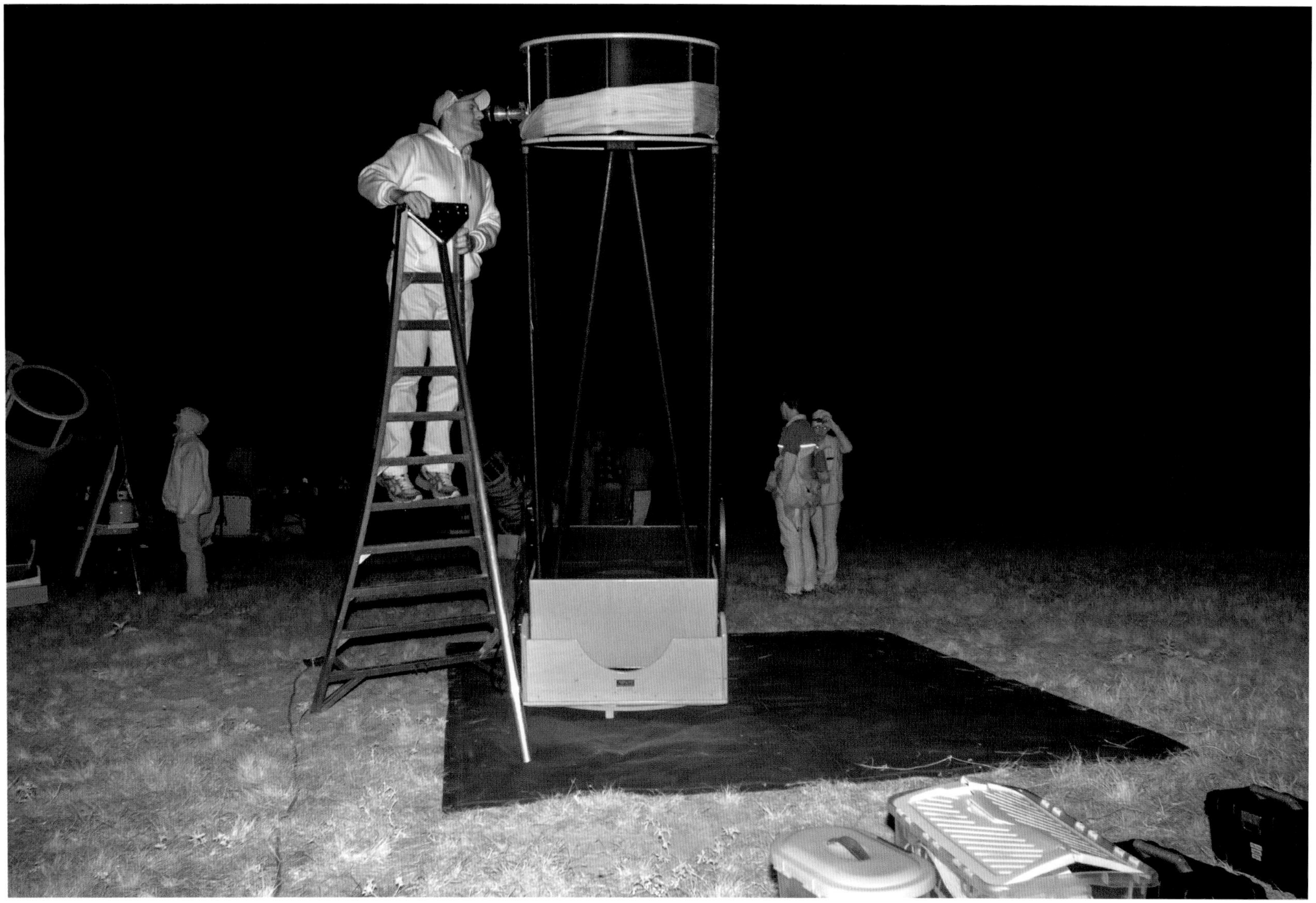

106. *Tall Dob, Okie-Tex Star Party, Kenton, Oklahoma*, 2013–15.
Archival pigment print, 13⅓ × 20 in.
In the collection of the Museum of Texas Tech University, Lubbock

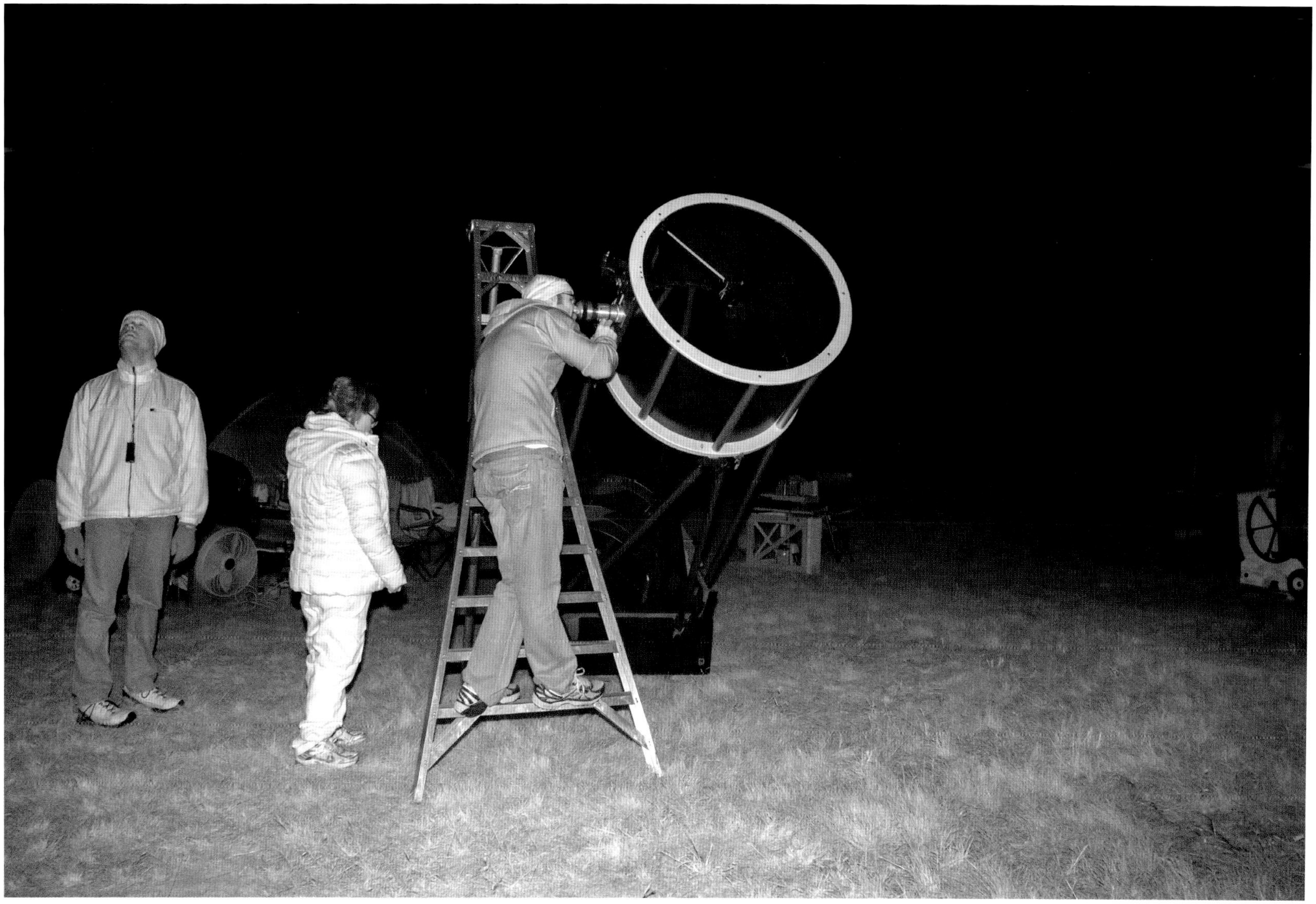

107. *Elaborate ATM, Okie-Tex Star Party, Kenton, Oklahoma*, 2013–15.
Archival pigment print, 13⅓ × 20 in.
In the collection of the Museum of Texas Tech University, Lubbock

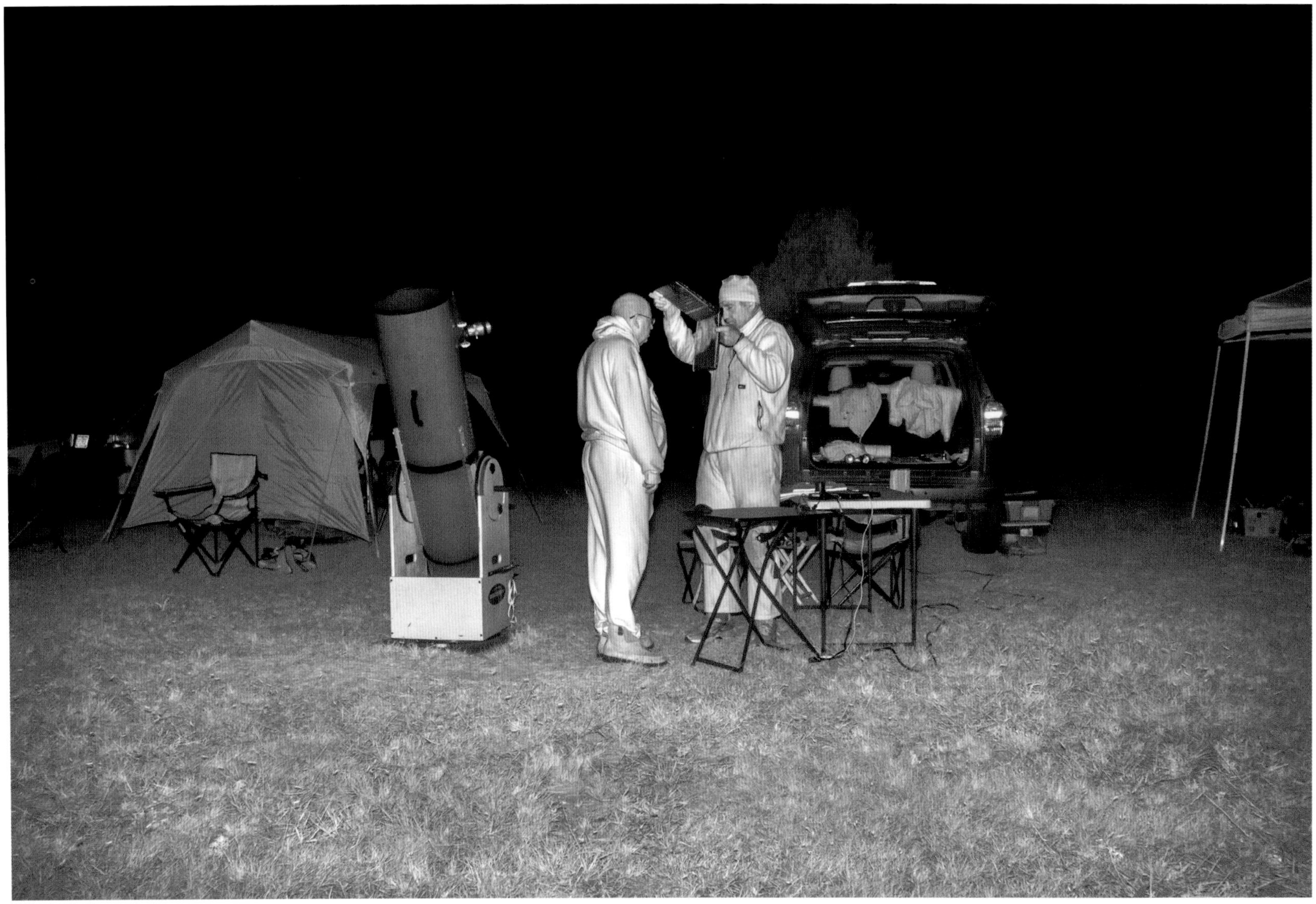

108. *Shared References, Okie-Tex Star Party, Kenton, Oklahoma*, 2014–15.
Archival pigment print, 13⅓ × 20 in.
In the collection of the Museum of Texas Tech University, Lubbock

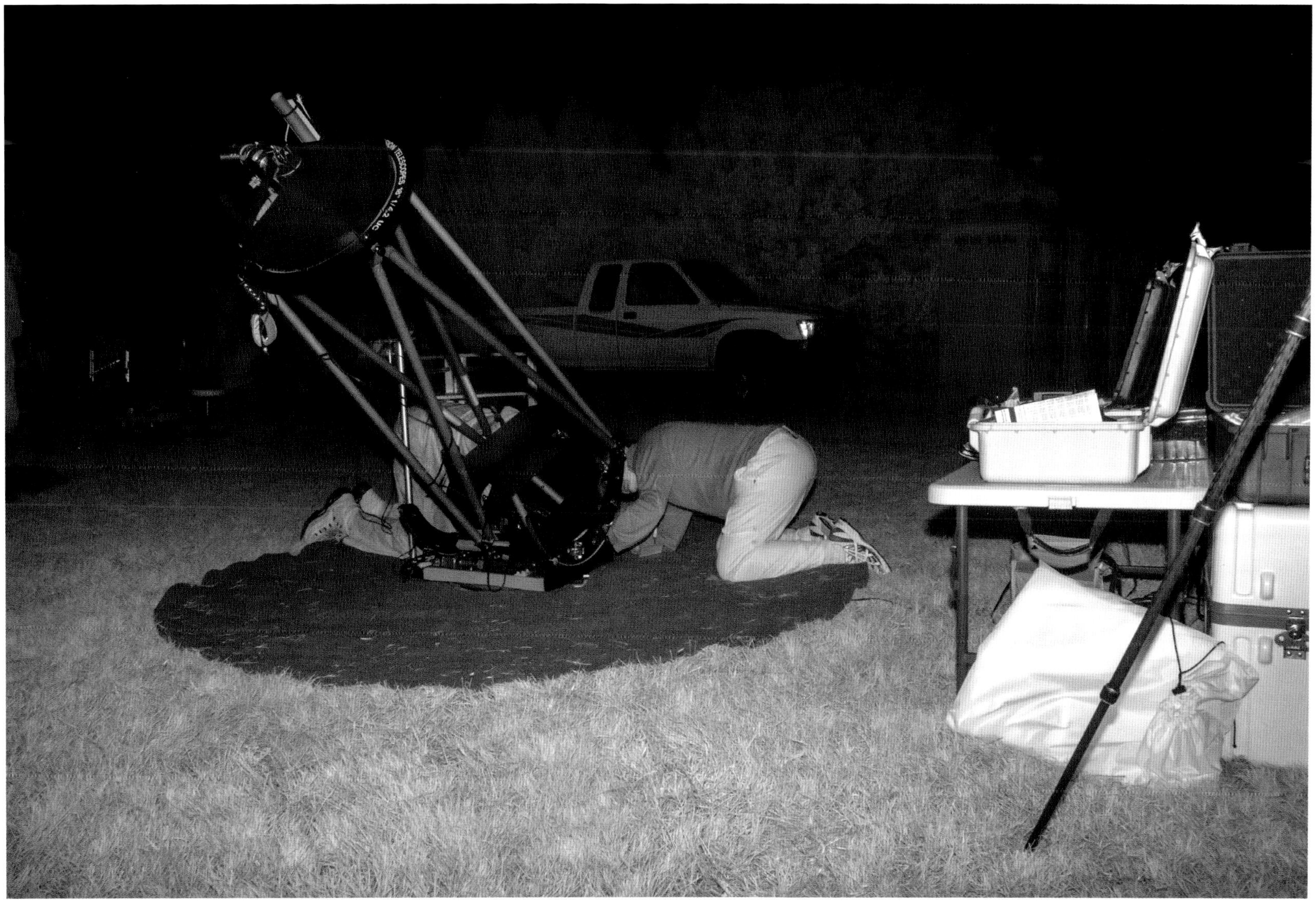

109. *Tracking Adjustments, Okie-Tex Star Party, Kenton, Oklahoma,* 2014–15.
Archival pigment print, 13⅓ × 20 in.
In the collection of the Museum of Texas Tech University, Lubbock

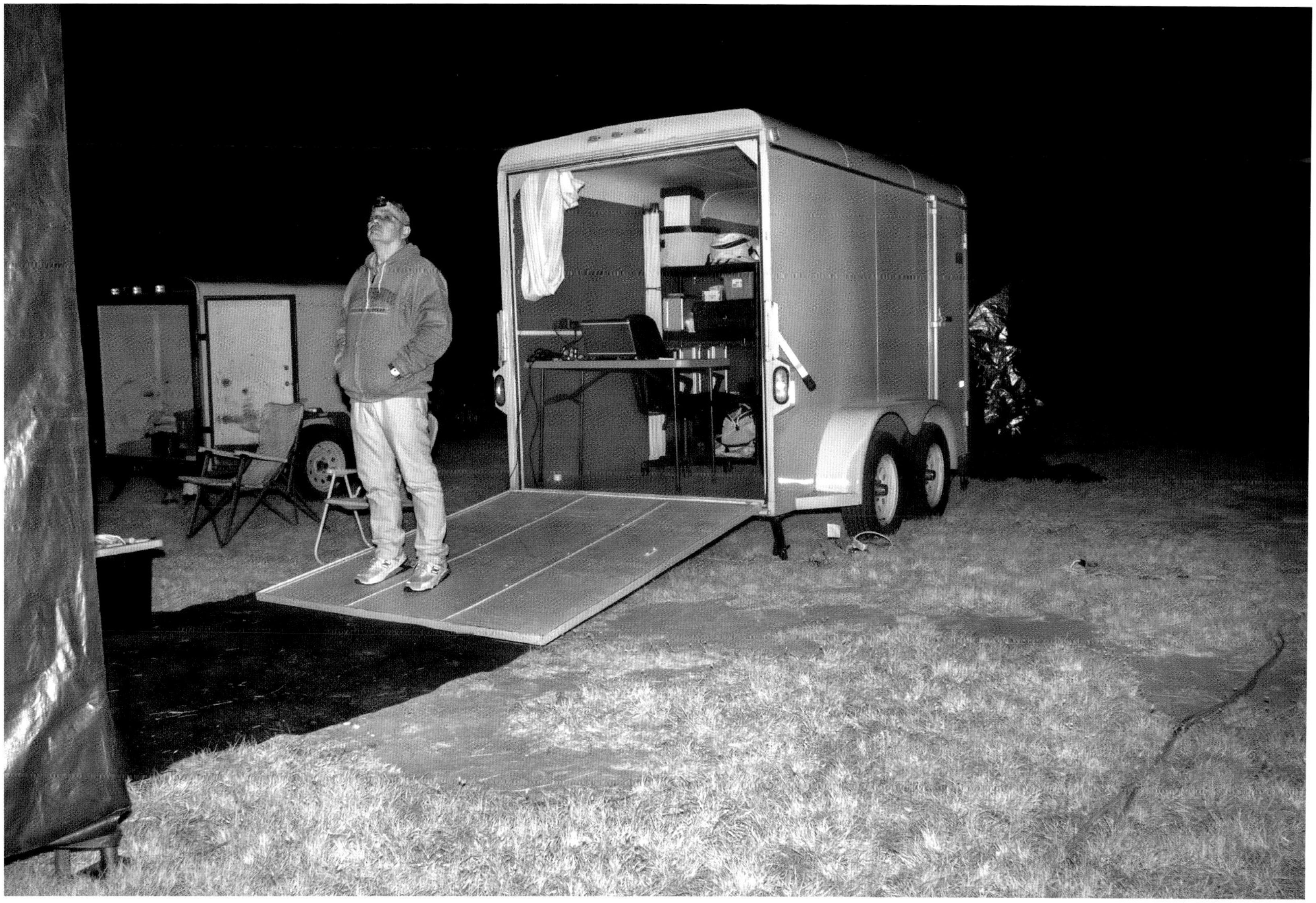

110. *Observation Trailer, Okie-Tex Star Party, Kenton, Oklahoma*, 2014–15.
Archival pigment print, 13⅓ × 20 in.
In the collection of the Museum of Texas Tech University, Lubbock

IR Aerials

The IR Aerials were shot in bright daylight with an infrared filter behind my lens, looking down at the earth from commercial passenger airplanes. The infrared sees clearly through the smeared windows of the airplane and atmospheric haze, revealing sharp details in the landscape and making evidence of human activity visible in unexpected ways.

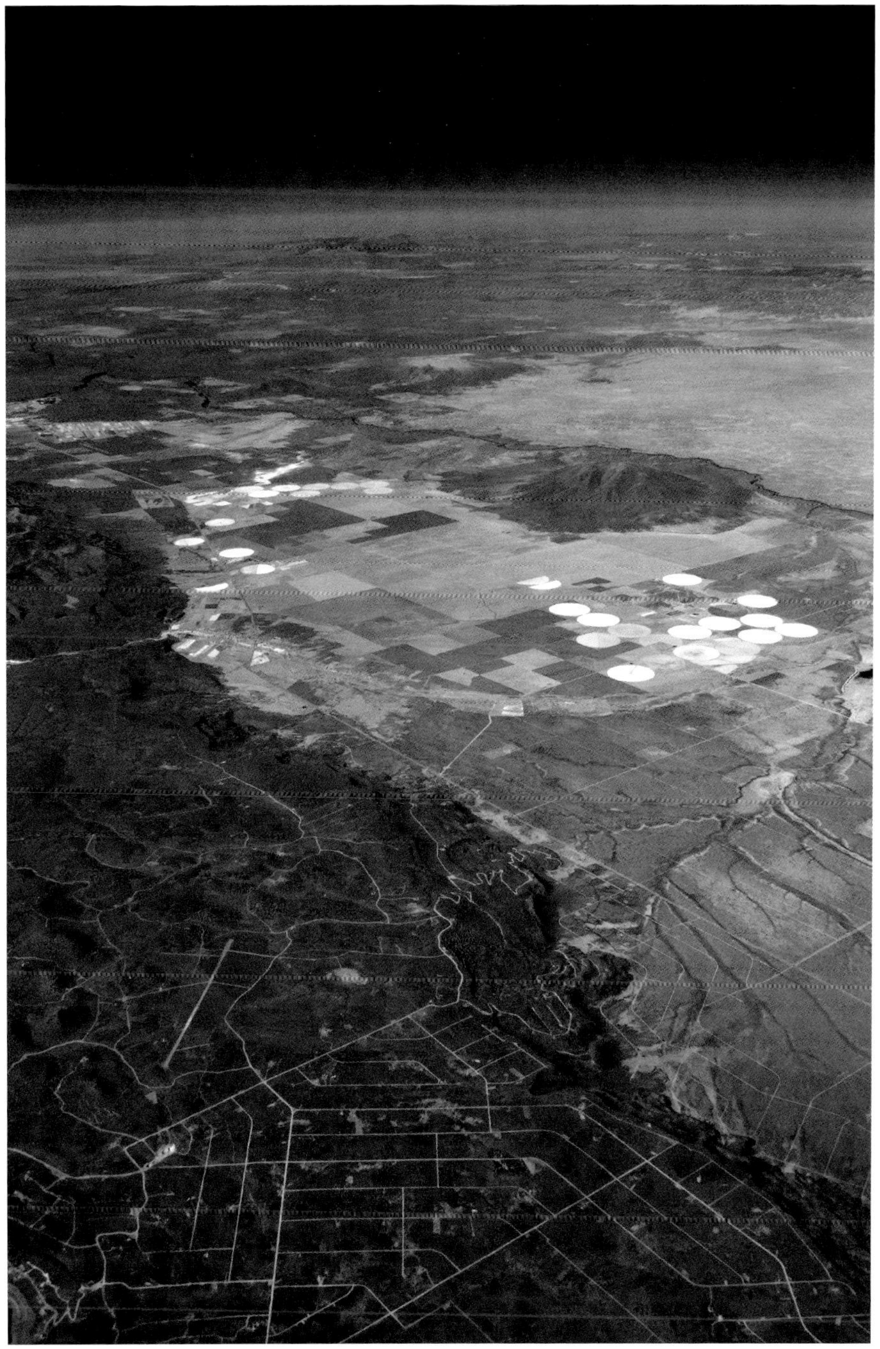

111. *Lined Escarpment and Circles (SLC→DFW→LBB)*, 2012–15.
Archival pigment print, 33 × 22 in.
In the collection of the Museum of Texas Tech University, Lubbock

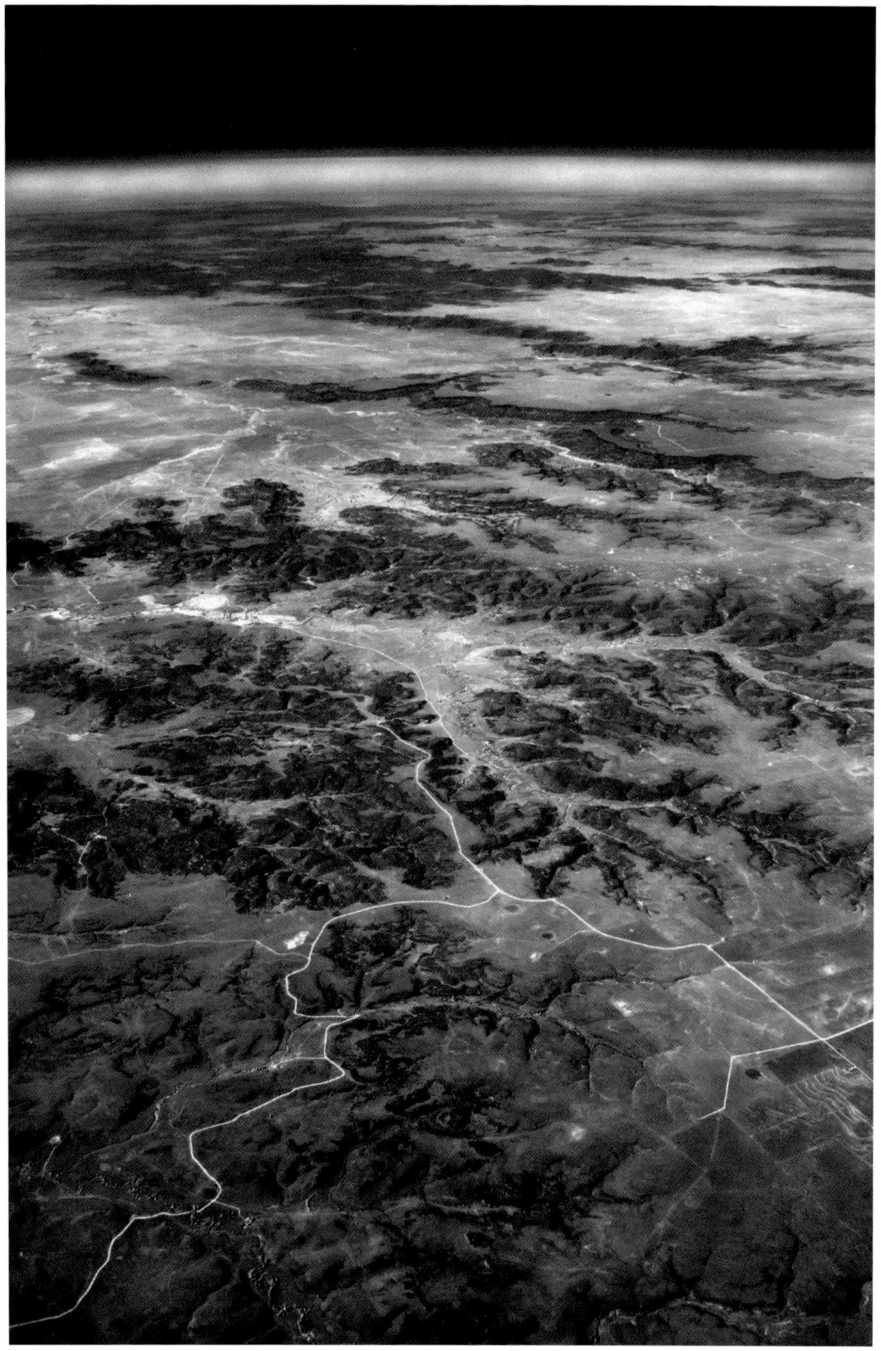

112. *Circumvented Canyons (SLC→DFW→LBB)*, 2012–15.
Archival pigment print, 33 × 22 in.
In the collection of the Museum of Texas Tech University, Lubbock

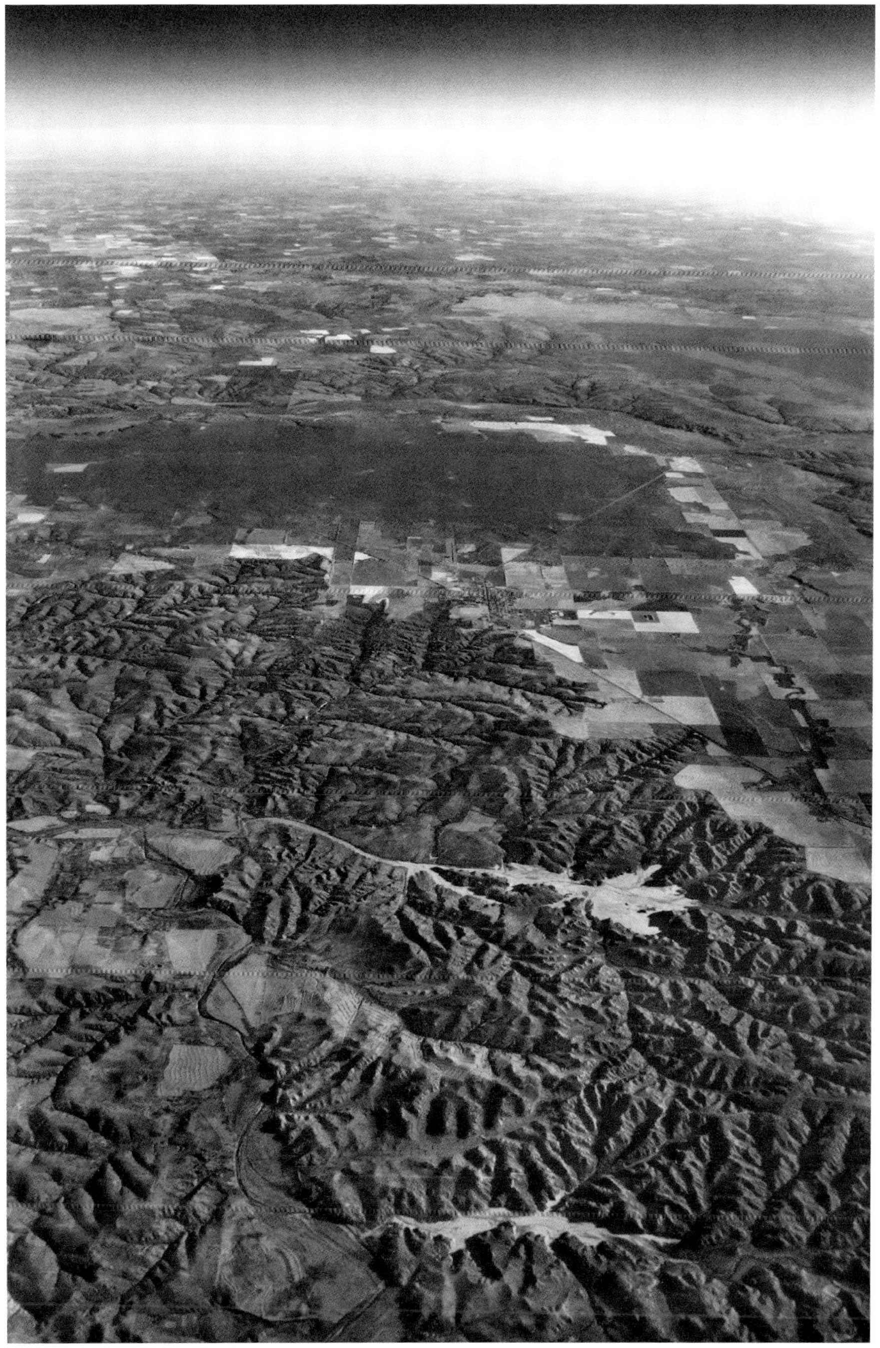

113. *Fields and Gullies (MDW→DAL→LBB)*, 2013–15.
Archival pigment print, 33 × 22 in.
In the collection of the Museum of Texas Tech University, Lubbock

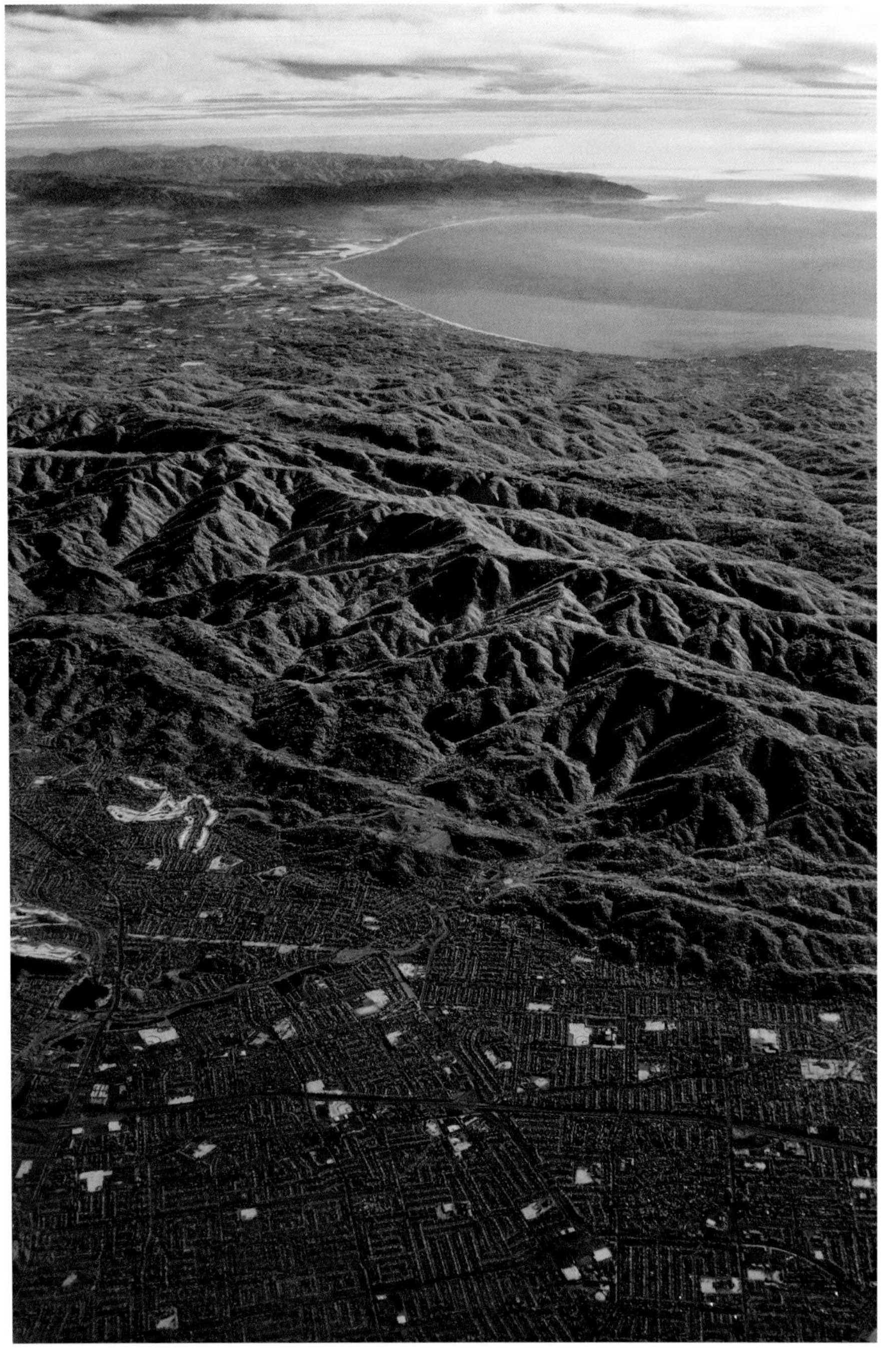

114. *Silicon Valley (OAK→LAS→LBB)*, 2014–15.
Archival pigment print, 33 × 22 in.
In the collection of the Museum of Texas Tech University, Lubbock

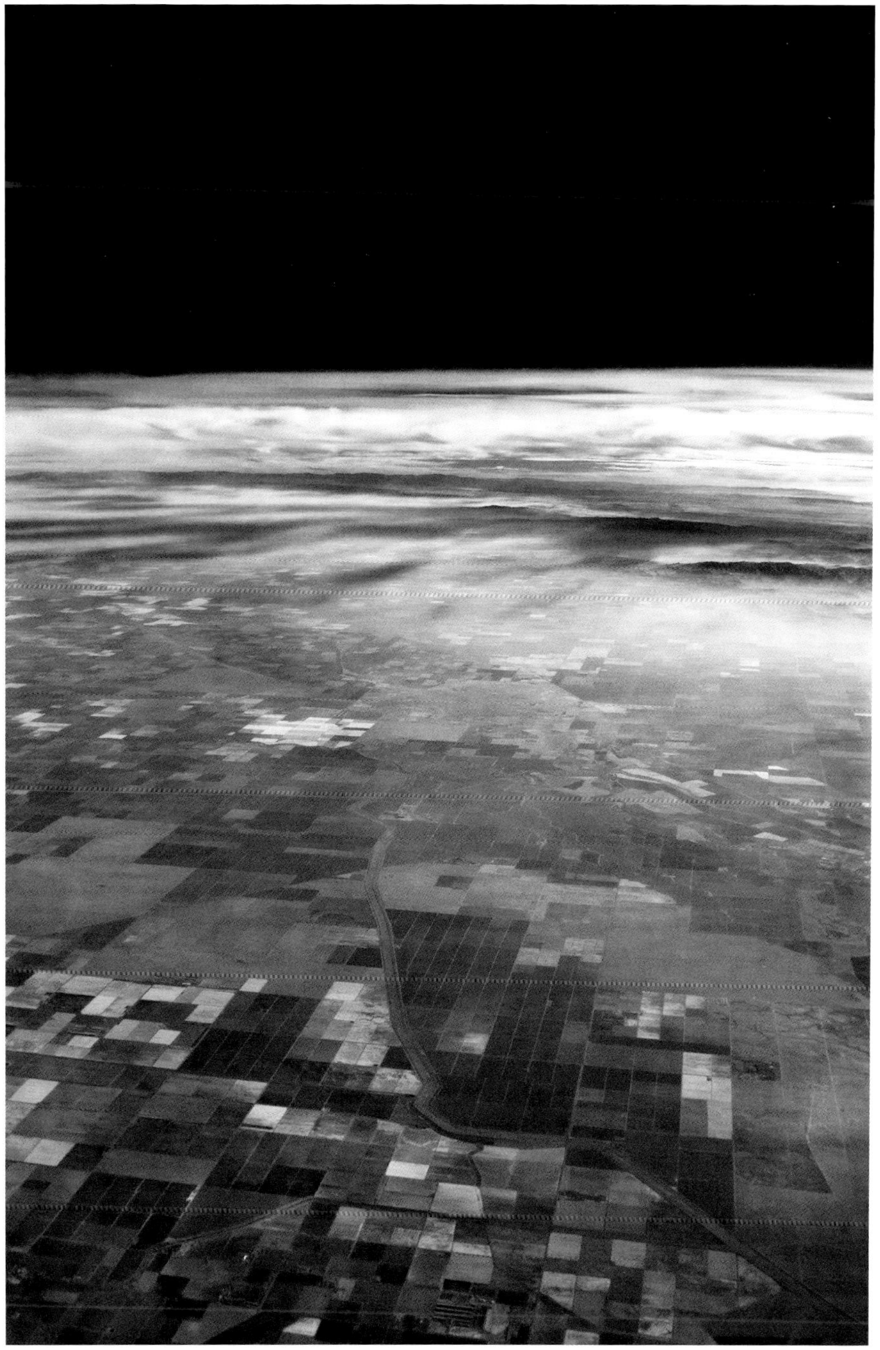

115. *Irregular Flatland Grid (OAK→LAS→LBB)*, 2014–15.
Archival pigment print, 33 × 22 in.
In the collection of the Museum of Texas Tech University, Lubbock

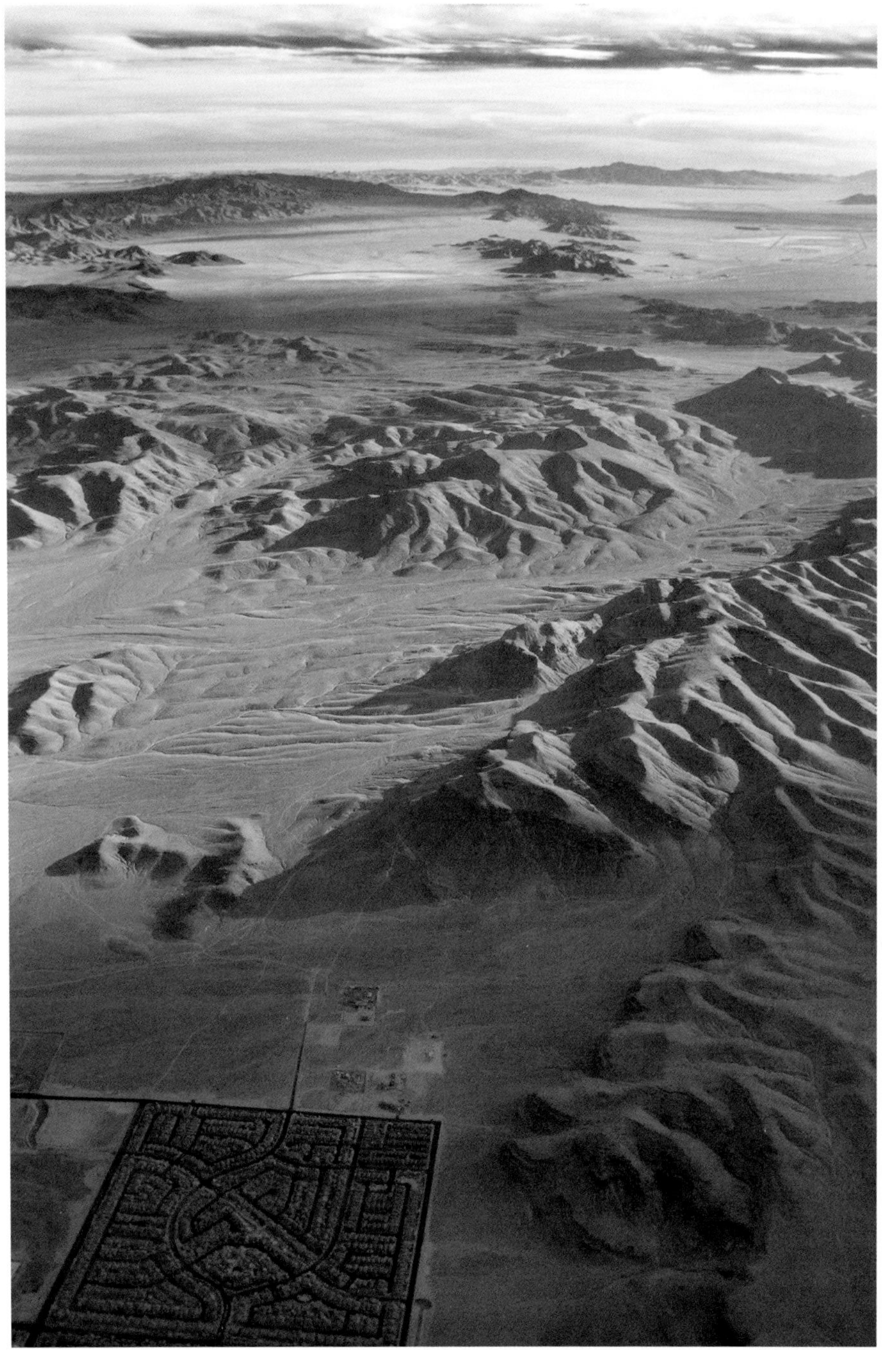

116. *Suburban Maze (OAK→LAS→LBB)*, 2014–15.
Archival pigment print, 33 × 22 in.
In the collection of the Museum of Texas Tech University, Lubbock

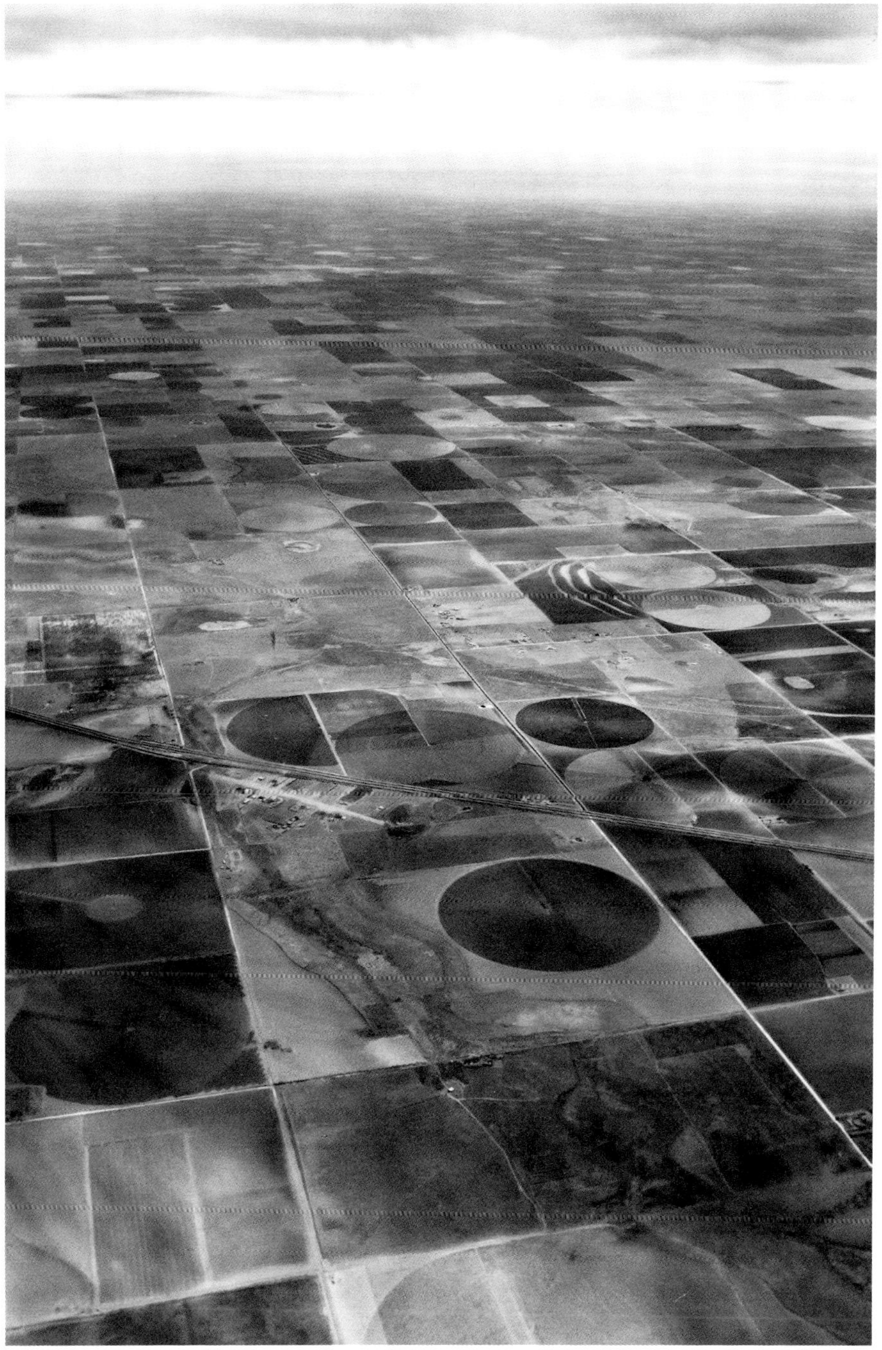

117. *Reworked Fields with Circles (LBB→LAS→OAK)*, 2014–15.
Archival pigment print, 33 × 22 in.

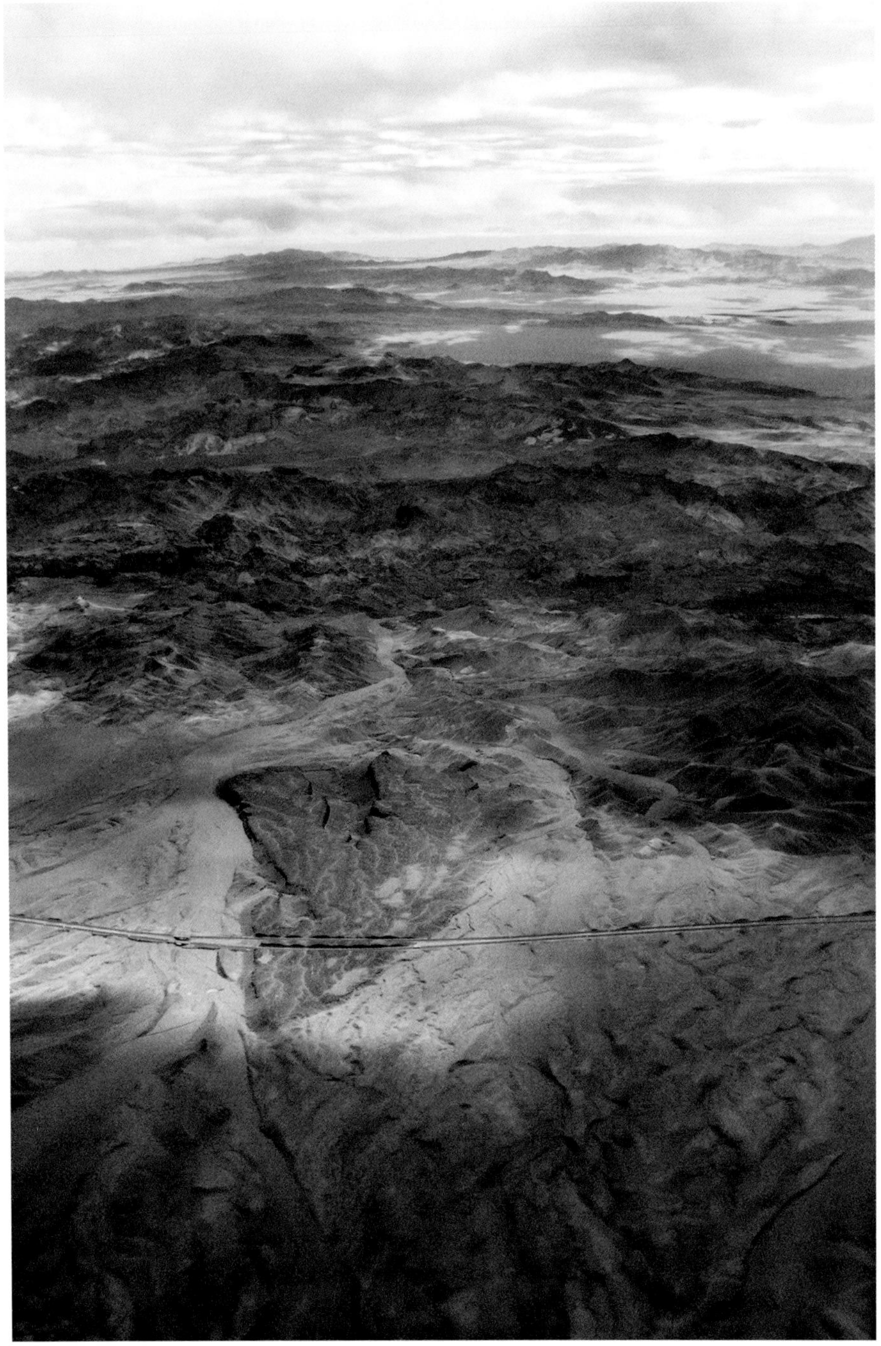

118. *Ridged Desert Highway (LBB→LAS→OAK)*, 2014–15.
Archival pigment print, 33 × 22 in.
In the collection of the Museum of Texas Tech University, Lubbock

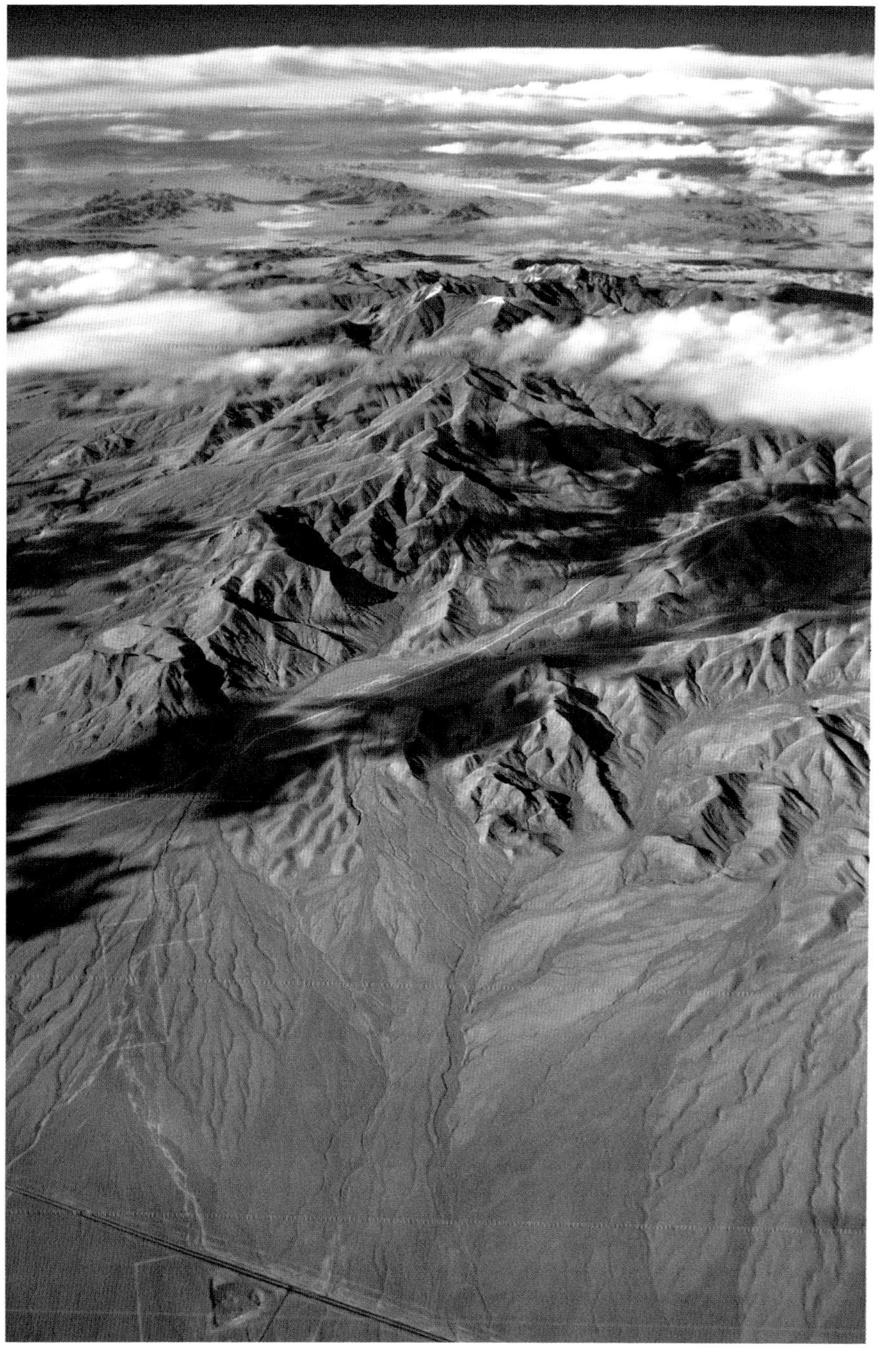

119. *Line Marked Mountains (LBB→LAS→OAK)*, 2014–15.
Archival pigment print, 33 × 22 in.
In the collection of the Museum of Texas Tech University, Lubbock

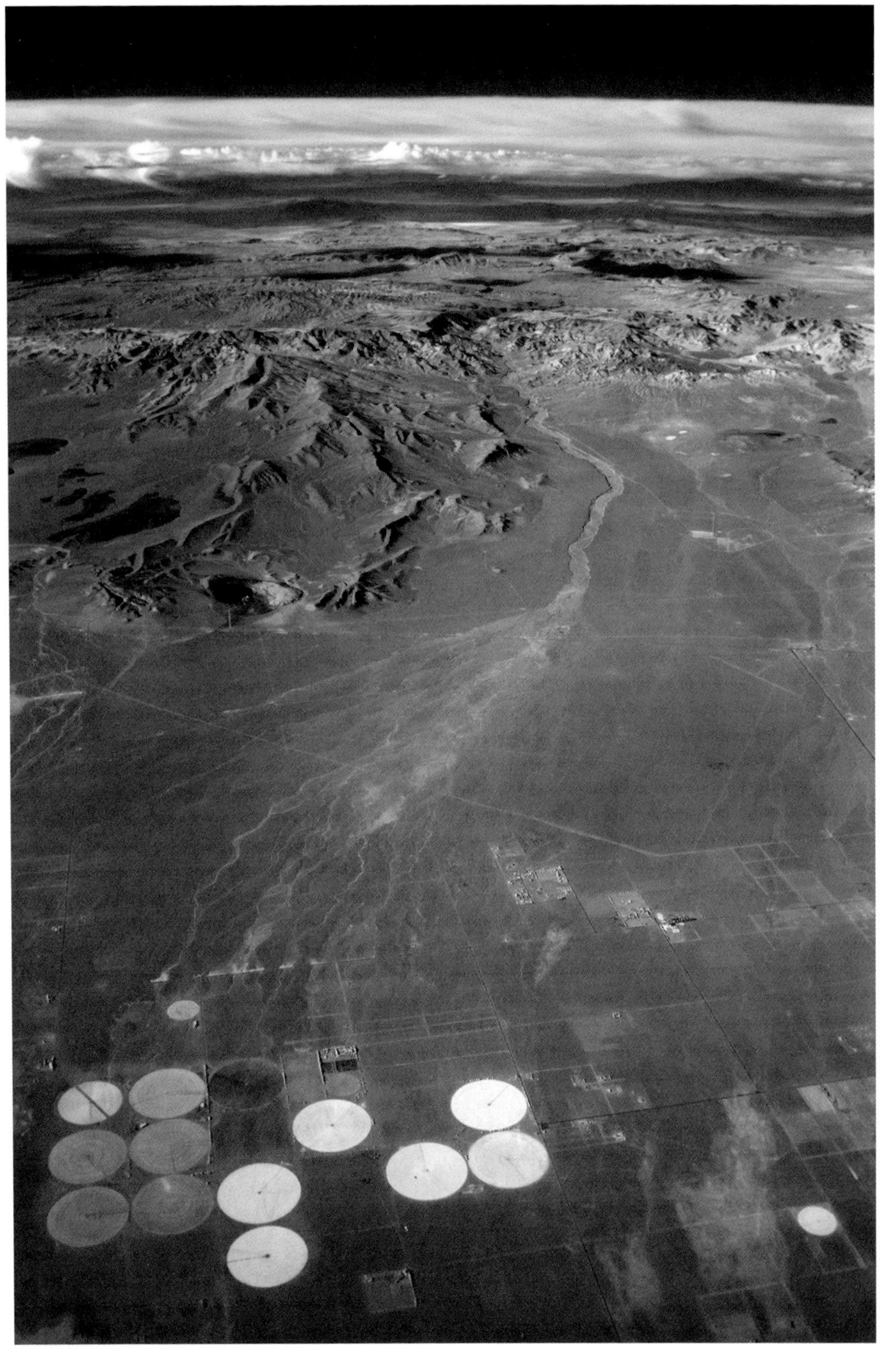

120. *Drainage toward Circles (LBB→LAS→OAK)*, 2014–15.
Archival pigment print, 33 × 22 in.
In the collection of the Museum of Texas Tech University, Lubbock

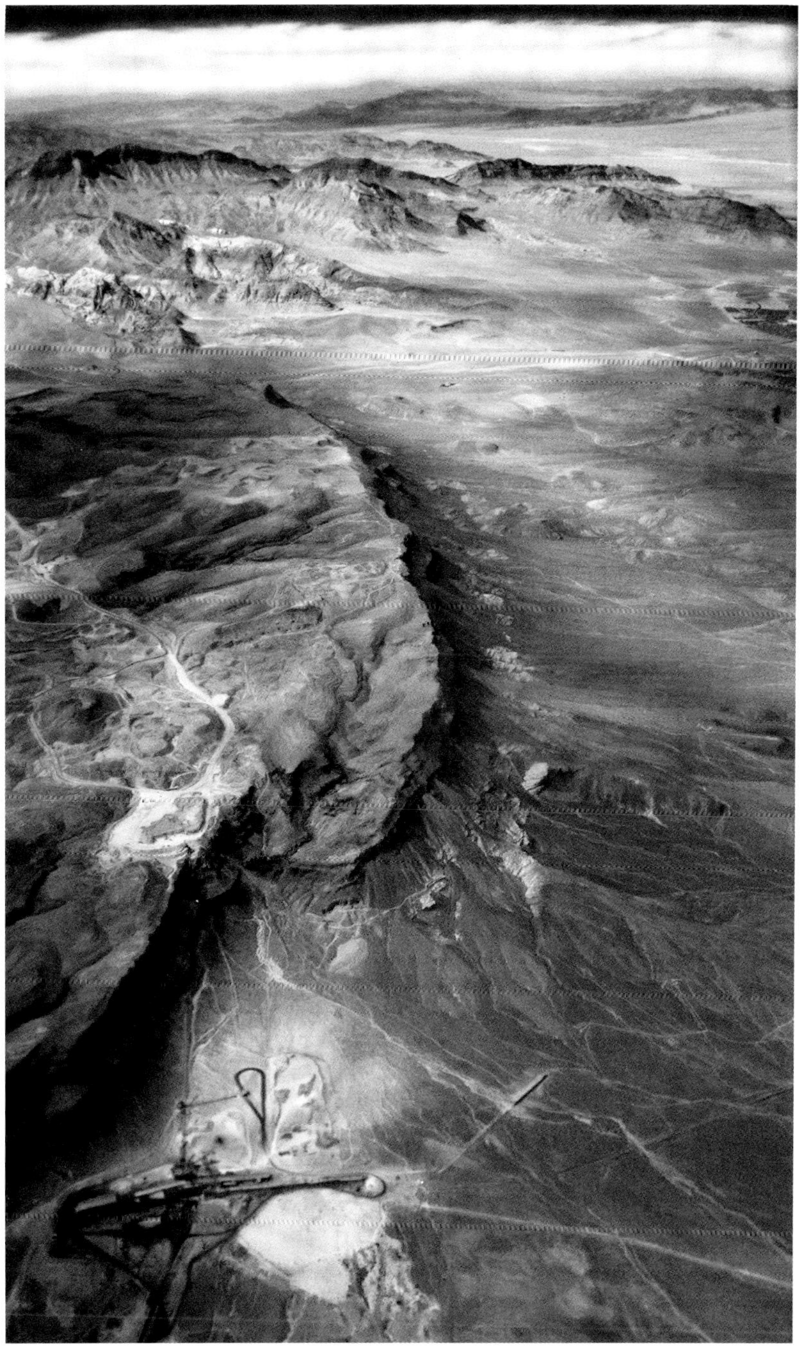

121. *Ridges, Roads, and Runway (OAK→LAS→LBB)*, 2014–15.
Archival pigment print, 33 × 22 in.

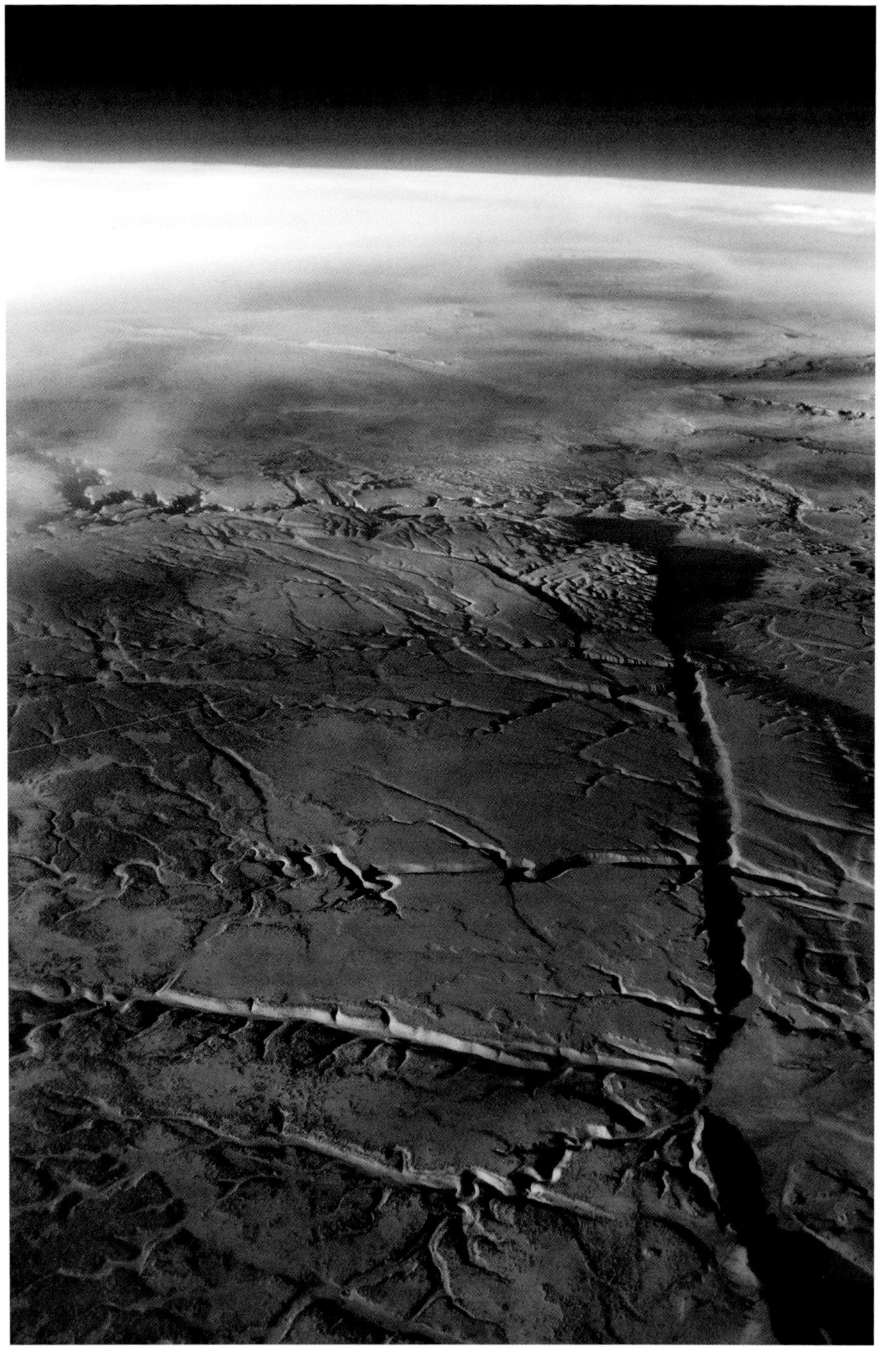

122. *Straight Line over Fractured Ground (OAK→LAS→LBB)*, 2014–15.
Archival pigment print, 33 × 22 in.
In the collection of the Museum of Texas Tech University, Lubbock

Chronology of Photographs

This list of photographs is organized by the year in which an image was completed. The title of each photograph is followed by the page number on which it appears in this volume.

About the Author & Contributors

Rick Dingus's photographs have been widely exhibited, published, and included in public and private collections since the 1970s. Dingus is author of *The Photographic Artifacts of Timothy O'Sullivan* (1982). He has worked on a variety of collaborative projects that include the Rephotographic Survey Project; Marks in Place: Contemporary Responses to Rock Art; Dinétah-Hajiinei: Place of Emergence; and Llano Estacado: An Island in the Sky. He helped establish the Millennial Collection archive at the Southwest Collection/Special Collections Library at Texas Tech University in Lubbock, where he is a professor of photography in the School of Art.

Shelley Armitage is a Roderick Professor Emeritus at the University of Texas at El Paso. She has published widely on photography, the visual arts, and landscape. Her most recent work is *Walking the Llano: A Texas Memoir of Place* (2016).

Peter S. Briggs has organized more than 150 exhibitions and authored more than sixty articles and books, mainly on twentieth- and twenty-first-century art in the western United States. He is the Helen DeVitt Jones Curator of Art at the Museum of Texas Tech University and founder and curator of the Artist Printmaker and Photographer Research Collection.

Toby Jurovics is chief curator and Holland Curator of Western American Art at Joslyn Art Museum in Omaha, Nebraska. He has organized more than sixty exhibitions and is the author of *Framing the West: The Survey Photographs of Timothy H. O'Sullivan* (2010), as well as essays on New Topographics, Thomas Joshua Cooper, John Gossage, and William Sutton.

Lucy R. Lippard is the author of twenty-three books on art, politics, place, and culture, most recently *Undermining: A Wild Ride Through Land Use, Politics and Art in the Changing West* (2014). She lives in Galisteo, New Mexico, where she has edited her monthly community newsletter for nineteen years.

INDEX

Page numbers in italics indicate illustrations.